2/86

NEIGHBOURS

**The work of
PHILIP ABRAMS**

NEIGHBOURS

The work of
PHILIP ABRAMS

MARTIN BULMER
Senior Lecturer in Social Administration,
London School of Economics and Political Science

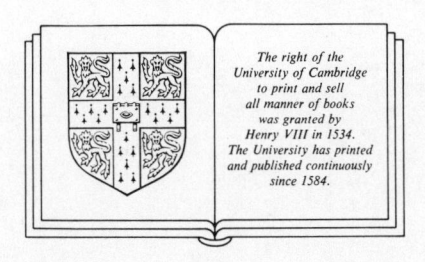

CAMBRIDGE UNIVERSITY PRESS
Cambridge
London   New York   New Rochelle
Melbourne   Sydney

Published by the Press Syndicate of the University of Cambridge
The Pitt Building, Trumpington Street, Cambridge CB2 1RP
32 East 57th Street, New York, NY 10022, USA
10 Stamford Road, Oakleigh, Melbourne 3166, Australia

© Cambridge University Press 1986. Chapters 8, 9 and 10 are Crown Copyright 1986.
No part of these chapters may be reproduced in any form without the permission of the
Department of Health and Social Security.

First published 1986

Printed in Great Britain at the University Press, Cambridge

British Library cataloguing in publication data

Bulmer, Martin
Neighbours: the work of Philip Abrams.
1. Abrams, Philip   2. Neighbourhood – Great Britain
3. Cities and towns – Great Britain
I. Title
307'.3362'01   HT133

Library of Congress cataloguing in publication data

Abrams, Philip.
Neighbours: the work of Philip Abrams.
Bibliography: p.
Includes index.
1. Community. 2. Neighborhood. 3. Interpersonal
relations. I. Bulmer, Martin. II. Title.
HM131.A25 1986   307.3'362   85–16569

ISBN 0 521 32005 4 hard covers
ISBN 0 521 31296 5 paperback

CE

Contents

Preface   *page* ix
Glossary: Places studied which are referred to in the text   xvii

Introduction
1. Neighbours, neighbouring and neighbourhood care: the significance of the work of Philip Abrams   3

Part I Informal neighbouring
2. Defining the field   17
3. Making sense of neighbours and neighbouring   27
4. Neighbouring in six localities: the Street studies   44
5. The sociology of informal neighbouring   83

Bridge
6. Altruism and reciprocity as sources of neighbouring and neighbourhood care   103

Part II Organised neighbourhood care
7. Neighbourhood care as a form of organised care   121
8. Ten Neighbourhood Care schemes   134
9. Ventures in neighbourhood care: the perspectives of Helpers and Clients   160
10. Limitations of neighbourhood care   182
11. The relationship between informal and formal care   206

Conclusion
12. Neighbours and neighbourhood care: a forward look   223

Appendix
The methodology of studying six streets and ten neighbourhood care schemes   245

Bibliography   267
Index   278

A note to the reader

Two different typefaces are used throughout this book to distinguish between what was written by Philip Abrams and what by Martin Bulmer.

Material by Philip Abrams is printed in Times typeface, which is the type used for this sentence.

Material by Martin Bulmer is printed in Univers typeface, which is the type used for this sentence and for most of the Preface.

Preface

Between 1976 and his death in October 1981, at the age of 48, Philip Abrams, Professor of Sociology at the University of Durham, directed three projects on neighbours, neighbouring and neighbourhood care. When he died, he was about to commence writing up this research in book form. The present work is an attempt to present posthumously a unified account of the results of this Durham research by Philip Abrams. The author was asked to undertake this task by the Joseph Rowntree Memorial Trust, who supported the first and (in part) the third phases of the work. Most of the material in this book is drawn from manuscripts written by Philip Abrams and members of his team during his lifetime. These have been selected, edited and integrated by me with addition and commentary where this seemed necessary and appropriate. All material in the book by Philip Abrams is set in Times typeface, the same as this sentence is set in. All passages written by Martin Bulmer are set in Univers typeface, as is this sentence and the rest of the page.

At first sight, Philip Abrams was perhaps rather an unlikely person to make a close study of the interpersonal world of neighbours. Both by academic background and interests he had previously concentrated on history and macro-sociology. Born in 1933, he took a first in both parts of the Cambridge history tripos, graduating in 1955. After six years as a research student and then research fellow at Peterhouse, he was awarded his PhD in 1961 for a thesis on John Locke as a Conservative, subsequently publishing a critical edition of Locke (Abrams 1963). These postgraduate years were also spent in the study of sociology, particularly political sociology, which he taught in his first job as assistant lecturer in sociology at LSE from 1961–62. He then returned to Cambridge as assistant lecturer, teaching political sociology in the Faculty of Economics and Politics. In 1965 he was appointed University Lecturer and Fellow and Tutor at Peterhouse. Between 1968 and 1970 he was Chairman of the Social and Political Sciences Committee, which was responsible for setting up and then running the new Part II tripos in social and political sciences, which became the main instrument for introducing substantial sociology teaching into the university (cf. Bulmer 1984a:23–7). From January 1971 until his death in October 1981 he was Professor of Sociology at the University of Durham (British Sociological Association (BSA) 1982; Brown 1982; McCulloch 1982).

Philip Abrams's scholarly interests ranged widely. Political sociology was his first love and remained a major centre of interest. Historical sociology was an abiding interest (cf. Abrams 1972; Wrigley and Abrams 1978), culminating in his posthumous *Historical Sociology* (1982). An early interest, too, was in the sociology of the military (cf. Abrams 1962, 1965, 1970), which led to an invitation from Morris Janowitz to spend the year 1966–67 at the University of Chicago. There he wrote *The Origins of British Sociology 1834–1914* (Abrams 1968), a classic essay and standard source of reference. He continued to work on the development of British sociology after 1914, holding a Social Science Research Council (SSRC) personal research grant in 1979–80 to investigate the utilisation of British sociology in the present century (cf. Abrams 1984a) and organising the thirtieth anniversary conference of the British Sociological Association with its theme of the history of the discipline (Abrams *et al.* 1981b).

A more practical strain was however evident in his work, which may be traced back to interests developed while spending the year in Chicago. There he was attached to the Centre for Social Organization Studies in the Department of Sociology, directed by Morris Janowitz, and rubbed shoulders with Albert Hunter and William Kornblum, absorbing some of the themes and interests of the Chicago school which are apparent particularly in chapters 2 to 4. He saw a good deal also of Lloyd and Margaret Fallers and of Edward Shils, whose interests in primary group relationships may have influenced his later work. What is most evident is the connection between the kind of applied sociology encouraged there by Morris Janowitz, combining an interest in sociology and social policy (cf. Janowitz 1970; 1977) and Philip Abrams's own developing interests in social policy and policy research apparent in chapters 7 to 12 of this book.

Among his earlier books, this tendency was most evident in the wide-ranging survey of contemporary British society which he commissioned and edited. When he came to Durham he carried on an earlier series of research projects spanning sociology and social policy, starting with studies of regionalism and regional development. The immediate antecedents of his work on neighbours may be found in the SSRC-funded project on communes in Britain, which explored empirically contemporary alternatives to the nuclear family, the nature of friendship in capitalist society, and sociological theories of social solidarity and cohesion. There he quoted approvingly Durkheim on the moral necessity for collective life, the perils and pains of social isolation and the need to nurture social cooperation (Abrams and McCulloch 1976:219–20). The communes project led directly to a study (funded by the Department of Health and Social Security (DHSS)) of the effectiveness as a type of care of therapeutic communities, particularly those concerned with the mentally and emotionally disturbed and with unsupported mothers. (This work remained unfinished at his death.)

This book does not attempt to give a personal portrait of the man, nor to assess the significance of his historical and sociological work as a whole. Such a task would be too complex and, in the case of his scholarly work, premature. The focus here is exclusively upon the research on neighbouring and neighbourhood care. The sources of his interest in these subjects were varied. During his year in Chicago he became familiar with the classic sociological studies of the urban neighbourhood. He had a long-standing interest, apparent in the communes research, in the basis of social solidarity, and was much influenced by Durkheim's *Division of Labour in Society* (cf. Abrams and McCulloch 1976:152–88). The communes research raised questions about the relative roles

Preface

of friendship and of the family as foundations for social relationships. Through his interest in political sociology he came to issues of community power and neighbourhood control with a fresh eye. And it may be that his active involvement in the Cambridge Labour Party up to 1965 was also a contributory factor.

The immediate origins of the research on neighbours lay with the Joseph Rowntree Memorial Trust. The Trust's Associate Director in the mid-1970s, Robin Huws Jones, had identified a number of areas for research under the umbrella of the effectiveness of social care. One of these was a study of neighbourliness.

> We read in the paper of people who die alone. Being alone before you die can matter greatly, and sometimes this happened in areas where statutory and voluntary social services were very active. In any society, but especially one with an increasing proportion of people who are old, or handicapped, or in community care because they are mentally ill or handicapped, we need more good neighbourliness, however well the statutory and organised voluntary services performed. (Interview with Robin Huws Jones, 23 November 1983.)

When the opportunity came, Philip Abrams hesitated at first, then, with his wife Sheila's enthusiastic support, he seized it. From this began a series of studies in which he became progressively involved, so much so that shortly before his death he had committed himself to a career move into policy research as Deputy Director of the Policy Studies Institute.

Writing in 1980, Philip Abrams said that three reasons had impelled his own interest in neighbours and neighbouring. In the field of social policy a number of major initiatives, conspicuously the Seebohm Report, had directed attention to the desirability of strengthening 'informal', 'community' or 'neighbourhood' care in relation to the organised statutory and voluntary services. And, rightly or wrongly, such developments had been seen as involving actual neighbours in being 'neighbourly'. In sociology a whole tradition of community and neighbourhood studies seemed to have come to a dead end so far as firm knowledge about neighbouring was concerned. Indeed, apart from a number of truisms about 'working class community', neighbouring appeared to be a relationship which had elusively defied analysis. And in society as a whole there was a widespread belief that for obscure reasons we were living through a major decline of neighbourliness. New styles of architecture and planning, social and geographic mobility, working wives, television and a host of other reasons for the decline were proposed, but the essence of the argument seemed to be that the costs of neighbourliness to the individual had come to seem excessive in relation to the apparent cheapness of other relationships and other sources of support and care. It was an argument cogently set out by Fred Hirsch (1977) in his image of an emerging 'society of bad neighbours'. Faced with such challenges and opportunities, above all with the prospect of social policy moving boldly into the unexplored territory of 'neighbourhood care' and often firmly behaving as if it knew its way, he could not resist the temptations of research.

The results of this research up to the time of his death are presented here. A considerable quantity of unpublished material arising from the first two phases of the research survives, together with a number of published papers listed in the bibliography. This forms the basis of the present book. Material already published has been drawn upon sparingly, since it is already in the public domain. Particular attention has been paid to presenting the results of empirical research and to tracing the evolution of Philip Abrams's ideas about neighbourhood care. Some 21 case studies were completed in the course of the two projects, and 16 of them are referred to frequently here. A considerable body of data resulted. The Street studies (chapter 4) involved about 165 interviews, the Neighbourhood Care studies (chapters 8–10) about 570 interviews with Helpers, Clients and Residents. To aid the reader in identifying places, a glossary appears on page xiv. All places and persons are referred to by pseudonyms; no real names are used of local people studied. To complicate matters, more than one pseudonym was sometimes used for a particular place or street. Thus the Durham pit village whose Good Neighbour scheme was studied was variously referred to as 'Sunniside', 'Pitside' and 'Slide'. The alternative pseudonyms are shown in the glossary, but only one pseudonym is used for each place in this book.

The form of this work is somewhat unusual, for the posthumous exegesis of someone else's unfinished scholarly work is comparatively rare. There were scarcely any models to follow. There are one or two posthumous reconstructions of a social scientist's lectures from student notes (e.g. Mead 1934) but that is a rather different exercise. On the other hand, critical assessments of the work of leading figures like Tawney or Titmuss (cf. Terrill 1974; Reisman 1978) can take for granted that their work is already well-known. This was not the case here, since much of the work was unpublished. The task seemed a worthwhile one to me personally because of my dual interest in the sociology of community and the relevance of social network analysis on the one hand, and the nature of informal social relationships and the extent to which they can be built upon to provide social care on the other. Moreover, the bridges which Philip Abrams was seeking to build and maintain between theory and policy need constant reinforcement, particularly in Britain where sociology and social policy have become unnecessarily distant as academic subjects.

Philip Abrams left a number of unpublished manuscripts which form the basis of the book. These, however, have been drawn on in different ways in preparing individual chapters, so that some chapters can be more closely related to a single unpublished work than others. Thus chapter 4 is largely based upon research reports of the six 'Street studies' prepared for the Durham advisory committee, as well as re-reading of the original interview schedules. Chapter 6 reproduces his influential paper 'Altruism and reciprocity: altruism as reciprocity'. Chapters 8 to 10 and the second half of the methodological appendix draw heavily upon the report which Philip Abrams, Sheila Abrams, Robin Humphrey and Ray Snaith submitted to the Department of Health and Social Security in March 1981, for which Robin, Ray and Sheila carried out all the fieldwork. Chapters 1–3, 5, 7, 11 and 12 are more composite, drawing upon several sources among the unpublished writings. Thus, for example, material from two draft chapters which Philip wrote for a projected book entitled *Neighbours, Sociology and Social Policy* is incorporated in chapters 1, 2, 3, 5 and the first part of the

Preface

methodological appendix. In the autumn of 1979, Philip Abrams gave four lectures at the Volunteer Centre on neighbourhood care, dealing with definition, relations, values and policy. Material from the first of these is used in chapter 2; from the first and second in chapter 5; from the fourth in chapters 7, 11, and 12; and from the third in chapter 12. Chapter 7 also contains an extract from an account of the Stonegate Street Warden scheme which was produced as a research team working paper. Where a published source written by Philip Abrams is drawn upon in the text, this is cited as such and the publication listed in the bibliography. Where material comes from an unpublished source, this is not cited in order to avoid cluttering up the text with references to unpublished reports and working papers which are not accessible to the reader.

Not only is the form of this work somewhat unusual, but the reader will become aware that it is the work of two different people, the first speaking with a clear and modulated voice, the second putting the unfinished work of the first together, filling gaps and setting the Durham research on neighbours in its wider context. In places, there is some reference by the second voice to other research work on related issues, and the raising of critical questions. Occasionally, certain inconsistencies are pointed out. If the work is one of reconstruction and critical exegesis, the exegesis looms largest. There has been no attempt to achieve a unified prose style as between the two voices. Philip Abrams's writing style was his own, clear, subtle, winning, distinctive, and marvelled at by his colleagues. The reader is therefore asked to bear with the two rather different voices, and such disjunctions and even incompleteness which must in places inevitably result.

Nor is the book by two people only. Philip Abrams conceived, guided and directed the research from his department with the assistance of several research staff whose contribution to the finished product was considerable. Sheila Abrams (1976–83), Janice Davinson (1976–78), Fred Robinson (1976–77), Robin Humphrey (1978–83) and Ray Snaith (1978–83) worked on the project at different stages and for varying lengths of time. Sheila Abrams's influence is discernible throughout, reflecting participation in team meetings over five years, continuing involvement in fieldwork and the salience of neighbouring as a regular topic of conversation at the family dinner table. Janice Davinson's contribution as a creative fieldworker is particularly apparent throughout chapter 4; she drafted the reports of fieldwork in Boswell, Congreve Hall and Dryden Square. Fred Robinson laid the groundwork for chapters 2 and 3 and also contributed to chapter 4. Robin Humphrey and Ray Snaith worked on the studies of Good Neighbour schemes at the second phase, where their contribution has already been publicly recognised (Abrams *et al*. 1981a; Abrams *et al*. 1982). This was followed by the ten detailed case studies reported in chapters 8 to 10, for which they and Sheila Abrams carried out all the fieldwork (see p. 255). This work will be reported in full in an HMSO monograph (Abrams, Abrams, Humphrey and Snaith forthcoming) and is also drawn upon in a practitioner-oriented publication edited by Diana Leat (Abrams, Abrams, Humphrey and Snaith 1985b). Philip Abrams did not work on his own but directed a research team, and their contribution to this account of his work is the foremost acknowledgement to be made. I should also like to thank Sheila, Janice, Fred, Robin and

Ray for their helpfulness to me personally at various stages along the road to preparing this account of Philip's work.

Without the support of the Joseph Rowntree Memorial Trust, which enabled me to take leave from my teaching duties to carry out this work, this book would not have been possible. To the Trustees and especially to the Trust's Director, Robin Guthrie, a particular debt is owed. Robin's determination to see that Philip Abrams's work was brought together and his contribution to sociology and social policy remembered led directly to this book being written. As indicated earlier, Robin Huws Jones, when Associate Director of the Trust during the 1970s, was the person who originally suggested that work on the topic of neighbours and care would be fruitful, and initiated the discussions which led to the first grant from the Trust to Philip Abrams.

The present work to write up the neighbouring research benefited from the existence of an advisory committee, and it is a pleasure to acknowledge their helpful contributions at various stages to the completion of the task. Ably chaired by Alan Little, the other members were Mark Abrams, Sheila Abrams, Jack Barnes, John A. Barnes, Richard K. Brown, James Cornford, Robin Guthrie, Robin Huws Jones, Dennis Marsden, John Pinder, Robert Pinker, Alan Walker and Peter Willmott.

Certain acknowledgements are customarily left until last, but they deserve more prominence. Throughout the year spent preparing this book, Valerie Campling provided admirable help with all manner of typing work, including this manuscript itself, which she prepared with her customary accuracy and efficiency. Gay Grant provided very effective general secretarial support.

The first stage of Philip Abrams's research in Durham also had an advisory committee, and four members of that previous committee shared with me their recollections of the development of Philip's work: Esther Goody of the Department of Social Anthropology, University of Cambridge, Fred Philp, Assistant Director of Cumbria Social Services, Erica Vere, a Rowntree Trustee, and Sir Derman Christopherson, former Vice-Chancellor of Durham University.

In the research community, others working on different aspects of informal social care provided information and advice. Particularly helpful were Peter Stubbings and Giles Darvill at the Volunteer Centre, Tilda Goldberg at Berkhamsted, and Peter Willmott and Diana Leat at the Policy Studies Institute. Also consulted were Michael Bayley and Hazel Qureshi at Sheffield, George W. Brown of the Medical Research Council (MRC) External Staff, Sally Baldwin and Gillian Parker at York, Michael Power at Bristol, Clare Ungerson, Claire Wallace and Bleddyn Davies at Kent, Clare Wenger at Bangor, Marie Johnson at Newcastle and Ian Sinclair at the National Institute of Social Work. The opportunity to make presentations at Colin Bell's Economic and Social Research Council (ESRC) Workshop on Community Studies in January 1984 and at the Social Administration Association conference in July 1984 was also valuable. Jack Barnes and Hazel Canter in the Office of the Chief Scientist, Department of Health and Social Security, facilitated the use of the 1981 Report to DHSS.

Several friends of Philip Abrams talked to me about his entry into sociology and the Cambridge years, and I would like to thank James Cornford, Liam Hudson, Morris Janowitz, Sonia Jackson, Peter Laslett, Andrew McCulloch,

Preface

Jonathan Steinberg, Edward Shils and Ken Woollard for doing so. John Barnes, Maurice Cowling, Sir Moses Finley, Jack Goody and W. G. Runciman also talked to me more generally about the development of sociology at Cambridge and Philip's role in that growth.

A visit to the United States in the summer of 1984 provided an opportunity to trace the influence of Philip Abrams's year in Chicago in 1966–67, and to learn more of related American work on neighbouring. At the University of Chicago, Morris Janowitz, Margaret Fallers, Donald Levine, Richard Taub and Gerald Suttles all provided fresh insights, and a conversation with Albert Hunter at Northwestern University was especially valuable. In New York, discussions with Herbert J. Gans and Eugene Litwak at Columbia were very useful. Meeting Diane L. Pancoast, Nancy J. Chapman and Alice H. Collins in Portland, Oregon, and Barbara Laslett of the University of Minnesota was also helpful. The view of the world from the campuses of the University of Chicago, Northwestern University and Columbia University is a very different one from that in London or in Durham, and a refreshing one. As Philip Abrams himself found in Chicago, the stimulation provided was beneficial.

The responsibility for the interpretation of Philip Abrams's work on neighbouring presented here lies with me. Based as far as possible on his own writings, it has nevertheless involved selection and piecing together, as well as engagement with the issues with which he was engaged. The experience of the year preparing the book has been for me an exciting one intellectually, which has enlarged my perspectives upon social policy and sociology. At the same time, the experience of completing someone else's work posthumously is a rather unusual one. Counterfactuals are of limited usefulness, but I am bound to say that I wish it had not been necessary for me to prepare this book. Philip Abrams's death in 1981 was a sad loss to British sociology and social policy.

London MARTIN BULMER
November 1984

Glossary: Places studied which are referred to in the text

Place (under pseudonym)	Location	What was studied	Where referred to
Alphaville (Reaching, Zoom)	Large northern city	Good Neighbour scheme	Chapter 1; and Abrams 1978b, 5–14; Abrams et al. 1981a, 66–72.
Austen Avenue (Balaclava Road)	Yorkshire woollen town	Informal neighbourliness	Chapter 4
Boswell village	Cumbria	Informal neighbourliness	Chapter 4
Bradbury	Suburb of northern city	Neighbourhood Care scheme	Chapters 8–10
Brandling	Inner London Borough	Neighbourhood Care scheme	Chapters 8–10
Congreve Hall (Manor Court)	Cambridge	Informal neighbourliness	Chapter 4
Dryden Square	Leeds	Informal neighbourliness	Chapter 4
Easethorpe	Village on South Downs in Sussex	Neighbourhood Care scheme	Chapters 8–10
Etherege Terrace (Prospect Terrace)	Durham	Informal neighbourliness	Chapter 4
Fielding Close (Hutton Crescent)	County Durham New Town	Informal neighbourliness	Chapter 4
Grantley	Central area of a northern city	Neighbourhood Care scheme	Chapters 8–10
Hope Green	London Borough of Camden	Good Neighbour scheme	Abrams et al. 1981a:87–94
Parsons Green	Suburb of an East Anglian town	Neighbourhood Care scheme	Chapters 8–10
Riverside	Inner London Borough	Good Neighbour scheme	Abrams 1981a:94–8
Skeffington	Commercial and industrial city	Neighbourhood Care scheme	Chapters 8–10
Southfield Park	Suburb on edge of GLC area	Neighbourhood Care scheme	Chapters 8–10

xviii *Glossary*

Place (under pseudonym)	Location	What was studied	Where referred to
Stonegate	District of a great steel city	Neighbourhood Care scheme	Chapters 8–10
Sunniside (Pitside, Slide)	Durham mining village	Good Neighbour scheme	Chapter 1; and Abrams 1978b, 5–14; Abrams *et al.* 1981a:59–66
Task Force	London Borough of Greenwich	Good Neighbour scheme	Abrams *et al.* 1981a:72–9
Tattworth (East Kinley)	Inner area of a midlands city	Neighbourhood Care scheme	Chapters 8–10
Trimdon (including Darnton, Bream and Strathburn within it)	District of a large city in south of England	Neighbourhood Care scheme	Chapters 8–10

Note: The localities studied are given pseudonyms. Where Philip Abrams used other pseudonyms for the same place in other publications, these are given in brackets.

Introduction

1 Neighbours, neighbouring and neighbourhood care; the significance of the work of Philip Abrams

Everyone, even in the remotest rural area, has neighbours. Social relations between neighbours are a significant form of social exchange. In addition to sociable contact, neighbours may provide tangible assistance for each other in the form of tasks performed or services rendered. For certain social minorities neighbours may be a source of social support and provide some types of social care. And in recent years there have been a number of attempts to foster more organised neighbourhood care by capitalising on such neighbourly feelings and the existence of neighbourliness as a social phenomenon. This book presents the results of empirical research and theoretical reflection on these topics to provide a picture of neighbours and neighbouring in contemporary Britain. Informal care – care provided by neighbours, friends and relatives – is a particular focus, and one of the threads that runs throughout. The frames of reference used are predominantly but not exclusively those of sociology and of social policy, with contributions from history, social anthropology and economics. The book both analyses how relations between neighbours are changing at the present day, and highlights the main problems facing policy-makers in trying to mobilise informal care and make it a meaningful complement to, or substitute for, statutory care paid for by government.

The study of neighbours, neighbouring and neighbourhood care is important for several reasons. 'We can do without our friends, but we cannot do without our neighbours', goes the popular saying. Certain groups in society – notably the infirm elderly – depend on various forms of support and care in order to maintain an independent existence and not enter institutional care. That only one in twenty old people in Britain live in institutions shows the importance of support networks in which neighbours may play a significant role. The growing proportion of 'old' elderly people, aged 75 and over, makes such support of even greater importance for the future (cf. Goldberg and Connelly 1982). For the politics of social policy, neighbourhood care provides an illuminating case study of the potential for community care and of the merits of shifting attention and resources from statutory services to the family and the community. If such policies are to be pursued, what can one expect the informal sector to provide, and how will the boundary between statutory responsibility and voluntary and informal care be drawn? Sociologically, the study of neighbours is rewarding because it focusses upon social relationships intermediate between the macro and the micro levels, between the political, economic and value systems of society as a whole, and the level of interpersonal relations where two or more people interact in settings such as the family, the workplace or the pub. To what

4 Introduction

extent, and for which sections of the population, does the neighbourhood provide a basis for significant social relationships?

It will be helpful at the outset to make some basic distinctions, although definitions are discussed more fully in chapter 2. As Philip Abrams pointed out to the Downing conference in 1977, 'social care' refers to 'all forms of care and treatment in institutions and elsewhere other than medical care and direct cash support' (1978a:78). It includes various activities along a continuum from visiting, providing transport, doing shopping and befriending to washing, lifting and taking to the toilet. The psychological dimension of support is important in addition to practical help. It may be provided in a variety of ways: by government through Local Authority Social Services Departments (referred to here as statutory care); privately on a commercial basis, for example, in homes for the elderly; by volunteers working for voluntary organisations such as Age Concern or the Women's Royal Voluntary Service (WRVS); and informally by relatives, friends and neighbours helping people known to them on a personal basis. A basic difference, reflected in the structure of this book, is between care in the informal sector, which is personal and particularistic and unorganised, and on the other hand voluntary, commercial or statutory care which is usually care provided universalistically by people who are initially strangers and who work within a formal organisation of some kind (cf. Wolfenden Report 1978:22–9). Part I of the book is concerned with neighbours and neighbouring and with informal care in this context. Part II of the book discusses Neighbourhood Care schemes which are more formally organised, although trying to bridge the gap between voluntary and informal care, and to harness the strengths of informal caring among neighbours and friends on a broader basis. One of the questions it seeks to answer is whether such aims can be achieved.

Formal care is provided within the ambit of bureaucratically structured agencies; it is a matter of tasks to be performed by specified persons whose work it is to carry out such tasks, within an overt hierarchy of accountability. By contrast, informal care is rooted not in commitment to tasks but in attachment to persons; it is a property of relationship, not of jobs; its dispositional base is involvement with other people, not the conscientious performance of a role. It is personal involvement that gets the contracts enforced – indeed a major problem about informal care from the point of formal caring agencies is just that so many contracts (between spouses, parents and children and so forth) are persistently not fulfilled. It is the dispositional base (of involvement with other persons) and the social context (relationships perceived as chosen or natural) that matter, not any specific form of care. Among informal carers there are further distinctions to be made between kin on the one hand and friends and neighbours on the other. Relatives in general assume the main burden of informal caring, but friends and neighbours also perform important tasks. One purpose of the research was to establish what help and support neighbours do provide, and what are the limits to the help they can be expected to offer.

These distinctions may be clearer from a brief history of the Durham research directed by Philip Abrams. The projects had three phases. The first project on The Social Contexts of Neighbouring, was supported financially by the Joseph

The work of Philip Abrams

Rowntree Memorial Trust and ran from 1976 to 1978. Fred Robinson, Sheila Abrams and Janice Davinson were the research staff. The first aim of the project was to explore patterns of neighbouring, the nature of mutual help in different types of local community, and the second to determine the circumstances under which more sustained and substantial types of neighbourly help were provided. The earliest product was a literature review, *What We Know About the Neighbours* (Robinson and Abrams 1977; see also Robinson and Robinson 1982). Empirical research focussed upon six contrasting streets, with different characteristics, in different parts of the country, in which an attempt was made to interview all residents to study patterns of contact between neighbours. The results are reported in chapter 4.

As the first phase developed, the research team became increasingly aware of the significance of efforts being made by a number of voluntary and statutory agencies to develop systems of neighbourhood care by exploiting the informal neighbouring presumed to be latent in different localities. Grass-roots Neighbourhood Care projects of many kinds were coming to be an increasingly favoured form of community action and were increasingly being seen as a possible means of linking and coordinating formal and informal caring systems. One particular stimulus came from the political arena. David Ennals, Secretary of State for Social Services, launched in the autumn of 1976 a national Be A Good Neighbour campaign, with exhortations to individuals to 'pluck up your courage and be a good neighbour'. The campaign gave direct encouragement to local residents to form organisations in order to promote mutual help and care, and equally direct encouragement to Social Service Departments and voluntary organisations to support such efforts. 'Within the larger movement to cultivate neighbourhood care, it gave an explicit role to grass-roots helping and caring, to direct action by local residents within their localities' (Abrams *et al*. 1981a:10).

The Good Neighbour research began in 1977 with two case studies of a Durham mining village and a prosperous middle class area in a Yorkshire city, together with a national survey by postal questionnaire of Good Neighbour schemes. Starting with a list of about 3,000 schemes, most though not all of which included 'good neighbour' or 'neighbourhood care' in their title, the Durham team obtained information about 1,000 schemes in some detail.

The second phase of the Durham research, between 1978 and 1981, into Patterns of Neighbourhood Care, shifted the focus to these semi-organised Neighbourhood Care schemes. It was supported financially by the Department of Health and Social Security. Sheila Abrams, Robin Humphrey and Ray Snaith were the research staff. Their first task was to analyse the data about the 1,000 Good Neighbour schemes, the results of which appeared in *Action For Care* (Abrams *et al*. 1981a). The following year, a *Handbook* of such schemes appeared (Abrams *et al*. 1982. See also Humphrey and Snaith 1982.)

Philip Abrams and his team had been developing hypotheses (set out in chapter 8) about the social sources of informal care and about the sorts of relationship between formal and informal care which might be expected to be conducive to mobilisation of the latter at a neighbourhood level. Many different types of project were being set up under many different auspices and apparently with widely differing results. But it was clear that rather little was known about these ventures in general terms – that, for example, no one seemed to know which type of scheme might be best suited to what type of situation, locality or need. The main empirical research at this phase, reported in chapters 8 and 9 (and in more detail in Abrams, Abrams, Humphrey and Snaith, forthcoming) focussed in depth upon ten particular schemes in different parts of England, to assess their effectiveness as forms of community care and as possible means of linking and coordinating formal and informal care. They were selected in terms of a number of theoretical criteria related to degrees of statutory intervention and the basis of the scheme. Prior to this, five other case studies were carried out (of Sunniside, Alphaville, Hope Green, Riverside and Task Force Greenwich) which were reported in *Action For Care* (Abrams *et al.* 1981a). In all, including the six Street studies at the first phase, 21 localities were investigated. These are set out in alphabetical order in the glossary on p. xii.

Between 1977 and 1981, Philip Abrams developed close contacts with the Volunteer Centre, which was then involved in a five-year programme on neighbourhood care. His evolving ideas on the neighbourhood care policy were first presented to Volunteer Centre audiences in 1978 and 1979, and at the time of his death he was involved in planning a joint project in which a Durham team would have evaluated an information training programme for Neighbourhood Care schemes run from the Centre. The research element in this project was continued in a different form after 1981 by Michael Power at Bristol (Power, forthcoming). The very definite applied, policy-oriented, thrust to the programme of research on neighbours intensified as the years passed. The interest in neighbourhood care, already apparent in his writing, was reflected in the field research being carried out from an early date. Philip Abrams's continuing preoccupations with the relationship between formal and informal care are discussed in chapters 7 and 11, while the limitations of Neighbourhood Care schemes are considered in chapter 10.

Although the two phases of the research followed each other, to some extent there was a hiatus between them. The first was concerned with informal, unorganised, 'spontaneous' neighbouring (though Philip Abrams came to doubt whether it was useful to invoke spontaneity as an explanatory factor (cf. 1978a:80–2)). The second, focussing on organised Good Neighbour schemes, crossed the boundary into more formal provision, which properly speaking was outside the informal world of kin, friends and next-door neighbours. New issues appeared, such as what degree of accountability to expect of Organisers, whether Helpers should be paid, and if so how much (token amounts or real wages), and what relationship to establish with statutory services. To some extent, though not entirely, the first phase of the project was more sociological and the second phase more concerned with social policy. To reflect these differences, this book is arranged in two parts, grouping together chapters 2 to 5, and 7 to 11, with an introduction, a bridging chapter (6) and a conclusion (chapter 12).

When Philip Abrams died in 1981, a third phase of the research on neighbouring was beginning, funded by SSRC (now ESRC) with some further Rowntree Trust support. This work on 'The Caring Capacity of the Community' started from several findings from the first two phases. The caring capacity of the community appeared to be severely limited. The provision of care by the community was not directly or adequately related to the incidence of need in the community but reflected the needs and interests of care-givers to a considerable extent. Nine-tenths of 'community' care was in fact given by kin, almost all of them women. Community care-givers themselves needed considerable and varied forms of support. For the 5% to 10% of local residents without available kin, most needs short of institutionalisation were met through the provision of 'surrogate kin' (fostering) or a package of care involving a fine division of labour between many helpers. This required mobilisation, and the basic problem of how to mobilise and sustain community involvement remained seriously underresearched. It was therefore proposed to carry out three projects: an exploratory study of problems and possibilities of mobilising and sustaining community involvement in social care activities; a study of the costs of community care in personal, relational and financial terms, focussing on daughters looking after their mothers who were living with them; and a contrasting study of the relationship between formal organisations and informal networks, specifically concerned with the extent to which the former could foster the latter among the elderly.

After Philip Abrams's death, these three projects continued until 1983 under the general guidance of Professor Alan Little. Ray Snaith worked on the first, Sheila Abrams on the second and Robin Humphrey on the third. The results are reported in Snaith (1985), S. Abrams (1985) and Humphrey (1984).

This, then, is the way in which the research reported here developed. The twin themes of this book are neighbours and neighbouring as sociological phenomena and neighbourhood care as an issue in social policy. These themes were apparent in the original research proposal to the Rowntree Trust, which emphasised both practical and academic objectives and implications. A better understanding of what sorts of people were willing to give what sorts of help in what circumstances would contribute appreciably to society's ability to develop alternatives to institutional care for the partially dependent. At the same time, a careful study of the forms and contexts of neighbouring would enlarge knowledge of the nature of social solidarity and community in modern industrial societies. In the first phase, the research was accordingly organised around three main questions concerning the idea, practice and contexts of neighbouring. Firstly, what ideas, expectations and beliefs did people have about their own willingness to help their neighbours or their neighbours' willingness to help them? What sort of relationship did people expect neighbouring to be? Then, what sorts of help were actually given or not given to what sorts of people in what sorts of situation? What was the practical experience of neighbouring? Thirdly, how far could variations in the idea and the practice of neighbouring be related to variations in such contextual factors as kinship, class, hardship, length of local residence, age, availability of public services, and so on? What were the social sources of neighbouring?

By seeking answers to each of these questions in a number of different types of social milieu and r , seeking to relate the answers to each question to one another, it was hoped to develop a body of fairly precise, substantive and empirically grounded propositions about the resources of practical altruism available in British society and about the circumstances in which altruism might be effectively mobilised.

Such questions had a close affinity to general questions about the sources of cohesion and solidarity in society which sociologists from Emile Durkheim onwards had sought to answer. Durkheim saw what he called the corporation as a means of fostering communal life without weakening the nation-state. Industrialisation had swept away the 'little aggregations' (including the neighbourhood) in which people existed in the past and which were the centres of their lives (1952:386–92). (Bloch's evocation of the localism of feudal society illustrates this earlier state vividly (1962:64).) The result was a polarisation between the centralising state absorbing all activity of a social character on the one hand, and the mass of individuals on the other, moving formlessly 'like so many liquid molecules'. Some intermediate structure was required between the two to provide a focus for social activity and a point of attachment.

> The absence of all corporative institutions creates, then, in the organisation of a people like ours, a void whose importance it is difficult to exaggerate ... Where the state is the only environment in which men can live communal lives, they inevitably lose contact, become detached, and thus society disintegrates. A nation can be maintained only if, between the state and the individual, there is intercalated a whole series of secondary groups near enough to the individuals to attract them strongly in their sphere of action and drag them in this way, into the general torrent of social life. (Durkheim 1933:29, 28)

The consequences of organic solidarity were analysed by a number of sociologists, both European and American, including Toennies, Simmel, Cooley, W. I. Thomas and Robert Park. A reflection is found in twentieth-century theories of mass society (cf. Bramson 1961). A modern version, more explicitly addressed to policy and articulating the concept of mediating structures, appears in the recent writings of Peter Berger (1977, 1980), who discerns a dichotomy between the megastructures of society – remote, impersonal and hard to understand – and private life, where meaning and identity are discovered and enjoyed. The relative lack of intermediate institutions not only leaves the individual vulnerable in time of crisis – as when, for example, in need of social care – but threatens the political order by depriving it of the moral foundations on which it rests.

The neighbourhood or local community is one type of mediating structure. 'The question of how residential solidarities are keyed into other social arrangements bears on almost all the problems of societal integration' (Hunter and Suttles 1972:45). Durkheim had dismissed its potential as a basis for collective action. Neither the locality, nor the department, nor the province had in his view enough influence to exert moral authority over the individual. 'It is impossible to artificially resuscitate a particularistic spirit which no longer has any foundation' (1952:390). Some modern sociologists are not so sceptical, for they see the potential politically-integrating role of the neighbourhood or locality.

At the outset, a theme which was to recur appeared, the contrast between neighbouring in the traditional working class community and 'modern' neighbouring. In Philip Abrams's view, neighbourliness and the moral attitudes sustaining it developed in the past in situations where people helped each other because there was no alternative way of surviving. Neighbouring was essentially a response to economic insecurity, lack of financial resources and the absence of public welfare services. The best-documented patterns of strong neighbouring in the past were directly associated with chronic collective deprivation, class consciousness and powerful and extensive kinship attachment. He was also struck by studies of disasters (cf. Barton 1969) which showed that altruism could be generated spontaneously in such crisis situations. Both kinds of evidence pointed to the view that neighbourliness should be considered as a relatively unnatural phenomenon in the normal circumstances of fairly prosperous societies. Neighbouring was what people did when they could neither afford to buy professional services nor claim an effective entitlement to them from the state.

Philip Abrams enjoyed playing with ideas, putting alternative viewpoints, and showing the paradoxes of different positions. There was an element of that here, but nonetheless he was serious in questioning a certain tendency among sociologists towards an idealised view of the traditional working class. He wanted to insist very firmly that neighbouring was not something 'natural', to be taken for granted, but very definitely had to be explained in sociological terms. The aim of the first phase of the research was to do just this. At the outset he identified three types of theory which might be used to explain neighbourliness.

In one view, patterns of neighbouring were strongly determined by sheer physical proximity. Neighbours are nigh-dwellers, and those living next door or a few doors away are *ipso facto* more likely to enter into neighbouring relations than those living further away. The fact that neighbouring is typically highly localised behaviour (even if its sources are unrelated to locality) gave ecological explanations of neighbouring a continuing cogency. Though theories of this type were out of favour with sociologists, they enjoyed a certain standing among geographers and urban planners and deserved serious consideration.

A second type of theory clearly had some appeal to Philip Abrams. This involved recognising that there was a balance between necessity and choice as alternative bases of altruism, and identifying the conditions under which people would help one another because they could 'afford' that choice rather than because they felt they had to in the absence of any other choice. There was a good deal of evidence to suggest that, other things being equal, people preferred neighbourly altruism to public provision as a means of coping with dependency and personal misfortune. Enjoying the paradox, he pointed out that people appearing to *choose* neighbouring if they could possibly afford it was directly at odds with the view that traditionally neighbouring arose from economic constraint. Everything turned on what was understood by the idea of 'affording it'. (The idea of the opportunity-costs of relationships may have come from economic anthropology.) It could of course have literal financial implications, as in cases where informal carers were paid for the care provided; this was one way of exploring the working balance of altruism and self-interest that individuals maintain. However, for most people it was unlikely that financial need would be the prime determinant. Many different values, attitudes and experiences would play a part in determining the point at which any given individual would decide to choose altruism, decide that he could 'afford' to be neighbourly. An understanding of how and why different sorts of people put different prices on neighbouring seemed called for, once neighbouring was seen as potentially something more than the traditional concomitant of a certain kind of harsh class situation. The social cost of neighbourliness was a theme running through the first phase of the research.

Implicit in this theory were elements of a third, which became in many ways the lynchpin of the Durham research and a bridge between the first and second phases of the research. It developed gradually during the course of the first two years of the research, aided by lively exchanges between Philip, his team, and members of the Rowntree Trust's advisory committee for the research. It is discussed fully in chapter 6. Linked to the costs of neighbouring were the benefits, and coming from this the idea of neighbourly relations as social exchange rather than a one-way transfer. Philip Abrams came to attach central importance to the idea that the moral basis of neighbourliness could best be understood as an expression of reciprocity rather than of altruism. Care was meaningful as an exchange rather than as a gift. The obstacles to neighbourhood care at the local level were to be found in the ideas of cost and benefit, and around doubts about the possible existence of a flow of help in which the individual could be recipient as well as donor. Unhelpfulness could be a defence against the perceived failure of reciprocity.

To anticipate slightly some of the discussion in later chapters, two years into the research Philip Abrams was suggesting that there were more forms of reciprocity than met the eye. One did not have to think in terms of exchange of strictly equivalent services or even of exchanges within immediately given bilateral relationships. Informal care was given by many to others who could themselves give little or nothing in direct return, because the donors had a deep sense of debts of care they had incurred to quite different people in different contexts and often in the quite remote past. Four distinct bases of active informal helping could be discerned: *altruism* (the acceptance of a norm of beneficence as an absolute guideline for personal life), *tradition* (a practice of taken-for-granted helpfulness strongly implanted in childhood or earlier experience in adult life and carried over as an unconsidered principle of present activity), *status* (the culling of self-esteem from the patronage aspect of the relationship between donor and beneficiary or from the honorific connotations of being seen as a caring agent by the larger society) and *reciprocity*. Not only did they find in the first phase of the research that reciprocity was the most widespread and influential of these bases for care, but they were forced to the conclusion that reciprocity was in some important respects a matter of possibilities within the caring relationship which some perceived and many did not. If that conclusion was justified, it would follow that a great deal more informal care could in principle be unleashed by appropriate social policies.

These three sets of theoretical ideas are explored further in the first part of the book. They are implicit in a good deal of the conceptual discussion in chapter 2. The literature review in chapter 3 is focussed with these issues in mind, trying to answer quite specific questions about the social basis of neighbouring. The evidence from the Street studies in chapter 4 was likewise analysed in the context of theoretical issues. The threads of the sociological analysis of informal neighbouring are drawn together in chapter 5. The bridging chapter discusses altruism and reciprocity and the issue of whether beneficence or exchange lie at the heart of informal, unorganised, help and support provided by neighbours to one another.

The background to the study of Patterns of Neighbourhood Care reported in the second part of this book was rather different from that of the studies of informal neighbourliness in the first part. It centred on neighbourhood care as a type of community care and grew out of the studies of Good Neighbour schemes. These may be defined as any organised attempt to mobilise local residents to increase the amount or range of help and care they give to one another. The key word is 'organised'. Such schemes were distinctively different from informal care between kin, friends and next-door neighbours, in that they involved the local provision of care by comparative strangers within an administrative framework, however tenuous. In one sense such schemes had a long history. Many projects sponsored by churches, voluntary bodies and community groups, such as the Good Companions of WRVS or the link schemes of Age Concern, had been around for a long time. In the 1970s, however, the theme of encouraging good neighbourliness by drawing an ever-wider range of local residents into an ever-wider variety of caring and helping activities, acquired dramatic new emphasis, including endorsement by the Seebohm and Wolfenden Reports (1968, 1978).

Good Neighbour schemes are quite distinct from conventional voluntary work. 'The Good Neighbour scheme is an organisational Cheshire Cat; it comes into being in order to put itself out of existence. Success for such a scheme would have to be measured in terms of the degree to which the scheme [i.e. the formal organisation] was no longer needed' (Abrams *et al*. 1979:21–2). The principal analytic object of the research as a whole was to examine what some called the 'interface' and what Philip Abrams preferred to call the 'frontier' between informal and formal care, and to enlarge understanding of the possible traffic across it. There is currently much enthusiasm for 'interweaving' formal and informal care, the Barclay Report (1982) being but one example. Philip Abrams was more sceptical, at least initially, and made a trenchant critique of optimists who believed that the formal and informal sectors formed a seamless web. He saw clearly some of the social obstacles and barriers to interpenetration. These difficulties are further discussed in chapter 11.

The initial studies of Sunniside and Alphaville Good Neighbour schemes were carried out alongside the Street studies, throwing up ideas about reciprocity and altruism. In Sunniside, a traditional Durham working class mining community, the scheme had some difficulty in becoming established, and this suggested the need to study not only the Helpers, but also their Clients and community members *not* involved in the scheme. More importantly, comparative studies were needed. In early 1978 Sheila and Philip Abrams wrote:

> Again and again the Sunniside Good Neighbours told us that it was in large towns, tower blocks and more generally the unfriendly 'south' that Good Neighbour schemes were really needed and where they would be really difficult to establish. There are good sociological reasons behind such commonsense judgments and their validity should obviously be explored.

After the contrasting study of Alphaville, where there was a flourishing scheme heavily dependent on the contacts and energy of the local organiser, they and Janice Davinson drew both practical and analytic conclusions early in 1978. The practical conclusions were that the Alphaville scheme has succeeded remarkably well within the limits of possibility set by the needs and capacities of its central personnel. As Peter Jarvis, the energetic local Organiser, put it: "There's a really strong community spirit here now; the place is like a village; I can walk down the street and everyone knows me; people feel a need to belong and we're meeting that need." At the same time the care-giving offered by the scheme has not typically developed into a matter of neighbourly relationships between the members and their clients; a majority of the Volunteers feel desperately under-used; and much of the at-risk or in-need population of Alphaville appears to be unaware of the existence of the scheme. The frustration of many of the Volunteers stems from their lack of referrals and from a consequent need for the scheme to expand on a more decentralised, localised basis. The scheme requires more advertising and more support from local medical and ecclesiastical agencies; perhaps the original plan of organising on the basis of streets or groups of streets each with its own organiser should be revived; plainly, the organiser cannot maintain contact with all the Volunteers he has recruited – at the very least some possibility of drawing the Volunteers as a whole together for meetings and exchanges of ideas and knowledge seems highly desirable. Some Volunteers clearly want to develop long-term personal relationships, often on an implicitly reciprocal basis, with those they help and it seems that the scheme ought to build this possibility into its organisation. Yet many of the Volunteers in the core group – for whom the point of the scheme was to get to know each other as much as to help the Clients – are quite clear, as one might expect from such competent businesslike and mobile people, that the one thing they do not want is to get involved with the Clients; "I don't mind doing anything that's needed, but I don't want to get involved." Some Volunteers want to relate, others simply want to give help; if the scheme is to maximise its potentialities it must plainly be able to use both types fully.

Analytically, we are driven to the conclusion that the study of Good Neighbour schemes and Neighbourhood Care projects is indeed, as we originally hoped, a fruitful detour so far as the study of informal neighbouring is concerned. We think our studies of Sunniside and Alphaville have shown that these projects provide a defined point of access in terms of which both the social functions of neighbouring and the varieties of demand for neighbourliness in contemporary society can be effectively identified. We are impelled towards the view that class is after all one of the most important sources of variation in accounting for the ways in which people actually succeed or fail in securing the neighbourly environment they desire. But we are also impelled to the view that in one form or another neighbourliness is a deeply cherished, strenuously pursued value of all social classes and groups and one which social policy ought to be more constructively seeking to realise.

A change in direction of the research was already being signalled in these two case studies (for fuller details of them, see Abrams 1978b; Abrams *et al.* 1981a:59–72). They were followed by a social mapping exercise to establish nationally by means of a postal questionnaire the extent of Good Neighbour schemes. This national survey overlapped the end of the first phase and the beginning of the second, DHSS-funded, phases of the research. There are passing references to this national study in the following chapters, but the material is not reproduced here, since it is already available in published form (Abrams *et al*. 1981a, 1982). It was intended that these data would provide a framework of hypotheses and propositions for analysis in the main stage of the second phase of the research, concentrated on a limited selection of case studies. These were intended to permit a comparative appraisal of the success or non-success of a variety of highly local, neighbourhood projects in mobilising different forms of service, help, support or care in certain types of setting and through certain types of organisation.

Of some interest is a description written in 1979 of what an ideal Good Neighbour project might look like. The paper stressed that in reality only a tiny minority of schemes began to approximate to this ideal. Such a scheme would cover a small area – probably not much more than 2,000 households; each street would have its own Good Neighbour or Street Warden who would be, eventually if not initially, accepted as merely a Resident but would also be sufficiently 'trained' in the ways of the health and welfare services to be able to give instant specific advice on how to handle problems when asked to do so by her or his neighbours. The scheme would thus be highly localised and require little formal organisation. It would, though, contain a mix of types so far as the Good Neighbours were concerned – male and female, young and old. The organiser or coordinator would be paid (part-time) and one member, either the coordinator or someone else, possibly someone themselves disabled or housebound, would be available at all times to receive messages and pass on problems with which the Good Neighbours could not themselves cope. To make rapid contact and response possible Good Neighbours who did not have telephones would be supplied with them. Social Services offices would make referrals and be ready to offer advice and information but would not interfere in the running of the scheme. Doctors and other relevant professional people in the area would play a similar supportive role. The Good Neighbours would meet regularly with the organiser and perhaps with social workers, doctors, clergymen and others with whom the work and problems of the scheme could be discussed. The meetings would have an important function for the morale of the scheme in allowing the professionals to indicate their appreciation of the work being done and allowing the members generally to 'pat each other on the back'. Expenses would be made available to meet necessary transport costs and perhaps also to ensure a certain amount of publicity for the scheme (a postcard in every home and occasional circulars are the favoured methods). Emphasis in the scheme would be placed on supporting and gradually extending natural neighbouring networks and stressing the value of informal as against formal caring – thus members would try to bring together residents who might be able to help each other as well as providing help themselves. The scheme would have a fairly intense social life over and above any specific giving of care (Abrams *et al*. 1979:22–3).

Part II of the book presents the main results of the case studies of neighbourhood care. Some of the questions addressed included: what was the caring

14   *Introduction*

capacity of the community, and of neighbours in particular? To what extent were ties between neighbours relatively weak, involving low commitment? If this was the case, who provided the bulk of informal care of the dependent young and old? How far did community care predominantly mean care by female kin? What were the implications of variability in the amount of care available? If some people belonged to relatively dense and close-knit kinship networks, and others had few or no local kin and were socially isolated, how could support be provided most effectively to the latter? Care, particularly of the incapacitated elderly, could be very demanding; who could care for the carers, and provide them with support? Neighbourhood care clearly required organisation; what were the merits of alternative forms, with varying admixture of statutory, voluntary and local leadership? If projects were to be local in origin and management, how was the necessary local support to be mobilised effectively? What were the alternative forms of mobilisation?

A detailed study was made of ten particular Neighbourhood Care schemes selected on the basis of type of locality, type of need and the type of linkage sought between the formal and informal sectors (see chapter 8). The researchers sought to establish how each scheme worked, the characteristics of its members and Clients and of members who had withdrawn as well as of local Residents who had not joined; more fundamentally they tried to understand the successes and problems of each scheme in the context of the broader pattern of informal neighbourliness in its locality, the input of resources and support received from the statutory and organised voluntary sectors and the relationships between the Good Neighbours and those they were helping. To develop analytical portraits of this type it was necessary for the researchers to spend a considerable period of time with each of the schemes they were studying and to involve themselves with the scheme, its members and Clients and the whole milieu in which it was active, as well as undertaking more formal interviewing. As in the first phase, the semi-structured interview in the context of extended observation and a measure of participation was found to be the most fruitful and appropriate method of working (for a fuller discussion, see the methodological appendix).

This work, then, is a reconstruction of the book which Philip Abrams was intending to write, but it is not that book. It is a selection and interpretation by another of the two phases of his research on neighbours and neighbouring, the sociological and the policy-oriented. It emphasises the fertility of the link between the two and the bridges which he was able to build. The structure of the work, in two parts, emphasises that the two phases were at once separate but linked, and therefore complementary. There is no way of knowing what Philip Abrams would have thought of the account which follows. The reader has the reassurance, however, that the majority of the following chapters are in Philip Abrams's own words.

Part 1

Informal neighbouring

2 Defining the field

What do we mean by a neighbour, or by neighbourliness? This chapter provides some terminological clarification about both the informal neighbouring studied in the first part of the book and the more organised forms of neighbourhood care examined in the second half. It draws largely upon unpublished manuscripts. The discussion emphasises the distinction, highlighted in the previous chapter, between informal care among next-door neighbours and more organised forms of local care, while at the same time showing that the two are not completely antithetical.

It may seem a little incongruous, if not pedantic, to discuss such commonplace terms as 'neighbour' and 'neighbourhood'. However, problems of definition appear time and again in the research literature, notably in the framing of questions and the interpretation of answers in survey work. It is often difficult to discover exactly what is being measured and described and, consequently, serious problems are encountered in attempting to compare one study with another. There is considerable ambiguity in the meaning and use of terms such as 'neighbour', resulting in widespread conceptual confusion (Keller 1968:15). The literature is scant, predominantly atheoretical and not sufficiently advanced to have produced a debate on concepts, let alone a consensus.

Much of the difficulty stems from the fact that people themselves differ in their conception of neighbour and neighbourhood; some respondents, for example, conceive of neighbours as those living next door to them whilst others will adopt a less restricted definition and include people living within the same street. The term 'neighbourhood' is notorious for the variety of meanings attached to it and hence its use is almost as hazardous as that of the term 'community' (cf. Bell and Newby 1971, chapter 2). Of course, these differences between personal perceptions and definitions are in themselves of considerable interest in research on neighbouring, but in most studies they are taken at face value. Thus, in a typical survey, respondents are asked when they last visited one of their neighbours and provide an answer within their own definition. Data may then be collected which under- or over-estimate the extent of neighbouring activity and which conflict with the researcher's own conception of neighbouring. The resulting confusion may mean, for example, that 'by confounding the distinction between neighbour and friend, studies often report less neighbouring in cities than would be shown to exist were other definitions of neighbouring used' (Keller 1968:15–16).

In some studies attempts have been made to avoid the problem by imposing operational definitions: thus Wallin preceded the administration of a questionnaire with instructions to the interviewee, who was told that:

> In the questions you are now going to answer the word *neighbourhood* means all homes within one block in any direction from the block where you live. *Neighbour* means any person living that distance from you. (1953:343)

However, it appears that respondents found difficulty in thinking along the same lines as the researcher, and frequently answered within their own more restricted terms.

Formal 'objective' operational definitions have, however, been usefully employed in studies of areas physically and socially distinctive where it was possible to assume that neighbouring was contained within a chosen area. In McGahan's (1972) study of an apartment block in New York City no difficulty was encountered in restricting the use of the term 'neighbour' to fellow residents in the block. Similarly, in the work of Festinger and his colleagues (1950) and Caplow and Forman (1950), neighbour interaction could be considered within the isolated student housing projects they studied. In the latter study the problem of defining neighbours was, in a sense, avoided because each respondent was asked to evaluate his relationship – or lack of it – with every other resident in the project.

Neighbour

All studies agree that *proximity* is an essential and key attribute of a neighbour. Indeed, the root of the word is in the Old English word for 'nigh-dweller' or 'near-dweller'. The spatial distance between oneself and one's neighbours varies, but within limits. Most of the literature suggests that neighbours live within walking distance and that face to face contact is possible. Neighbours are rarely regarded as further afield than the street, block or apartment building. A second common suggestion made throughout the literature is that the neighbour relationship is a relatively limited one. Although accounts of the limits vary, it is generally agreed that being a neighbour is something much more specific, more narrowly framed, than being a relation or friend, just as it is noticeably less specific than being an employer or a social worker. Its occupation of this indeterminate relational middle ground is no doubt a principal source of its resistance to tidy operational treatment in social research. It is neither universal nor specific; it is framed by propinquity and in general terms by little else.

Being a neighbour, then, is a matter of location. Unfortunately, in common use the term has become saturated with emotional and normative connotations which obscure this simple truth. In seeking a definition of neighbours and neighbourhoods one must begin by eliminating these prescriptive moral and evaluative overtones that have come to surround everyday notions of neighbouring and neighbourliness. Neighbours are quite simply people who live near one another. Living near to others is a distinctive context for relationships – nothing more. And the most obvious special feature of nearness as a setting for relationships is the exceptional cheapness with which it can

Defining the field

permit good relationships and the exceptional cost it can attach to bad ones. Relationships are constructed within many different spatial and institutional settings – each of which provides a peculiar context of opportunity and of constraint so far as the character and content of actual relationships are concerned. The family, the workplace, the neighbourhood, the school, the church, the voluntary association are all familiar examples of such settings, settings within which actual networks of positive or negative interaction are or are not created. Obviously, the properties of the setting influence the nature of the networks that are created within them. But it remains essential not to confuse the settings with the relationships – and unfortunately the everyday connotations of terms like neighbouring, neighbourliness and neighbourhood can do just that. Workmates are people who work in a common norm-governed organisational setting; co-religionists are people who seek salvation in the same norm-governed system of belief; but neighbours are merely people who inhabit the same locality, and by comparision with co-workers and co-religionists their interactions are distinctly *not* norm-governed. Co-workers, co-religionists and co-residents may or may not form friendships. If they do, the nature of the friendship will in part reflect the distinctive character of the interactional setting in which the relationship arose; occupation, belief, local residence – the more so the more the setting is experienced as an autonomous normative system. But it will not be determined by it. Nor, so far as the commitment of the friends to caring for each other is concerned, will it be peculiar to it. Friendships are both constrained (by settings and other opportunity structures of the individual's environment) and chosen (on the basis of values, costs and rewards). The question explored further in chapter 5, therefore, is about the relationship between the character of social networks and residential nearness. More specifically it is a question about the conditions under which neighbours become friends – given that 'nighness' is, normatively, a peculiarly weak basis of attachment.

Neighbourhood, neighbouring and neighbourliness

The term 'neighbourhood' appears to be even more elusive in meaning than that of 'neighbour', not least because, in addition to a variety of personal and social definitions it has also encompassed technical meanings in urban and social planning. As Roderick McKenzie of the Chicago School of Urban Sociology observed in 1921:

> Probably no other term is used so loosely or with such changing content as the term neighbourhood, and very few concepts are more difficult to define. The word neighbourhood has two general connotations: physical proximity to a given object of attention, and intimacy of association among people living in close proximity to one another. (Hawley 1968:73)

Many attempts at defining neighbourhood have been made, incorporating ideas of physical demarcation, self-containment in respect of certain services and atmosphere or sentiment. Ruth Glass's definition is widely quoted. A neighbourhood is a distinct territorial group, distinct by virtue of the specific physical characteristics of the area and the specific social characteristics of the inhabitants. (1948:18)

Definitions of this kind have been particularly associated with those concerned to make sense of the city by dissecting it into its constituent neighbourhoods. The foundations of this approach can justifiably be said to stem from the work of the Chicago School, which sought to demonstrate the ecological interrelations between the sub-areas – the 'Gold Coast', the zone of transition, the slum, 'Little Italy' and so on – of the urban 'organism' (see Robson 1969; Hunter 1974).

Others have taken the perception and demarcation of neighbourhood as the central concern of their inquiries. Typical of this is the work of Terence Lee (1968) who questioned residents of Cambridge about their conception of neighbourhood. This, and other studies, showed that individuals differed very considerably in their perceptions. In a similar exercise Reimer (1951) had shown a marked lack of consensus when asking respondents "what do you consider 'your' neighbourhood?", 53 respondents, out of a total of 197, defined their neighbourhood as an area of one block or less, whilst as many as 78 thought it to be greater than seven blocks. A fundamental objection to the use of the term emerges from the fact that many were unable to associate with it.

> People were not only vague about the subject of discussion, but felt actually forced to make a choice between different types of experience to which the term 'neighbourhood' could be applied. (Reimer, 1951:35)

Finally, the term 'neighbourhood unit' has been formulated and received widespread attention in urban planning. Apparently first espoused by Clarence Perry in the early 1920s, the idea of developing towns on the basis of neighbourhoods became something of a vogue in the inter- and post-war years, producing a substantial literature (see especially Dennis 1968; Mumford 1954; Goss 1961; Hallman 1984). The concept of neighbourhood units was, above all, functional. The intention was to create fairly self-contained sub-areas of the city, containing some 5,000 to 10,000 people, sufficient to support a primary school, shops and some services, yet small enough to foster a 'sense' of neighbourhood, engendering community 'cohesion'. In Britain this was given official backing in the 1944 Dudley Report on the design of dwellings and such neighbourhood units are a feature of many New Towns (see Goss 1961).

Nearness, or neighbourhood, is itself an ambiguous concept. It is not, for example, as easily specified as occupation or religion. Rural nearness involves distances very different from those that constitute urban nearness. Car-ownership and even telephones notoriously revolutionise the meaning of nearness. More generally, proximity is a matter of costs, facilities, technology and logistics. So how is one to determine the nature of neighbourhood or the boundaries of nigh-dwelling? There will always be some lack of fit between subjective and objective maps of locality – indeed, within any postu-

Defining the field

lated neighbourhood the subjective maps of different individual inhabitants are likely to vary dramatically. For purposes of analysis, neighbourhoods must be defined, however arbitrarily, in terms of some external (even if not objective) measures of deployment, concentration and distance.

The 'streets' studied (in chapter 4) were neighbourhoods as defined by architects, planners and officials who lived elsewhere – determinate, named and bounded territorial settings for the domestic life of others. They were settings in which people were forced into an externally specified spatial nearness to one another. The research problem was to see what they made of that fact in terms of relational nearness. For that purpose it was essential to start with spatial not relational neighbourhoods. Then it would be possible to consider how far and in what ways externally specified neighbourhoods of different types were realised subjectively as neighbourhoods by their inhabitants, how far strong personal attachments arose among people within given types of externally specified neighbourhood as compared to people in other types and, conversely, how far the attachments formed in any type of externally specified neighbourhood were shaped by the fact of proximity within it rather than by other structures of cost, opportunity and value in the lives of the people concerned.

To sum up by means of encapsulating definitions:

Neighbours are simply people who live near one another.

Neighbourhood is an effectively defined terrain or locality inhabited by neighbours. Subjective and objective designations of neighbourhood in these terms will in almost all cases fail to fit. Research and policy must build on the probable distance between the two.

Neighbouring is the actual pattern of interaction observed within any given neighbourhood whether objectively or subjectively defined. Indeed, the term neighbourhood has been used to refer to that area 'where neighbours reside and in which neighbouring takes place' (Keller 1968:12).

Neighbourliness, by contrast, is a positive and committed relationship constructed between neighbours, a form of friendship. It is not a special type of good relationship peculiar to neighbours but an instance of a larger type of relationship contingently arising, in some circumstances, between nigh-dwellers. The crucial question is that of the relationship of the particular local setting to other settings of the lives of the individuals in question. Being a neighbour is a role, not an existence. The study of neighbourliness involves assessing the relationship between the given world of nigh-dwellers as proximate persons and the larger systems of social networks and relationships in which individuals are also involved.

The extent of neighbourliness may be accounted for in terms of the characteristics of neighbourhoods as settings, *or* in terms of the characteristics of the individuals involved, *or* in terms of the social networks through which individuals and settings are locked together. Social networks are discussed in more detail in chapter 3. The point to emphasise is that the actual networks of neighbouring among any given aggregate of neighbours, ranging from neighbourliness to hostility, indifference and neglect, can be understood only as fragments of the complex systems of networks in which all concerned participate.

Informal neighbouring

There has to be the possibility of explaining the local in terms of the constraints and choices of a non-local world. The six 'streets' were studied not only in terms of the ethnography of neighbourliness but in terms, too, of networks quite other than those of neighbouring.

A further useful distinction is that between *manifest* and *latent* neighbourliness, proposed by Peter Mann. Manifest neighbourliness is characterised by overt forms of social relationships, such as mutual visiting in the home and going out for leisure and recreation. Latent neighbourliness is characterised by favourable attitudes to neighbours which result in positive action when a need arises, especially in times of crisis or emergency. These two forms can be thought to occur in combination, together capable of describing the pattern a relationship takes (Mann 1954: 164). Notions of manifest and latent neighbourliness have the advantage of establishing some links between attitudes and behaviour. There are many indications in the literature of the importance of latent neighbourliness which only comes to the surface in certain situations; Mogey, for example, noted that in Oxford:

> Although the most general strand in the pattern of neighbouring both in St Ebbe's and in Barton is the 'keep myself to myself' one, all these individuals have great reserves of friendliness. Any emergency will uncover this willingness to help. (1956:93)

This and other examples suggest that potential neighbourliness is no less important than neighbourly activity manifest in everyday life. A caring environment, for example, may be felt to exist but not be revealed until a particular situation of need calls it into play and neighbourly help is mobilised. Attitudes, expectations and contexts must be addressed as much, or more than, actions alone. From the point of view of policy and practice, little has yet been done to demonstrate the nature and sources of this latent element, let alone to suggest the conditions under which it is or could be made manifest. One development which has attempted to capitalise on it has been that towards various forms of neighbourhood care.

Neighbourhood care

Neighbourhood care is a type of community care. 'Community care' may be defined as the 'provision of help, support and protection to others by lay members of societies acting in everyday domestic and occupational settings' (Abrams 1978a:78). This meaning is rather different from that used, for example, in the health services, where it refers to the transfer of those suffering, in particular, from mental illness and handicap from institutions into non-institutional settings (cf. DHSS 1981a,b; Walker 1982:13–39). Philip Abrams distinguished community care from some of the other main forms of social care – institutional care, institutional treatment and community treatment – by both its typical agents and its typical milieux. The agents of community care were unspecialised and the milieux are open; both were socially given rather than administratively constructed. It could be shown diagrammatically as in table 2.1.

Defining the field 23

Table 2.1. *Settings and milieux for community care*

		Setting	
		Closed	Open
Personnel	Professional/ specialist	Institutional treatment	Community treatment
	Lay/non-specialist	Institutional care	Community care

For practical purposes, however, any separation of community care from other forms of social care is a relative matter. In practice some of the most representative and many of the most innovative forms of social care combine, blur or bridge the modes isolated: several types of hostel provision, therapeutic communities and sheltered villages, home helps and most community workers would all be mixed or impure types of social care in these terms. And it may be just these hybrid forms in which community care overlaps with institutional care on the one hand and with community treatment on the other that will prove the most fruitful sites for research. That is especially likely to be the case if one assumes any deep conflict of principles between community care and other forms of provision.

Community care must be understood as a complement not as an alternative to other forms of social care. It may be seen as the base on which more specialised forms of provision build or as the ideal which the more specialised forms underpin and sustain. But from either point of view the meshing together of community care and other forms of provision seems bound to become a major issue for policy and therefore for research. The place and function of community care within the overall pattern of social care has implications for both values and resources which compel attention.

The concept of neighbourhood care (as a form of community care) remains curiously vague, ambiguous and *ad hoc*. Much of the appeal of the call for neighbourhood care has been a matter of ill-defined sentiment and imprecise rhetorical resonance. It feels like a good thing; it sounds, nebulously, like the sort of thing we would want to value. Yet in practice it covers an enormous variety of projects and possibilities. Almost any sort of provision for almost any sort of need can, so long as it is offered at or near the place of residence of the beneficiary, be identified as neighbourhood care. So if enthusiasm for neighbourhood care is to be more than a diffusely sympathetic posture, if it is to become a matter of specific social policies achieving specific results, a more precise definition of the term is required. But once one begins to think about possible definitions of neighbourhood care it seems impossible not to recognise that the idea is profoundly ambivalent, moreover, that the ambivalence is intrinsic and cannot easily be resolved. On inspection the call for neighbourhood care appears to be a call for two quite different, and in some ways antithetical, developments of social policy. Neighbourhood care is a term which can refer to the intensity and extent of neighbourliness achieved in a neighbourhood. Or it can refer to the provision of social services to the inhabitants of a neighbourhood with no necessary reference to neighbourliness at all. It can be a call for the extension of neighbourliness, or it can be a call for the extension of the welfare state. The idea of neighbourhood care crosses a frontier between formally organised social action and essentially informal social relationships. In the language of the Wolfenden Committee (1978) it has one foot firmly in the informal sector of social care, the world of kin, friends and neighbours, but the other is no less firmly planted in the formal sector, the world of voluntary organisations, professional services and statutory agencies. Yet there are fundamental senses in which the world of neighbourliness and the world of the welfare state, far from being complementary, are deeply at odds with one another, founded on incompatible principles, even mutually exclusive. Those who favour neighbourhood care overlook the extent to which they are attempting to bridge alien worlds, to cross the difficult and problematic frontier between formal social action and informal social relationships.

There is no reason why neighbourhood care should not be defined in terms of pursuing both neighbourliness and localised service delivery. Indeed, there is an overwhelming consensus among those for whom neighbourhood care is a project that that conjunction is just what the project is about; that the whole point is to provide services in ways that elicit neighbourliness while eliciting neighbourliness in ways that provide services. It allows us to recognise that by far the strongest form of social care in our (and probably any) society is provided within relationships of kinship (and to a lesser extent of proximity, friendship, race and religion), while also identifying a rather large category of people for whom, for different reasons, that form of care is going to have to be a matter of both supporting natural caring networks and creating artificial networks where the former do not exist.

So we arrive at a definition. Neighbourhood care is a mobilisation of local energies and resources to achieve levels of indigenous concern and support which complement, supplement and progressively contain the need for external statutory and voluntary services in specified respects. 'Mobilisation' is a key term in this definition because it refers both to the ideal end product (high levels of neighbourliness) and to the preferred means of getting there (all sorts of collective action to invoke, evoke and provoke localised concern and support).

In this sense neighbourhood care may be seen as a cunning independence movement of the informal sector which seeks to create and hold a territory for itself by exploiting the resources, using the methods and emulating the standards of the formal sector. Thus, to quote one example, 'by linking people, groups and services together ... having a visiting scheme to befriend anyone who is lonely or isolated ... giving practical or emergency help where needed ... running local and social groups ... the aim is to use local people as a resource to help one another in an informal way'. Or it may be seen as a cunning extension of social control which seeks to advance the frontiers of public surveillance and service by appropriating the rhetoric and forms of private life. Thus, as one Social Services Department puts it: 'the aim is to help organise neighbourhoods to meet the personal and social needs of their less fortunate inhabitants ... quick referral to the Social Services Department will enable the deployment of centrally based volunteers or social workers ... the ultimate aim will clearly be to have a Good Neighbour Cell (*sic*) for every street within the Authority (*sic*)'. Most versions of the project hover uneasily between these extremes and it may not matter where on the spectrum they are. The projects are defined not by their commitment to either neighbourliness or service delivery but by their insistence on the idea of promoting both jointly through one and the same measures. That would be the critical test of whether any given enterprise was or was not a Neighbourhood Care project.

The alternative route to a definition, particularly from the point of view of an interest in voluntary action, would be to 'unpack' the notion of neighbourhood care, substituting for it a more mundane concern with each or either of the two main elements of which it is composed namely: (1) voluntary action to promote neighbourhood involvement – regardless of care, and (2) voluntary action to promote informal care – regardless of neighbouring. In both cases what is known of neighbouring and of the relationships and values involved in informal care can provide examples of this differentiation. It is made by less utopian voluntary agencies interested in either neighbourhood involvement or informal care, but not the more ambitious 'package' of neighbourhood care which attempts to combine both elements in one. Such an approach would, however, amount to watering down the concept to the point of disappearing.

One major analytical issue which has invariably confused discussion of neighbourhood care in the past has been the question of spontaneity. It is often held that such care is somehow dependent upon the spontaneous action of members of a community. Celebration of spontaneity is above all to be found in accounts by members of voluntary caring agencies of the reasons for their own activity. By contrast, it is necessary deliberately and specifically to avoid any suggestion that spontaneity is a defining feature of neighbourhood care. The reasons that lead volunteers to volunteer are indeed obscure and a proper object of research. But, quite apart from the fact that spontaneity is a wholly mystifying and unsociological conception in this context, there is no evidence that would suggest that spontaneity is in any way an important source of the type of sustained altruistic practice which neighbourhood care embodies.

The relevant distinction is between formal and informal organisation, *not* between organisation and spontaneity. Just as the 'altruistic' suicide is impelled to self-destruction not by a spontaneous self-expression but by social norms from which he cannot escape, so neighbourhood care appears to be a product of strong and persuasive informal social organisation culminating in the feeling that one ought to help, not in the feeling that it would be fun to help. Indeed, in social analysis generally it is noticeable that while it is now quite acceptable to explain 'bad' behaviour in terms of social constraints, it is regarded as preposterous to explain 'good' behaviour in the same way;

individualism has survived much more effectively in the analysis of goodness. Specifically with relation to community care the tendency has been to hope for an adequate supply of good, or bribable, persons rather than to ask about the conditions that *make* good communities.

Where effective systems of intensive community care have been discovered, there is an interesting contrast between the form of the caring relationship and its basis. The form of the relationship is indeed seen as mediated by rhetoric of spontaneity. But its practice and predictability, the fact that we can talk about relationships and not merely about encounters, result from the involvement of actors in some system of entrenched and impelling social norms. It is the normative basis of care that is stressed again and again in these studies.

These issues about neighbourhood care are discussed fully in the second part of the book, beginning in chapter 7. The point to be brought out here is that there is a distinction between informal care by kin or friends or 'nigh-dwellers' and neighbourhood care. While the latter seeks to build on the sentiments and relationships of informal care, it goes beyond them and takes on different forms – more organised, in particular, and more oriented to service delivery. At the same time, there is some degree of overlap between informal care and neighbourhood care, at least so far as neighbours (rather than kin) are concerned, just as there is overlap between the first and second parts of this book. The concept of neighbourhood care is a dual, even ambiguous, one.

The basic dilemma is that neighbourhood care as service delivery does not have to have anything to do with neighbourhood care as neighbourliness, or vice versa. Indeed, these two types of neighbourhood care could perfectly well be thought of as irrelevant to one another. Accordingly, if neighbourhood care of the first type – neighbourliness – is thought desirable in its own right as an objective of policy, neighbourhood care in the second sense – service delivery – will have to be designed and implemented in specific appropriate ways, which could prove an expensive, even inefficient, business. Neither type of neighbourhood care is going automatically to achieve the other. If both are wanted, policies must be developed specifically tailored to that double purpose. Left to themselves neighbourhood care policies of the second type do not do the sorts of things that would cultivate neighbourhood care based on neighbourliness – that is perhaps the heart of the problem. The method of formal organisation, the distinctive mode of service delivery, may not actually subvert informal care but neither is it an easy or sure way to promote it.

This brief discussion of the definition of key terms clears the way for the next chapter, discussing previous research on informal, unorganised, neighbouring. The results of the Street studies are then presented in chapter 4.

3 Making sense of neighbours and neighbouring

The Street studies in the next chapter aimed to establish the social conditions under which neighbourliness in the form of day to day helpfulness was likely to occur. At the outset of the research, a review was undertaken of relevant studies to find out what were the most significant aspects of neighbouring and neighbourliness for investigation.

This is not an exhaustive literature survey. That has been done on a number of occasions elsewhere: Keller (1968), Boissevain and Mitchell (1973), Fischer *et al.* (1977), Robinson and Abrams (1977). Instead only those selected aspects of earlier works are discussed which were found to be particularly pertinent and helpful in relation to the problems of neighbouring and neighbourliness. Specifically, this chapter draws together work on the basic elements of neighbouring, on some of the formal properties of neighbouring, and on place, class and time as contexts of neighbouring.

The basic elements of neighbouring

Fortuitously, the search began with the discovery of Peter Mann's paper on 'The Concept of Neighbourliness' (1954). Along with most of the authors whose work was examined, he used the terms neighbouring and neighbourliness in an intuitive manner giving them definitions at odds with those proposed in the last chapter and, more pertinently, devoid of an alternative considered theoretical meaning of their own. Throughout this chapter the usage of the authors discussed is therefore 'translated' to make it consonant with the definitions given earlier. Mann's paper was really about the concept of 'neighbouring' – about interaction between neighbours rather than about a relationship of positive attachments. He saw manifest neighbouring as characterised by all sorts of practically enacted social intercourse: visiting, joint outings, amiable greetings, recriminations, vandalism. Latent neighbouring, by contrast, was a matter of dispositions, of a reserve of sentiment not normally enacted but brought to life in appropriate specific circumstances, especially in times of crisis or emergency.

He drew attention to the fact that a great deal of neighbouring was probably situational or context-specific and not therefore readily observable in the conditions and activities of routine everyday life. Studies such as the Kingston inquiry (1972) leave little doubt that there is indeed a reserve of judgements and beliefs about the desirability and propriety of neighbouring beneath the surface of everyday interaction which sustains a potential for positive or negative action far beyond anything that can be directly observed in the ordinary course of normal life.

Nevertheless, it is of course actions that seize the researcher's attention in the first instance. Virtually all the studies reviewed focussed on neighbouring *activity*, and moreover on the positive forms of such activity typified by acts of helpfulness, as what neighbouring is all about. Mann's 'negative' pole was virtually ignored. This line will be followed for the moment, while noting suspiciously the lack of information provided on the nature, forms and bases of un-neighbourly action. Several writers – for example, Kuper (1953), McGahan (1972) and Shulman (1967) – advance the view, adopted implicitly by almost all authors, that there are two basic elements in positive neighbouring: *friendliness* and *helpfulness*. Both are seen as very inclusive categories, and the specific actions which they embrace are treated as being to a large extent prescribed in variable ways by local, historical and culturally specific personal and collective standards and conventions. Thus, individuals and groups differ dramatically in their understanding of, for example, the significance and value of given forms of greeting. There are different indicators, salient symbols and interpretations for both friendliness and helpfulness in milieux which have different norms and resources and histories so that it becomes virtually impossible to assign fixed values to any given actions. The modes of friendliness and helpfulness are, as it were, the common denominators of positive neighbouring whatever their specific, locally enacted content may be. Table 3.1 tries to summarise the main types of action most frequently identified as exemplifying each of these common basic components of positive neighbouring.

Friendliness is generally thought of as a matter of forms of action which are more diffuse and involve lower levels of commitment than those implicit in helping. It has been treated as a type of interaction requiring little more than a minimal degree of personal engagement. '"We're friendly", says Mr Wild, "... but we don't get too involved because we've found that causes gossip and trouble ..." People are wary, though polite' (Young and Willmott, 1972:148). Friendliness has been discussed most regularly in studies of new estates and developments, many authors having now disputed the widely held view that these are somehow peculiarly unfriendly places – thus Bracey (1964), Mogey (1956), Thorns (1972). Yet the precise point at which one might distinguish friendliness from, say, mere civility or interest at one extreme or a deep concern and involvement at the other in these or other settings remains highly obscure.

Trying to clarify it brings one back to the crucial problem of distinguishing neighbouring from neighbourliness or neighbours from friends. What is clear in the literature is that, in the understandings of everyday life, there is a world of difference between any mode of friendliness and friendship; that the former, but *not* the latter is a conventional idiom of neighbouring; and that unlike the latter it involves distances as well as closeness. Pfiel (1968:147) provides a sensitive illustration in discussing greetings between neighbours: 'a greeting is a turning towards *and* a turning away ... it implies both good manners and social distance ... to some people the element of turning

Table 3.1 *The principal forms of positive neighbouring*

	Friendliness
Mode	Examples
1 Acquaintance	Awareness of who neighbours are and some casual greeting.
2 Cordiality/sociability	Chatting. Visiting. Going to shops together.
3 Communication	Exchange of information. Gossiping.
4 Participation in individual or family events	Neighbours being invited to weddings or funerals.
5 Participation in collective events	Street parties. Local celebration organised by neighbours for neighbours.
	Helpfulness
6 Services for convenience	Holding money for rent-collectors, etc., keeping the key for meter-readers, relations.
7 Watch and ward	Keeping an eye on a neighbour's house during absences. Checking that 'all is well' with old people.
8 Routine, recurrent helping	Babysitting. Child-minding. Taking a neighbour's children to school.
9 Specialist services	Skilled neighbour helping with plumbing, electrical repairs, decorating.
10 Borrowing and lending	Routine loans of equipment, foodstuffs, et.
11 Help in individual or family crises	Response to fire, flood, etc. Offering comfort to the bereaved. Looking after the sick.
12 Help in collective crises	Aid in the face of natural disasters, war, general economic insecurity, etc.
13 Help in collective events	Joint harvesting.

towards is the important one, to others it is that of distance'. Friendliness is a medium of casual sociability and routine interaction; stylised, superficial, at once outgoing and restrained; it connects by presuming separation. Friendship, discussed in chapter 5, is something altogether different.

Helpfulness ranges from relatively minor acts such as passing on the rent for a neighbour who is out, through to saving life in a disaster or persistently caring for the lonely or disabled. The literature focusses mainly on the former types of activity – borrowing sugar is the classic instance – but writers such as Form and Nosow (1958) and Barton (1969) document the upsurge of very substantial forms of help given by neighbours in major disasters and crises. Form and Nosow note that as high a proportion as three-quarters of people involved in major natural disasters may be rescued in the first few hours by neighbours or kin living nearby, while Barton discusses the more general appearance of 'local therapeutic social systems' in the wake of calamity – an extreme demonstration, perhaps, of the release of latent positive neighbouring.

Disasters apart, one important aspect of neighbourly helping is its relation to help from other sources. In what circumstances, that is, do people seek or receive help from neighbours rather than from friends, relatives, voluntary or statutory agencies? Evidently, the answer depends once again on perceptions, norms and resources in any given setting. Litwak and Szelenyi have produced an exceptionally persuasive discussion of the tasks which are 'the special province of neighbours'. Firstly, there are those in which speed of reaction is important – ranging from the quick convenience of *ad hoc* borrowing and lending, to help in an emergency when time is of the essence. Secondly, there are ranges of problems common to, and based on, the sharing of a common territorial location – situations in which people help each other and themselves by grouping together to improve shared services and local amenities, for example. And thirdly, there are tasks necessary for socialisation, continuous and everyday learning experiences and 'watch and ward' functions involving constant local presence but no specific helping activity – such as the informal pooling of knowledge of child-rearing or 'keeping an eye' on solitary dependants. 'Time emergencies, services based on territoriality, and activities which require everyday observation' (Litwak and Szelenyi 1969:470), are seen as constituting the distinctive modes of neighbourly helpfulness.

There is one feature of neighbouring which seems to be enormously valued as a component of positive neighbouring, respect for privacy. So regularly and emphatically does this emerge from the literature that it must be placed alongside friendliness and helpfulness as one of the essential components of positive neighbouring. The placing of respect for privacy on the same footing as friendliness and helpfulness is hardly controversial; it occurs in almost all studies.

> It appears that people value helpfulness and privacy more than personal qualities in their neighbours. It can be seen in fact that the role of neighbours is a fairly general one in that it does not demand a particular type of person, but rather someone who is prepared to be helpful, friendly *and* to respect their neighbours' privacy to a greater or lesser extent. (Kingston 1972:95)

The suggestion that privacy should be regarded as more fundamental than friendliness or helpfulness is more debatable but it does have substantial support. Bracey, for example, (1964:79–86) found that English householders clearly recognised that neighbours constitute a threat to privacy. In both England and the United States he found general agreement that neighbours are best kept at arm's length, even though hardly any of the people he studied had themselves ever had any direct experience of intrusive or prying neighbours. He was impelled towards the view that neighbouring began with the guarding of domestic secrets. [For a further discussion, see Bulmer 1985b.]

Throughout the literature in fact there are constant echoes of the folk wisdom quoted by Robert Frost: 'good fences make good neighbours' – and not just good fences, but stout walls, thick curtains and discreetly averted heads, too. We are, however, left with Frost's nagging question: '*Why* do they make good neighbours?'

Neighbouring, then, seems to be a type of interaction constituted in a rather enigmatic three-dimensional space. Insofar as it is positively evaluated the evaluation appears to be made typically in terms of friendliness, helpfulness and privacy. Two of these elements would seem to be essentially sociable and other-regarding; the third is plainly disengaging and self-regarding. Good neighbouring could be said to be a matter of finding a point of equilibrium in a highly unstable field of contrary forces. Indeed, the conflict of inclinations is nowhere more apparent than in accounts of what people understand 'good neighbours' to be. Hole's study of tenants is representative:

> Great value was placed on helpfulness, such as practical assistance in times of illness or keeping an eye on children when the mother was out. At the same time there was an almost equal emphasis on withdrawal. The ideal neighbour was neither too interfering nor too intimate, and did not repeat confidences (1959:167).

Bracey (1964:74) notes that a standard feature of the good neighbour was being ready to talk but not too talkative, 'nobody wanted "the real gabby type" as one American housewife described the neighbour who did not know how to stop talking'. All but 10% of the people Kuper (1953) interviewed made reference to some form of helpfulness in their definitions. But thereafter the vast majority also pointed to the importance of some combination of closeness and distance. Positive aspects included: "Always happy to speak to you when they see you"; "Pleasant; doesn't interfere"; "Friendly, without being too familiar"; "Someone for a chat, but in and out all the time I can't bear"; "Always acknowledges you but respects your privacy." Negative aspects mentioned included: "Minds her own business"; "Doesn't interfere"; "Not nosey"; "Don't believe in going into each other's houses"; "Respects your privacy." The problem of course, both for neighbours and for those who study neighbours, is to tease out what Paine (1969) and Allan (1979) have called the 'rules of relevance' for accomplishing the balancing out between involvement and withdrawal. (See also Ginsberg and Churchman 1983.)

Although these studies tell us very convincingly what neighbours can, and do, do they still leave us a long way from an explanation of why they do such things. The literature indicates other properties of positive neighbouring of a less other-regarding nature. Litwak and Szelenyi, for example, themselves introduce larger questions of the functions of neighbouring in creating and enforcing social cohesion and social control. One can go further and ask where the standards and conventions that are so enforced come from in the first place; of considering whose standards and conventions were being imposed on whom. How far and in what circumstances is social control through neighbouring a matter of mutual regulation; how far and in what circumstances do the mechanisms work to enable some neighbours (or even some non-neighbours) to control others?

Bailey's work on the local-level politics of reputations (1971) has been centrally concerned with these aspects of neighbouring. Neighbouring has been found to maintain cohesion by evoking a sense of identification with and obligation to locality and the cultivation of what are perceived as 'neighbourhood' values (Smith 1975; Boissevain 1974; Bracey 1964). Social control can similarly be enforced through myriad forms of neighbouring such as gossip, casual conversation and informal surveillance – all of which subject individuals to purportedly collective sets of norms and expectations.

Most of the literature, moreover, quite ignores both bad neighbouring and the razor's edge that divides it from good neighbouring. Oddly, there are few references to trouble between neighbours and indeed, one gains the impression that conflict and other forms of bad neighbouring are rare, or uninteresting, occurrences. Yet the few studies of negative neighbouring that we have – Collison's saga of the Cutteslowe Walls (1963) for example, or Bailey's study of malignant gossip (1971), or the appalling world of 'amoral familism' discovered by Banfield (1958) – all suggest that such situations and styles of interaction would richly repay research. Not least because they imply that bad neighbouring involves only a very slight tipping of the relational balance that sustains good neighbouring. Quite marginal changes in people's resources, quite trivial and unconsidered infringements of convention, even the modest over-performance of approved patterns of neighbouring can precipitate torrents of bad neighbouring. Mr and Mrs Crudas in Austen Avenue (p. 50) found themselves launched on a bleak career as bad neighbours for just such reasons.

An affectionate picture of bad neighbouring is provided by James Mearns's nineteenth-century Tyneside song, *The Neighbours Doon Belaa (Down Below)*:

> Oh – they'll borrow your onions, leeks and peas whenever the pot's to boil
> They'll ask for ha'penny candles if they canna get parafin oil
> Whatever they borrow they'll never return
> Such folks I never saa,
> The skin is wrapped for its hide in fact for the neighbours doon belaa.
>
> I'll tell ye the deeings of some of the folks that live in wor neighbourhood
> They're a lot of lazy good-for-nowts and meest of them is far from good,
> From Sunday morn to Saturday neet they're cadging neet and day,
> And whatever they borrow they'll never return so you might as well hoy it away.
>
> Oh, they'll borrow your onions ...
>
> Yon Misstress Smith set up her gob and asked us what I meant,
> Cos I wouldn't lend her half a crown to help her pay the rent,
> I've lent her money and one afore but I'll never die it again
> For she called us hotty a fiery fool and she hit us with a steen.
>
> Oh, they'll borrow your onions ...
>
> I started a shop but oh dear me, of that I soon got sick
> It was like a clock that wadn't gan without its favourite tick,
> The mainspring broke, the clock was then hoyed out into the street,
> I often said the clock would gan if the neighbours wad be reet.
>
> Oh, they'll borrow your onions ...

Many of the cases of bad neighbouring in the Street studies arose either from overstepping perceived boundaries of privacy, or from the exercise of social control. The latter was very clear, for example, in the case of Mrs Cousins in Dryden Close, the outcast of the estate (p. 54). The extent of mutual surveillance by neighbours deserves more attention, as does the social significance of gossip (cf. Gluckman 1963). As Mr Bennett remarks in *Pride and Prejudice*: 'For what do we live but to make sport of our neighbours, and to laugh at them in turn?' At a recent trial of members of a drug smuggling ring uncovered as a result of the interest taken in their activities by local villagers on the Pembrokeshire coast, the prosecuting counsel observed that the accused forgot one thing, 'a characteristic you may think of rural life. Some call it neighbourliness, some call it over-curiosity, and some would say it is nosiness' (*The Guardian*, 6 June 1984). Recent studies of unemployment, the informal sector and the 'hidden economy' provide some evidence of negative neighbouring. Bell and McKee (1984) found that unemployed people felt inhibited in engaging in activities outside the home because they believed they were under constant scrutiny by neighbours, so that breaking Social Security rules would lead to punitive action. Wallace and Pahl's study of the Isle of Sheppey (1984) showed similar inhibitions among the unemployed, who feared being reported to the DHSS by jealous neighbours, as well as at least one case in which a local shopkeeper carefully watched the amounts of money his unemployed customers had to spend in order to report unusual affluence. In other cases, like neighbours who suspect parents are being neglectful or cruel to their children, interference may be justified in terms of protecting the weak.

Some cases of bad neighbouring (the Cutteslowe Walls, for example) arise from conflicts of interest between groups, and some – such as Banfield's amoral familism – from the pursuit of self-interest at the expense of the wider group. Fred Hirsch's analysis (1977:71–83) of the 'economics of bad neighbours' goes some way to explain breakdowns in neighbouring. If people treat neighbouring relationships as relationships of exchange, and assess the costs involved, they really may shift their commitment toward those that they find substantially more profitable. In modern industrial society, making friends with the neighbours tends to become a high-cost ("she's always round here wanting something"), low-reward ("you can't rely on her") business – that is to say, bad business. People can get the rewards they need, the relationships they value, more cheaply elsewhere.

The formal properties of neighbouring

Solidarity, as Durkheim long ago observed (1893, 1933:67), may be the most interesting element of social relationships and for many purposes the one most worth knowing about, but it is also one that cannot be observed directly. To the extent that the focus is upon ties of solidarity in neighbouring, the approach has got to be oblique. And in the case of neighbouring, as distinct from, say, kinship or commerce, the ties of solidarity are so peculiarly elusive and variable that almost any vantage point of relatively secure knowledge is to be welcomed – including that of relatively secure knowledge about variations in the formal characteristics of neighbourhood interaction. These characteristics might include intensity, style of transaction, density, 'multiplexity', range, frequency of contact, location of contact and clustering.

Intensity is without doubt the most intriguing of these. The assumption is that the intensity of interaction in neighbouring provides a measure of the commitment of neighbours to one another. Intensity would appear to be a bridge from action to relationships. If one could measure the intensity of neighbouring and then related levels of intensity to variations in the contexts, content or even other formal properties of neighbouring, surely one would have cracked the mystery of solidarity among neighbours? The trouble is that the relational side of intensity is, like solidarity itself, a moral rather than a formal property of interaction and has no immediately obvious empirical reference. To ask people directly, 'How intense is your relationship with the neighbours?' would be somewhat like asking, 'How much do you love your spouse?', and likely to evoke somewhat similar replies – objectively meaningless even when they were not subjectively rude. Qualities such as intensity can perhaps be discerned through close and prolonged observation but could they possibly be elicited directly? Caplow and Forman (1950) dealt with the problem by combining frequency of interaction and (presumed) closeness of contact between households to constitute an indicator of intensity. They scaled six combinations of frequency and closeness and asked each resident of their study area to locate her or his relationship with every other resident accordingly. What is achieved is a mapping of interaction in terms of frequency plus closeness. But the question of whether or not that indicates intensity in the sense of commitment for the people concerned has not really been broached. The bridge from forms of interaction to the substance of relationships has not materialised. The description of interaction in terms of its formal properties can be a useful way of formulating questions about neighbouring – so long as the questions are not mistaken for answers.

One of the more common ways of describing interaction in terms of its formal properties involves focussing attention on styles of transaction. Here the move towards precise and unambiguous terms of description is much greater, although it is still not complete. In a sense statements about style are merely generalisations about content: to talk of a joking-relationship is to talk of interaction which must include jokes, either a lot of jokes or jokes which effectively define the relationship for those concerned. The formal property implies a substantive content. Some of the work that has been done on variations in style of transaction (greeting, borrowing, joking, scandal-mongering and so forth) has been remarkably productive. It seems possible, for example, to relate variations in style both to variations in the contexts of interaction (larger structures of power, norms, resources and opportunity) and to variations in the probability of many specific actions or relationships or conditions in which one might be interested (such as mutual aid, friendship, reliable information about the circumstances of others). The conspicuous example of work of this sort is that of Kapferer (1969) who, having first differentiated five styles of transaction (conversation, joking, job assistance, personal service and cash assistance), was then able to build up a network map in terms of the

Making sense of neighbours and neighbouring

stylistic diversity (or 'multiplexity') of the links between each of the network's members and so to account cogently for the course and outcome of interaction and events within it.

One thing that earlier research has made extremely clear is that it is very difficult to know relationships between neighbours in any detailed or reliable way. And although Allan (1979:11) suggests that in the study of kinship and friendship one should direct attention to the specific content of interaction, to what happens in particular jokes or visits as it were, because categories of style are too imprecise to 'differentiate between essentially similar relationships', in studies of neighbouring those categories might well provide the finest differentiations one could hope to achieve. So far as one can tell neighbouring relationships, unlike those of kinship, perhaps, are not 'essentially similar' but enormously and minutely varied. A further important theme of recent considerations of neighbourhood and network cohesion has been concerned with the problem, posed most clearly perhaps by Elias and Scotson (1965), of the rules of bonding. This has centred on the normative construction of attachment, on the ways in which different orders of rules for relationships are worked out, known, enforced or broken. Traditionally this is the problem of norms: more recently it has been presented as the problem of the 'rules of relevance'; in either form the assumption is that under certain circumstances, supportive other-regarding behaviour comes to be widely expected in social groups or collectivities and the individuals making up those groups or collectivities experience such expectations as cogently valid for themselves. The research task, less simple than it sounds, is to establish in any given case what the rules are, how they have come into being and how they are maintained or changed. One problem is that although norms can be overtly prescribed (as in books of etiquette and manners) and sanctioned (as in codes of law), their validity is a subjective and frequently unconscious matter.

This is more definitely so the more the interactions and relations in question are ostensibly 'chosen' by the parties concerned as in, say, neighbouring or friendship. Thus, the study of norms becomes less a matter of identifying overt shared standards and more one of determining the subjective probability of various forms of action effectively implementing standards which may well be unperceived. A further difficulty, highlighted by both Paine (1969) and Allan (1979), is that norms (of which rules of relevance seem to be a special instance) must be understood as at once fixed and fluid. In effect, they map the territory of relationships but the map is one which the travellers concerned continually re-draw as they travel. The degree of freedom travellers have to re-draw the normative map in any given relationship is of course the obverse of the strength of the norms surrounding and defining that relationship. The idea of norms or rules as a point of access to the study of the cohesion of relationships is attractive just because such concepts appear to unite social organisation and individual action in a persuasive duality. As Allan puts it, 'it is this duality that makes the concept useful for analysing the solidarity present in different types of relationship'. Yet it is that very duality which the concept catches so well that seems to baffle research efforts to identify the rules of relationships empirically.

Nevertheless, the literature on neighbouring reveals a persistent wish to discover norms. Among others Mogey (1956), Bracey (1964), Keller (1968) and Smith (1975) all argue strongly for the existence of discernible neighbourhood 'codes'; 'neighbouring' according to Keller (1968:44) is a 'socially defined relationship ranging from highly formalised and institutionalised rules and obligations to highly variable voluntary exchanges'. Smith (1975:147) seizes on the same idea of normative variation as a springboard for research, emphasising the way normative bonding appears to range 'from a relatively extensive subscription to a common set of values, as in older, ethnic or working class neighbourhoods, to agreement (only) on a minimal set of behavioural codes involving the preservation of privacy'. The idea of strong norms is usually associated with the idea of strong cohesion and high levels of other-regarding activity. Yet that connection is in fact not at all obvious – once again we would argue that it is not the strength but the content of the rules-of-relationship that distinguishes, say, the socially extrovert people of Ashton described by Dennis, Henriques and Slaughter (1956) from the compulsively introvert people of Alor described by Kardiner and Prebble (1962). Evidently norms can be stronger or weaker – Bracey (1964) and Pfiel (1970) both discover norms of helping which have acquired the strength of acknowledged tradition. But equally strength and weakness can exist in relation to a universe of different values and actions – Bracey (1964) and Kuper (1953) both discovered unwritten but meticulously observed norms of *not* lending and borrowing among groups of financially hard-pressed council tenants.

The most striking instance of neighbourhood bonding achieved through strong norms is that reported from Tokyo by Ronald Dore (1958:255). The Japanese *tsukiai*, or five-household-group, is a system of mutual responsibility among neighbours within which members express complete trust in each other, lend and borrow freely and act as guardians for each other's houses, health and reputations. Moreover this nexus of social care between households is anything but informal. Rather, the relationships of involvement and support and the whole etiquette surrounding them are conceived of as an objectively established body of rules, subject to local variation and capable of being learned and taught, not simply as natural ways of behaving which can safely be left to the spontaneous promptings of the individual heart. In such circumstances norms can be said to evoke social cohesion with all the force of a social fact. The rules of neighbouring would seem to be both overt and paramount. Yet what the rules are regulating is of course a complex of relationships of exchange in a context of engrained need.

In other words while accepting the relevance of the problem of norms to any understanding of neighbourhood cohesion, explanation in terms of norms and rules must be seen as a complement to explanation in terms of exchange, not as an alternative. And both rules and exchanges need to be located contextually.

The contexts of neighbouring

The content of neighbouring constantly invited explanation in terms of the contexts of neighbouring. Two types of context seemed especially pertinent.

Making sense of neighbours and neighbouring

First, there was the larger pattern of sociability provided by association with kin, friends, co-workers, co-religionists and so forth. Secondly there were the obstacles, inhibitions and taken-for-granted realities provided by the 'facts' of place, time and social structure. Within limits, the first may be seen as a context of choices, the second as a context of constraints; one as what individuals make of the resources available to them, the other as the ways in which the resources available to them are limited by matters beyond their immediate control. In relation to the latter, the literature was unanimous in stressing the influence on neighbouring of urbanism and built form (place), length of residence and stages in the life cycle (time) and class (social structure).

The significance of urbanism – in effect, of whether the degree of urbanism of different neighbourhoods affects the pattern of neighbouring of their residents – has always been and still remains strenuously contested. The disposition of recent authors such as Pahl (1966), Pickvance (1978) and Castells (1977) is to insist that urbanism as such – as an ecological property of spatial milieux distinguished from, say, ruralism or suburbanism – lacks the precision and substance to be a useful explanatory variable (see also Abrams 1978d). Yet as Keller (1968), Morris (1968) and Butler (1976) have pointed out, there is a compelling body of evidence which does seem to link patterns of neighbouring to the specifically urban or non-urban character of the milieux in which neighbouring occurs. Thus Keller, whose scrutiny of the whole body of relevant work is by far the most thorough yet attempted, concludes that the existing evidence does point to definite relationships between urbanism and the closeness and positiveness of neighbouring:

(1) As crises diminish in number and kind where, that is, self-sufficiency increases, neighbour relations will diminish in strength and significance.
(2) As new forms of social control arise, the significance of neighbouring as a means of social control will recede in importance.
(3) Where neighbouring is a segmental activity in an open system rather than an integral part of a closed system, it will be a highly variable and unpredictable phenomenon.
(4) Since all three of these conditions are more true of urban than of rural or suburban areas, neighbouring should diminish in extent, significance and stability in cities.

There is of course no doubt that neighbouring assumes a peculiar frequency, closeness and helpfulness (and also perhaps a peculiar vindictiveness and authority) in rural settings. Arensberg and Kimball (1940), Rees (1950), Williams (1956), Frankenberg (1966), Newby (1979) have all underlined the high levels of mutual assistance to be found among neighbours in rural settings – while also pointing out that assistance is linked to economic interdependence and that rural in this analysis also means isolated, closed and long-standing. Frankenberg (1957) directly questions the extent to which contemporary villages in industrial societies can properly be regarded as 'rural' in such terms, suggesting that it is the structural implications of a certain kind of ruralism *not* the ecological fact of being in the countryside that provide the relevant context of neighbouring.

The problem is that while towns, villages and suburbs do indeed display dis-

38   Informal neighbouring

tinctive patterns of neighbouring, no specifically urban, rural or similar locational feature can be found to cause those patterns. The discovery of 'urban villages', city neighbourhoods displaying all the characteristics of neighbouring supposedly typical of the countryside, by Young and Willmott (1972), Gans (1962) and Suttles (1968), and of 'rural urbanism', villages in which the pattern of neighbouring reproduces that held to be characteristic of towns, by Frankenberg (1957), Pahl (1968) and others, plainly undermines any notion of a direct locational influence on neighbouring of the sort envisaged by Simmel (1969) and Wirth (1938). The failure of a string of authors to find any single pattern firmly associated with suburbia carries that subversion forward and has also pointed to a solution to the difficulty: Gans (1967), Berger (1960), Whyte (1963), Willmott and Young (1960), Thorns (1972). Statements such as Keller's 'the sociology of village life makes neighbouring mandatory' (1968:48), while profoundly misleading in themselves, can be made acceptable if the term 'village life' is de-coded to mean not ruralism but a *distinct social division of labour* which often is, but need not be, found in villages and which can be found elsewhere.

Urbanism and ruralism loosely indicate variations in the division of labour; they do not affect patterns of neighbouring by virtue of their intrinsic characeristics as settings but only insofar as they point to variations in the lifechances of their inhabitants, variations, that is, in the possibilities, opportunities and costs of both local and extra-local social interaction. An interesting further question then arises as to the sort of division of labour that is conducive to positive neighbouring and cohesion. Keller's account of the 'sociology of village life' points in several different directions: 'In the small rural village with long-established traditions, a common way of life, an intertwining of work, family and social relations, and a common destiny, neighbouring is a by-product of life itself.' But is it the mechanical solidarity implicit in the notion of a 'common way of life and common destiny' or the organic solidarity behind the 'intertwining of work, family and social relations' that is important? Or the combination of both types of division of labour in a single distinctive real world?

Meanwhile, if the gross properties of place indicated by notions of town, country and suburb fail to account for variations in neighbouring, what of the subtler characteristics associated with physical design? Several studies do argue that proximity, an essential condition for neighbouring, is a functional as well as a strictly spatial matter which can be affected by built form and layout insofar as these provide or fail to provide opportunities for face to face encounters. Admittedly it is usually recognised that the effects of physical features were often not at all those intended by the designer. Kuper, for example, (1953) noted that design factors meant to induce proximity, and thus positive neighbouring, commonly did no more than facilitate superficial interaction and sometimes seemed actually to promote withdrawal from interaction because people were afraid to run the risk of involvements which could prove *too* intense, or turn sour. Festinger *et al.* (1950), Hole (1959) and Pfiel (1968) have all documented the ways in which design features can influence the frequency of contact, and thence opportunities for interaction. Yet these

Making sense of neighbours and neighbouring

and other authors, such as Willmott (1963) and Whyte (1963) have also shown that the *sort* of interaction that ensues remains remarkably variable. Willmott, for example, draws attention to the way in which an arrangement that involved tenants of semi-detached houses in sharing the use, and cleaning, of joint front porches gave rise both to exceptional friendliness and to exceptional animosity. He also notes the fact that 'banjo' street designs were associated with more neighbouring than was found in conventional street patterns *and* the fact that many people avoid living in banjos precisely because they find them too neighbourly.

Once again, neighbouring emerges as an effect of constraint *and* choice; of people choosing for (as yet obscure) reasons not determined by place what they will make of the opportunites for neighbouring that place supplies. Place in both senses thus seems to provide at best a very weak 'frame' for neighbouring. Knowing something of the influences physical arrangements can exert tells us little about whether or not people will succumb to those influences. And knowing the patterns of neighbouring often but by no means invariably found in towns, villages, suburbs and so forth tells us equally little about the causes or meanings of those patterns.

Can one, then, substitute class for place as a decisive contextual influence on neighbouring? Class is certainly more directly bound up with the division of labour and the social structuring of opportunities and costs than is place. And some writers, such as Gans (1968), Pahl (1970) and Castells (1977), have certainly urged such a substitution. Gans, for example, concludes a discussion of neighbouring in suburbs by ruling bluntly (1968:112) that 'the behaviour and personality patterns ascribed to suburbia are in reality those of class and age'. And Rex and Moore (1967) move still more to emphatically reconstruct both urban and community sociology in terms of a theory of class and class conflict. Yet the precise influence of class on neighbouring – or even the precise co-variance of class and neighbouring – remains elusive and hard to gauge. The great strength of the work of Rex and Moore is that they do adopt a very tight, empirically accessible and unambiguous definition of class in terms of position in the housing market, and go on to demonstrate definite relationships between class in that sense and the resources, constraints, needs and opportunities out of which local sociability is constructed. Very few other studies achieve comparable clarity. Indeed, one of the main problems of many studies is a pervasive tendency to use the idea of class in a quite impressionistic, multi-dimensional and unstandardised way. While this no doubt aptly reflects commonsense usage – and also those theories of class which insist on its many-faceted, variable and historically specific nature – it also makes it quite remarkably difficult to determine the extent to which different patterns of neighbouring can properly be explained as distinct class constructs.

What emerges from the literature is not a clear and grounded theory of the relationship of class and neighbouring but, rather, a set of more or less confirmed generalisations about co-variances between class (loosely and variously defined) and neighbouring which themselves cry out for further explanation. A good example is provided by Allan (1979) who dwells at length on the ways in which working class sociability differs from middle class sociability in being context-specific, confined to particular and segregated settings, such as the street, the club, the workplace, whereas 'when middle class persons find they like someone, the tendency is, other things being equal, for them to interact ... with that person in a variety of settings'. Moreover, these

> organisational differences are matched by conceptual differences which are, if anything, even more marked. The rules of relevance which shape sociable relationships emphasise the personal relationship whatever the social setting in which it occurs for the middle class but affirm the primacy of the interactional setting in which the relationships develop for the working class. (1979:82)

These differences in class patterns of sociability are well documented across a wide range of interactions including neighbouring. But why do streets, fences or neighbourhoods 'bound' working class relationships so much more strongly? The importance of class as a context of neighbouring is undeniable but how does class work? What are the mechanisms by which the class effects are so constantly achieved?

Most authors deal with such questions by pointing to the element of choice in middle class life. Thus Keller draws the conventional contrast. Neighbouring is more extensive, solidary and generalised, and in that sense de-individualised, in 'the solid working class areas ... where need combines with fellowship to make neighbour relations almost as close and nearly as necessary as family relationships [while] middle class areas ... are marked by neighbouring that is more selective ... and more likely to emphasise personal sociability and compatibility' (Keller 1968:53). And she goes on to stress the fact of choice, especially of hedonistic choice, as itself accounting for the whole pattern of variation. But although her general formula, 'working class solidarity, middle class selectivity and suburban sociability', has found wide acceptance, the emphasis on choice is unsatisfactory unless certain concomitants of choice are given equal emphasis.

The stress on choice obscures the extent to which choice is linked to power and to constraint. Working class patterns of neighbouring are also chosen. The difference is that they are chosen on the basis of different resources and in the face of a different order of costs and opportunities. Class not only permits or denies choice but also shapes and structures it. This was the theme which the Durham research on neighbouring sought to explore. The possibility that the bounded, context-specific sociability of working class people was in fact no less chosen, and certainly no less a matter of valued and important relationships, than the 'flowering-out' of selective attachments within the middle class was left open. For all classes, neighbouring is chosen in the face of some order of costs and opportunities. The ordering of costs and opportunities, not selectivity, sociability, solidarity and so forth, was what one should understand by the class context of neighbouring.

From that point of view, the contrast between pure and mixed class residence became a vital focus for research. In selecting the six streets discussed in the next chapter, instances were sought both in the pure and mixed cases in which class was displayed in relatively extreme form.

Over and above place and class, earlier research has paid considerable attention to time as a possibly significant context of neighbouring, particularly length of residence, and stage of the life cycle. So far as length of residence is concerned most studies seem to agree that positive neighbouring takes time to develop or, as Shulman (1967) puts it: 'Since a primary relationship involves the right of one person to invade the privacy of the other, most people will require some assurance that such a right will not be abused before entering into such a relationship. This assurance is gained through experience with the person.' And not only does it take time to work out the conditions for positive neighbouring, but the longer established a neighbourhood is the longer it will take for a new 'neighbour' to find a stable place in the network of neighbouring (Frankenberg 1966).

What does emerge very clearly is that patterns of neighbouring have their own careers and histories which are related closely to the stability and mobility of residence. For example, several studies of suburbs and new estates have displayed the sequence of very busy neighbouring, followed by withdrawal and home-centredness, followed eventually by the consolidation of levels and forms of neighbouring between the two. From Durant (1939) to Keller (1968), McGahan (1972) and Allan (1979) this patterning over time has been repeatedly documented. The higher the proportion of the residents involved in short-run mobility, the more evident but also the more complex the pattern appears to be. Newcomers, unguided by valid norms, engage in rapid and wide-ranging exploration of the possibilities of neighbouring. The exploration serves not only to solve immediate problems of moving-in but to construct norms; a cogent understanding of an appropriate level and range of interaction is achieved. Furthermore, the excesses of the early days have exacted their costs in extremes of closeness or demand; as Durant puts it: '"Watlingitis" sets in ... the patient is attacked by a sudden desire to do nothing, see nothing, help no one and go nowhere.' A much more cautious but this time increasingly norm-guided second round of exploration ensues in due course as neighbours discover, within the framework of norms, costs and rewards, a manageable mode of friendliness with and distanced from others. Residential mobility will pose problems for the stabilisation of such patterns in a variety of ways; but if the rate of individual coming and going is itself fairly stable it can, as Bracey (1964) and Willmott (1963) have shown, be managed by more or less explicit mechanisms of induction such as greetings, the welcoming cup of tea, offers of assistance in moving-in, popping in with small welcoming gifts, parties for newcomers or seemingly very informal but actually extremely regular and uniform signs of acceptances and goodwill. The difficulty posed for research by such findings is of course that time is both an individual and a collective matter; within any neighbourhood individuals will be at different stages of their several different neighbouring careers which as a whole constitute the historical moment of development of the neighbourhood as a whole. The essential thing is somehow to allow for the fact that except in the most static settings both individuals and neighbourhoods are moving through a calendar charted by the vagaries of residential mobility.

The implications of the life cycle for neighbouring centre around two themes. First there is the sense of family traditions of neighbouring reported by so many informants in so many studies. People appear to re-enact the forms of neighbouring they learned to regard as normal during their own childhood. They refer again and again to what their mothers did or what it was like 'when I was a child' as a norm for their own practice in later life. And this invocation of the past as a guide to the present seemed to be particularly marked among those particularly caught up in positive neighbouring, those most likely to be judged 'good neighbours'.

The other major influence of the life cycle on neighbouring is through children. Children increase the incidence, and on the whole the positiveness too, of manifest neighbouring. Children simultaneously raise the costs for parents of interaction outside the neighbourhood and increase the opportunities for and rewards of interaction within it (Kuper 1953; Bracey 1964; Shulman 1967). Gans (1961) goes further and suggests that many young adults may organise their lives, and pick their homes, directly with a view to solving the problems presented by children through neighbouring. Young adults with children are widely acknowledged to be the age group most actively caught up in localised mutual aid and it could well be that children brought up in settings in which localised mutual aid is normal are especially likely to become bearers in later life of the norm of localised mutual aid. Using the locality in childhood could be a key to the creation of neighbourly adults.

Over and above place, class and time, certain other significant contexts of neighbouring bound up with the overall pattern of sociability available in different neighbourhoods are also stressed in the literature. Two in particular deserve further attention: the question of homogeneity and the question of alternatives to neighbouring. Homogeneity as a source of neighbouring is interesting because it clearly points to mechanical rather than to organic solidarity as the significant basis of interaction. Gans (1961) among others has argued very emphatically that homogeneity – either real or perceived – among neighbours is a decisive source of positive neighbouring. Whatever the basis of friendship and other attachments, positive neighbouring is held to depend on the neighbours being 'just like us'. Propinquity is indeed an occasion for interaction but making something valuable out of propinquity 'requires homogeneity'. Its essential form is, however, subjectively defined, the propensity to see other people as like oneself (Gans 1961:137). The issue requires further clarification, but reaches to the very heart of the problem of social solidarity.

Alternatives to neighbouring have two aspects. The first is the way in which other types of informal interaction, interaction with friends and kin for example, compete with neighbouring both as forms of sociability and as forms of social care. The second is the extent to which formal social services displace or reinforce helpfulness and care between neighbours. The evidence is somewhat contradictory. On the one hand Litwak and Szelenyi (1969), Tomeh (1964) and others appear to have documented a division of function between neighbouring, kinship and friendship so far as informal helping and caring are concerned. And Young and Willmott (1972), Townsend (1963) and others have reported a similar division of function between neighbouring and interaction with kin and friends in respect of sociability. That is to say, in neither

Making sense of neighbours and neighbouring

case does one form of interaction tend to drive out either of the others because each is relatively specialised in terms of its content. Though one would expect class variation, such studies which have compared classes in this respect hold that the complementarity of neighbouring, friendship and kinship is maintained across the board.

On the other hand there has been a persistent line of commentary which has expected neighbouring both as interaction and as social care to decline and wither with the advent of formal welfare provision, membership of voluntary associations and friendship on the 'selective' middle class model. The literature does not point to clear conclusions in these respects but simply suggests issues which require further research. Such consensus as there is would seem to indicate that, when opportunities for multiple modes of sociability are available, the segregation of types of interaction and helping within distinct types of relationship is associated with more overall interaction and helping, not less. At the same time, rather different conclusions are reached about the relationship between the informal and formal provision of help, support and care. Although there are a few dissenting voices – for example, Goldberg *et al.* (1970) – the main thrust of interpretation is exceptionally clear in this respect. Thus Keller (1968:58) quite simply identifies 'better social services' as one of the 'reasons for the decline of neighbours and neighbourhood as primary sources of material and moral support'. Dore (1958:255) considers that 'the expansion of social services . . . will certainly have the effect of further reducing the importance of the *tsukiai*'. Hirsch (1977:82) spells out the economic logic underpinning this negative relationship in a compelling way. From a public point of view the provision of expert services is very costly and the provision of neighbouring very cheap. But from the point of view of the individual the balance is reversed; the costs of positive neighbouring are very high, often exorbitant, those of the welfare state are low, or at least unavoidable. Thus positive neighbouring is subverted by 'the economics of bad neighbouring'. The overall tendency of such research and speculation as there is about the relationship between neighbouring and formal social care is plainly to suggest that the former will decline as the latter advances. Whether this is in fact the case is one of the central hypotheses to be explored in later chapters.

4 Neighbouring in six localities: the Street studies

This chapter is an account of research into informal patterns of neighbouring and neighbourliness carried out between 1976 and 1978. We began by accepting both the intellectual and the practical credentials of the 'problem of neighbouring' as we found it in the world at that time. We took on board both the claims of the popular sociology which envisaged a decline of neighbourliness and the hopes of the popular social policy which – most overtly in the Be a Good Neighbour Campaign launched by the government in 1975 – proposed a revival of neighbourliness. The vital issue, for both research and policy, seemed to be to discover 'good neighbours'. 'Good neighbours' we took to be people who could be relied upon to help when help was needed. Being a good neighbour, we argued, might be a matter of many tiny acts of helpfulness – lending and borrowing sugar – or of prolonged and strenuous caring – looking after a child or an invalid or an old person while someone else is at work or away. But in either case we saw good neighbours as both an important qualitative element of social life and a reserve of 'practical altruism' which could have significant implications for policy. Yet, we were bold enough to assert, social science had at that time no more than a sketchy picture of the extent and forms of neighbouring in our own society and hardly any understanding at all of the conditions under which it develops. And so we proposed an exploratory research project to map out two broad areas of the problem of neighbouring: we set ourselves, first, to identify what might be called the 'patterns of neighbouring', or the extent and forms of interaction, in different types of local social system; and secondly, more specifically, to determine the circumstances under which the more sustained and substantial types of neighbourly help are provided. Our first set of 'findings', made even as we tried to draft a coherent research project, involved discovering that even in its simplest sensible terms the 'problem of neighbouring' was a great deal knottier and more elusive than that.

We saw the research as having both practical and academic objectives and implications. A better understanding of 'what sorts of people are willing to give what sorts of help in what circumstances' could contribute appreciably to our ability to develop alternatives to institutional care for the partially dependent. And a careful study of the forms and contexts of neighbouring would at the same time enlarge our knowledge of the nature of social solidarity and cohesion in modern industrial societies. Accordingly, we planned to organise the work around the three main topics and related questions set out in chapter 1 (pp. 7–8): the idea of neighbouring, the practice of neighbouring and the contexts of neighbouring. By investigating these questions in a number of different types of social milieu it was hoped to develop a body of fairly precise, substantive and empirically grounded propositions about the resources of practical altruism available in our society and about the circumstances in which that altruism might be effectively mobilised.

The 'myth of community studies' having been debunked by Margaret Stacey (1969) the conventional wisdom of sociology on the question of neighbouring was in a somewhat disordered state. People seemed, in effect, to have dropped locality studies without any very conclusive attempt to reduce the mass of evidence on strictly localised relationships such as those of neighbouring to any very helpful propositional form. On the other hand, certain generalisations were common. The 'myth of neighbourliness' and the 'decline of kinship and community' were rampant. It took some effort to break through this miasma and discover that, for example, Mogey had in fact shown in 1956 that residents on a newish estate were *twice as likely* to have friendly relations with their next-door neighbour as inhabitants of a traditional working class community. Or that Woodford had been found to be 'a very neighbourly place' compared to Bethnal Green (Willmott and Young 1960). Quite simply the myth did not facilitate the unpacking of the notions of locality, kin, class, friendship or neighbours and neighbouring, let alone those of care, help, altruism and reciprocity which ideally should have been unpacked as a prelude to research. The results of our examination of the available evidence are discussed in the previous chapter.

If one is interested in the *whole* of a relatively untheorised social phenomenon, say, neighbouring, naive observation is often much to be preferred to the spuriously sophisticated testing of hypotheses within a curtailed framework of theory. In the absence of a solidly-based theory of neighbouring, we judged it wise to start simply. We carefully avoided questioning or clarifying the notion of altruism – later, we were to conclude that hardly any of the actual behaviour (helping, supporting, caring and so forth) in which we were interested could be understood adequately in such terms. And with equal care we refrained from facing up to the methodological issues involved in separating out our several postulated contexts of neighbouring from one another with a view to testing their interrelations. We justified our refusal to unpack the phenomenon of neighbouring analytically before trying to look at it empirically in terms of the positive merits of naive observation at some junctures in the creation of sociological knowledge.

Our view of how social science proceeds towards knowledge follows that outlined by Wallace in his well-known image of the wheel of theory and method (1969:ix; Bulmer 1984b:21). In certain settings of theoretical confusion and methodological excess, wilfully innocent observation may well be the best way to get the wheel moving. Specifically, in relation to neighbours, neighbouring and neighbourliness we felt the need for immediate evidence, for a body of data with which we could feel directly familiar, which was relatively uncontaminated by other people's ideas and which we could use as a resource to think about those ideas as well as for generating ideas, even generalisations, of our own. So without more ado we turned to ethnography:

we proposed a study of six streets (for a similar approach, see Bytheway 1979).

The locales for the study: six 'streets'

In the event the 'streets' turned out to be a mixed bag of residential entities of which three were indeed streets, two were small estates and one was a village. The selection of these areas was guided by our central interest in two types of variation which were reported to be closely related to neighbouring: social class and residential stability. Each of these terms is in fact abstracted from a cluster of properties and characteristics and lacks any strict theoretical or empirical reference. Class in this context indicates only gross and loose groupings of occupation, income, lifestyle and milieu; and stability refers variously to measures of length of residence, patterns of migration, relation of place of residence to place of work, incidence of certain kinds of social problems and so forth. Each was determined on the basis of externally-perceived social characteristics of areas and not in terms of the subjectively-perceived attributions of individual residents.

The resulting two-dimensional classification of types of area was not unlike that proposed by Baldock (1974:48–53). Three types were envisaged on each dimension: working class, mixed class and middle class; and stable, unstable and disintegrating. And of the nine possible variations we decided to concentrate on the six closest to, and fanning out from, what conventional wisdom told us was, so far as neighbourliness was concerned, the stable working class pivot (table 4.1). We looked for and eventually satisfied ourselves that we had found residential entities that we could confidently describe as stable working class and stable mixed class; as unstable working class and disintegrating working class; as unstable mixed class and as unstable middle class. We decided to ignore the other three possibilities, not because they were theoretically uninteresting or empirically undiscoverable but because we wanted to concentrate on residential stability and working-classness as especially relevant contexts of neighbouring (and wanted therefore to include all the types that possessed *either* of these properties). Moreover, our resources did not allow us to do everything, and we wanted to achieve depth rather than breadth wherever possible.

The particular relationship in which we were interested was that of neighbourliness – a form of friendship constructed between neighbours. We assumed that neighbourliness would be explained by the particular properties of the immediate individuals, settings, networks and contexts among which neighbourliness occurred. The individuals, obviously, would be neighbours – defined simply as nigh-dwellers. But being a neighbour is a role not an existence. The role is prescribed, by nearness, but what is made of it, how it is taken and played is 'up to the individual' in the sense of involving all the other aspects of her or his life. In much the same way neighbourhoods, defined in terms of externally given and specified residential proximity, are the obvious setting for neighbourliness, but the neighbourhood is only one setting among others in which the lives of residents are enacted.

Table 4.1 *Six settings*

	Working class	Mixed class	Middle class
Stable	Austen Avenue (Yorkshire woollen town)	Boswell village (Cumbria)	X
Unstable	Dryden Square (Leeds)	Etherege Terrace (Durham)	Congreve Hall (Cambridge)
Disintegrating	Fielding Close (Co. Durham New Town)	X	X

The networks of neighbouring, further discussed in chapter 5, are the actual patterns of interaction among any given aggregate of neighbours ranging from neighbourliness to hostility, indifference and neglect. They can be understood only as fragments of the complex systems of networks in which all concerned participate. In all three respects, therefore, our approach directed our attention not only inwards to the details but also outwards to the contexts of neighbouring provided by the whole life of those studied. Implicitly at least we had accepted the need to explain the local in terms of the constraints and choices of a non-local world.

Style of neighbouring also needed to be taken into account. Dramatic variations in the style of neighbouring were to be evident in each of our six streets and the pattern of variation itself varied from street to street. In Fielding Close, for example, a great deal of time and energy was spent in mutual recriminations of various sorts. One might speak of a wrangling style. And the style in turn is plainly an immediate, felt, obstacle to extensive mutual help and support. Moreover, Congreve Hall with its carefully convivial style of interaction also turned out to contain a conspicuously unhelpful pattern of neighbouring. Style appeared to mediate various connections between action and context, content and setting, as filtering the relationship between social structure and individual action.

It is now time to turn to the first of the 'Street studies'. Their methodology is discussed in more detail in the appendix.

Austen Avenue, Yorkshire woollen town

Austen Avenue lies three miles north of the town centre in an area consisting of rows and rows of small terraced houses mainly built around the beginning of this century. There are several textile mills within walking distance; two of them adjoin the back lane behind the street, and some of the families moved into the street to be near their work. Occasionally people referred to the local area as a village. All shopping can be done locally, though many of the women went into town to meet a friend or relative at least once a week.

There are 42 houses in Austen Avenue, which were built in or shortly after 1910. The houses are terraced, two-storey, and solidly built from Yorkshire stone. Each house has a small front garden and a long narrow back garden. Privet hedges separate each house at the back and the front, but are for the most part cut very low which makes it possible to see from house to house the full length of the street from the top to the bottom.

Only the Crudases at number 9 had made any attempt to keep the privet hedges high. Mr Crudas, a retired watch repairer who used to have a small shop, remarked:

> "When we moved into this house the hedge was very high on either side. We liked it that way as it was a great protection from the wind blowing through the back door. We got up one morning and the people next door had chopped it down very low, and then they called across to the people below, 'We'll put a pair of shears in his coffin when he goes...'" (Mr Crudas added: "I'll never talk to them again as long as I live.")

The houses were quite small inside. Downstairs there was a large kitchen in which the families had their meals, and a sitting-room. Upstairs there were two bedrooms originally. However, many of the houses had been modernised and had a bathroom, so that now several houses had a large bathroom and one bedroom, and others had a small bathroom and two bedrooms. The lack of garages (though there are some at the bottom of the back gardens) and consequent parking of cars in front of the houses, created a lot of tension in the street. One of the few rows that threatened to come to physical violence in Austen Avenue was caused by a dispute between neighbours about the parking of a car outside their houses.

Some of the houses were built as an investment. Mr Bingham, for example, owned eight houses in the street and seven houses in the road situated along the top of the avenue. Mrs Taylor once commented: "You can tell which houses are owned by Mr Bingham, they all have turquoise painted doors." By contemporary standards the size of the houses suggested a couple with either one child or no children. A high percentage of people lived by themselves. The feeling that the houses were small and compact, plus the fact that most people found it reassuring that they could hear their next-door neighbours through the walls gave a sense of security to those living alone.

There was some sense of distance, even of antagonism, between the longer-term inhabitants of Austen Avenue and the newcomers; and these feelings were possibly compounded by differences of age. Thus one resident who had lived in the street for 61 years and knew a lot of people, said, "but there's a lot of young couples moved in recently; I don't really know them". A relatively young newcomer to the street when asked how she got on with the older people replied,

> "I wish some of them would die and younger people move in. A lot of them are just nosey and want to know everything. I like Amy [Mrs Derbyshire] and she made sure we got to know her; but she's never a good word for anyone. I never tell her anything because I think if she's like that about others, she might be like that about us, so I listen to her."

No professional people lived in the street. Residents were for the most part skilled or semi-skilled manual workers; about half were retired or widowed.

The Street studies

There were two or three junior managers in the textile or engineering trades. The painter and decorator at number 39 had the largest house and garden with a garage at the side of the house for a van and a car. Miss Martin, a retired clerical worker – now living on Social Security – felt that she had come down in the world to end up living in Austen Avenue. On the other hand Mrs Smith, a hospital clerk, said, "ever since I came to live in this area, I've wanted to live in Austen Avenue, it's not posh but it's right for me". The street existed in a no-man's-land between the working class and the lower middle class and its residents were quite keenly aware of the status implications of living there.

Austen Avenue represented one modern version of the traditional working class neighbourhood. The most striking findings showed the ways in which traditional patterns are broken down by geographical mobility, increasing state provision and relative affluence and greater frequency of husband and wife both working.

The idea of neighbouring was perfectly well understood in common sense terms; people believed that they knew what neighbouring was and could quite readily give an account of themselves as neighbours:

> "Well, this street isn't what you'd call neighbourly ... where I come from in Wales – the Rhondda Valley – that was different. Our neighbours would come in – they might sit all night in our house. There's no popping in and out of each other's houses in this street; they're friendly but not neighbourly." (Mr Thomas)

and

> "I'm not the neighbourly type; I wasn't brought up that way." (Mrs Crutchley)

Similarly, there is a widespread consensus as to what one would mean by a 'good neighbour'; and that consensus reflected the main ambiguity in the academic conception of the neighbour-relationship that emerged from the literature search; it was a matter of friendliness and helpfulness on the one hand, *and* distance on the other; "Someone you can rely on but who doesn't live in your pocket" (Mr Thomas). "A good neighbour is someone you can rely on, and someone who doesn't interfere and pry into your private life" (Mrs Thomas). For Mrs Askew, the basis of neighbouring was "keep your distance and don't live in each other's homes". "A good neighbour would be someone you could ask for help but didn't live in your pocket" (Mrs Crutchley). Conversely, a bad neighbour was likely to be too intrusive. "A bad neighbour is someone always coming into the house" (Mrs Edwards). "A bad neighbour would be someone who's nosey" (Mrs Hitchin).

The pattern of a typical day for several of the occupants of the street nevertheless involved a great deal of casual helpfulness.

> "In winter I usually get up between eight and half past. This morning first of all I came to see if Mr Light was all right; then I went next door to make sure Mr and Mrs Henry were O.K., then Mrs Weir who lives at the back, I went to see if she wanted any shopping done." (Miss Wright)

However, *distance* was equally important:

> "I go into the Hawley's once a day, and that's it for the day, I don't go in again." (Miss Wright)

Several respondents made a distinction between day to day contact, or lack of it, and emergencies. "We're not neighbourly, but in any kind of crisis we would help anyone" (Mr Thomas).

Neighbouring was nevertheless a 'weakly framed' role, not expected to carry much practical action. The most important relationship from the point of view of dependable/expectable support was that of spouse. Then came that blood relation – especially, mother, daughter or sister. Neighbours came a poor third. Organised helpers, whether voluntary or statutory, were very plainly also-rans, whose help it was almost something of a personal failure to receive. Within this hierarchy the greatest distance was that between relatives and everyone else. As Mrs Hitchin at number 14 put it: "If anything happened to me I should knock on the wall to number 16 and they would go and get my sister." Neighbours were intermediaries not principals in the process of social care (cf. Townsend 1963:140).

Altruism – a personal willingness to help others, a store of credit for help to be given in future need by others – was plainly understood as an outcome of a long experience of reciprocity – not necessarily within any particular relationship but rather within a subjectively perceived *set* of relationships:

> "We have good neighbours here; we're lucky ... before Mrs A. died I always used to listen; one day I heard such a bang and I went round to see if she was all right – it was a picture that had fallen off the wall – but she thanked me for coming round ... and during the summer Mr and Mrs Hyde noticed that Mrs Allison's curtains upstairs were still drawn; they went across to tell Mrs Taylor and she came to me to ask if I'd heard anything. Everything was all right, as it happened Mrs Allison had gone out early in the morning shopping."

Mrs Hitchin went on to say, "My sister who is ill has a wonderful neighbour and we feel very grateful to her – we show how grateful we are by buying her grandchildren little presents – now she goes in to see if my sister is all right three and four times a day; of course she has to have a home help as well."

The best exchange relationship did, however, need to be an established one, and could backfire. Mrs Crudas, who was relatively isolated in the street, said:

> "Where I used to live before, the people were friendly, they'd do anything for you. If I'd made too much of anything, I'd give it to one of my neighbours and it used to be appreciated. When we first came to live here [17 years previously], I made too many fish cakes ['It was lovely halibut too', piped in her husband] and went to the next-door house and offered them to the elderly couple. They asked: 'What are they? How much do you want for them?' That was the last time I did that."

There was – and this again is something the literature on neighbouring had led us to expect – a noticeable contradiction between expressed and practised norms, attitudes and behaviour, so far as neighbouring was concerned. People

The Street studies

claim to disapprove of visiting neighbours or to approve of keeping themselves to themselves or to have friends in the street. But they were constantly observed and reported visiting their neighbours, involving themselves in other people's troubles and having close friends a few doors away. Phyllis Cheswright was representative in this respect: "I know that I couldn't stand people popping in for a chat" she said, but a moment or two later Joan Roper called and settled down for a chat and a cup of tea. It is not clear how this ambivalence should be interpreted or explained. Are people under some sort of social pressure to deny that they are effectively attached to and involved with others?

Festinger's suggestion that there is a continuum of types of neighbour ranging from the isolate to the sociometric star was borne out in Austen Avenue. Everyone in the street knew that Mrs Taylor was a sociometric star: "Now Mrs Taylor knows everything and everybody. She always has something to say; whereas I never know what to say, I feel envious of her really." Mr Crudas was an isolate: "They're a bit toffee-nosed. They have their little world – the daughter and her husband and the four of them do everything together – which is fair enough if that's what they want" (Mr Thomas). But the residents' own explanations of these differences were not wholly satisfactory if only because they sat so uneasily between the social and the personal. On the whole commonsense does not get beyond psychological stereotyping. But the interviews suggest the possibility of at least a slightly more sophisticated social interpretation. Respondents' accounts did *seem* to be related to consistent variations in social position and social practice. Mr Crudas's social relations – as a small entrepreneur – actually were different from those of everyone else in the street; Mrs Taylor was – as a widowed resident of long standing – socially situated in a way that made her involved with *and* usable by others around her. To this extent the interviews contained hints of a *sociology* of neighbouring independent by psychological interpretations of personality.

Nevertheless, personality factors and personal experience were hard to dismiss altogether. It did seem that the immediate personal circumstances and psychological make-up of the individual played a large even if ephemeral and changing part in shaping day to day patterns of neighbouring in Austen Avenue. Mr Goldthorpe at the age of 93 was friendly and very ready to help others: "It's people who turn to me – not me to them – I'm always doing odd jobs for people nearby." Life had treated him kindly; when his wife died there was Miss Wright who lived next door ready to become involved and look after him. For Mr Shrimpton this was not the case. He was aggressive and when asked "have you a few minutes to spare", his response was "have I bloody hell." His wife died a year ago and in a stubborn but proud way he was determined to live in isolation asking nothing from anyone. Underneath this rather sharp exterior, one had the impression that he would have liked very much to talk. He said that he didn't see anyone, but his neighbour told me that she goes round each day to make sure that he is all right.

Physical proximity and distance were also clearly significant influences in the pattern of neighbouring in Austen Avenue although it was not clear how far they could really be distinguished from personality and *social* distance.

52 Informal neighbouring

Rather it seemed that physical proximity and distance mattered only if something is made of them. Thus Miss Martin mentioned several times that she was lonely being in the end house at the top of the terrace; whereas Mrs Taylor could be seen on any fine day talking to people as they passed her house at the bottom end of the street when they were walking to the bus stop or shops on the main road.

In sum Austen Avenue was a relatively stable setting in which neighbouring relationships were well developed and constituted a significant, taken-for-granted and pervasive background dimension to the lives of most inhabitants. Neighbouring was, however, contained within a framework of the stronger attachments of kinship and was limited by considerations of personality, of status, and of self interest. For this reason few of the residents in Austen Avenue would ever rely on the neighbours for help, even though most neighbours were in practice very helpful on a day to day basis.

Dryden Square, Leeds

The village in which Dryden Square is situated lies six miles on the northern side of Leeds. Originally it was a small mining village surrounded by fields. After the war it expanded with the building of a large council estate and a private housing estate situated at either side of the main street. In the past 10 to 15 years, two huge private housing estates have been built on the outskirts of the village, the majority of people living there travelling to work outside. The area is now within Leeds City boundaries. The houses and bungalows in Dryden Square constituted a small new council housing estate situated near the old council estate, but quite separate from it. It was a quarter of a mile from the main street in the village, which has a good selection of shops, banks etc., and a new library.

The estate was 'open plan' – the houses having a small area to the back and to the front a larger fenced garden. The houses were arranged in two cul-de-sacs, with two blocks of garages. Old people's bungalows were placed alongside the road leading to the houses. The majority of houses were three-bedroomed; in one street they were two-bedroomed. Both the houses and bungalows had a kitchen, lounge and bathroom with solid fuel central heating. The houses and bungalows were rented from the council. The occupants of the houses had the option of buying them if they wished, and only one person was doing this. Most people interviewed worked within a five mile radius, plus a few in Leeds.

The houses and bungalows were two completely separate social entities. In the houses, there was a predominance of young married couples – most in their early twenties – all with young children. Three-quarters of the women interviewed were 30 or under, one or two of them had part-time jobs but no one worked full-time. Of the women in their forties with full-time jobs, two were separated from their husbands and supporting a family. The majority of women in these two cul-de-sacs were at home all day. As is usual on new estates, this had resulted in intense interaction when they initially moved in. They were all of the same age and class and all moving into new houses. They

The Street studies

also had the shared interest of, and common concern with young children. Many of them had moved from the village of their birth, attracted by the new houses. The result was that they were constantly in and out of each other's houses, having coffee, exchanging and borrowing and, most important of all, gossiping.

This pattern of neighbouring, however, did not last, illustrating some of the problems of creating neighbourliness in new communities. Since those early days, many of the women had withdrawn from these activities because of the malicious nature of this gossip. When discussing neighbouring with them there were numerous references to this; Mrs Cousins: "They can't mind their own business and keep themselves to themselves ... They're all young and naive and don't know their own minds." Or Mrs Thompson: "I was friendly – and too soft really. They were always in borrowing things ... it got to be a bit much. Then they were gossiping about each other and being nasty about other people in the street and you began to realise that as soon as they'd finished talking to you they'd be off telling other people what you'd said – except they'd exaggerate it and make it worse." Or Mrs White: "I used to at first, but it's not worth it. You'd tell someone something in confidence and the next thing you knew it would be around the whole estate that you'd said it." Or Mrs Maxton: "I wouldn't go to no.— if I were you. We call her 'rent-a-mouth'."

The outcome was a split between the younger people on the estate. There was still a group of 'about six' who were always in and out of each other's houses but those who had withdrawn from the group tended only to have neighbouring relationships with one or two selected people on the estate. This could involve quite substantial help in time of crisis, as when Mrs Hill was in hospital and her children needed looking after, or when Mrs Long had her last baby at home and neighbours brought in meals.

All the older women who worked had little time for neighbouring. Mrs Christie's attitude was typical: "There was a time – when I was first married and the children were young when I had time to chat with my neighbours and go round for tea but I haven't time now – it just depends on the predicament you're in." The older women at home all day regarded everyone as being friendly but normally weren't involved in the visiting, lending and borrowing syndrome characteristic of the young newcomers.

Definitions of a good neighbour reflected very clearly the balance between involvement and distance noted earlier. They included:

> "A good neighbour is somebody who'll help out." (Mrs Maxton)
> "Someone you feel at ease with and who is not put out if you ask them a favour and vice versa." (Mrs Wright)
> "A good neighbour is someone who's friendly and who you can turn to in an emergency." (Mrs Bell)
> "Someone who isn't always in the house. I like having a neighbour, but not to live with." (Mrs Peterson)
> "A good neighbour is someone who's friendly but not nosey and knows when not to come." (Mrs Smith)
> "A good neighbour is someone who minds their own business." (Mrs Carpenter)

Informal neighbouring

"Someone who knows when they're wanted and when to disappear." (Mr Collins)
"One who doesn't interfere." (Mrs Green)
"They're alright in small doses." (Mrs White)

These definitions obviously reflected the bitterness felt by many as a result of the gossiping. The use of phrases such as "one who kept herself to herself", "doesn't gossip", "doesn't borrow", "minds her own business", "is not nosey" or "doesn't interfere" was common. However, this was always balanced by a more positive attitude to 'latent' neighbouring – for example, the hope of help in a crisis. Sentiments such as "there if you need them", "could go to in trouble", "pleasant and thoughtful" and "can turn to in an emergency", were also commonly offered as accounts of the good neighbour.

The relatively weak character of neighbouring ties were evident in the much greater reliance upon kin in times of domestic difficulty. Without exception, everyone said that in a crisis they would rely on their mother, or if they were older, their daughter. All lived near enough to their parents to be in regular contact with them. Friends did not appear to have a great significance in their lives – many of the younger couples did not have much of a social life – mainly because of lack of money and having young children.

In the houses, there were two couples who were ostracised from the community. The husband of the first family had been unemployed for a long period and they were obviously finding it difficult to cope. No one mentioned them as being neighbours they'd visit and they were only ever referred to by their immediate neighbours – one disliking them, the other feeling sorry for them. The other family which was excluded from the community was a constant object of criticism. Mrs Cousins, a divorcee, had alienated neighbours by having noisy parties and "different men" in her house. She had genuinely been a good neighbour in the past and was one of the few people to visit the old people in the bungalows – providing a useful hairdressing service. She herself commented: "I used to do all sorts for them but I don't now – because I'm a divorcee they think I'm poison to their husbands." She had annoyed some women because she had asked favours of their husbands, such as to give her a lift to work.

Finally, it was interesting to note the impression gained by the families in the houses of the old people in the bungalows. Only three women ever visited any of the old people although most were quite confident that they looked after each other. When asked if anything could happen to the old people without anyone knowing, an interesting response from one woman in the houses was: "I don't think anyone could die here alone – they're too nosey – they'd soon miss you." However, Mrs White, who did visit an old woman contradicted this: "I think that someone could die there without knowing because no one bothers with them." In other words neighbouring in this part of Dryden Square was highly pragmatic, conditioned and rooted in self-interest. There was intense activity but shot through with mistrust. Life was organised in terms of personal convenience and short-term need. Those who most needed the help of their neighbours were, as a result, those least likely to receive it. There was no historical depth of reciprocity here. Comments such

The Street studies

as: "Neighbours aren't the same as they used to be when I was younger – they'd do anything for you then" (Mrs Brown, aged 45), need to be interpreted in the context of predominantly younger families being thrown together for the first time and having to create somehow a workable informal pattern of interaction. The endless flow of malicious gossip indicated the dilemma of people who both wanted to be involved with others and had no confidence that others wanted to be involved with them.

The bungalows were situated parallel and at right angles to the road leading to the houses, as a completely separate entity, without a warden or community centre. The majority of the old people were in their 70s or 80s, quite a few of them being housebound or only able to walk with help. Although they had all come to know each other, their immobility and age restricted the quality and quantity of neighbouring. There were many indications that these people would have benefited from the services of a full-time warden.

Many of the old people were not from the local area but had moved there to be near their children, leaving friends and neighbours of long standing behind. Those who were able to walk visited the British Legion old people's flats nearby and participated in the activities organised by the warden there. But many of the old women living alone told us bluntly and candidly that they were lonely. For example, Mrs Elger (aged 80) remarked, "I'm very isolated here – you don't see many people about ... no one comes to visit me." And Mrs Weaver – a sprightly 76 – said, "It's very lonely ... I like people to come in for a cup of tea but they're all too old around here and a lot of them can't get out." Mrs Weaver's solution was to walk everywhere in the hope that someone would speak to her.

Some definitions of a 'good neighbour' by this group reflected this feeling of isolation:

> "Someone who'll come and have a word with you and see you're alright." (Mrs Elger)
> "One who inquires after your health and has a chat now and again, but who doesn't come to live with you." (Mrs Dickinson)
> "Someone who will help you if you need it." (Mrs Moore)
> "One who is willing to come when you really need them." (Mrs Black)
> "One you could call on but who didn't live with you." (Mrs Forster)

Without exception all the old people had children living in the village and all relied *solely* on them for help and company. Obviously this placed a tremendous burden on sons and daughters: Mrs Weaver told us: "I have one son ... he comes every dinnertime ... and has his dinner with me – otherwise I wouldn't bother – it's no good just cooking for one." And Mrs Black said simply: "My daughter comes every day." This burden did not go unnoticed by the old people themselves and many made a positive attempt not to be too demanding. Mrs Weaver, for example, talking about her son and his family, recognised that "they've got their own lives to live as well".

Although a warden was not employed, Mrs Dunn, a retired warden, lived in one of the bungalows and carried out many of the duties of a warden simply through being a good neighbour. Her rather idealised account of mutual support in part reflected her own very active role: "In the bungalows we're a good little community – we're a community that care. We all make sure that each other's curtains are opened in the mornings and get things at the shops for each other." She was the old people's 'sociometric star' and everyone mentioned her as being a friend and someone who would help in a crisis. Through her experience as a warden and an appreciation of the importance of activities to the elderly, she had organised a Thursday Club which many of the residents of the bungalows attended and also organised day trips in the summer. But because of her involvement in numerous voluntary schemes, she was extremely busy and many of the old people recognised that, as with their children, they could not be too demanding. In the absence of either a professional caring agent or a neighbouring community of people younger than themselves, the village old people could only scale down their demands: they settled for a socially impoverished old age.

Although these bungalows were on the edge of a housing estate there was little contact or opportunity for contact between the old and young people. Mrs Weaver regretted leaving her house to move into the bungalow because she had had to leave her young neighbour: "When I lived in Kippax I had a young neighbour with two children – that was lovely – one day she'd come to me for tea and the next day I'd go into hers for a cup of tea. Then if we were having fish and chips she'd go to the shop and get them and I'd make the tea and butter some bread and we'd have them together. I do miss her."

A short-term solution could be the use of volunteers to visit both the elderly and single parents like Mrs Cousins, who felt she could have taken her children out of care if she'd had the support of someone calling every day to ensure all was well. But in a community or non-community such as the village, it was not at all clear where the volunteers would come from. If organised, a few of the middle-aged women would have been willing to help – but then they had their own family, parents and jobs to cope with too. And who was going to organise them?

The residents of Dryden Square shared a number of characteristics – common residence, proximity to each other, (in the houses and bungalows separately) common age and stage in the life cycle, (in the houses) being mothers with young children. Dryden Square consisted of an aggregation of people who needed each other but had no way of making contact with each other. Their needs were inhibited by their lack of any confidence in the goodwill of the others with whom locally they had to relate if they were to have any neighbouring relationships at all. Their houses were clean, polished, neat and well equipped. But the world of the other houses around them was one in which they didn't "feel as if you belong". Relationships were at best friendly, intense but guarded. It takes a long time and a lot of experience to develop the sort of trust many of them associate with "a pre-war street". Until that sort of trust developed, neighbouring seemed doomed to be superficial, provisional and a matter of hoping for, not counting on, the best. Mrs Cousins, the outcast of the estate, actually spoke for all the residents when, from her extreme position, she said: "The main trouble is the walls are too thin." More specifically, she pointed to the way people in the village wanted to help each other, but in their desperation they used rather than helped those around them:

> "I don't speak to any of the neighbours. They can't mind their own business and keep themselves to themselves. I used to do all sorts for them but I don't now. I used to cut people's hair – it was a favour done for a favour. I wouldn't ask for money because if I did it would go straight back to Social Security – someone would tell them – so I'd say, 'buy a vest for Dene or a pair of socks'. But I don't do it now. Because I'm a divorcee they think I'm poison to their husbands. Also I sometimes have men coming to have their hair cut and I'm sure they all gossip and get the wrong idea. In fact I've only had three or four boyfriends in the last two years but they don't think that. They're all young and naive and don't know their own minds. Instead of staying at home and looking after their husbands and children, they go into each other's houses to gossip. And if they run short of talk one of them will knock on my door and ask to borrow something so that they can talk to me and try to find out what I'm doing. But since I've had this bad back and not been able to lift things I've come to realise what sort of neighbours they are. Not one of them's come to offer me help . . . I always thought people would help – I get no help from no one. So now I don't bother with anyone on this estate. I go to the club and I stand on my own."

In the context of an aggregate of newcomers such as exists in the village, neighbouring was at once an essential form of activity and an activity in which, rather too obviously, everyone was in it for themselves.

Fielding Close, County Durham New Town

Fielding Close was chosen because it was thought desirable to include a 'problem area' within the research programme of street studies. The street is located in a County Durham New Town, one of the 'first generation' designated in 1948. The main initial objective set for the town was to provide new housing, principally for miners employed at the nearby long-life Durham collieries. The aim was that most of its population should be drawn from the surrounding pit villages; it was felt that the villages did not justify expansion but should, in fact, decline in population. With the ultimate population of 30,000, the town was expected to serve as an 'urban focus' for the surrounding area, providing services and employment. During the 1950s, the industrial development accent was largely on the provision of employment opportunities for women but local pit closures in the late 1960s and early 1970s meant that the creation of alternative jobs for men became a major priority.

The town succeeded in attracting a considerable number of families from nearby pit villages. Restrictions on house-building in the villages ensured growth and meant that the majority of new households – usually young couples – had little choice but to move to the town in order to obtain a house. The Development Corporation, which owned more than four-fifths of the New Town's housing stock, accorded priority to these local newly-formed households in allocating houses. Because of this, and also on account of high turnover which tended to result in older families leaving, the town still had a very youthful age structure. In 1971, more than half the population was aged under 25 (compared with nearly two-fifths in England and Wales). Only 8% of the town's population was aged over 60, compared with a national figure approaching one-fifth.

The Development Corporation had a great deal of difficulty in attracting new firms to the town. Manufacturing industry provided only 2,000 male and 2,500 female jobs; consequently many people travelled to work elsewhere. About one in ten working men living in the town were employed at the remaining collieries and many others worked in industries in neighbouring towns. Unemployment remained persistently high from the mid-1960s on, and in 1977 more than 11% of local men were registered unemployed, a figure slightly above the regional rate. There was evidence of hardship and deprivation stemming from high unemployment and, not infrequently, low wages. More than one-third of Corporation tenants received rent rebates and literally hundreds of families were solely dependent upon Supplementary Benefit. At the same time, the cost of living in the town was appreciably higher than in the villages, the New Town tended to have less well-developed 'natural' support networks and there appeared to be serious deficiencies in social and welfare provision. The town was one of the least 'successful' New Towns and was clearly not a 'self contained and balanced community' providing, in the words of Lord Reith, an opportunity for all its residents to 'lead a happy and gracious way of life'.

It was known, from the results of a survey conducted in 1974 and also from studies undertaken by Dr Fred Robinson, that this was undisputedly an area suffering considerable problems. Fielding Close was one of the most 'notorious' streets in the town. The 1974 survey showed that it was widely considered to be of very low status and the present study showed that many of its residents felt that they were stigmatised for living there. Unemployment was exceptionally high, car and telephone ownership very low. Several residents had been in trouble with the police. The street – and much of the rest of this estate – looked somewhat neglected; there was some vandalism but the area certainly appeared less run down than the stigmatised problem estates of the major towns and cities.

The houses in Fielding Close were constructed by and rented from the Development Corporation. The street consisted of short terraces and semi-detached houses containing three bedrooms, bathroom and inside W.C. Built in the early 1950s, the houses were traditional, brick-built with pitched roofs, fringed by open-plan front gardens. There were no signs here of experiment in architecture, construction or planning as found in the newer parts of the town.

Fielding Close was little more than ten minutes' walk from the town centre and the area was also served by neighbourhood shops. Residents were fairly well placed for access to social facilities but provision was very limited. There was a common-room at Bishop Road but this was now used for little more than jumble sales. The most important and active social facilities in the town were the pubs and clubs, reinforced by the fact that there were few alternatives.

The study included 22 houses in the street. One, however, had been

The Street studies

boarded up and another was in a state of neglect and appeared to have been abandoned by tenants who had 'flitted'. Of the remainder, 17 households were successfully contacted and interviewed. 11 of the 17 households comprised couples, mainly in their twenties or thirties. All but one of these households contained children. In addition, there were five single-parent families and one woman, recently widowed, living alone. Nearly one-third of the children were under school age and one-quarter of them had left school but continued to live with their parents. 10 of the 14 male heads of household were employed, all in manual occupations, and 4 were unemployed. There were 7 sons of working age, of which only 2 had been able to find work. 4 of the 13 women went out to work, although in only one case did this involve full-time employment. 3 of the 12 working men were employed at local collieries. All households possessed a television set, but only two had telephones. Five households had a car – a proportion well below the 43% recorded for the town as a whole in the 1971 census.

Fielding Close was characterised by a high turnover in population. The average length of residence of the present tenants was less than four years and, although the houses were completed over 20 years ago, no one had been living there for more than eight years. Partly, this was accounted for by high turnover in the past when the longer-serving tenants transferred quite easily to newly-completed estates. More recently, as the Corporation's house construction programme had come to an end, residents wishing to transfer found great difficulty in doing so because they were now dependent upon mutual exchange arrangements – and almost no one wanted to transfer to a house in Fielding Close. Yet high turnover continued, not by transfer but by moving away from the town altogether. The 'moonlight flit', which accounts for about 15% of tenancy terminations in the town, was not an uncommon phenomenon in Fielding Close and was often considered a suitable response to problems of rent arrears and threats of eviction. High turnover, entailing frequent changes of neighbours, was noted by several respondents, some of whom may have considered it disconcerting; but there is little to suggest that it seriously affected the formation of neighbourly relationships.

Most people maintained at least minimal contact with their neighbours, they knew them by sight and acknowledged them in the street. One man, however, recently in trouble with the police, had a strong dislike for his 'nosey' neighbours and repeatedly stressed his concern to keep himself to himself – but his wife maintained neighbourly contacts. And a housewife, whose house had been burgled whilst she had been on holiday, had understandable reservations concerning the helpfulness and watchfulness of her neighbours, but nonetheless admitted that some of the neighbours had been good friends to her. Generally, the people of Fielding Close were in contact with their neighbours and, quite often, this contact was close. The attitude of several respondents can be summed up by Mrs Thorpe's comment that "the neighbours are quite friendly, but they have their ups and downs . . . you can depend on them if necessary".

The most active, 'positive' – and perhaps 'useful' – neighbouring relationships were those between women who had children at school or below school age. Most of these women were at home all day and many seemed to enjoy quite close contact with their neighbours. In some cases the neighbours provided them with 'company' and in several instances helped each other by babysitting, borrowing and lending and so on. This included two lone parents, Mrs Clapper and Mrs Ryder, whose husbands had left them with young children. They babysat for each other, went out shopping together, and saw each other at least once a day. "I don't know what I'd do without her", said Mrs Ryder. 8 of the 11 women in this group had relatively close, friendly relationships with one or two neighbours whom they saw quite frequently and with whom they exchanged visits and help. Beyond these close relationships there was a less intense and broader network of neighbourly contacts; on several occasions this was seen in operation as a group of women chatted together, congregating on a small patch of lawn in front of the houses at the end of the crescent. There was also some evidence of help in times of crisis. Mrs Smith, recently widowed, was in close touch with her next-door neighbour Mrs Dickinson. When her husband was in hospital, Mrs Dickinson used to sit with her, and was "a lot of comfort" when he died. "She helped me get over it and got me on my feet again."

It is more difficult to classify the least active neighbours. It appeared that men were, as a whole, uninvolved with their neighbours. One divorced man, living with his two sons, said that he had little to do with the neighbours and considered that this was because neighbouring was a female activity: "it's the women who do a lot of that sort of thing, gossiping and that, isn't it?" Another man, unemployed, disliked going out during the day because "you get watched by the neighbours, they gossip about you". Mr Collins made an unfavourable comparison between the friendly and trusting relationships in the first village he came from and the town, where "everyone's out for themselves and neighbours wouldn't think to help out". Of one of his next-door neighbours he remarked: "He's a queer one and I keep out of his way." Mrs Davies felt that some neighbours constituted a threat and were best avoided, otherwise "you get too involved in their troubles". She gave an example of a woman who used to live in the street who had become friendly with another woman whose husband "was always beating her up". The neighbour got so involved that in the end the husband had threatened her too, and she became so upset that she left the area as soon as she could.

There were, however, exceptions. Two men worked at the same colliery and knew each other on a friendly basis and some of the men met their neighbours at the local pub or the club. The development of close relationships with neighbours stemmed from a number of factors, the most important of which appeared to be shared interest and/or needs. Several of the women with children noted that their most intense contacts were with others in similar circumstances. Added to this were common needs, notably for babysitting. Two women whose husbands both worked shifts relied on each other for company in the evenings when the husbands were away at work. The two divorced women, bringing up children alone, were particularly close. And a slightly different example was that of the Chappells who had most contact with the two or three other neighbours who, like themselves, had an interest in dogs and exhibited at dog shows.

The Street studies

Borrowing and lending seemed much more common in Fielding Close than in most of the other areas studied. It was generally an accepted element in neighbouring and was usually included in 'helping' relationships. Some respondents suggested that they were plagued with requests to borrow things; one said that "people come round asking for scissors, half a loaf and all kinds of things that all households should have". Most said that they lent items but few admitted to borrowing. Those who lent things tried to keep the practice within limits; they never lent money, for instance, or made sure it didn't "get out of hand". Some were unhappy about lending but seemed unable to avoid it entirely. Five people expressed strong views against borrowing; they sought, for example, to be "independent" and not have to borrow. But borrowing and lending were widely expected and commonplace, even though a minority said that they did not approve of it.

One indication of residents' attitudes was their ideal picture of the neighbour. Nearly all respondents thought of "the good neighbour" as one who was friendly and helpful. About two-thirds of respondents said that good neighbours should not be nosey, disruptive or continually visiting. This underlined the limits to neighbouring and the concern to protect privacy. Three people defined the good neighbour solely in negative terms, as someone who leaves you alone, doesn't bother you or disturb you. Four respondents, who had developed close friendships with their neighbours, regarded them as good neighbours. Replies included:

> "Someone who's friendly and helpful." (Mrs Clapper)
> "Someone who doesn't bother you, but is friendly; someone you could ask for help from if you were really stuck." (Mrs Davies)
> "I like neighbours to be friendly and not always wanting things or wanting to find out your business." (Mrs White)
> "Someone friendly and helpful and who doesn't cause you any trouble, with noise or gossiping about you behind your back." (Mrs Fox)
> "Those that are quiet and don't bother you, but you could ask them for help if you were really stuck." (Mr Short)
> "There if needed, but don't trouble you. Not always in and out." (Mrs Chappell)
> "Someone who doesn't cause you any trouble. Isn't nosey or always coming round." (Mr Collins)
> "Good neighbours should be seen and not heard." (Mrs Smith)

These references to "nosey" or "interfering" neighbours, or those "always in and out" parallel those in the other street studies. Relations with neighbours were understood as involving distance and privacy as much as friendliness or helpfulness. But there was a further element in Fielding Close of neighbours who, for various reasons, had a poor reputation or were labelled 'problem families'. Some respondents noted that they tried to avoid becoming involved with these people; one woman, in particular, seemed to be trying hard to maintain the respectability of herself and her family by being very selective in her choice of neighbouring relationships. However, although some avoided *close* relationships with people they considered disreputable this does not mean that they ignored them, nor does it mean that these people were isolated. In most cases those who might be thought to be problem fam-

62   *Informal neighbouring*

ilies had developed some close contacts and were, generally, accepted. The case of the man who had been in trouble with the police and sought to avoid contact with the neighbours appeared to have been an exception. The low status of the area was keenly felt; as one man said, "this area is where they say everyone's thieves and vagabonds". Some said that they were embarrassed when asked where they lived and there was a strong, justifiable, suspicion that the Corporation housed its 'problem tenants' in the street. But everyone shared the stigma attached to living in the area and this seemed to foster a sense of togetherness. It gave an element of cohesion and also created an environment which quite readily accepted the 'problem family', the lone parent and the unemployed.

In the street, geographical mobility was the norm. Only three residents had been brought up in the town. Of the rest, a majority came from the surrounding pit villages and some from nearby towns. Consequently, they were able to compare the town with older-established, working class communities. More than two-thirds of respondents thought the town was less friendly or neighbourly than the 'traditional' places in which they had been brought up. "It's not like the colliery village where everyone knew everyone" or where "the same people have lived in the street for years", were typical comments. Mr Taylor had always wanted to go back to his village, where people were much friendlier and more settled. "You know where you are with — people, not like here." Mr Mason was of the opinion that "neighbours round here are not real neighbours, not the old style neighbour. It's quite different from the colliery village – people aren't so close." People recalled a past of intense neighbouring which contrasted with the more private, home-centred styles of life in the new town. Possibly the past and the pit villages were viewed somewhat romantically but the difference was, nonetheless, strongly perceived. One important and distinctive difference was that Fielding Close, unlike most other areas, did not have any old people. High turnover also meant that there was no sense of continuity and stability; "it's not the same as where everyone's known each other, and their families, for years", said Mrs Ward, whose mother living in a pit village had had the same next-door neighbour for 20 years.

Some people, however, thought the New Town had advantages over the close-knit village communities. Though Mr Short missed the pit village where everyone knew everyone else, at the same time the village people could be too nosey. "They knew all about you – you couldn't move without someone watching you." One woman felt that people in the villages tended to pry and pass judgement. When her husband had left her she noted that neighbours "didn't all talk and get nosey" as they would have in the village: "here there are lots of people who get divorced, it's no big thing".

The pattern of migration in this part of County Durham, involving the movement of young families into the New Town clearly resulted in some dislocation in the ties between parents and their married children. However, 11 of the 15 households with surviving parents maintained reasonably close contact with them. In nearly all cases parents lived in the surrounding villages and towns and could be visited without undue difficulty. Most visited their parents at least as often as once a month. Help was usually given and exchanged, typically the parent would babysit and, in return, receive help with odd jobs, household chores and so on. The problem of distance seemed to limit the amount of help which could be given; it was not usually possible, for instance, for mothers to regularly visit their married children in the town to babysit for them. By comparison with Austen Avenue or Dryden Square, the residents of Fielding Close had much less contact with kin, and kin were not nearly such a significant source of social support, partly but not entirely due to distance.

The move to the New Town had also broken friendship ties. School friends were rarely seen and most depended on friends they had made in the town. The majority of the women had neighbours as their closest friends, while the men, as far as could be ascertained, had wider networks of friends or acquaintances whom they met at work, the pub or the club. It was difficult to gauge the relative priority accorded to the three primary networks. For the women, especially those tied to the home by young children, neighbours who were also friends made up a major part of their social networks. It might be argued, too, that for many of them the neighbours were a vital source of friendship and that their helping function was often secondary.

By comparison with the traditional mining village, leisure activities were relatively home-centred and privatised. For many, television provided almost the only leisure activity. Every household had a television set and it was by no means unusual to find it turned on in the morning. Several of the men and a few women visited pubs or clubs in the evenings, but it was naturally difficult for them both to do so if they had young children, unless a babysitter could be arranged. No one belonged to any formal organisations apart from the occasional leek club member. People were asked if they knew about Good Neighbour schemes and respondents' knowledge about them was very limited. The operation of these schemes was, however, explained and opinions were sought. Nearly everyone thought that they were a good idea, although finding difficulty in relating them to the New Town situation in which there are few old people.

Fielding Close was a problem area, judged by commonly accepted criteria and also according to the opinions of local residents. But despite this – and, one suspects, partly because of it – there existed strong, satisfying relationships between neighbours. This study suggested that common adversity, including a shared stigma, served to draw the people together and not keep them apart.

Boswell village, Cumbria

The village of Boswell lies inland from the Solway Firth, just off the main road between Carlisle and Whitehaven. Very few cars pass through unless they are specifically coming to the village. There are four buses a week to a nearby town or one has to walk a mile to the main road where the buses run every half hour to Carlisle or Whitehaven. Buses take the children to schools which are all out of the village. Village amenities include a public telephone, post office, small shop, travelling shop, a pub, a church and a village hall still in use and a chapel and school not now in use.

At the turn of the century Boswell village was completely self-sufficient. It had a carpenter, a blacksmith, a shoemaker, a shop, two pubs and a village school with an attendance of over a hundred children. The majority of men worked on the farms in the village, only one or two travelling to work at the nearby pit. The farming life was very much a community enterprise. Wives and children helped in the fields, made butter and cheese, etc., and it was traditional for those who finished sowing or harvesting first to help those who had not finished. The village was well-known for its dances in the village hall, many of which were connected with the farming cycle – dances after the harvest was brought in, etc. At this time in the village there was a small group of 'professional' people to whom villagers could turn for help and advice – the vicar, the headmaster, a nurse and an unqualified nurse who helped with births. These people had lived in the village all their lives and for this reason were always approachable. In 1977 none of these people remained in the village – the vicar and doctors were based two-and-a-half miles away and the school was two miles away. Mrs Peters, who was born in the village 60 years ago remarked, "It was a real blow to the village when we lost our vicar and at the same time the village school closed."

The physical appearance of the centre of the village was much the same in 1977 as it was a hundred years ago. All the old cottages and farms were built around the large green in the centre of the village. New bungalows, all built in the last ten years, stood in a ribbon development at either end of the village. In the centre of the village there were three working farms with their fields spread out around the village. This resulted in herds of cows being driven through the village at least twice a day. Boswell Castle stands at the edge of the village, set back from the road and surrounded by woodland. Built in the fourteenth century it was, until the end of the nineteenth century, inhabited by the lords of the manor. Since then it has been used as a working farm, employing people in the village. The village green and moorland behind the village still belong to the Holt family, who were at one time lords of the manor, and they allow it to be used as common grazing land.

Most changes in the population of the village had occurred over the previous ten years. The old people living in the centre of the village had worked and lived in the village all their lives. If their sons and daughters still lived in the area, then they usually lived in the council houses at East End – half a mile out of the village. If the large houses in the centre of the village became vacant, then the trend had been for newcomers to buy them and commute to work in nearby towns. There were a few small unmodernised cottages still owned by farmers in the village and these were, in general, rented to newcomers – young families attracted by the low rents.

The practice of neighbouring was highly developed in Boswell – both intensively and extensively. Although some people received rewards or help in return for their neighbouring activities, their motivation was usually an altruistic one – they were prepared to give without thought of, or desire for reward (cf. chapter 6). A story told by Mr Peters illustrated this very well. Mr

The Street studies

Peters married into the village 25 years ago and started a milk business, bottling and delivering the milk with a little help from his neighbours:

> "Len Brooks worked 365 days a year here for years without taking payment. He used to come and help before going to work. When he finished work [retired] he helped me deliver the milk as well as doing the bottling – I give him a few pounds and milk, butter and cheese but he won't take anymore. I've always felt in his debt."

Len was now in his 70s and as well as helping with the milk he also helped Mr Peters's brother-in-law on his farm at weekends.

Newcomers could find such altruism disconcerting, as Mr and Mrs Jones (a 30-year-old couple from urban Lancashire) explained:

> "Mr Pile came over and did our garden over with his tractor, then yesterday dumped a load of manure in the garden. We didn't ask him to, he just did it to help. We feel a bit bad about it really because where we come from (urban Lancashire) you pay people to do things for you then you know where you are. Here people won't take any money and we've not really got anything to give them in exchange, except maybe the odd pint in the pub."

The range and variety of neighbouring activities engaged in are exemplified by the case of Mr and Mrs Davies. Although this old couple were very independent, they were the most obvious case of need in the village. Until his retirement Mr Davies was a roadsweeper. Three years ago, Mrs Davies had to have her leg amputated and was now housebound. Many villagers regularly visited them and offered help. Every week Elizabeth George, a woman in her early thirties, baked for Mr and Mrs Davies, and her mother set Mrs Davies's hair and took her out in her wheelchair. Mrs Spring, a newcomer to the village, took Mr Davies to the nearby town to shop every Friday, and in the middle of the week Mr Pringle, another newcomer, brought them meat and any other groceries they needed. If Mr Davies had to go out, even if only to chop wood in the yard, a neighbour would always come in to sit with Mrs Davies. Flowers and pot plants, gifts from various individuals in the village, were very much in evidence in the house and the children in the village were always calling to chat to Mrs Davies. Neighbours ensured that they were well stocked with coal and wood for the fire, and at Christmas they received a large amount of potatoes and turnips from the family at the Castle. These types of activities occurred in varying degrees between neighbours throughout the village. If newcomers moved into the village the locals visited them, helped dig the garden and tried to help them settle in. As Mrs Straw, who had lived in the village for five years, remarked: "The people in Boswell are very neighbourly. When we first came they all came round to see that we were alright. They weren't being nosey or trying to get into the house – they were just being kind."

The standard definition of a good neighbour in Boswell was someone who was there when you needed them but didn't sit around your house all day. Locals (those who had lived in the area all or most of their lives) emphasised this balance between caring and privacy particularly.

Informal neighbouring

> "A good neighbour is someone that doesn't make a nuisance of themselves but is there when you need them." (Mrs Martin)
>
> "A good neighbour is someone who's friendly and is there when you need them but not somebody who sits around the house a lot and smothers you." (Miss Mars)
>
> "A good neighbour is someone who's completely honest with you. We're like one big family in this village, well, the older ones are who have always lived here. The new ones – we call them foreigners – they don't know the mode of life of the country." (Mr Roberts)
>
> "A good neighbour is someone who's willing to help out." (Mrs House)
>
> "Someone who is friendly." (Mrs Vernon)
>
> "A good neighbour is one who doesn't sit around your house but is there when needed. Boswell people have never been ones to sit around in each other's houses. It's when people are around all the time that quarrels start." (Mrs Lloyd)
>
> "'Love thy neighbour as thyself.' A good neighbour is friendly and caring. I know what a bad neighbour is because we had one once – they were always accusing you of things you hadn't done, then other times she'd be sweetness itself. Well, that's no good, you can't rely on people like that." (Mr Prime)
>
> "Good neighbours are those who are always popping in and lending a hand." (Mr and Mrs Davies)

Newcomers emphasised reserve slightly more:

> "A good neighbour is someone who keeps themselves to themselves and doesn't force themselves on you." (Mrs Spring)
>
> "A good neighbour is someone who's always ready to help in a crisis but is not in and out of the house all the time." (Mrs Straw)
>
> "A good neighbour is someone who would help out when you needed help but who wouldn't be in and out of the house all the time – that would get on my pip." (Mrs Field)
>
> "Bob [age nearly 80] is my idea of a good neighbour. He's not nosey and he doesn't come around all the time but he's always ready to lend a helping hand, even before we have to ask him." (Mr Kelly)
>
> "A good neighbour is someone who's there when you need them." (Mrs Miller)
>
> "Someone who's always ready to help out." (Mrs Smythe)
>
> "A good neighbour is someone who's there when you need them, is honest, and is willing to accept help – because it's nice to be able to help someone, sometimes." (Mrs Brody)
>
> "I don't know. I wasn't used to neighbours before we came here. We lived in a farmhouse about two miles from anywhere else." (Mrs Jones)

In practice neighbours were often found sitting in other people's houses. Potential neighbourliness in Boswell was no less important than manifest neighbouring. Many people did not see their neighbours for weeks but were confident that they could be relied on in a crisis. Mrs Dower, a busy farmer's wife and a newcomer, summed it up by saying: "It's not a village where you would sit around all morning having tea with your neighbours, but if you needed it they'd always be there to help. It's very quiet and also very friendly." Similarly, most people said that they would not borrow on principle, but if it was urgent then they knew that they could ask their neighbours without hesitation. Amongst locals, and especially the older ones, there was an overwhelming feeling of trust and reliability of neighbours. One of the overt signs of this was their habit of walking into each other's houses without knocking, a habit which some of the newcomers found difficult to cope with. The social basis of this degree of trust needs further exploration and explanation.

There were few limits placed on what kind of activity neighbouring was; in general it was all-embracing. Only one local suggested that there might be acceptable limits to neighbouring by saying: "I don't make close friends of my neighbours, I don't agree with them knowing all your business." This woman originated from a nearby village and so was able to distinguish people in that village as her friends and people in Boswell as her neighbours. In contrast, people who had always lived in Boswell found this distinction between friends and neighbours difficult to define. Having grown up, gone to school and worked with their neighbours, they all knew the intricacies of each other's lives, had nothing to hide and therefore had open friendly relationships. Only if neighbours had moved out of the village could they then be definitely classed as 'a friend'. Newcomers to the village tended to choose their friends and neighbours from two distinct areas. Neighbours were usually described by their proximity, friends were chosen both in and out of the village because of a bond of common interest or similar social background. 'Neighbours' were exclusively kept within the village boundaries; this included the outlying farms.

Amongst the locals, most of whom were farmers or retired farmworkers, the practice of neighbouring was a fairly haphazard but taken-for-granted activity which had to fit in with the farming way of life. They did not want it to be bounded by rules or limits. Ann Connelly, a farmer's wife, explained this when talking of one of the newcomers – Elizabeth Field.

> "Mrs Carruthers and I had an arrangement where we took it in turns to take our kids to the playgroup at —. It was fairly haphazard and we were often late – usually with having to round up the cows before we left – or something would always turn up. Anyway, Elizabeth would come in with us. First she organised us into a rota, then started to complain if we were late."

Newcomers are much more selective in their neighbouring and for them it is not really a spontaneous activity. They would go for coffee to a neighbour's house if they had phoned up and organised it beforehand. They would take one of the old people into town shopping but it was a regular arrangement every week. Newcomers in the 'professional' middle classes seemed to prefer helping through organisations rather than casual helping within the village. The Field family took this to the extreme:

> "I think to get into a village you have to make the effort and go out and make contact. I'm the local meals-on-wheels organiser ... I'm a member of the National Housewives Register ... I'm on the Children's Treat Committee, and the children are in the Cubs and Brownies, Mr Field is secretary of the local Conservative Association, treasurer of the Boswell Church Council, secretary of the — Band and the local Blood Donor Organiser."

68 Informal neighbouring

Of all these activities only the Children's Treat Committee and the Church Council involved Boswell village, and the Field family were only marginally involved in neighbouring in the village.

There was little difference between men and women in neighbouring activity in Boswell. In rural communities men seem to take as significant a part as women in promoting neighbourliness. Farmers met their neighbours at work, had common work experiences and ambitions and helped each other out by lending tools or expertise. In a wider context, the men went to the cattle marts, a very social occasion, and returned home with gossip about friends and neighbours.

Unneighbourliness was rarely referred to in discussion and not one of the locals was ever classed as being unfriendly. Only one person was referred to more than once as being unsociable and this was a newcomer who had built dog kennels in her garden. She was out at work during the day and the dogs often made a loud distressing howling noise. As Mrs Straw, another newcomer, remarked: "The people nearby should get a petition up but they won't – they're not that type of people."

There are many distinguishable variables affecting the practice of neighbouring in Boswell. It is relevant to note these at this point, for when they are are taken together they indicate a definite pattern.

Length of residence was the most important of these variables. Mrs Peters, a women in her sixties whose family had farmed in Boswell as long as she could remember, pointed this out by saying: "I still automatically think of people who may have lived in the village for 30 years as newcomers – if we haven't grown up with them and gone to school with them then they're newcomers." This does not imply any animosity towards the newcomers. In fact the locals were welcoming and tolerant of them. However, those families who had lived in Boswell all their lives and grown up in this close-knit community seemed almost to be related to each other. Mr Davies, aged 73, actually said, "We're all one big family in Boswell." This situation obviously fostered a feeling of dependency and reliability which was found lacking in the newcomers. One young newcomer, Mrs Lloyd, who had married a local, thought that outsiders could find it hard to be accepted. "Just because one person in the village didn't get on with them, then nobody liked them. You either get on with everyone or no one in this village."

Age was another evident variable in Boswell's neighbouring. Neighbouring tended to take place between people of a similar age group. Miss Snow, in her late fifties and born in Boswell, remarked: "The old ones know what good neighbours are ... if I'm ill and laid up in bed that young woman next door would never pop in and see how I was." Age as a variable was difficult to distinguish from length of residence – "that young woman" referred to by Miss Snow also happened to be a newcomer. She married a farmer in the village and although she had lived there for 15 years she still regarded herself as a newcomer. Neighbouring was more intense between the middle aged and the old but they were also those who had lived in the village for a long time. It seemed general that the young women were less interested in neighbouring, being more mobile and more dependent on their families. Children were an important feature of neighbouring in Boswell. Many visited Mrs Davies, who was housebound, and young mothers came together through their common interest of children. A Children's Treat Committee was formed a few years ago and although only the younger mothers and fathers attended the meetings, there was a combination of newcomers and locals on the committee. With the newcomers, children were an aid to integration into the village. Several times newcomers said to me: "Well I'm not involved in anything in the village but my daughter is." Older children were much keener to partake in village life than their parents.

Related to the question of age was that of common interest. Most people were on neighbourly terms with people in a similar age group who had interests similar to theirs. If there was an age difference between two friendly sets of neighbours then the bond was usually that of shared interest, e.g. a common interest in what the old family would call a smallholding and the younger family call self-sufficiency.

Class, as usual, was one of the most ambiguous variables in Boswell's neighbouring. With the locals there was a definite feeling of heirarchy in the village. This did not result in conflict but seemed to be accepted as the natural order of things. Over the last century, two or three families have owned most of the land around the village, provided the employment and provided much of the money to build the church. So, it was accepted that these same families still dominated the Parish Council, Church Council and, in 1977, the Jubilee Committee. This difference in status did not, however, affect social interaction. People in the village chose to interact with each other because they were of similar age, had common interests or lived next door; wealth and status were not significant determinants. It was the newcomers in the village who made the distinctions. Instead of taking individuals on their merits they tended to choose with whom they wished to interact in terms of class. If the new professional class in the village wished to partake in village life, then they chose to do so with the wealthier farming families or the vicar or the headmaster. This was resented by the farming community.

It is difficult to assess the impact of religion on neighbouring as most people who were good neighbours went to church, but this correlates with the fact that they had lived in the village all their lives. Do they neighbour because it is their spiritual duty or is it because it has always been the norm in their community? Certainly, the older locals expressed strong criticisms of Roman Catholics, Nonconformists and Jehovah's Witnesses – a family of Jehovah's Witnesses lived in the old vicarage. Yet, in contrast to their emotional defence of the Church of England, they were tolerant of nonconformity in everyday life. The new vicar in the village was shocked to discover a woman who had been on the Church Council for 30 years and in that time had two illegitimate children by her sister's husband. The attitudes and behaviour of the locals to each other and to outsiders expressed norms of tolerance, kindness and honesty which they themselves were not unhappy to recognise as springing from 'Christian' values.

Mobility at all levels was an important concept in Boswell. At the practical level, it was reiterated many times by the locals that they never saw anyone in the village street to talk to because everyone had a car. They go to work out of the village in their cars, they do all of their shopping out of the village and they travel for their entertainment.

Related to this and to the class variable was the idea of social mobility. Those of the newcomers to the village who were in the professional class were all socially mobile and for them Boswell and West Cumberland was just a rung on the ladder. A few of the wives emphasised this by saying, "I wouldn't mind moving tomorrow." They were prepared to move if it meant improved job prospects for their husbands. Most of these families, before moving to Boswell, had lived on middle class housing estates and so had deliberately chosen to live in the country for the independence and peace of village life. A typical response was that of Mrs Jones when discussing their previous home on a housing estate in Blackburn:

> "The thing we didn't like about it was that you always had to keep up with the Jones's – there was competition for who had the most expensive cars – it was terrible. It's nice here because you can do what you like – you can be more individual and nobody bothers you. Mind you I don't think I could live here for more than a few years."

It seemed that the average length of stay in Boswell for the upwardly mobile was about five years. In this time most of them didn't bother to become too involved in village life. If they did make the effort, like the Field family who joined everything available and were now leaving after five years, then it was resented. Mr Mars, aged 74, made this point when discussing the church: "The new people aren't interested – they got that man across the road [Mr Field] to be treasurer of the Church Council and now he's moving. They only stay a couple of years and then move on – well that's no good."

Finally, there was the influence of the family on neighbouring. Both locals and newcomers said that with a long-term crisis a relative would come and stay to help. If it was a small problem then they would turn to their neighbours and their neighbours would be prepared to support their relatives in a long-term crisis. The young families and the newcomers, those who were least involved in neighbouring, were more familistic than the older locals. Their relatives were the focal point of their lives and everything else was peripheral to the family. Most of the locals' families lived either in the village or within a small radius of the village, but they were much more taken for granted. As a farmer's wife pointed out: "If you've got relatives nearby you don't see them much – especially if your husband works with them – you don't see them socially much as they'd get sick of each other."

All of the farms both in and around Boswell were farmed jointly by either father and sons, or nephew and uncle or father, cousins and sons. The extended family played a very supportive role. If the families of the older residents had either died or moved a long way away then neighbours usually fulfilled the role of the extended family. Miss Snow and Mr Mars are an interesting case in this respect. All of Miss Snow's immediate relatives were dead, but she had cousins and uncles living in and around the village. Mr Mars, who lived next door, had worked most of his life on her father's farm and she had

The Street studies

come to regard him almost as a brother. She had very little to do with her own family in the village and although Mr Mars's sister lived in the same small terrace of houses, she in fact also played the role of sister to him. She washed and ironed his clothes and lit the fire for him if he had been out.

It was apparent throughout the interviews that the main divide in attitude was between recent newcomers and locals. Those newcomers who had lived in the village for over ten years, and who were usually involved in the farming life, were undistinguishable from the locals as far as neighbouring went. Those who had moved into the village with no long-term prospects of staying, either hoping to move to better jobs or better housing conditions, were less influenced by village norms and less committed to the community life.

If one accepted that it was the locals of Boswell who were involved in the most prolific, supportive, reliable and altruistic forms of neighbouring, then it is important to identify the determinants of this situation. A long experience of shared involvement and interdependence through work, the relative insulation of the village as a distinct and self-contained society, acceptance of a settled way of life largely indifferent to the monetary and status ambitions of the larger world, and an assured confident sense of common interest have merged together to sustain the growth of a norm of mutuality in Boswell which evokes neighbourliness without regard to considerations of separate private advantage. In these circumstances we could almost say that altruism had become a social fact (cf. chapter 6). But it seemed to be a social fact only for those whose lives had been set wholly within Boswell's special social system, as in Mr Mars's definition of a good neighbour, quoted earlier.

In Boswell, although social services and specialised services such as meals-on-wheels were available to the village, no one took advantage of them or even knew of their existence. Very few people knew the meaning of 'social services'. The general feeling was that Boswell people could take care of themselves and each other without outside help, although the loss of the village nurse was frequently regretted. She had played an important role visiting the more infirm members of the community in their homes.

Etherege Terrace, Durham

Etherege Terrace consists of a row of 24 houses in a village on the periphery of the built-up area of Durham City. Patterns of neighbouring were investigated by two methods: residents were visited and interviewed informally and the researcher also had the opportunity to observe (and, to a limited extent, to participate in) neighbouring at first hand, being himself a resident of the terrace. Two houses were empty. Residents in 21 out of the other 22 houses were interviewed at least once.

Until the sinking of a colliery there in the 1830s, the village was an insignificant agricultural hamlet. With the advent of mining came the rapid expansion of the village and several rows of pitmen's cottages were built on a cramped site adjoining the village's main street. Etherege Terrace, completed in the 1860s, was one of the last of these colliery rows to be built. Gradually the basic institutions of the typical Durham pit village developed – four pubs,

72 Informal neighbouring

three Methodist chapels, a Board school, a co-operative store, a miner's Reading Room and Institute and, in the early 1900s, a working-men's club. Pigeon and dog racing, handball and pitch and toss were common activities. Village life was dominated by the pit, since nearly all the men worked there.

In 1924 the colliery closed and subsequently the village changed radically. Many miners left to work elsewhere – but the unemployed and old remained. The Depression brought prolonged hardship, hardly alleviated by relief schemes. The Jarrow marchers were welcomed and encouraged as they passed through in 1936. In the late 1920s, the collier rows were sold to a local builder. Many of the cottages – including those in Etherege Terrace – were improved by the addition of a second storey. As these houses became vacant they were sold, bringing a steady influx of newcomers. The longest-established resident of Etherege Terrace in 1977 had bought her house in 1930, at the beginning of this period of transition.

Towards the end of the 1930s, the village was considerably extended by the addition of a large Council estate. Then after the war, the main street developed further as a shopping centre to serve the enlarged population, especially after through traffic was diverted. In the early 1950s, the roadway in Etherege Terrace was, at last, made up.

Recent years have seen further additions to the main street which now serves a wide area, including substantial new private estates. Residents of Etherege Terrace are well placed for virtually all services. The main street now possesses a Community Centre, church, chapel, three pubs, working men's club, recreation ground, garage, fish shop and cafe, post office, bank, doctor's and dentist's surgeries, opticians and wide range of shops, including a new supermarket. The main street is on a major bus route, with frequent services.

Etherege Terrace was thus very conveniently located. It was also a relatively cheap place to live, house prices being low for the area. They varied depending upon the extent to which houses had been modernised. Respondents stressed the importance of both these factors as reasons for coming to live there. Many had modernised their houses by their own efforts, providing themselves with cheap and comfortable accommodation and giving these old colliery houses a new lease of life.

The four longest-established residents of Etherege Terrace, who had lived there for over 25 years, were all of retirement age, widowed and living alone. A further three households – a middle aged couple, a middle aged man and a retired couple – had been established there for periods of 16, 14 and 12 years respectively. All the rest – constituting two-thirds of the households – had moved into the Terrace during the last five years or so. Eleven of these 14 newcomers were young couples, half of whom had children. These families were small – none contained more than two children. Although only four adult residents were born in the village itself, most of the remainder were born and brought up within County Durham – mainly in villages close to Durham City. Only three households originated entirely from outside the north-east and these were the three connected with the university as students and research staff.

The Street studies

Fifty years ago the tenancy of a house in Etherege Terrace was tied to employment at the colliery. In 1977 there were no miners living in the terrace – only two retired men who had left mining many years ago. The present residents are engaged in a wide variety of occupations; they include factory workers, drivers, professional entertainers, university students and staff, a self-employed mechanic and a second-hand dealer. Etherege Terrace is therefore predominantly working class but contains a small and young middle class minority. Half of the households had a car and rather fewer had a telephone; only two households did not possess a television set.

Most people were found to be on friendly terms with at least one or two neighbours – usually including those living next door. These relationships were sufficiently close to involve mutual helping and, in the majority of cases, visiting. The kinds of help provided varied very considerably and ranged from passing on money to the milkman to assistance with car repairs. Visiting in the home was not as common as helping – which could often be transacted over the garden fence. Visiting tended to be infrequent although the group of four very close neighbours mentioned above engaged in formal, frequent and pre-arranged visiting. Some saw visiting as an opportunity for sociability and welcomed it; others saw it as an intrusion and potentially hazardous. Mrs Brooks, for example, now a widow, had lived next door to the Whites for 28 years and was on very good terms with them, both with Mrs White, who had recently died, and Mr White. They would meet and chat in the garden or street every few days, but Mrs Brooks had never been into their house, even when Mrs White was alive, and they had not been into her home. Mrs Brooks attributed this to her urban upbringing in Newcastle. When she first came to the village in 1935 everyone was in and out of each other's houses. She and her husband didn't follow this practice, they always kept their neighbours "at a bit of a distance", and she had not been into any of the neighbours' houses in all the years she had lived in the street.

Beyond these one or two close neighbours, most respondents claimed to be acquainted with, on average, about half a dozen others. The Smiths at number 15 were exceptional in being able to give the name and job (or other characteristic) of almost all the residents of the street and of the next terrace. The intensity of these relationships varied greatly – from knowing that the person lived in the street, knowing their name, greeting them, through to stopping for a chat in the street. About half of the respondents included, within this subsidiary network, people living in another terrace across the road. Others claimed that the other terrace – built so that the backs of the houses face the fronts of houses in Etherege Terrace – was quite separate and did not consider its residents as 'neighbours'. Two respondents could be described as 'isolates' since they had not developed any close neighbourly relationships, although they did have a passing acquaintanceship with a few of their neighbours.

In common with findings reported in previous studies of neighbouring, most respondents defined the good neighbour as someone who was both friendly and helpful – but did not invade their privacy. Four respondents cited their own neighbours as examples of the good neighbour. Several, incidentally, mentioned their awareness of the national 'Good Neighbour' campaign.

> "Someone who you can rely on if you need help or company. The best neighbour is someone you're close friends with." (Mrs Harrison)
> "Someone who would help you out if there really was a serious emergency and is someone who generally lets you get on with your own life." (Mrs Whiteside)
> "You never see them and never hear them. They are pleasant and don't hassle." (Mr Welch)
> "A good neighbour is someone who's tolerant and easy-going, not always coming round and complaining about little things." (Mr Leach)
> "Good neighbours are sociable and friendly, but they don't get too involved with you and you don't get too involved with them. They don't find out about and tell everyone about your dirty washing." (Mr Murphy)

The bad neighbour was typically one who "interfered", was "pushy", "nosey" or, on the other hand, refused to be sociable. Some complained that the resident who operated a backyard car repairs business was a bad neighbour because he parked old cars – in varying states of disrepair – along the street and made it look untidy. One respondent referred to a former bad neighbour who, he felt, was unpleasant and had an "unstable" personality. Another example of unneighbourly behaviour reported was Mrs Parr's reporting to the police an untaxed, broken-down car which belonged to someone else in the street. The owner was subsequently fined. Some thought this a mean thing for a neighbour to do. The majority of people, however, did not offer examples of bad neighbours or unneighbourliness.

A comparison was made between the significance of neighbours and that of the other primary social networks, friends and relatives. It was difficult to discover much about contact with friends. A few bluntly remarked that they had no friends, some were perhaps puzzled by the concept itself and a group of four especially close neighbours cited each other as friends. However, eight respondents clearly felt that they had friends – whom they saw frequently. Friends seemed to be of greater importance to those without accessible relatives; to the old lady living alone her best friend was almost a substitute relative and to the young university people friends constituted the main part of their social network.

One of the most important findings, however, was the significance and strength of links with relatives. All except four households (the university people and an aged widow living alone) had close relatives living within easy reach. Several lived within the village and most of the rest in the vicinity of Durham City. Young people had their own and/or their spouse's parents, and older people had their siblings and/or children and grandchildren. In nearly all cases contact was maintained by frequent visits – on average about once a week, but in several instances virtually every day. Although it was the young who usually helped the old there was a number of cases of mutual help; older people received help from, or enjoyed the company of, their grown-up children and also served as babysitters by looking after their grandchildren. In most cases the old were highly dependent upon their kin both for sociability

The Street studies

and help, while the young expresssed responsibilities for the old; several young people had been concerned to live near their parents and in two instances mothers had moved in with their daughters to be nursed until their death. Like the residents of Austen Avenue and Dryden Square, residents of Etherege Terrace maintained close kinship ties which were much more salient as a resource than those with either friends or neighbours.

There were various sources of variation in the nature and extent of neighbouring. Age and stage in the family cycle was most important for the elderly and young families with children. The old people were mainly concerned with help from neighbours in times of crisis; all pointed to their dependence upon neighbours to raise the alarm if they fell ill. For all four old people living alone their most intense neighbourly contacts were with each other (each had one of the others as a next-door neighbour) so their abilities to help each other were limited by reason of their age and their own health problems. All the old people, including the retired couple who lived next door to a young couple, were mainly involved with their neighbours on the level of friendliness; their expectations of help did not extend much beyond the need for immediate help in a crisis. After that, their kin or secondary agencies would take over.

For the young families the presence of children, rather than similarity in ages, seemed to draw them together. Mothers met each other when collecting their children from school or playschool (at the Community Centre nearby) and their children played together in the street. A related point was that mothers who remained at home to look after their children tended to develop close visiting relationships with others in the same position. Finally, the presence of young children often gave rise to the need for a babysitter and two or three neighbours helped others in this way. Most, however, relied on their kin – usually the grandmother – for babysitting.

In Etherege Terrace age and stage in family cycle were closely correlated with length of residence. Insofar as it is possible to isolate length of residence as a specific variable, it has significance in dividing the relatively long-established residents (seven households) from the newcomers. All the long-established residents knew each other, in the majority of cases quite closely. Family backgrounds were known and recollections shared. Most of them disapproved of the changes which had occurred with the arrival of the newcomers to the terrace. Only two of them had really made much effort to get to know who the newcomers were. Amongst the newcomers themselves, length of residence was important only inasmuch as it takes time for relationships with neighbours to develop. The two 'isolates' were, in fact, the most recent arrivals, having lived there for only a few months. It would seem, however, that the time taken to develop such relationships varied between individuals and with circumstances; two of the university couples, for example, established close relationships with their neighbours within a few weeks of moving in.

In Etherege Terrace women were undoubtedly more active in neighbouring than men, partly because the opportunities for neighbourly contact were greater amongst women, particularly if they did not go out to work. Only four of the 20 adult men engaged in visiting neighbours in their homes, but the majority of women did so. Neighbouring between men, insofar as it occurred, tended to involve help with specific problems or the loan of a particular tool or machine. At another level, the two men with their own businesses enlisted the help of one or two of their neighbours. The advantages of the two 'employers' was that neighbourly help was immediately available, but it was rewarded by cash rather than by help in return.

Social class differences within Etherege Terrace between the working class majority and the handful of (lower) middle class people were widely recognised but did not seem to prevent the development of close relationships between neighbours of different classes; at most they produced discomfort or misunderstanding.

Physical layout also played some part in influencing neighbourly contacts. Etherege Terrace was virtually a cul-de-sac opening out onto the main street and terminating at the other end in a rough ballast track leading to playing fields. Consequently, the number of residents passing by was greatest at the top end of the street and least at the bottom; opportunities for contact varied with location along the street. This was reflected in differences in people's knowledge of their neighbours; those living nearest the junction with the main street generally had a fuller knowledge of who lived in the street than those at the bottom end of the street. Moreover, the terrace was constructed in such a way that front doors were located together in pairs and these next-door neighbours could hardly avoid each other. Arising from this it seemed that the relationships between these next-door neighbours were significantly more likely to be intense than those between the more distant next-door neighbour. In addition, the terrace was broken by a gap half way along its length, produced by a driveway. For several respondents this formed a boundary to their knowledge of neighbours, so that they knew few of the residents on the other side of this gap.

Although kinship networks remained of vital and prime importance to most of the people of Etherege Terrace, neighbours did play some part – varying in significance – in the lives of most residents. To the old people the watchfulness of others was essential and comforting; it was also a function which requires proximity and thus can best be performed by neighbours. Amongst the younger people many seemed to enjoy a close and friendly relationship with a neighbour which, as well as being pleasant, could be of value in providing everyday assistance and the assurance of help in times of crisis.

Although people in Etherege Terrace lived in close physical proximity and necessarily came into frequent contact with each other, they had their own lives to lead and were mainly home-centred. This was no longer the occupational community it once had been nor was it held together socially by continuity of residence. For most, their major concern was with their families and their work; neighbouring relationships were for the most part satisfactory for those involved – but of subsidiary importance.

Congreve Hall, Cambridge

By contast with the other five Street studies, this one focussed upon an unstable, though relatively new, middle class locality in Cambridge. Congreve

The Street studies

Hall was an architect-designed development near the centre of Cambridge. It was very secluded from the surrounding area but was convenient for the centre of town and for transport. The houses were arranged around a central area of trees and lawns with no roads running through the middle. Constructed in terraces of four to six, they were divided by huge white fences and high walls. Prices were high. Each house was surrounded by abundant vegetation. The houses, built in the early 1960s, were two- or three-storied with a garden at the front, and a yard and garden at the rear. All the houses had underfloor central heating. Some had garages attached to the houses, others had them in blocks away from the houses. At one side of the development was a block of one- or two-bedroomed flats facing onto a main road. The houses and flats were highly-priced by national standards. The property was leasehold, so all occupants had to pay ground rent, and in the houses they also paid a full-time gardener to maintain the grounds. The flats had their own maintenance man. A residents' committee was formed to administer the employment of the gardener and to encourage all the residents to live in harmony. To this end they had rules about how loud you could play radio or television and how high you could hang your washing – hanging washing out on a Sunday was strictly forbidden. Most people interviewed thought the Residents' Association was a good idea.

Congreve Hall was a very mobile community. Many people worked abroad for long periods and rented out their houses – usually to the families of visiting academics. This practice was frowned upon by the Residents' Association but legally they could not do anything about it. In the summer many families went away for the whole of the long vacation period and rented their houses out to foreign families. Many people commented on the large turnover of families on the estate; for example, Mr Harrison remarked, "I would say between two-thirds and three-quarters of the families here had moved in the four years we were away." Reasons given for this were that many academics living in Congreve Hall moved on to better jobs; that families with children found the houses too small, and that with rising prices many people found they could not afford to continue living there. According to one resident, Miss Price, rising prices had resulted in a changing social composition: "The social composition of Congreve Hall has changed very much since I've been here. When I first came it was mainly university people who lived here. Prices have gone up so much that it's only the wealthy who can afford to buy houses here now – businessmen and retired people."

This mobility resulted in many people not knowing their neighbours, or not bothering to find out who they were when they knew they were only staying for an academic year. The following response from Miss Murray was typical: "I don't really know anyone in Congreve Hall. The people next door are away a lot, I think." Or from Miss Klein: "I don't know my neighbours yet as they've just moved in. We had an American couple living there last year . . . I didn't get to know them all that well as I was away much of the time", and from Mrs Harrison: "I know the people who have lived here a long time well, but there's such a high turnover in the other houses that I don't know some people. Since I've been here there's been seven or eight families living next door", and Mr Wilson: "we have owned this house for three years but we don't actually live here – we rent it out during the year through the university so that it's always just for eight months, then we come here for two or three weeks in the summer." One or two residents were resistant to talking about neighbouring at all in the interview, not finding it a very meaningful subject.

With such a mobile population, comparisons could be drawn with experience elsewhere. Mrs Barnes had lived for a time in a flat in the Barbican, where "you could be in the lift with the same people every day and they'd just look through you and never smile." She thought Congreve Hall compared very favourably. Others who came from the north or Wales took a different view. Miss Cleaver observed of the difference between Yorkshire and Cambridge: "It's not the same here as in the north. You can't just go up to someone and start chatting to them, or being too friendly, because they'll think you're funny." Mr Hutton from Wales took a similar view: "I suppose it has a lot to do with the type of background you come from. We come from one where you pop in for cups of tea and look after each other. Most people here come from wealthy backgrounds where they have been more independent and not been involved in communities." Miss Pumphrey agreed, though with a note of reservation: "It's not like in the north. I come from Manchester and it was much more intense there, but also a bit too interfering." Mrs Benson summed the situation up aptly: "When you come into a middle class intellectual type of place there are rules. There's no popping in and out, like with your working class."

Residents in Congreve Hall were divided into two categories – those who had lived there since it was built or for a reasonable length of time, and those who had lived there only a short while. There was closer contact between those who had lived together in the early days – as Mrs Lockwood said: "When we first came here everything was new and we all got to know each other and shared the problems that come with new houses." Mrs Watson endorsed this: "There was the novelty of living on a new estate – we were always in and out of each other's houses – the children would all play together and we'd stand talking to the other mums." Mrs Robinson moved a few years later and viewed it more objectively: "They weren't madly friendly but I got to know some of the mothers through collecting the children from school and there were things organised at that time – like a bonfire and a party organised by the residents' committee. There was a general feeling of being among similar people – middle class intellectuals."

However, over the intervening years, with the children growing up, this intense interaction declined and although quite a few of the original families still lived there, they had little to do with each other. Mrs Watson went on to say: "That's all receded now that the children have grown – we don't mix or share things anymore", and Mrs Robinson continued: "I would say that people are still equally friendly now but as the children grow up people get jobs and you're too busy to see anyone."

With the changing social composition in Congreve Hall there were fewer people with families. Those who did exist were never observed chatting by the sandpit or partaking in the intense neighbourliness of "the old days". People who had moved into Congreve Hall in the intervening years without the common bond of young children were polite and superficially friendly with neighbours, but if there was a relationship between them then it was usually because they were colleagues at work or had other common interests rather than that of just being a neighbour. Where neighbouring existed it did so on a more formal level. As Mrs Wright said: "This is definitely not a pop-in-for-a-chat place, but everyone is friendly."

Neighbours would be invited in for the occasional 'drink' which was always arranged beforehand. Reciprocal arrangements were between friends rather than neighbours in Congreve Hall. When they occurred between neighbours then they were mainly concerned with the protection of property. For example, Mrs Blewitt interacted with her neighbour when "we exchange keys if we're going away and things like that". Miss Schloss was very content with the Congreve Hall community: "We help each other a lot in Congreve Hall but I never go into anyone's for coffee – we don't waste each other's time – we are all very busy professional people – there's no housewives here so we don't have time to chatter."

Miss Klein had been taken ill last year and been forced to ask a passer-by to call an ambulance. She had been taken to hospital and when she was finally released again she returned home with no one in Congreve Hall even realising that she had been away. Mr Harrison explained the attitude to neighbouring as follows: "Reciprocity occurs where it is needed. Here there is little need. Not many people work on their houses so there is little need for borrowing tools. The shops are just around the corner so there is no necessity to pop next door to borrow a cup of sugar."

However, there were individuals living in Congreve Hall who would have benefited from a more caring community. Ironically, Mr Harrison's immediate neighbour was one of the most extreme cases. Mrs Murray, in her early thirties, was left by her husband after moving to Congreve Hall. After two years she knew hardly anyone on the estate. At that time she desperately needed someone to talk to – "I really had to face this problem of who to turn to when I was left alone." In fact she turned to her family and eventually the doctor. To see her family she had to travel to London, so the doctor gave her a number to ring if she needed to talk to someone immediately. She would go to her neighbours in a crisis – which she explained was "if I'd been burgled", but hadn't been able to go to them when "it's just needing someone to talk to really".

Definitions of a good neighbour shared elements in common with those in the other Street studies – friendliness, helpfulness and keeping oneself to oneself, but a few also made geographical and class comparisons.

> "Someone who doesn't intrude but is kind and helpful – like my neighbours here." (Mrs Jefferson)
> "A good neighbour is easy going and sympathetic, a balance between friendship and interfering. A person who will give you a hand if you really need it." (Miss Pumphrey)
> "One you can go to without having daily contact with them." (Mrs Wilson)
> "Never to intrude but be ready to help." (Mrs Benson)

"A good neighbour is someone who respects your privacy and shows consideration." (Mr Dixon)

"A neighbour in the Christian sense of the term. Someone who is willing to share their problems, someone to whom you can turn, someone with a ready smile who is kind and helpful." (Mr Tweddle)

"Someone who doesn't peer out of the window at you and ones who don't object to children." (Mrs Bennett)

"Someone who doesn't shop you for having tenants (strictly confidential). The [professional man] at no. 3 said that if my children didn't behave, he'd shop me to the residents' association for having tenants." (Mrs Murphy)

"A good neighbour is someone who is always around to help out. Well, that's not what it's like here, but at least in theory." (Miss Cleaver)

"In my opinion, the richer people are, the less neighbourly they are." (Mrs Barnes)

"I like to think the London way about neighbours, and that is you don't know and you don't want to know them. It never occurs to you to speak to the person in the flat next to you in London." (Miss Ponsonby)

The lack of community spirit in Congreve Hall was readily excused. Mr Hughes remarked that: "The type of people who choose to live in Congreve Hall aren't really interested in a community life I don't think. Most of them have friends through work." The importance to residents of preserving their social space and independence was manifested in the high walls and abundant shrubbery surrounding each house. As Miss Pattinson remarked, "you can't have much to do with the neighbours because the walls are too high – you can't chat to them over the wall".

Mr Laidlaw's attitude was typical of many of the older residents: "We don't have much to do with the neighbours. We like our privacy and peace and quiet ... most of us have moved around in our lives and have no difficulty settling in a new area and making friends – or not – as we choose." Unfortunately this independence and seclusion made it difficult for those who would have liked to meet their neighbours. The Michells, a young couple both out at work during the day, were unhappy when first moving to Congreve Hall: "It really wasn't very satisfactory when we first came here. Coming from Wales I wasn't too happy about it – for nearly 18 months we didn't know any of our neighbours at all – none of them came to introduce themselves or invite us in for coffee ... now that we have go to know people they're very friendly." Mrs Allison, a widow in her late seventies, with very few visitors, left her six-foot-high garden gate open so that she could see people walking past.

Very few people in Congreve Hall knew anyone in the flats – which were mainly inhabited by old people – and no one visited any of the old people. When asked about the old people, responses from the people in the houses were always similar: "I think they look after each other"; "I've always assumed that they employ the caretaker to keep an eye on them." However, Mr Harrison, who had in the past had some contact with a few of the old people remarked: "Many of them in fact are very lonely – even though they appear independent – I always think it's a mistake to separate old and young people."

Although families with children had the advantage of having more contact

The Street studies

with each other, children also presented a problem in Congreve Hall. The development is high density living and all the children played in the central area of grass and trees. The resulting noise and 'unruliness' had caused a marked split between residents with and without children. Many of the inhabitants, especially the older ones, felt threatened by this 'unruliness' and one old woman had remarked that, "I feel as if I'm living in a goldfish bowl in a children's playground." The conflict was expressed as two opposing theories of child-rearing. The older residents believed in discipline and the dominance of parental authority whilst the young parents talked of concepts of 'free expression'. This dichotomy resulted in many emotional scenes between the children and the older residents, and the parents and their older neighbours. Mrs Watson, a parent of one of the children most objected to, explained her view:

> "The elderly seem to have a stranglehold on Congreve Hall now – they don't have children themselves and they strongly object to the older ones. They didn't mind the children when they were small but it's as if they're a threat now that they're older and doing the normal things older children do. I suppose when they were young they were brought up in public school and they have set ideas – they don't like the children playing – they expect them to be restrained."

Miss Pattinson, in her late thirties, was perhaps more objective about the situation:

> "This estate hasn't really worked as they thought it would do. They expected old and young to mix but in fact there's a lot of trouble. The old people think that the kids are too noisy and the kids are always arguing. Also they bring in kids from outside and there are fights. The space outside here isn't big enough for them to play football but they do. Yesterday they were climbing the pear trees and throwing pears at each other but as the trees don't belong to one particular person there's nothing you can do about it . . . the main problem is that there's so many broken homes on this estate. We overheard one child ask another, 'Have you a mother, *or* a father?'"

The implications of that question did not wholly misrepresent life in Congreve Hall.

There appeared to be a lack of consideration for the other's view on both sides of this dispute. But these tensions were nevertheless set within a curiously strong sense of local community. As an architect's experiment in community building, Congreve Hall has both succeeded and failed. The success lay in the fact that almost without exception the residents were pleased to be living there and were strongly aware of it as a special and especially desirable place to live. They had a distinctly positive view of both the place and in general terms the sort of people who lived in it. The failure, however, lay in the fact that this sense of place has not grown into a sense of neighbourliness, attachments to or involvement with people. The residents of Congreve Hall were, to put it crudely, irredeemably bourgeois: property, privacy and status were the concerns that dominated their relations with their neighbours. These concerns both prescribed a general belief that Congreve

Informal neighbouring

Hall residents were 'nice people' and ensured that actual relationships would be shot through with reserve and a jealous defence of each family's private life space. Comparing this study with those conducted in Boswell, and the Yorkshire woollen town and Durham seems to impel, rather brutally, a class view of neighbouring.

5 The sociology of informal neighbouring

What is the sociological significance of neighbouring? The material in the three preceding chapters now permits some threads to be drawn together and conclusions drawn. These will be discussed under four headings: factors accounting for variations in neighbouring; the significance of social networks; a theory of neighbouring in the contemporary world; and the relationship between neighbouring and friendship. Philip Abrams's own synthesis of these issues was never completed, but an outline is presented here, a good deal of it in his own words.

The factors accounting for variations in neighbouring can be considered in the light of the six Street studies. A broad distinction may be made between those social influences in the foreground and those in the background. The most obvious foreground factor is the longevity of the settlement and the length of residence there of particular households. At one rural extreme Boswell was an ancient village with a substantial proportion of residents born there or nearby. At the other, urban, end of a continuum was Congreve Hall, built less than 20 years ago and bringing together a mobile section of the middle class. Even relatively similar streets could be quite different. Despite the fact that many of its inhabitants were not unambiguously working class, Austen Avenue was a remarkably close approximation to a typical traditional working class community. Dryden Square, similar in terms of class composition and urban type, differed markedly both in patterns of neighbouring and in the situation of the elderly. There are clearly differences between long-time residents and newcomers in terms of contact with neighbours and sort of help exchanged. And the pattern that emerges is likely to be different in a long-established community to that in a new one. New settlements, whether working class or middle class, face more severe problems in fostering neighbourhood ties.

A second foreground factor in accounting for neighbouring is proximity. This sounds like a truism, particularly if neighbouring is defined in terms of 'nighness'. In the Street studies, however, the most frequently mentioned influence upon whether neighbourly relations developed with neighbours was proximity. Being next door to somebody *is* different from living in the next street to them. Several earlier studies (Kuper 1953; Mogey 1956 and Hole 1959) emphasised the difference between next-door neighbours and other neighbours. In the Street studies the people next door were the most salient relationship, both positively in terms of friendliness, help and reciprocity – and negatively in terms of problems over noise, fences, car parking or social distance.

Though small variations in built form can have some influence on attitudes and behaviour – as in Etherege Terrace where pairs of front doors were side by side and led to closer contact – the physical layout on a larger scale proved a more important influence. In Dryden Square and Congreve Hall, there was clear evidence that the segregation of the elderly in bungalows in the former and flats in the latter cut them off from neighbours other than people of their own age and accentuated social isolation, while in Austen Avenue and Etherege Terrace neighbours of all ages lived side by side and there were more opportunities for mutual aid between different age groups. At Congreve Hall another aspect of layout promoted more formal neighbourly contact. The common central play areas, and the employment of a gardener to maintain the environment, was tied in to the existence of the Residents' Association, which attempted to exercise a degree of social control over residents' activities – for example, in restricting noise and vetting house extensions.

Apart from proximity, the most salient influence mentioned in the interviews as promoting neighbourliness was age and stage in the life cycle. In several streets, young mothers with young children had particularly close contacts, and young children in particular often were the cause of cooperation and reciprocity among nigh-dwellers. The elderly, too, more restricted in their mobility, tended to develop close neighbourly ties particularly when living in housing occupied by people of their own age. Similar life cycle stage does not necessarily promote neighbouring. One group for whom neighbouring ties were notably weaker were married couples both of whom were working, where the wife did not have time to foster contacts with those living nearby. Similar circumstances might foster neighbouring, between young divorced mothers with young children, for example, or between elderly widows or widowers who could give each other support. Mixing different age groups was not, however, always an unalloyed blessing, particularly in Congreve Hall where the existence of communal play areas led to conflicts between residents with children and some of those without, particularly the elderly.

A fourth foreground factor should be briefly mentioned. Particularly in the working class streets, contacts between neighbours involved women rather than men, and the social world of the men was much more likely to be found elsewhere, through work, or a hobby, or pub or club. These gender differences should not be exaggerated, but they were a continuing theme in all the Street studies. Women, too, were the principal carers in cases of dependency.

Lying behind these influences are what may be termed background factors, which influence people's propensity to become involved in neighbourly relations and affect whether the opportunities provided by common gender, age or life cycle stage or proximity or length of residence, are mobilised or not, and if so, how.

Personal history is clearly one influence. The opportunity to develop neighbourly relations at one stage in one's life may be important in influencing future behaviour. This was clear in the contrast at Congreve Hall between the former Londoner who thought it rather a neighbourly place, and the northerners with a different frame of reference who didn't. There were suggestions in some of the interviews that neighbouring might be influenced by socialisation and one's parents' behaviour. In Leeds Mrs Skinner said: "I suppose it's the grounding your mother gives you" and Mrs Davis commented: "I was never brought up to go in and out of each other's houses." Very similar comments were made in Boswell: "I've never been one for going into other people's houses. My mother was the same and so is my daughter. I suppose it's the way you're brought up." (Mrs Kelly). "My mam didn't go in and out of houses. She said: neighbours should be there if you need them." (Mrs Jones).

People clearly differ in their propensity to interact with others, which some students of neighbouring have attempted to explain in terms of personality. Kuper (1953) suggested a distinction between 'reserved' and 'sociable' types. Festinger *et al.* (1950) postulated a continuum between the 'isolate' and the 'sociometric star'. Certainly in the interviews there were a number of remarks to the effect 'I'm not a neighbourly type', but these needed to be interpreted in the context of the speaker's social situation and social networks. Personality differences may be one contributory factor – though very difficult to separate from personal history – but as the concept of 'sociometric star' suggests, neighbourliness is often rooted in the social structure.

The clearest evidence of this in the Street studies was the marked class difference in behaviour between the one middle class case, Congreve Hall, and the rest. Even within predominantly working class streets like Etherege Terrace, the middle class residents had a different role and a different relationship to their neighbour. Typically, their range of social contacts was wider, their friends and family were more likely to be geographically distant, they were more likely (as several incomers to Boswell demonstrated) to be actively involved in voluntary associations, and relations with neighbours were more likely to be on a formal basis. The middle class in general did not 'pop' into one another's houses, least of all without knocking; witness the shocked reaction of incomers to Boswell. Class may also be associated with aloofness and the making of social distinctions about whom it is appropriate and not appropriate to 'know'. On the evidence of Congreve Hall, affluence appeared to be associated with a greater desire for privacy and a greater sense of social distance.

There may also be distinct class differences in the need for reciprocity; at least, this was suggested by Mr Harrison at Congreve Hall, who had lived for some years in Turkey while doing scientific research:

> "Being a good neighbour involved cooperation, both negative and positive, and it must be a reciprocal service ... Living in Turkey, one could see that the whole system was built on reciprocity. If a farmer broke his leg, then he must rely on his neighbour to help out. Also there was a sharing of skills. In Turkey you knew how much you could afford to ask for from each individual. Indeed, people often did things to build up credit for a later date. It was a very cohesive force. In a place like Congreve Hall neighbouring isn't very strong. Here there is a mobile community with a rapid turnover rate. Reciprocity occurs where it is needed. Here it isn't needed. The more affluent a community, the less reciprocity is practised."

Class on its own, however, is insufficient. It needs to be related to wider trends towards privatisation, to dominant social norms, and to the nature of support networks. The most striking uniformity in the interviews was the universal ownership of television and the extent to which it dominated people's leisure time. Changes in leisure patterns toward more home-centred entertainment have inevitably somewhat attenuated neighbourly relations, particularly in more traditional working class urban areas such as Austen Avenue. And this needs to be linked to the social value of privacy. Very many respondents mentioned neighbours who called without invitation and hung around as an unwelcome bugbear. Many respondents were clearly aware of the boundary between their home or family and the outside world, which should not be transgressed. Here, perhaps, personality and social influences come together to determine the extent to which members of different social groups erect barriers to protect their own personal living space. Neighbours can be too friendly, to the extent that privacy is threatened, as the study of the houses in Dryden Close showed. The mechanisms available for maintaining social distance were very evident in Congreve Hall. It is clear – for example, from definitions of a 'good neighbour' – that neighbouring is held in check by many people who fear it may get out of hand. Gossiping, for instance, may develop into nosiness and rumour-mongering and cause unpleasantness. Consequently, some, like Mr Crudas in Austen Avenue, took the attitude that contact with neighbours should be kept to a minimum, not least because if animosity develops one could not escape it except by moving away. The complexity and contradiction of neighbourliness lie precisely in this combination of closeness – through passing the time of day, visiting, mutual aid, emergency help – with distance. And such contradictions have important implications in trying to draw on neighbourliness as a source of neighbourhood care.

Dominant social norms, perhaps but not necessarily class related, are also to be considered. The reticence so characteristic of Congreve Hall contrasts with the promiscuous gossiping of the young mothers in the early days of Dryden Square on the one hand, and the friendly but somewhat distant tone of life in Boswell, where people nevertheless were very well informed about what their neighbours were doing. The evolution of neighbouring among the young mothers of Dryden Square is perhaps the most interesting case. Young and Willmott (1972) quote Hazlitt approvingly: 'with change of place we change our ideas; nay, our opinions and feelings'. This was true of Dryden Square, but veering from over-involvement and the ultimately destructive amount of gossip to withdrawal and the cultivation of a few contacts on the estate.

Equally clearly, neighbourly relations cannot be looked at apart from the existence of other support networks. In the interviews there was a good deal of talk of friends, but they did not appear to be a major source of social support in times of crisis. What was most striking was the extent of contact with kin, both on a day to day basis and in times of difficulty. By comparison with kinship ties, neighbouring relations were weak relations. In the light of the earlier literature review, this is a not unsurprising finding, though it requires explanation.

The limited nature of the neighbouring relation arises from the fact that there is no basis for functional interdependence between modern neighbours other than proximity or kinship. Unlike the members of a caste system, for example, they do not work for each other but for impersonal outside bodies. There is no positive sense in which people regularly need each other's services in day to day matters. Being a neighbour is something much more specific, more narrowly framed, than being a relation or a friend, just as it is noticeably less specific than

The sociology of informal neighbouring

being an employer or a social worker. It occupies an indeterminate relational middle ground. It is neither universal nor specific; it is framed by proximity and by little else. Most neighbours do not choose to make their friends among their neighbours. Most neighbourhoods do not constrain their inhabitants into strongly-bonded relationships with one another.

By comparison, local kinship ties are (on the evidence of the Street studies) much stronger. With the exception of the geographically mobile middle class minority in Boswell and Etherege Terrace, and the majority in Congreve Hall, contact with kin was regular and for most respondents on a daily or weekly basis. This was true as much of the newer as of the older settlements, though Fielding Close was something of an exception. One can think of support networks as ranged on two continua shown in figure 5.1

NEAR

	Boswell village	
Fielding Close		Austen Avenue
	Etherege Terrace	Dryden Square

INFREQUENT CONTACT ——————————————— FREQUENT CONTACT

| | Boswell (middle-class incomers) | |
| | Congreve Hall | |

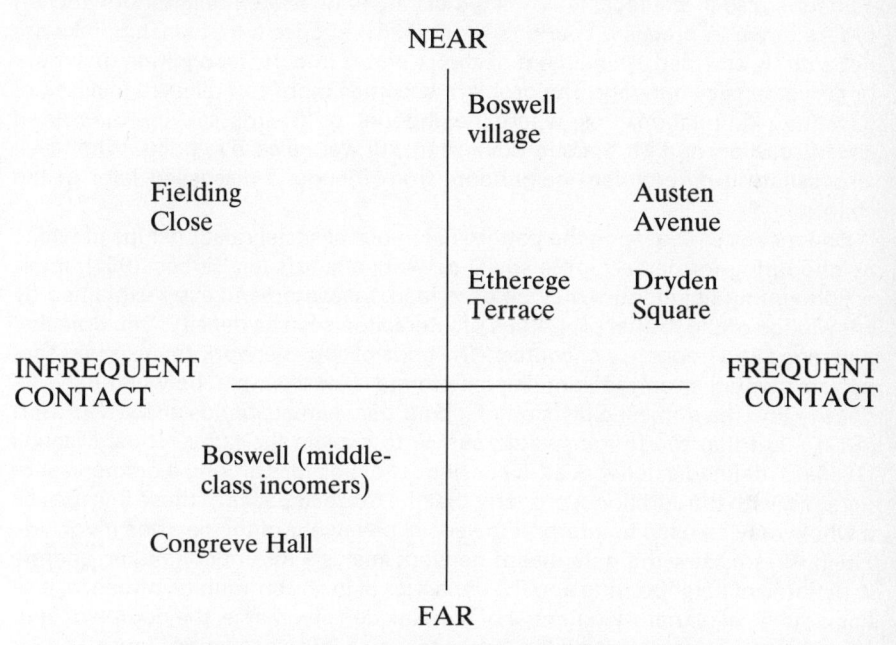

FAR

Figure 5.1 Characteristics of family support networks

One is geographical propinquity between kin – nearness or distance – the other frequency of contact. There was a marked difference between the working class residents of Austen Avenue, Dryden Square and Etherege Terrace (as well as the locals in Boswell) and on the other hand the middle class spiralists of Boswell and Congreve Hall, whose kin tended to be far away and be seen infrequently. Fielding Close was an exception, in that although most people had kin living within the county, they saw them less frequently, perhaps due to poverty and possibly (though this is only a suggestion) a degree of social estrangement.

If this sort of pattern were generalisable, it would have very significant implications for the provision of social services. For it suggests that informal care might, potentially at least, be most forthcoming for the less geographically mobile sections of the population who have kin living nearby, and least forthcoming for the mobile middle class on the one hand and the disadvantaged lower working class on the other. Economically, however, it would be the working class kin who would most need financial support if they were to be expected to provide care on a long-term basis. These tentative hypotheses will be further explored in later chapters.

Several of the 'streets', Boswell in particular, raise the question of how far it is possible to distinguish meaningfully between kin, neighbours and friends in practice. Studies of small rural communities (cf. Frankenberg 1966) make clear there are some localities where virtually everyone is related by blood to someone else in the locality. Thus the distinction between neighbours and kin breaks down in practice. Loudon's work (1961) suggests that kinship links are not entirely ascribed; an element of choice enters into the recognition of a more or less extensive network. The problem becomes more complicated in cases of substitute kin relationships, where 'neighbours' or 'friends' take on the role of kin. Miss Snow and Mr Mars in Boswell (p. 70) were a case in point. Whether it is possible to differentiate neighbours from friends is discussed later in the chapter.

One means of analysing the patterns of informal social relationships of which neighbouring formed a part is social network analysis (cf. Barnes 1954). Interaction among neighbours may be described, measured and even explained by knowledge of the formal properties of interaction such as density, 'multiplexity' and range and frequency of contact. The hope of early network analysis was that not only would strong relationships be found – for example, between network density and the domestic division of labour between husbands and wives (Bott 1957) – but that the former would suffice to explain the latter. Thus, Mitchell (1969a:2) defined a network as 'a specific set of linkages among a defined set of persons, with the additional property that the characteristics of these linkages as a whole may be used to interpret the social behaviour of the persons involved'. Philip Abrams saw the potential of network analysis for understanding change in patterns of neighbouring and the dynamics of local community influence, particularly the explanatory potential of network density, that is, the degree of connectedness of a network and the extent to which it is close-knit or loose-knit.

The image of the traditional working class community as, among other things, a milieu of intense neighbouring is, more than anything else, an image of a network of very high density. Arguments about the decline of community are in large measure arguments about an unavoidable decline in the density of local social networks and the unavoidable consequences of that decline – as Bulmer (1977) and Frankenberg (1966) have made very clear. High density has been generally associated with solidarity, commitment and normative consensus – also with a host of other more specific relational effects. Low density, by contrast, is held to bring about all sorts of contrary conditions. It is through the erosion of density that modernisation and urbanisation are said to wreak havoc with traditional social solidarities including those of the caring neighbourhood (see Bott (1957), Henry (1958), Frankenberg (1966), Craven and

Wellman (1973), Laumann (1973)). By far the best known and most extensive debate on the effects and concomitants of density is that launched by Elizabeth Bott around the hypothesis that variations in network density promote variations in relationships between spouses. Fifteen years later, Bott (1971) allowed that density might not be an adequate independent variable and that density itself has to be explained in terms of factors which subsist not in the formal properties of networks but in the social contexts, relationships and individual careers out of which networks are assembled. Thus, she concluded that at least the following variables (which may or may not act through network density) would have to be taken into account: occupation, social mobility, geographical mobility, ecological factors, subculture and ethnic grouping, education and phase of individual and family development.

One of the main reasons why so many of the proposed relationships between density and other factors cannot be found effectively in the real world is, as Harris (1969), Fallding (1961), Kapferer (1972) and Allan (1979) have argued, precisely because density, insofar as it is taken seriously as a formal property of interaction, has to be measured in terms of *all* the links in a network. The varying content of actual links is deliberately ignored; equal weight is given to all links regardless of the varying significance they might have to those concerned. If one recognises that different links can have widely different values for individuals within a network, one may get much closer to an explanation of the relationships in which one is interested but the explanation is no longer grounded in the notion of density as a formal property of interaction; it is an explanation in terms of the significant content of relationships, not of the structure of networks.

The relevance of outside links – of context – also needs to be considered. The shift of emphasis from density to cohesion is largely an effort to respond to the force of such arguments. Discussions of the cohesion of neighbourhoods, and other networks, typically do proceed in terms of the interrelation of content, form and context. Here the work of Kapferer (1972) has been especially influential, not just because he has tried to develop explanations of the closeness or connectedness of members of networks in terms of the significance or value of their interactions but because he has in addition drawn attention to the *exchange* element in relationships in trying to account for their significance.

It is the three themes of exchange, costs and rules which seem to dominate attempts to identify and account for network cohesion; cohesion in turn being held to be crucial to the understanding of such matters as mutual aid, support, care and helpfulness insofar as these are found among people who are neither friends nor kin. Kapferer's contribution was primarily to establish the pertinence of ideas of exchange, costs, investment and reward as ways of relating the content of interaction to the importance of relationships and both in turn to the extent to which individuals experience relationships as entailing obligations to act in certain ways. Such actions – helping, joking, not gossiping or whatever – are likely to be routinely exacted, to acquire the force of social facts, in close-knit groups, not because the groups are close-knit but because the reasons that have made them close-knit have also made them fields of personal investment in which all concerned are permanently in debt. As Allan (1979:132) comments: 'when an individual is embedded in a close-knit set of relationships of a particular type, he is indeed embedded'.

C. S. Fischer has carried this line of argument forward to propose that 'neighbourhood cohesion ... will exist when people find social relations in their localities more rewarding than those outside their localities' (Fischer *et al.* 1977:32); and he goes on to identify three particular conditions which have been found to produce such a state of affairs:
(1) The existence of other, overlapping ties, as in ethnic enclaves ... and factory neighbourhoods.
(2) Logistical difficulties in developing or maintaining extralocal relations, as in isolated hamlets ... and among carless suburban housewives.
(3) An external threat that increases the functional importance of neighbourhood ties, as in the case of urban redevelopment and busing.

Such perceptions, centred on the idea of cohesion as an outcome of profitable exchange, have radical implications for the whole range of traditional theorising about both community and neighbouring. Inspired primarily by the work of Blau (1964), they have been trenchantly elaborated by Fischer and his colleagues and by several other authors. Wellman (1979), for example, has carefully discredited the view that there is a strong relationship – or in his view any relationship – between frequency of face to face contact and closeness or helpfulness. Here, too, the evidence points towards the costs and rewards of interaction as being the decisive factors. In other words, positive neighbouring can less and less be explained in terms of the mere fact of people being neighbours. What is needed is an explanation of why some neighbours are *chosen* for close relationships and others are not. Or to quote Allan (1979:139) once more: 'it is not neighbours as a category who are relied on but particular neighbours who have developed a sufficiently close relationship'. The strongest statement and development of these ideas is that provided by Anderson (1971), whose work is discussed in chapter 6.

Philip Abrams acknowledged the ingenuity and technical skill devoted to network analysis, but argued that there had been little progress with the main project of explaining content in terms of form. This perhaps explains why his use of the term (for example, Abrams 1980) remained a metaphorical one, without any attempt to analyse in detail actual networks on the ground or even to measure the extent of respondents' contacts in the Street studies. A good deal of the now considerable literature on support networks and helping networks was published after the Street studies were in the field (cf. Froland, Pancoast *et al.* 1981; Gottleib 1981; Warren 1981; Gottleib 1983; Maguire 1983) and it is only recently that Wenger (1984) has studied support for the elderly in North Wales through analysing their social networks. These studies have produced hypotheses which deserve further investigation. Wenger, for example, suggests a relationship between network size and loneliness among the elderly, those with smaller networks being more likely to be lonely. Warren suggested a relationship between local network characteristics and propensity to seek professional help. Pathways to help were related to different types of network, and this partially explained the reliance of working class communities upon kin and neighbours rather than outside assistance.

The sociology of informal neighbouring

In one specific respect, Philip Abrams made direct use of an idea from network analysis, and suggested its wider application. Both in the Street studies and Neighbourhood Care research, the concept of the 'sociometric star' or key individual at the centre of a dense local network of help, was invoked. For example, Mrs Dunn played this role among the old people in Dryden Square as did the coordinator in the Parsons Green Neighbourhood Care scheme (p. 155). Philip Abrams was particularly impressed by *Natural Helping Networks* (Collins and Pancoast 1976), which developed out of American action research on day care, and the observation that many of the neighbourhoods studied had natural networks through which mutual aid was channelled. In a 1979 seminar he put it this way.

We really ought to take steps to follow up the lead offered us by Collins and Pancoast and oddly neglected so far in this country – by beginning a serious hunt for what they call 'central figures' in neighbourhoods. They are precisely the people whose position and activities enable them to fuse and mediate both neighbourhood involvement and informal care. And quite often, luckily for social policy, such people are not obscurely hidden in unexplored informal social networks but the quite visible incumbents of quite obviously central formal roles – that is, again, they are doctors, priests, post-mistresses, publicans, teachers (not usually social workers or social service administrators, though). Their centrality reflects the *functional* substance of social networks and that is obviously where the structuring of neighbourhood care should begin.

For the sociological explanation of neighbouring, however, Philip Abrams was inclined to discount the value of network analysis by itself, and to turn to more historically-grounded theories drawing on ideas of cost and exchange as the basis of relationships. The nearest that he came to a general theoretical statement of the development of neighbouring was the contrast which he drew between the traditional neighbourhood and modern neighbourhoodism, in industrial society. To do this he again turned to network analysis.

There are two types of social network, which I will call the traditional neighbourhood and modern neighbourhoodism. We probably all have a fairly definite idea of what the traditional neighbourhood was like. There are also enough pieces of fairly strong social and historical research around to suggest that what we are probably thinking of is more than a mythical beast: the densely woven world of kin, neighbours, friends and co-workers, highly localised and strongly caring within the confines of quite tightly defined relationships, above all the relationships of kinship. What is found in empirical research is a rough approximation to the ideal type – the sort of thing that turned up again and again in the famous 'community studies' of the 1950s; in Bethnal Green, in North Wales, in St Ebbes in the old centre of Oxford, in Yorkshire mining villages, in mid-nineteenth century Preston and even in mid-twentieth century Dagenham. In all these cases localities were found permeated with informal social networks sufficiently dense, complex and extensive, and evoking sufficient commitment from residents, for a high proportion of local needs for care to be met within them. Nor are such networks entirely a thing of the past. In our own current research we have come across two, possibly three, localities in which something plainly identifiable as an attenuated

Informal neighbouring

version of the traditional neighbourhood system of relationships could be recognised.

The problem with the traditional neighbourhood type of social network is not to my mind that it is a thing of the past, rapidly being eliminated by the forces of social change – although as I shall argue shortly, it is – but that when one considers the social conditions that made it possible one is forced to the conclusion that on balance it is probably rather undesirable. This is a matter of looking at the social *contexts* of the networks rather than at the caring and supportive relationships within them. Internally, the networks of the traditional neighbourhood were indeed marked by collective attachment, reciprocity and trust. Externally, they were no less plainly marked by constraint, isolation and insecurity. Moreover, the internal characteristics were in large measure a product of the external characteristics, a way of life worked out to permit survival in the face of them. The so-called natural helping networks of the traditional neighbourhood – not actually natural at all, of course – developed as a response to certain highly specified social conditions which one would not wish to see reproduced today.

Two or three generations ago, the majority of the population, particularly the working classes, inhabited local areas within which most of their lives were lived and activities centred. Class homogeneity combined with neighbourhood 'provincialism', a high degree of endogamy and sometimes shared religion to create tightly-knit neighbourhood units. Powerful links between both men and their workmates, and between women and their kin and neighbours – links often involving substantial exchanges of services and money – bound together households in the same local area.

> Poor women did indeed share extensively and unsentimentally. Small sums of money, like a penny for the gas, were passed back and forth between households, and even on these cash-poor streets, women could launch collections toward such major expenses as funerals. Domestic paraphernalia circulated too between women: linen, washtubs, clothing or other pawnable items which the borrower could use to raise immediate cash. In emergencies like serious illness or eviction, neighbours could be counted on for major services, something not contingent on having maintained cordial ties, but on the obligations people viewed as part of 'the neighbourhood role'. Women giving birth, and their children, would be cared for. Battered wives could get shelter for a night. . . . Custom reserved special treatment for the sick. Neighbourhood women did their laundry, built (and provided) their fires, prepared their meals. (Ross: 1983:6)

Such self-help networks at the local level were a realistic response to low incomes, economic adversity and unpredictable domestic crisis. In the absence of state support for the relief in the home of illness, old age or unemployment, the 'safety net' for most families was the neighbourhood itself. 'A family who have lived for years in one street are recognised up and down the length of that street as people to be helped in times of trouble' (Pember-Reeves 1913:39). There were limits to the extent of aid. It was useful to meet small-scale or very short-term material needs, and to deal with various forms of domestic crisis for a week or two. Neighbours could not provide adequate support for a household with too few wage earners – unmarried or deserted women with small children,

The sociology of informal neighbouring

widows and the elderly were more likely to have to move to the workhouse. Other forms of care, however, were commonly provided on a neighbourhood basis. Neighbours and even neighbourhoods could act as auxiliary parents, keeping an eye on children when parents were not there. When a mother of young children was ill, neighbours as well as extended kin would help out.

In the United States in the late nineteenth and early twentieth centuries, such mutual aid became to a degree organised and formalised. The ward unit of the American political machine delivered a form of neighbourhood care to urban ethnic groups recently arrived in a country without significant welfare provision by government. Help was provided through elaborate networks of personal relations, not by the socially distant professional social worker.

> In our prevailing impersonal society, the machine, through its local agents, fulfilled the important social function of humanising and personalising all manner of assistance to those in need. Food baskets and jobs, legal and extra-legal advice, looking after the bereaved – all these found the ever-helpful precinct captain available in the pinch (Merton 1957:74).

The machine declined as state welfare provision grew during the twentieth century (cf. Callow 1976:233–318). It provides an interesting historical model of neighbourhood care, however, particularly in relation to Philip Abrams's discussion of neighbourhood political organisation in chapter 12.

Such a system of neighbourhood interdependence was a practical response to a world in which there were few alternative forms of support to going into the workhouse in times of need. These community networks of mutual aid developed most strongly in Britain in the period before the advent of significant welfare legislation, prior to World War One. The expansion of state activity, however, only slowly influenced the character of such networks. Some state provision – for example, universal primary education – actually increased the demands upon families for mutual support. Other measures, such as old-age pensions, helped specific groups. Until well into the twentieth century, among the semi-skilled and unskilled manual working class, mutual self help remained a significant source of short-term and emergency social care.

The bulk of sharing was on the basis of reciprocity. You gave back what you borrowed. Some services – childcare, maternity nursing, tending the sick, running errands – were compensated by money payments, an important source of income for those with meagre resources. Self-interest was also a motive in offers of assistance. 'Gifts' created obligations, and to be able to count on the goodwill of several other nearby households might mean help or money when one was in difficulty in one's own household. Not all neighbours, moreover, were treated on the same basis. Some women regarded themselves as socially superior; others could rely on their kin network; stigmatising factors influencing the provision of help included drunkenness, slovenly housekeeping or sexual promiscuity. Tension and conflicts were not infrequently the other side of the coin of mutual aid (Ross 1983:14–16).

Reciprocal care between neighbours grows where information and trust are high and where resources for satisfying needs in other ways are low: in relatively isolated, relatively closed and relatively threatened social milieux with highly homogeneous populations. In effect, when closely examined, the networks of the traditional neighbourhood usually proved in any case not to be primarily networks of neighbours, not territorially based networks at all but, rather, either kinship networks or networks rooted in religion, occupation or race.

This older pattern is important because it provides a baseline from which change in the social context of neighbouring can be measured. Three features of the older system need to be underlined. Its stimulus lay in want and economic privation. It rested on a system of short- and long-term reciprocity, tempered by a degree of compassion, but also by fine distinctions of social status and recognition of social worth. There was a considerable overlap between kinship ties and neighbouring, since a high proportion of close relatives lived near each other. Philip Abrams contrasted this traditional pattern with what he called 'modern neighbourhoodism' which developed in a society with greater geographical mobility, diversity, low-cost state provision of services and social choice. With the post-1945 welfare legislation and the growth of local authority social services, providing more adequate income support and health services, the mutual aid born of economic adversity becomes less salient, though in the recession of the early 1980s the pace of change may have slowed down.

Most neighbourhoods today do not constrain their inhabitants into strongly bonded relationships with one another. Those that do are either exceptional or regrettable. Generally the old equation of problems, resources and closure which produced the diffuse trust and reciprocity of the traditional neighbourhood type networks, within which care in 'critical life situations' could effectively be provided for and by local residents, has plainly collapsed in the face of new social patterns. Most neighbours are not constrained and do not choose to make their friends among their neighbours. Those who do tend to be seeking highly specific solutions to highly specific problems which they cannot solve elsewhere and which make them 'expensive' people to befriend from the point of view of their neighbours. In general terms perhaps only two features of the social networks of the traditional neighbourhood type have survived the social revolutions of industrialisation with sufficient strength to serve as significant sources of informal social care today. These are close kinship relationships between parents and children (at both ends of the life cycle) and siblings on the one hand, and on the other the networks of local information sustained by the more or less idle, more or less benevolent or malicious talk that people engage in in their efforts to construct a known and comfortable socio-spatial setting for their own lives, namely gossip.

Two of the social products of industrialisation which have worked their way through to the local level are greater mobility and choice. Better transport, longer journeys to work, geographical dispersal of kin and friends, a wider range of shopping and recreational opportunities, and the privatisation of the family, have all reduced the centrality of the neighbourhood as a locus of social interaction and social support. It is not that the neighbourhood has ceased to be important. For young children, their mothers and for many elderly people, particularly those who are less mobile, it remains the centre of their social world. The growing proportion of the very old among the elderly makes the provision of informal social support even more important than hitherto. There is still a significant amount of social exchange between neighbours. Such exchanges are, however, qualitatively different from those which took place in working class neighbourhoods eighty to a hundred years ago. 'Local self-sufficiency and local self-reliance are diminishing everywhere. Concentration of the local area seems to be most strongly correlated with lack of alternatives' (Keller 1968:116).

Philip Abrams saw the implications for neighbourhood care as being to find ways of enabling people to renew their involvement in caring relationships despite the mobility of careers, distance from their own kin, and comparative strangeness of the areas in which they lived. There was little prospect, however, of networks of the traditional type playing a major part in the future provision of neighbourhood care. On the other hand, the networks of modern neighbourhoodism were potentially important as sources of neighbourhood care and were products of the social changes which had eroded the traditional neighbourhood.

If mobility and choice are two distinctive features of the social effects of industrialisation, formal organisation and a vastly enlarged sphere of public, political life are two others. And it is precisely these four properties – mobility, choice, organisation and politics – that identify and precipitate modern neighbourhoodism and mark it out as something quite unlike the traditional neighbourhood. Modern neighbourhoodism is in its purest form an attempt by newcomers to *create* a local social world through political or quasi-political action. Great organisational skills and ingenious organisational devices are often used in attempts to mobilise old and new residents alike in order to protect amenities, enhance resources and, to a greater or lesser degree wrench control of the local milieu from outside authorities and vest it in strictly local hands. Much of the driving force and most of the success of the enormous diversity of Neighbourhood Care projects up and down the country springs from these sources. Traditional informal networks are dying and should be allowed to die.

Neighbourhood care today means working out a constructive relationship between the state, nationally and locally, and neighbourhoodism, the politicised voice of local attachment.

The implications for neighbourhood care are discussed further in chapters 7 to 11, but this later phase of the research was rooted in a sociological theory of change in the character of neighbouring. There was a convergence, moreover, in the critique of network analysis and the theory of modern neighbourhoodism. The latter emphasised the role of choice in local social relationships, the former the nature of the solidary relationships involved. Both pointed to the importance of friends, and of seeing neighbourliness and positive neighbouring as a form of friendship. This was a further contribution which Philip Abrams made to the sociology of informal local relationships.

Friendship can be thought of, not as primarily norm- or affect-governed but, in Etzioni's term, as a calculative involvement rooted in actual or prospective exchange (1964). In a sense this is perhaps no more than the theme of reciprocity in a new guise. The slight shift of emphasis away from norms and towards opportunities and costs, choices and constraints which it encourages usefully

Informal neighbouring

directs attention away from the moral properties of institutions, places or 'communities', to the interactional properties of relationships – that is, to the question of what makes local relationships sufficiently rewarding for them to be consolidated as friendships.

The literature review and Street studies probed the extent to which it was possible to distinguish meaningfully – in theory and practice – between neighbours and others living nearby, notably friends and kin. Could one postulate a specific social network of *neighbours* which excluded friends and kin? Attempts to differentiate between neighbours and friends are hazardous. Studies of working class areas (Mogey 1956:95; Bott 1957:69) indicate the term 'friend' is not often used. Kuper (1953) and Bracey (1964) attempted to distinguish between 'friendly' relationships and close friends. The essential differences have been summed up in the saying: 'you lose a neighbour by moving away; you lose a friend by failing him; you never lose a relative except through death' (Keller 1968:27).

In everyday life the distinction between friendship and friendliness is well understood and widely taken for granted. Friendliness is a desirable quality of casual, contingent interaction; it involves a restricted conviviality which flourishes by carefully respecting each party's right to preserve the privacy of a 'back-stage' realm. Friendship, by contrast, is chosen, committed and encompassing it; it flourishes on the knowledge each part has of the 'real self' of the other. In a sense the difference between friendliness and friendship seems to be a matter of trust. Becoming friends, as Suttles (1970), Bates (1964) and Allan (1979) have all pointed out is a matter of progressively breaking down the barriers of privacy so essential to mere friendliness and steadily increasing the 'secrets' with which one is willing to trust the other. It is precisely the guarded quality so characteristic of neighbouring that is absent from friendship. Yet at the same time it is clear that neighbours *can* be friends.

The sharp contrast between friendly neighbours and 'true friends' can also be thought of, no less realistically, as points on a sliding scale. Friendship after all is a *created* relationship; and it is created out of specific sorts of mutually rewarding interaction (which could be those of neighbouring), occurring initially in specific settings (which could be neighbourhoods). Neighbouring can *become* friendship if the change of rules needed to effect the passage from privacy to intimacy can be negotiated. Perhaps one of the reasons it does not become friendship more often is that the sheer proximity of neighbours makes that negotiation exceptionally difficult to control as it proceeds.

Both people and researchers have found difficulty in sorting out the fact that neighbours in principle are not, but in practice can be, friends. The entanglement is nicely described by Townsend (1963:140): 'Often a neighbour with whom there was a close relationship was no longer thought to be a neighbour but a friend. Thus a question about neighbours was interpreted by many people to apply only to those non-relatives living around them who were not friends.' The confusion is of course compounded by the fact that it also embraces kin. In virtually every study people are found claiming their mothers or sisters, or even their mothers-in-law, as their 'best friend'.

Friendship, like neighbouring, is a construct of actual or prospective exchange. And exchange, in the construction of friendship as in the construction of neighbouring, occurs not in a vacuum but in specific contexts structured in terms of needs and resources, opportunities and constraints. Individuals are constrained and choose to live in specific milieux for specific pasages of their lives. In those milieux they are constrained and choose to enter into interaction with specific others. Among those others they choose their friends or are constrained to remain friendless. And it has become overwhelmingly clear that within the constraints provided by their settings, and within the opportunities for interaction they offer and deny, friendship choices are made by individuals *not* on the basis of the intrinsic qualities of those with whom they make friends but on the basis of the discovery of actual or potential advantage to oneself. 'The value or *reward* of a friendship to an individual depends on the capacity of the other to provide certain "services", such as emotional support, economic assistance, information, allies and connections to resources outside one's immediate network' (Jackson 1977:61).

No doubt much neighbouring, patterned as it is by a distinctive blend of curiosity and caution, generosity and withdrawal, can be understood as a matter of explorations functioning to assess prospective mutual advantages and costs and so clear or close off the ground for eventual friendship. In this perspective friendship, far from being an antithesis to neighbouring is effectively an extension of neighbouring built around an enrichment of reciprocity. To anticipate the discussion in the next chapter, it is important to follow Blau here (1964:93) in distinguishing reciprocity as a basis of social attachment from strictly economic exchange. The claim that friendship is constructed through exchange has to be set against the recognition that social exchange, unlike economic exchange, can take many oblique, ramified and devious forms; that it is typically indirect rather than direct; that it can involve what in economic terms would be insanely generous credit-ratings derived from the accretion of trust or from norms of reciprocity which operate across whole collectivities or life cycles.

The other side of the process of making friends is the question of costs. Friendship also has costs: direct costs, such as the time spent helping a friend; indirect costs, such as the money spent to visit a friend; and opportunity costs, the value of the services a person could obtain in an alternative friendship. It was the recognition of the weight of a mass evidence to the effect that people really do shift their commitments toward those that they find substantially more 'profitable', that pointed to the 'exchange' interpretation of friendship. And that in turn pointed toward an understanding of why, in our sort of society, neighbouring only rarely turns into friendship. In the settings for interaction provided by the neighbourhoods of such societies, making friends with neighbours very easily becomes a high-cost ("she's always round here wanting something"), low-reward ("you can't rely on her when you need her") business. Life can be transacted more cheaply elsewhere.

The problems posed by exchange theory are largely problems of the circumstances under which reciprocity escalates into a generalised attachment or remains confined with more or less specific contexts in more or less instrumental forms. It is not just that friendship can be thought of as an extension of neighbouring (as of most other forms of interaction) but that the conditions involved in striking any given balance of reciprocity (whether at the negative pole of neighbouring where gossip and trouble-making prevail or at the positive pole where neighbours become friends) are themselves both positive and negative, a matter of both choice and constraint, of rewards as well as of costs. There has been a tendency in the literature to stress the negative side of these balances – to emphasise the importance of threat, closure and lack of resources in encouraging the formation of strong localised attachments, for example. Thus Anderson's model (1971:172) of the sources of caring networks among kin can be read as a bleak chronicle of poverty, isolation and insecurity. Yet there is always a reward side to the equation as well; the relationship is put together out of positive responses to negative circumstances. In Anderson's example attachment is favoured by the reliability of others (transformed into norms of trust) and a complementarity of skills as well as by the absence of other sources of support. And these positive and negative strands of reciprocity are both separable from one another and independently variable. That is to say, one does not have to think in terms of an increase in social insecurity and economic hardship in looking to an increase in helpfulness among neighbours.

Neighbourhood friendships in contemporary industrial societies are typically casual, not very intimate and based largely on the low cost of interacting with those nearby (Jackson 1977). In such conditions relations with neighbours take on the familiar features noted in so many investigations: the qualities of a low-cost, low-value relationship of convenience, sharply differentiated from the high-cost, high-value relationship of commitment characteristic of serious friendship. Neighbourhood friendships are in a sense too easily come by to develop that sort of strength – especially for people who can choose their friends fairly freely outside as well as inside their neighbourhoods; which means most of us nowadays. But high values are also associated with high rather than low costs. Paradoxically, their low cost may itself be one reason why neighbourhood friendships do not for the most part develop the strength, intimacy or commitment that would be needed to sustain high levels of widespread and reliable neighbourhood care. Neighbourliness of that sort presupposes a relationship which is highly valued.

As settings most neighbourhoods do not constrain their inhabitants into strongly bonded relationships with one another. Those that do are either exceptional or deplorable. There is some evidence that the spatial structure of neighbourhoods influences the frequency of interaction with neighbours. But it does not appear to influence its intimacy or level of commitment. 'Community' may or may not have declined but the sense in which the neighbourhood as a compelling socio-spatial environment sustained 'community' – if it ever did – certainly has. The old equation of problems, resources and closure which produced the diffuse trust and reciprocity of the sort of local milieu within which care in 'critical life situations' could effectively be provided for and by the inhabitants has plainly collapsed.

As persons most neighbours are not constrained and do not choose to make their friends among their neighbours. Those who do tend to be seeking highly

The sociology of informal neighbouring

specific solutions to highly specific problems which they cannot solve elsewhere and which make them 'expensive' people to befriend from the point of view of their neighbours. Nevertheless, there is some evidence of a demand for a more generalised neighbourliness arising from mobility and of a willingess of some individuals especially at certain stages of the life and career cycles, to pay quite high prices for such relationships. The strength of the friendships created in neighbourhoods by such incoming neighbours as a resource for long-term neighbourhood care is an important question which needs further exploration. Certainly one does find relationships of deep and enduring commitment between neighbours and even some people whose lives seem to be governed by something approaching a morality of neighbourliness. But these cases are exceptional and on investigation seem to have their roots in long-standing relationships of reciprocity built up against a background of vexing problems and difficulties. People have to pay a high price for neighbouring (as well as receiving highly valued rewards from it) if they are to value their neighbours.

The peculiar hallmark of relations between neighbours in relatively open, mobile societies such as our own is frequent interaction coupled with *limited* commitment, helpfulness and distance. Nevertheless, within that framework some people will exploit neighbourhood social networks more actively than others. Specifically, these are the most likely to be the people who are most confined to those networks in terms of their general life-space, relatively deprived of friendship relations outside the neighbourhood or relatively committed to non-friendship relationships and projects within the neighbourhood. The sorts of people who are likely on such bases to have an interest in developing friendships within neighbourhoods, in cultivating neighbourliness as it were, can be identified without great difficulty and would include: (1) children, (2) young mothers, especially those without jobs or private transport, (3) the retired, especially again those without their own transport or without accessible kin, or who have lived most of their lives in the neighbourhood, (4) newcomers, especially those who are fairly young and/or without extensive kin attachments elsewhere and (5) those who have an active 'organisational' interest in mobilising social action within the neighbourhood – members of political movements, amenity societies, community associations and voluntary organisations.

In sum, having sifted three traditions of work – community studies, network analysis and exchange theory – which claimed to speak with some authority about neighbouring, it seemed possible to draw selectively on all three to explain neighbouring as a distinctive, variable balance of friendliness, distance and helpfulness, in terms of the social construction – and social restriction – of reciprocity.

Bridge

6 Altruism and reciprocity as sources of neighbouring and neighbourhood care

This chapter forms a bridge between the studies of informal neighbouring in the first part of the book and the studies of neighbourhood care in the second part. It examines the extent to which both informal and more organised neighbouring stem from altruism on the one hand and reciprocity on the other. In chapter 1 (p. 10), four sources of neighbourhood care were identified: status, tradition, altruism and reciprocity. Philip Abrams focussed his attention particularly upon the latter two, as of the most central theoretical and policy interest. Why did people offer to help those living near to them? What kinds of motivation could one discern in helping behaviour? Why do people provide care for others who are not related to them?

In discussions of social need and the relationship between the more self-sufficient and the more dependent members of society, altruism is frequently invoked as a norm and a value justifying and explaining the provision of social care. A common dictionary definition of altruism is 'an act done in the interest of another with no calculation of or thought for reward'. Eighty years ago Peter Kropotkin in *Mutual Aid* documented the propensity of both animals and man to help one another, and claimed that one of the central principles of morality was the propensity to 'freely giv[e] more than he expects to receive from his neighbours' (1915:222). In his research on neighbouring, Philip Abrams found ample evidence of the existence in contemporary society of a norm of beneficence. One of the characteristics of well established social norms is, after all, that they are reasons for action for which the individual does not have to give reasons. Simply, "it makes me feel good to do something for others"; "satisfaction, you know you've helped someone"; "I like to feel that you're helping someone else". Such assertions of the intrinsic value of helping and giving have been made too generally and persistently in our research to be ignored.

One of the most influential recent analyses of the role of altruism in social welfare was by Richard Titmuss, who argued that social policy extends opportunities for altruism in opposition to the possessive egoism of the market place. 'The grant, or the gift, or unilateral transfer – whether it takes the form of cash, time, energy, satisfaction, blood or even life itself – is the distinguishing mark of the social (in policy and administration), just as exchange or bilateral transfer is the mark of the economic' (Titmuss 1968:22). In *The Gift Relationship*, he concluded the analysis of the supply of blood with the words: 'Freedom from disability is inseparable from altruism' (1970:246). A free blood transfusion service is superior not just because it is more efficient but because its existence fosters social integration and positively encourages altruism. In industrial societies there was far greater scope for gift relationships than had previously been recognised. The limitations of family, community and class could be transcended to allow citizens to provide for the 'universal stranger', and it was in society's treatment of the universal stranger that altruism found its fullest expression. In modern society, more rather than less provision needed to be made for 'the expression of altruism in the daily life of all social groups' (1970:224).

In a Volunteer Centre seminar in 1979, Philip Abrams used these ideas as a starting point for a discussion of the philosophy of social care.

Richard Titmuss saw modern industrial societies as dominated by two types of value system, market values and bureaucratic values, and wished to see them counterbalanced by a third dimension, that of gift values. One might have expected that he would find the setting for gift values in the everyday settings of neighbourhood and community life. Yet in the event he repudiated these relationships and turned instead to the possibility of impersonal giving to strangers exemplified by blood donors and by patients who allow their bodies to be used for teaching and research purposes by doctors. He did so because he could not ignore the message of an overwhelming body of sociological and anthropological research about the profoundly 'impure' nature of giving in informal social contexts:

> The personal gift and counter-gift, in which givers and receivers are known to each other, and personally communicate with each other, is characterized by a great variety of sentiments and purposes. At one end of the spectrum economic purposes may be dominant ... At the other end are those gifts whose purposes are predominantly social and moral in that as 'total social facts' they aim to serve friendly relationships, affection and harmony between known individuals and social groups. Within all such gift transactions of a personal face-to-face nature lies embedded some elements of moral enforcement or bond. To give is to receive – to compel some return or create some obligation ... No such gift is or can be utterly detached, disinterested or impersonal. Each carries messages and motives in its own language. (Titmuss 1970:237)

It is not just that *Gemeinschaft* relationships are founded on reciprocity rather than altruism – and ideally upon the reciprocity of equals rather than upon the exacted reciprocity of patrons and clients. *Gemeinschaft* relationships are in any case a vanishing social form, and attempts to renew *Gemeinschaft*-like relationships in advanced industrial societies necessarily inject into neighbourhood settings values of a radically different nature.

Philip Abrams was particularly impressed by Fred Hirsch's analysis of the economics of bad neighbours (1977:71–84). This analysed the trends in modern industrial society pushing the individual toward those commitments that they found substantially more profitable, and undermining forms of sociability and mutual aid pursued as ends in themselves. Several factors were identified as contributing. Decreased dependency of the better-off on mutual aid might be one explanation; another was the higher valuation people set on their own time, in leisure for consumption as well as when working. 'Both elements may be tending to reduce friendliness and mutual concern in society as a whole as it

Altruism and reciprocity

becomes richer in material goods and ever more pressed for time' (Hirsch 1977:77–8). Increasing geographical and social mobility reduced the probability that those whom one helped would be in a position to return the exchange in future. Hirsch's analysis made a distinction between deep friendship and love, which involved a greater or lesser degree of altruism, and the element of mutual exchange and reciprocity which was present in many informal social relationships, including those of friendship.

Another study which Philip Abrams drew upon for ideas about altruism and reciprocity was Michael Anderson's study of the family in Lancashire during the industrial revolution. Anderson adopted exchange theory to explain patterns of mutual support in the family when faced with sickness, death or unemployment. His analysis emphasised strongly the reciprocity element, and was grounded in exchange theory.

> Though neighbours did provide some help, and though there were certain bureaucratically organised assistance agencies, each had major drawbacks as a reliable and low cost source of aid. Neighbours lacked a firmly enough structured basis of reciprocation in a heterogeneous and mobile society. Kinship, by contrast, could provide this structured link, and could thus form a basis for reciprocation. Kin did, indeed, probably provide the main source of aid. However, because this was a poor (and also a rapidly changing) society this aid ... was limited in cost, and family and kinship relationships tended to have strong, short-run instrumental overtones of a calculative kind. (Anderson 1971:171)

The motives that led kin to help each other were calculative. Parents aided their children with the expectation of receiving assistance in old age. More distant kin helped each other in the expectation of receiving assistance in return when they needed it. These calculative relationships were reinforced by strong social norms supporting mutual obligation among relatives. Assistance between kin is analysed as a series of exchanges arising out of self-interest and reinforced by social norms.

Neighbours did not play a central role in providing social support (Anderson argued) precisely because short-run instrumental exchanges between them were likely to break down. Given very high population turnover, actor A might on one occasion give up resources to his neighbour B. When A was next in need and sought reciprocation, B might have moved away and been replaced by C, who having no experience of relationship with A, and no debt to him, might not be prepared to assist. In this case, the lack of certainty of reciprocation and the uncertain timing make this source of support unreliable.

Anderson's emphasis on short-run reciprocation reflects a society in which, he maintained, the basis of action was a calculation of individual (or family) advantage which was maximised through balanced exchange. It is by no means clear that all long-term transactions between kin are motivated by rational calculation of this kind. Hareven argues in her important historical study of a New England textile manufacturing town that Anderson's model may explain short-run routine exchanges of service and assistance between kin in critical life situations. What it does not do is account for long-term kin assistance, especially when the rewards were not easily visible. Hareven postulated an overall principle of long-run reciprocity over the life course (1982:108).

The basis of Philip Abrams's approach to informal help and social care was, as the work of Hirsch and Anderson suggests, to see social care as a form of exchange and of reciprocity. This approach can be traced back to anthropological studies which showed that exchanges in primitive societies took the form of reciprocal gifts rather than of economic transactions, that these gifts were governed by a quite different morality from the market, and that they thus had a multidimensional meaning combining social with religious and utilitarian with sentimental elements. The classic studies were Malinowski's analysis of the *Kula* ring in the Tropbriands (1922) and Marcel Mauss's *The Gift* (1925). Mauss, for example, formulated a general theory of social exchange in which gifts appearing to be voluntary were in fact obligatory and subject to sanctions if not offered. The central obligation was making a return for the gift received (cf. Sahlins 1965). A direct connection can be made between these studies and those of informal exchange in industrial societies, for 'the exchange of gifts and favours between friends, neighbours and kin are strong and enduring threads in the social fabric' (Heath 1976:1). Outside the market one finds that 'neighbours exchange favours; children, toys; colleagues, assistance; acquaintances, courtesies; politicians, concessions; discussants, ideas; housewives, recipes' (Blau 1964:88).

Peter Blau's exchange theory was one which Philip Abrams drew on in developing his own ideas. Blau included within the category of social exchange all 'actions that are contingent on rewarding reactions from others and that cease when these expected reactions are not forthcoming ... [S]ocial exchange can be observed everywhere once we are sensitised by this conception to it, not only in market relations but also in friendship and even in love' (Blau 1964:6, 88).

Blau emphasised two central features of social exchanges. Firstly, reciprocity was involved. A fundamental characteristic of social exchange was that 'an individual who supplies rewarding services to another obligates him. To discharge this obligation, the second must furnish benefits to the first in turn' (1964:89). Secondly, there was an appearance of disinterested generosity. Social exchange differed from economic exchange in that, although a return was expected, this involved 'diffuse future obligations, not precisely specified ones, and the nature of the return cannot be bargained about but must be left to the discretion of the one who makes it' (1964:93). It followed from this that social exchange required individuals to trust each other. A banker giving a loan may assess the financial soundness of the borrower, but he does not have to trust him. The individual who provided an expensive gift does have to trust that the recipient will reciprocate. Blau argued that self-interest would lead to reciprocation for gifts received, and when this happened, feelings of gratitude and trust would be engendered. In this way the relationship between the partners would be transformed, establishing an enduring social bond between them (cf. Ekeh 1974:116–87).

The relationship between strong neighbouring patterns and length of residence may be explained by a further development of the theory.

> Typically ... exchange relations evolve in a slow process, starting with minor transactions in which little trust is required because little risk is involved ... By discharging their obligations for services rendered, if only to produce induce-

Altruism and reciprocity

ments for the supply of more assistance, individuals demonstrate their trustworthiness, and the gradual expansion of mutual service is accompanied by a parallel growth of mutual trust. (Blau 1964:94)

In such processes norms of trust are also progressively elaborated and so the possibility and probability of substituting indirect and delayed exchange for direct and immediate transactions grow. Interaction can be built into friendship, that is, into a relationship involving a deep fund of commitment, or credit, on the basis of a dramatic widening of the range of reciprocity. This echoes Malinowski's insistence that strict exchange and social reciprocity were not the same. The latter is broader, involving recognition of mutual obligation, and may be extended in time and uncertain of the return to be received.

In Philip Abrams's work on neighbouring and social care, these ideas were drawn upon and enriched to help understand the nature of altruism and reciprocity. A seminal unpublished paper in 1978, entitled 'Altruism and Reciprocity: Altruism as Reciprocity', argued that the relationship between the two was close and symbiotic. Dictionary definitions notwithstanding, altruism is in fact a form of reciprocity; and notwithstanding all fashionable scepticism about personal motives, altruism in *that* sense is a significant source of neighbouring in our society. One of the most striking things was the virtual unanimity with which members of Good Neighbour schemes insisted that they got great personal satisfaction out of the work they did, combined with their virtually universal inability to say precisely what that satisfaction was. There was, as it were, an *inexpressible* reciprocity involved. Good Neighbours got as much as they gave but they found it very difficult to give an account of what they got. The research team failed to find any way of asking Good Neighbours about the 'returns' they received for neighbouring that effectively penetrated the screen of statements to the effect that giving help was 'very satisfying'. In the Sunniside study respondents were asked simply 'what does the scheme offer helpers?'; and although probed in terms of personal motives and satisfactions, it was clear that the respondents found it an exceptionally difficult question to answer in any precise terms. Typically the answers simply repeated the question and asserted that giving help was intrinsically satisfying: 'it gives you a good feeling of satisfaction, helping others'; 'you have the satisfaction of helping someone'; 'I get a lot of satisfaction doing this kind of thing.'

One could argue that since a return for help *was* given, in the form of self-esteem and so forth, it would be better to abandon the notion of altruism altogether and instead try to develop some sort of distinction between, say, overt and covert reciprocity. To do this, however, would be misleading, since the actors considered that they were behaving altruistically. Altruism and reciprocity were thus both forms of exchange, but while some exchange relationships were understood by the parties as exchanges, others were not. In the latter the return to the donor was so exclusively provided to the donor's self-image and so contingent upon the nature of that self-image that an attempt to distinguish between benefits and identity was both subjectively inconceivable and objectively misleading. Our reason for adopting the procedure of treating altruism as a form of reciprocity was that, from the actor's point of view in the relationship in question, belief in the altruistic nature of the action and attachment to a norm of beneficence as distinct from a norm of reciprocity appeared to be crucial conditions upon which the acts of giving and helping depended.

From an objective sociological standpoint they involved reciprocal rather than altruistic action, even though the actors themselves explained their activity in terms of a principle of regard for others. But is there any inconsistency in suggesting that such a mode of action is in practice sustained by the way the activity itself and the relationship it involves affirm and validate the identity of the altruist?

Philip Abrams then drew on two papers by Alvin Gouldner (1960, 1973) concerned with the norm of reciprocity and the norm of beneficence, to illuminate his own research. Gouldner's formulation of the norm of reciprocity differed from that of Blau in that he postulated that the existence of a universal social norm led people to behave in particular ways (whereas Blau held that the norm of reciprocity merely reinforced and stabilised tendencies inherent in the character of social exchange itself). Gouldner's norm of reciprocity (1960:171) had two elements: (1) people should help those who have helped them; (2) people should not injure those who have helped them. In everyday life the norm is expressed, Gouldner suggests, in the attitude: 'people will usually help those who help them'; and, one would infer, in action patterned in terms of such an attitude – that at least is a possibility research might explore. Our own local studies by and large confirmed the impression that neighbourliness occurs with relatively closed networks of people who 'have helped' each other and is strongest within those networks where the debts of help are understood to run to and fro far back into the past within the same relatively closed network. The problem for the newcomer anxious to break into such a network is to establish unobtrusively the fact of having been helpful.

Reciprocity, then, enlists egoistic motives for social purposes. But because that is how it works it can develop only within relationships where each party has something of value to give to the other. On that basis the distinctive nexus of rights and obligations – X and Y both owe benefits to each other and are entitled to receive benefits from each other – that is the essence of reciprocity can develop.

Although he recognised that relationships of this sort do not have to entail the exchange of strictly matched benefits (equivalent exchange) and can take the form of exchanges of things dissimilar in kind but of equivalent value in the eyes of the parties concerned (which he calls 'heteromorphic exchange') Gouldner's line of analysis clearly implies that the web of reciprocity in any society will have rather firm boundaries. And specifically that those who have nothing of value to give will be left outside it and effectively unable to break in.

In his two papers, Gouldner made a firm distinction between reciprocity and altruism, and contrasted the norm of reciprocity to the norm of beneficence. Those who had nothing of value to give were treated according to a different principle.

> Clearly the norm (of reciprocity) cannot apply with full force in relations with children, old people, or with those who are mentally or physically handicap-

ped and it is theoretically inferable that other, fundamentally different kinds of normative orientations will develop in moral codes. (Gouldner 1960:178)

If such people are to be helped they will therefore have to be helped on the basis of the quite different principle of altruism, of beneficence, of 'something for nothing'. The problem of dependency, of having nothing to offer, was accordingly solved in Gouldner's eyes by the elaboration of the 'fundamentally different' norm of beneficence; the requirement that 'people should help those who need help'. As he argued, people must have some duties to others which are not the rights of those others; certain aspects of social relationships must be exempt from the norm of reciprocity if the dependent are to be cared for. Here either some form of 'moral absolutism' or a norm of giving must intervene to counteract the essentially calculative, marketing relationships of reciprocity.

> The norm of beneficence calls upon men to aid others without thought of what they have done or can do for them, and solely in terms of a need imputed to the potential recipient ... [It] is a diffuse one encompassing a number of somewhat more concrete normative orientations such as 'altruism', 'charity' or 'hospitality'. In short, the norm calls on men to give something for nothing. (Gouldner 1973:266)

This resurrection of the idea of disinterestedness was linked to a criticism of Mauss's formulation in *The Gift*. Gouldner agreed that Mauss correctly sensed the functional interdependence between beneficence and reciprocity, but failed to work out the conceptual distinctions between them. In particular, he failed to distinguish the *motivation* for beneficent actions from their *unanticipated consequences*. The intention of the donor was not always to initiate a pattern of reciprocal exchange, even if this was the consequence. If the donor was oriented to norms of beneficence, they might be motivated to give a gift without any consideration or expectation of a return from the recipient (1973:298–9).

Philip Abrams came increasingly to doubt this rather sharp distinction between reciprocity and beneficence and to examine it more closely. A comprehensive review by Krebs (1970) of the literature on altruism from a psychological standpoint, which would (it was hoped) clarify the disinterested motivation of those providing caring assistance on which Gouldner placed such emphasis, had not produced the expected result.

One of the most remarkable features of the very large body of research surveyed by Krebs was that hardly any of it seemed to have been concerned with the essential *dispositional* features of altruism, its other-regarding, selfless qualities. That is to say, the research had studied the situational concomitants of acts of giving and helping rather than their motivational background. The question of whether the acts studied were 'really' altruistic, or of whether the donor was in any sense also a recipient had barely been raised. Nevertheless, the research findings would seem to suggest rather strongly that a great deal of what has been studied as altruism was in fact reciprocity. Thus, it emerged that the incidence of giving and helping varies quite dramatically with a number of characteristics of donors, of recipients and of the situations in which they interacted. Some of these variations pointed fairly obviously towards an interpretation of altruism as a form of reciprocity: the positive relations between giving and 'the attractiveness of the recipient to the donor', the donor's previous experience of 'having been a recipient', the closure, isolation and homogeneity of the social setting in which giving occurs, the 'family experience' of the donor (which again turned out to mean experience of having been a recipient), all seemed to invite interpretations along those lines. Similarly, when Good Neighbours explained their own helpfulness by saying "my mother was always very helpful" or "we're all like that in Sunniside", let alone "people were very good to me when my parents died", the implication of some sort of ramifying subterranean nexus of reciprocity seemed at least as strong as that of a norm of giving. Not that the norm of giving was not there fairly near the surface, but beneath the surface something different and equally compelling was also suggested.

Krebs reported other variations, however, which at first sight seemed to call more powerfully for interpretation in terms of altruism. This was especially true of the findings of those studies that have focussed on the characteristics of recipients reporting, for example, a strong relationship between the incidence of giving and the donor's perception of the nature and extent of the recipient's dependency. If giving and helping are evoked by the perception of 'legitimate' helplessness (as these studies suggested) it was surely sensible to infer that here at least a norm of beneficence (people should help those who need help) really was operating and that genuine altruism was being observed. Once again, this was merely to scratch the surface of the problem. The altruistic explanation did not rule out the possibility of a more fundamental explanation in terms of reciprocity.

The trouble with normative analysis, as Krebs pointed out in discussing Berkowitz's suggestion that giving which is responsive to dependency could be explained in terms of a 'norm of social responsibility', is that it explained both too much and too little. Let us agree that at one level people do act in a given way because that way of acting is prescribed as or believed to be 'right' in that situation. There are always variations; the norm is never uniformly effective; even in crises and disasters some help unstintingly and others turn away; the problem of explanation is simply transferred to a different level. Moreover the cogency of norms itself varies from situation to situation; help is evoked much more readily for the old than for the mentally handicapped; here too normative analysis defines problems rather than explaining them. Krebs rather depressingly concludes that normative analysis is characteristic of sociology and that the real explanatory work is thus left to psychology – but that is not how we understand the progress of our own research.

Here it seems essential to distinguish between personal and social characteristics; and also between general and particular social characteristics. The authors of one of the very few carefully researched studies in this field, *Natural Helping Networks* (Collins and Pancoast 1976), answered the general question almost entirely in personal, psychological terms. For them the helping minority were distinguished from the indifferent majority not sociologically but psychologically. Natural helping networks are sustained by 'central figures' or 'primary caregiving persons' or again 'natural neighbours' who seem to provide a centre from which help flows to others without any directly

Altruism and reciprocity

comparable reciprocal return. This idea obviously corresponded to the earlier suggestion that caring agents play a critically active part in maintaining relatively intensive patterns of help among neighbours. But Collins and Pancoast resolved the mystery of these central figures by invoking the personal rather than the social attributes of the helpers: 'who are these central figures? ... not persons carrying their role because a title or a position gives them their importance; rather they have won the confidence of their associates because of their personal characteristics'. And to the question, 'what motivates individuals to involve themselves with others?', these authors find no definitive answer.

The conclusion reached was that while people certainly did invoke the norm of giving ("Well, it's the Christian thing, isn't it?") as an adequate account of their own action, the explanation of why some people were responsive to such norms while others were not (why some people are 'better Christians' as it were than others) was something that had in the first instance to be pursued through a social analysis of reciprocity. The important finding here was that even the 'best Christians' or the most dedicated Good Neighbours were not content to invoke the norm of giving; invariably they also speak of their own personal 'satisfaction'.

It is true that the notion of satisfaction was offered as an analytical full-stop. But if one regards this satisfaction as puzzling, the involvement of even the most helpful people in the business of helping at once takes on a new complexion. Why should these, few, people find helping 'satisfying' when so many others do not? "It's the same few people do everything in Sunnyside"; there must be something special about them – but what?

Going through the interviews, both of the Street studies and of the Good Neighbours, the answer that strongly suggested itself to this sort of question was one that pointed in two apparently different directions; there was a reference to absolute moral commitments: "I know God wants me to do something"; and there was a more common reference to what can only be called 'self-satisfaction' – an investment of identity in the idea of being helpful: "I wouldn't want to push myself on anyone but I'm pleased to know I can be helpful"; "I get a lot of pleasure from it – it makes me feel nice inside to do something for the elderly." Perhaps these two types of answer were not so very different; one was expressed in terms of a moral absolute and one in terms of an almost sensuous gratification. But both were astoundingly self-centred; both made the driving principle of action the condition of the self *not* the needs of the other. For both types of respondent giving was receiving and what was given was given because of what was received – the sense that *I* have done God's will or the sense that *I* am helpful. By being helped the dependant gave those sentiments to their helpers. But what made the helpers value such sentiments?

Whether or not a relationship involved reciprocal exchange depended on what the parties got from the transaction. Gouldner observed that theorists such as Malinowski (1922) and Homans (1961) tended to assume that the reciprocity norm stipulates that the amount of return to be made is 'roughly equivalent' to what had been received. He distinguished between two situations, one in which equivalence calls for 'tat for tat', the other 'tit for tat'. In the first, homeomorphic reciprocity, equivalence means that the exchanges should be identical in form, either with respect to the things exchanged or to the circumstances under which the exchange takes place. Historically, the most striking expression of this type of exchange was in *negative* norms of reciprocity such as the *lex talionis*, the idea that reciprocity demanded that injuries inflicted should be returned upon the person inflicting them. In the second type, heteromorphic reciprocity, things exchanged may be concretely different but should be equal in value, as defined by the actors in the situation (Gouldner 1960:171–2). This type of reciprocity clearly has greater relevance to the fields of neighbouring and social care.

If the claim that altruism is a special form of 'heteromorphous reciprocity' is accepted, this question must become the heart of the research. Happily, the work done so far both impels the question and suggests some answers. There *is* a norm of beneficence and at the level of motives it does impel action in appreciable ways – "you have the satisfaction of helping someone who needs help; you don't have a guilty conscience, you know, if you help someone". Among one set of Good Neighbours studied, the norm of beneficence would have to be recognised, indeed, as the principal motivational source of the help they gave. But that is a problem not a solution. Even in the fairly closed, homogeneous and neighbourly community of Sunniside, the Good Neighbours were an exceptional minority; they were eccentric in their responsiveness to the norm of beneficence. So the question arises, what makes the norm effective for them and not for others? This is where doubts about the strict distinction proposed by Gouldner between altruism and reciprocity become relevant.

In fact the distinction is already blurred in Gouldner's own writing. Once the idea of heteromorphic reciprocity on the one hand, and of generalised beneficence on the other, has been allowed, the separateness of altruism and reciprocity in principle begins to collapse in practice. Once one recognises the possibility of indirect, transferred, delayed returns one can hardly remain committed to the view that action that looks as though it is done for no reward, or action that is described subjectively as being done for no reward, is really either unrewarded or unrelated to debts incurred previously or elsewhere. The question of the possibility of an extended subterranean chain of reciprocity is bound to arise. And so is some sense of the possible complexity and diversity of the exchanges that could be hidden behind the notion of 'equivalent value'. As Gouldner himself put it, reciprocity sensitises the individual to the past and to the future; perhaps, then, debts can be suspended in time, carried to other, comparable relationships through the life cycle. And as a result reciprocity can look like beneficence at the moment it is enacted. Exchanges over time can replace exchanges now; giving to third parties can replace a direct return to a beneficiary one is unable to help directly. Having once received something for nothing from one person one can be obliged later to give something for nothing to another. And so forth. When so many people explain their helpfulness to others in terms of the helpfulness of their own mothers such ideas are bound to become persuasive.

In this context the notion of altruism as action done for no reward ceases to

Altruism and reciprocity

be a relevant point of reference for research. What remains relevant is the notion of action that is, for the actor, authentically other-regarding but which nevertheless receives real rewards, pays real debts – and would not be enacted unless it did so. Those who respond to the norm of beneficence, those for whom it really *is* a norm, seem (although it was not possible to study a control group of non-givers which would have been an important further step in the research) to be as keenly aware of what others have done for them (as children in different parts of the country or in otherwise distant crises and times of trouble) as they are of the 'satisfactions' they get from giving help now. The norm of beneficence is the *language* in which extended, transferred, indirect, or 'generalised' reciprocity is expressed. But it appears that it is the possibility of reciprocity that underpins the compelling nature of the norm. As Gouldner puts it in a revealing aside, 'reciprocity lurks in beneficence'. At the level of consciousness there is a structured disjunction; the Good Neighbours helped because "people should help those who need help"; at the same time they got the 'satisfaction' of repaying debts incurred long since to other helpers (so often their mothers) or of staking a claim to help themselves in prospective future predicaments – "well I just hope someone will do the same for me when I need it".

What are the conditions under which people come to be caught up in the reciprocities of what can be called 'as-if altruism'? In what contexts will the sort of reciprocity which proceeds under the banner of implementing the norm of beneficence arise? What circumstances, conditions and contingencies lead some people to conclude that enacting that norm and being known (if only by themselves) to enact it is a return of equivalent value to the gift of practical help they offer to others? Several studies provide insight into the *social* settings of beneficence.

First, caring agents, central figures or whatever one calls them are involved in generalised relationships of reciprocity with those they help and secondly the development of such relationships is facilitated by and directly related to a range of characteristics of social milieux, of which the most important is trust. Patterson and Twente (1971) have emphasised the first of these points ('mutuality is a distinguishing characteristic of the helper-helpee relationship') and a host of studies, perhaps especially the work of Anderson (1971), has documented the second. No less important than trust as a general property of the social milieu is predictability, or as Anderson calls it 'certainty'. Indeed, trust and predictability are obvious closely related to one another; generalised reciprocity can develop most easily in settings in which any one relationship can reliably be treated as a model for all others: "Sunniside people are like that."

Trust and certainty permit the postponement of debts – just as they ensure their eventual repayment. Communities in which high levels of trust and predictability are diffused among members will also be communities with high levels of generalised reciprocity, that is, of apparent altruism. In such communities, of which Sunniside is a striking example, voluntary Good Neighbour schemes will flourish; and at the same time they will be widely regarded as unnecessary, because "we'd do it anyway".

Over and above such general characteristics of social settings as trust and predictability it seems, however, that one can also identify a number of more specific, but no less social, properties which are again directly conducive to generalised reciprocity. These mainly take the form of *facilities* for beneficence. Perhaps training, an acquired capacity for appropriate sorts of action, is the most obvious and most important of these. Our own research led us to note the special role of people previously trained as nurses in Good Neighbour schemes – simply knowing how to lift an old person, confidence in reading signs of stress or illness, knowing one's way round the various specialised professional caring agencies, could be crucial enabling resources so far as helping others was concerned. Many of the people who initially joined Good Neighbour schemes and then dropped out appeared to withdraw precisely because they did not know *how* to be useful. The specific value of nursing training is of course also a major theme of the analysis of Collins and Pancoast (1976). However, appropriate training does not have to be provided through formal professional channels. Once more it seems that mothers can do just as effective a job as colleagues. Many of the Sunniside Good Neighbours, for example, stressed the fact that they had learned the detailed practicalities of helping, especially of helping the elderly and dying, in their own families as children. Conversely, the extent to which the untrained are frightened of helping, deterred by their own incompetence, also emerges strongly. The policy implications of such observed relationships between competence and action hardly need spelling out.

A second type of facility is akin to what Gouldner (1973:283-92) rather unfortunately calls 'moral absolutism'. We have been impressed by the degree to which the desire to help is inhibited in practice by a reluctance to intrude oneself into other people's lives. Once again, this aversion to cold-bloodedly knocking on the door, to visiting uninvited, to pushing oneself forward, appears prominently among the reasons given for dropping out of voluntary helping agencies. By contrast, significant numbers of those who do not drop out are manifestly enabled to bridge the distance between themselves and others by the belief that common membership of some moral community, typically a church, legitimate intrusion. This also explained why so many members of Good Neighbour schemes were happy to visit and help people who shared their own faith but reluctant to become involved in the same way with others. In other words their helpfulness was not a response to the need of others alone as the norm of beneficence would require; it was rendered possible by common memberships which were seen as giving the helper a right of access to the dependant. While the role of moral communities in facilitating helping in this way is quite clear, it is unfortunately not nearly as clear as in the case of the role of training what might follow from it in terms of policy.

A third type of facility for generalised reciprocity can be found in factors which are permissive of neighbouring rather than immediately conducive to it. The example that emerges most dramatically from our own research is time. Again and again the fact that "neighbouring is not what it used to be" has been explained to us in terms of the availability of time: "Women have to work now. When I was young we were always popping into someone's house – one woman

Altruism and reciprocity

used to bring her flour and things and bake her bread in our oven. Working women haven't the time"; "We would always help each other out. Now, with people working, they haven't the time." And conversely, of course, a crucial aspect of the situation of the people who become involved in Good Neighbour schemes is that they do have the time – an obvious point but one not, it seems, always realised by the organisers of such schemes; as the virtual halving of the membership of the Sunniside scheme following a decision to shift the main meetings from the evening to the afternoon made clear. Schemes plainly did vary in the extent to which their practical arrangements permitted such opportunities for helping as those implicit in the availability of time to different types of people to be seized. It would be useful to know whether there is indeed any relationship between such variations and the quantity and quality of help that is mobilised.

We have, then, at least a preliminary list of social conditions favourable to generalised reciprocity already suggested by our own and other existing research. Some of these conditions exist at the level of general social-structural conduciveness, others are a matter of more specific resources, facilities or permissive conditions. Analytically, the essential step is to substitute the notion of generalised reciprocity for that of altruism (or alternatively to treat altruism as a special, masked, form of reciprocity) as the thematic focus of research.

In the first study of a Good Neighbour scheme, at Sunniside in County Durham, the centrality of reciprocity was emphasised.

> The notion of 'ordinary people wanting to help each other' rests on a simple expectation of reciprocity. Whether the return is made now or in the future, there seems to be a fundamental belief that help can earn help. The negative aspect of this, of course, is a rather overt belief that help *should* earn help, that payment is due. But, even though the balance of help is not always maintained with sensitivity or symmetry, we were left in no doubt that, for most members of this particular scheme, the basis of neighbourliness is a well-understood 'norm of reciprocity'. Being a Good Neighbour is a way of activating the norm. Many of the problems of Good Neighbours Schemes in matching help to need are at bottom a question of striking the balance of reciprocity that will make helping worthwhile. (Abrams *et al*. 1981a:66)

The metaphor of a network of reciprocity has emerged in several studies from Collins and Pancoast (1976) onwards. A major national study in the U.S.A., *Helping Networks and Human Services* (Froland *et al*. 1981:42) found that reciprocity and mutuality served as motivating factors in many of the programmes observed. The time factor was particularly long-drawn-out, the expectation being that things would balance out in the long term. The studies of neighbourhood care schemes in the second part of the book throw further light on the returns which helpers receive from caring for others.

This chapter cannot, in the nature of the case, reach firm conclusions. It does, however, raise sharply certain philosophical issues about altruism and reciprocity in care which will continue to be contentious. 'Altruism' needs to be further considered. The economists who contrast altruism in the family with hard-headedness in the market place come close to equating altruism with love or affective relationships (cf. Becker 1980). Sociologist Pitrim Sorokin, whose later years at Harvard were devoted to fostering a Center for Creative Altruism, made the same equation in one of his main publications on the subject (1950). A commentator on Durkheim suggests that altruism is surely another name for love (Poggi 1972:240). Yet it is stretching the term 'love' to suggest that all 'other-regarding action' is of that type. The parable of the Good Samaritan is powerful and evocative, but its value is exemplary rather than a social norm. An appeal to pure love for one's fellow men and women can hardly be the general basis of social care, either informal or formal.

As Bernard Williams has pointed out, 'some of our decent actions come not from that motive which Christians misrepresent as our loving everybody, but just from our loving somebody' (Williams 1973:85). Even within the family, services and help for other members may be carried out from a sense of reciprocity, obligation or duty rather than affection as such (cf. Pitt-Rivers 1973:101). Mutual aid in the family occurs within complex networks of interdependency involving power relations between and within generations and the sexes (Pinker 1979:13–14). Given that altruism is likely to be interactive and conditional (cf. Pruger 1973), it is essential to understand the social contexts which shape caring behaviour. The difference between familial and non-familial ties is central here, as the dominant role of care by kin in most of the Street studies underlined.

In non-familial relationships, such as those between neighbours, more attention needs to be given to the relationship between reciprocity and trust. The sociology of trust has been developed in formal terms (cf. Luhmann 1979; Barber 1983), but empirical studies of helping and caring are needed to illuminate the role in fostering social care. The evidence quoted in chapters 8 and 9 about the role of home helps and Street Wardens in delivering care suggests that lack of social distance between Helper and Client is a very important factor in fostering trust between relative strangers.

A good deal of mutual aid, both within and outside the family, is undertaken out of duty and is not usefully treated as altruism. For example, in discussing the relative benevolence shown between firms in the Japanese textile industry, Dore suggests that the fundamental reason for this type of behaviour stems from a sense of duty. A particular sense of diffuse obligation to the individual trading partner leads to firms modifying profit-maximising behaviour to safeguard trading partners in a weaker position at a particular point in time (Dore 1983). Several current studies of care for the infirm elderly may throw important light on this question.

More generally, the nature of caring needs to be investigated sociologically and philosophically. Diana Leat's study of neighbourly helping made an explicit distinction between reciprocal and non-reciprocal forms of neighbourly care for the elderly. Reciprocal care referred to the existence of a complex web of unspoken understandings and responsibilities stretching back into the past and forward into the future. Non-reciprocal care was rather different and came closer to volunteering, but Leat agreed with Abrams that notions of reciprocity underlay the apparent norm of beneficence which was invoked.

> Adherence to the norm of beneficence was to our neighbourly helpers often a means of paying debts to some other member of the current recipient's family or

Altruism and reciprocity

of doing what they wished they had been able to do for parents, husbands and wives, brothers and sisters, or ... of staking a claim to help themselves in prospective future predicaments. (Leat 1983:29–30)

The ethical roots of reciprocal caring in Western societies have recently been traced by Nels Nodding (1984) to the bond between mother and child. She argues that this caring relationship, which provides a model in its way for all others, is not contractual but of a special kind rooted in human intuitions and feelings. Human beings carry with them the memories of and longing for caring and being cared for derived from the relationship between mother and child. The important point for the present discussion is that caring is not a one-way process but one in which the person receiving the care actively responds, and stores up basic experiences and ethical obligations which may emerge later as apparently purely 'other-regarding' behaviour. This kind of discussion links to discussion of what are the components of care (Parker 1981), questions about why women loom so large in caring (Finch and Groves 1980, 1983; Ungerson 1983a, b; Wilson 1982), and to studies of the motivations of carers (cf. Qureshi et al. 1979, 1983; Hatch 1983) which are particularly relevant to the non-institutional care of the elderly in a society such as our own.

Part II

Organised neighbourhood care

7 Neighbourhood care as a form of organised care

The second part of the book is concerned with issues of more direct practical and policy relevance in the provision of social care. While still sociologically grounded, this phase of the research was focussed on the provision of social care at the local level by means of collective local action. The history of the Durham research was recounted in chapter 1, but it is useful to repeat here the shift in emphasis between the first and second phases. The first phase, discussed in Part I, was concerned with informal neighbouring. The second phase was concerned with more organised attempts to promote informal local care. It began with the study of Good Neighbour schemes reported in *Action for Care* (Abrams *et al.* 1981a) and then developed into a broader-based study of Neighbourhood Care schemes, reported in chapters 8 to 10.

Neighbourhood care was defined in chapter 1 as 'a mobilisation of local energies and resources to achieve levels of indigenous concern and support which complement, supplement and progressively contain the need for external statutory and voluntary services in specified respects'. It can refer both to the intensity and extent of neighbourliness achieved in a neighbourhood and to the delivery of social services to local residents with no necessary reference to neighbourliness at all.

Neighbourhood care covers a variety of different forms. At one extreme, it could refer to the patterns of mutual aid characteristic in working class communities seventy-five to a hundred years ago, before the development of the welfare state, described in chapter 5. At the other extreme, it might by some stretch of the imagination be extended to cover highly decentralised delivery of social and health services such as 'patch' social work. In fact, the types of neighbourhood care discussed in this part of the book fall between these two extremes. All the schemes studied involve some degree of local *organisation* for the provision of care, so that informal mutual aid of the sort considered in Part I is not included. And all the schemes involve substantial contributions from local residents on a voluntary basis as distinct from professionals such as social workers, community nurses or doctors. In this respect, 'patch' social work (cf. Hadley and McGrath 1980, 1984) or decentralisation of local health and social services (cf. Bayley's study of Dinnington 1982, 1984) are distinctly different from neighbourhood care. A further distinguishing feature is the *local* character of the schemes studied. Neighbourhood care is different from the activities of more formal voluntary organisations such as Age Concern or WRVS. It is carried out locally by local people and usually the organisation to do this is of a rather limited kind. In short, neighbourhood care inhabits a middle ground between purely informal care on the one hand and statutory care on the other, and between care by professionals, by voluntary workers and by neighbours, friends and relatives. One of the main issues, indeed, concerns the extent to which formal and informal care can be combined successfully. The research on neighbourhood care also addresses the question of what scope there is for community care in contemporary society.

There can be little doubt that extensive and effective community care is uncommon and improbable in an advanced state-capitalist society such as ours. The combination of market moralities and official services which such societies typically achieve appears uniquely hostile to community care. Keller (1968) concluded quite unambiguously that in societies of this type we should expect a negative relationship between public welfare provision and community care arising from primary group and localistic involvements. Community care is subverted in advanced state-capitalist societies by what Hirsch (1977:71–83) aptly calls 'the economics of bad neighbours'. His argument fits remarkably well with the general trend of sociological analysis of issues related to community care, which almost without exception discerns a decline of effective community care, local attachment, neighbouring and so forth in these societies. The overall tendency of research and speculation about the relationship between community care and other forms of social care is plainly to suggest that the former will decline as the latter advances.

This inverse relationship was not, however, accepted as a fact of life, but treated as a hypothesis to be investigated. Were people in some areas more helpful than others? Why did some localities appear to be more neighbourly, able to respond to the needs of the elderly in particular, on an informal basis without organisation, while others did not? What different forms of organising neighbourhood care were there and how did they affect the outcome? What types of care could best be provided locally? These questions are tackled in the next chapter and the two following. The research on neighbourhood care also drew on the results of the first phase of the research to pose certain general questions about the capacity of the neighbourhood to sustain care.

Before turning to such issues, the sort of care provided will be illustrated by one example to give a flavour of the sorts of tasks performed by neighbourhood carers. The scheme is also discussed further in the next chapter (pp. 140–2). The Home Warden scheme in Stonegate, a steel city, is not typical of Neighbourhood Care schemes in that the carers were paid employees of the Social Services Department rather than volunteers. The activities undertaken are an instance of the sort of help and tending provided by members of Good Neighbour and Neighbourhood Care schemes to a more elderly, infirm and housebound client group, though in this case the recipients are more dependent than many of the clients in such schemes generally.

The Home Warden scheme was in effect an extension by the council of its Home Help service. Beginning in 1963 with 20 wardens, by the late 1970s there were 187, of whom 175 had been recruited from among home helps. The department described the scheme as follows:

> The wardens work a 40-hour week, mainly in the mornings and evenings and over the weekend on a rota system. As far as possible they work in pairs or

Neighbourhood care as a form of organised care

sometimes in a group of three to provide relief for each other in times of sickness and during holiday periods. 12 part-time wardens have been appointed to assist certain groups where there are particular difficulties. All wardens live within the area in which they work and most clients live within five to ten minutes of their home. Each warden assists approximately 25 people, some of whom require calls three times per day, once a day, twice weekly, and some are only visited once per week. Frequency of visiting and duties are discussed by the warden and home help organiser weekly. A general interpretation of their duties is the way they will carry out the more personal services such as would be given by an only daughter, for example helping people to get up and dress, lighting fires, giving meals, writing letters, helping to wash them or being on hand when the bath is taken. They do collect pensions and small amounts of shopping. In some cases where the client is confused the home warden will be responsible for managing her income, keeping strict accounts for checking with the Organiser weekly. In some measure it is hoped that the wardens foster a community spirit and self help amongst the people themselves.

Wardens receive special training, particularly in simple first aid, lifting of bedfast clients, physical and mental health of the elderly, practical health care, nutrition and budgeting, and home safety. Wardens are also encouraged to look out for anyone who may be in need within their area and to give the necessary attention required in an emergency. It is necessary to keep a balance between the various types of clients so the demand on the warden does not become unreasonable. The weekly rate of pay is £62.43 (in 1980) plus 60p allowance for incidental expenses. All wardens are on the telephone. Wardens are issued with overalls, mac, shopping basket, protection buzzer. Sheets, flasks and hot water bottles are available at the Divisional Office in case of need.

This diary of one morning's work by one Street Warden was compiled by Sheila Abrams, who accompanied Doris Marshall on her rounds, to give an impression of the kind of work done. Between 8.45 and 11.45 a.m. the warden visited 14 people.

1st call: Mrs A lives in a semi-detached house (probably the only house on the round that wasn't a council house). Usually Doris gives Mrs A her breakfast, washes and dresses her ready for the day. The home help was waiting at the house to help Doris lift Mrs A out of bed as she is crippled with arthritis. However on this particular morning a 'bath nurse' had arrived and there were no extras to be done. Mrs A had fallen the previous Christmas Eve and since that time her sister had stayed to look after her.

2nd call: Mrs B is also crippled with arthritis. Doris had some difficulty in lifting her from the sofa-bed where she had been sleeping. Slowly Mrs B got onto her walking frame and very slowly made her way to the kitchen. Doris had already put the kettle on and Mrs B, worn out by her efforts, sat down to drink the cup of tea, telling Doris that she would get something to eat afterwards. Doris put crepe bandages on Mrs B's legs and then put her stockings on for her.

3rd call: With the aid of two walking sticks Mrs C managed to walk to the door and let us into her flat. "All I do for Mrs C is to put on her stockings – she can make her own breakfast", Doris said. Actually that morning she also did some shopping. The kitchen of the flat was pleasantly warm and Mrs C explained that Doris had suggested that she leave the door of the cooker open to make the room warmer.

4th call: This visit was very brief. Mrs D was sitting in a chair and said several times that she didn't feel very well. She usually went to the community centre for lunch on Fridays but said she wasn't up to it that day. After a brief, reassuring chat with her, Doris left.

5th call: Mrs E had returned home the previous day from a nursing home where she had been staying for two weeks; she is blind. Doris let herself into the flat by reaching through the letter box for the key which was hanging by a tape behind the door. Mrs E was sitting on a chair in the living room in her nightdress; while Doris made her breakfast she explained that she had hated being in the nursing home; "it was strange, very strange, I missed not being in my own place. I couldn't find my food." She added that no-one had talked to her and that she had felt very lonely. She said that her daughter had called to see her the previous evening; "she waited till her husband came home from work so that she could leave the children with him; it gives me a headache when she brings the children". Doris brushed her hair, putting one or two hair grips in to keep the hair back from her face. She put Mrs E into her dressing gown, brought her some tea, chatted for a while and then left.

6th call: When we arrived the home help was in the flat and she told Doris that she was worried about Mrs F not taking her tablets. Doris was well aware that Mrs F was refusing the tablets and insisted that she take one while she herself was there. The home help also expressed horror at the chipped state of the mug Mrs F was using to drink her tea – it almost looked as if a piece had been bitten out. Doris asked Mrs F, "why don't you use the mug that I bought you for Christmas?" Doris's view was "well, you've got to buy them something, just a bit of something, I always do". She also told us that Mrs F's son was very good to her and called to see his mother every night after work; "she's got a daughter, too, but she doesn't come".

7th call: As we walked to the flat next door, Doris explained how she came to be visiting Mrs G; "Every time I went to see Mrs F I noticed that the windows in the next flat were getting dirtier and dirtier. I asked around and people said, "Mrs G keeps herself to herself; nobody sees anything of her." So I started calling round. To begin with the door was never opened beyond the chain stage. It took some weeks of persuasion before Doris was allowed in: "You've never seen anything like it. Mrs G's legs were badly burned and her hair was all matted together . . . I tried to talk to her a little but she couldn't understand what I was saying." Mrs G had been taken to hospital for treatment as a result of Doris's first visit and was now home again. A home help was there cleaning the windows. Doris and Mrs G had a brief chat.

8th call: Doreen said that Mrs H had multiple sclerosis. "She is just like a rag doll; she can't do anything for herself at all." When we arrived Mrs H's daughter was there and had given her breakfast and a cigarette which Doris usually does. Doris said she would do the shopping and come back in the evening to put Mrs H to bed.

9th call: Doris told us that Miss I had tried her patience more than once: "Everything has to be exactly as she wants it – if I move an ornament just a fraction she will go and put it back." The living room in the flat looked as if someone had just moved in and was awaiting furniture. There was only one wing-backed chair, and around that were suitcases piled on top of one another. Miss I was small and looked very frail, walking with the aid of two sticks. She had recently had an operation for cataracts. As she and Doris talked it became clear that the suitcases were filled with letters, that Miss I was a great correspondent and that she knew exactly where each of her hundreds of letters was. Doris told us "I hate shopping for her, nothing is ever right. Fortunately, the last time I got a bowl which wasn't right for her the shop let me change it; she can be a stickler."

10th call: Mr J was in his late seventies and feeling very sorry for himself, complaining of pains in his stomach. Doris had warned that she might be a bit sharp with him – and she was. Mr J hadn't washed or shaved for a couple of days and as Doris gave him a cup of tea and a tablet she said: "Here – you'll feel much better after this; and you'll feel even better if you get some of that growth off and wash the sleep from your eyes." Mr J groaned a bit and said he was going to get the doctor in. Doreen told him, "there's no need for that, the tablet will make you feel a lot better, and so would a bit of a walk". She explained to us afterwards that she had to start from scratch organising the house-keeping and getting the house clean and decorated for Mr J. His wife had died 18 months earlier: "She was a bit of a loose woman and quite a few years younger than him; when she died she was badly in debt, clothes on hire purchase and that sort of thing; Mr J knew nothing about it and it hit him badly." The sitting room had just been decorated and the kitchen was in the process of being painted. Mr J said it could be the smell of paint that was making his stomach upset. A record player was prominently installed in the living room and Doris commented: "He doesn't like television. There was some money over once we had straightened out the finances so I went to town and got him a record player and some records. He's a bit down now but tonight when I come he could be singing away while his records are playing." On one occasion Doris had been to the doctor with Mr J: "I was there an hour – of course, he knew the family very well and that was useful for me."

11th call: Mrs K has multiple sclerosis and was in an electric wheelchair. The bungalow was well designed to enable her to move around freely in her chair. Usually Doris puts Mrs K to bed at night and then "she has to stay there until I come the next morning" – this particular morning was different because the 'bath nurse' had been before we arrived. The flat had been very carefully designed to make life at home possible for Mrs K – with remote controls for the television and a 'possum alarm' to control the front door. Doris had organised much of the buying and placing of the furniture Mrs K wanted. "I would like one of those liquidisers next, Doris", Mrs K said, "it would make eating easier for me." Doris explained afterwards that Mrs K's husband had walked out on her in the early days of her illness.

12th call: Mrs L recently had two operations on her hip joints and can now just about get around her flat with the help of two walking sticks. We were told how Doris had washed and set her hair the night before she went into hospital; "it built up my spirits a lot". On the morning of our visit the home help was cleaning the flat when we arrived and as we were leaving Mrs L's daughter arrived – an unusual but much appreciated event.

13th call: Mr and Mrs M live in one of the council bungalows. Mr M is crippled and was in a wheelchair. Mrs M has angina and looked very frail. Doris shops for them and fetches library books. Mr M spoke at length and with difficulty (he has a speech defect) about the fact that too many people were sitting in offices (specifically, the Social Services Department's offices) doing nothing while people like Doris were "slogging their guts out" doing a worthwhile job for hardly any money. Doris said she had become fond of this couple and although in general "I never have a cup of tea with the people I visit", she does with Mr and Mrs M on occasion.

In sum, there is little sentimentality but a good deal of sensible humanity in the way the Home Warden Service as exemplified by Doris Marshall works on the ground. The area covered was fairly extensive, but there was a rule that no one should use cars on their rounds. To be seen and to observe what is going in the area was an important part of the work. People could approach Mrs Marshall if they needed help or she might see and approach someone she thought might need help from her. Overall, the object of the provision is to enable people to live at home 'with some dignity' virtually as long as they went to do so.

Almost without exception the Home Wardens were middle-aged working class women. Once selected they were given a fairly intensive induction by the relevant divisional Home Help Organiser who also introduced the new Warden to her 'round' of clients – never more than twelve to begin with. All the Wardens met every fortnight at the divisional office to discuss problems and those meetings were seen as important to the morale, enthusiasm and confidence of the Wardens individually as well as providing a check on the working of the project as a whole. The Wardens did have serious personal problems to overcome in doing the work. They were often received with a good deal of mistrust, resentment and jealousy. Far from being received as local 'saints' there was a strong probability of negative reactions, either from the clients themselves or from others in the neighbourhood who were not receiving the service. The Stonegate scheme is discussed further in the next chapter.

A general perspective on neighbourhood care suggested a sharp antithesis between formal and informal provision. The point can be made by invoking one of the best-known devices of sociological classification: the 'pattern-variables' identified by Talcott Parsons (1951:58–88). The pattern variables established a set of polarities in the forms of social action that mark out the frontier between formal and informal relationships with considerable clarity. What Parsons proposed was a systematic contrast between action based on principles that he called universalistic, achievement-oriented, functionally specific and affectively neutral and, at the other extreme, action based on principles that he identified as particularistic, ascriptive, functionally diffuse and affectively biased. He was contrasting the public world of the bureaucrat with the private world of mothers. In the context of social care the pattern variables drive a wedge between two types of care. The first is care given in terms of formal assessments of need, formal rules of procedure, sharply specified care-giving and care-receiving roles, general principles of treating all identified cases of need regardless of other personal characteristics of the individuals in need and outcomes measured in terms of objective criteria of success. The second is care given in terms of broad attachments between whole persons regardless of the needs of others, in ways peculiar to the particular relationships within which it is given, embedded in long-standing patterns of highly personalised mutual exchanges of care, and valued in terms of appreciations of the subjective relationship between the carer and the cared for.

These distinctions are not just abstractions of sociological theory. There are in our society two distinct systems of social care; one, the public sector, organised on principles that are in every crucial respect at odds with and incompatible with the principles governing the other, the private sector. There is the social care world of social administrators and their publics or of social workers and their clients; and set sharply against that there is the world of mothers and daughters, of caring neighbours and devoted friends. The trouble is that in terms of the standards of adequate and effective care that prevail in the first of these worlds, the world of public care, the second, the world of private, informal care, is something of a disaster.

Quite simply, the private sector persistently fails to provide enough care for enough people. However much one may value its emotional depth and the qualitative standards that at its best it sets, it cannot be relied on to provide care where it is needed or in the form needed for vast numbers of people. And faced with the manifest inadequacies of the private sector in terms of the universalistic (and so forth) criteria that prevail in the public sector, the inclination of well-intentioned policy-makers, entrepreneurs and activists in the public sector is quite understandably to colonise the private sector; to invade and reorganise it so that their own standards of effective care can be more thoroughly realised. Neighbourhood Care projects face an uncomfortable dilemma. Do they aim to reconstruct the informal sector along more formal lines, or strengthen and nurture the existing informal caring agents on their own terms?

In crossing the frontier between informal and formal care, one should recognise that informal care is profoundly unlike the sorts of services the formal agencies can provide and not deceive oneself that being a Good Neighbour (with capital letters) is in essence at all the same thing as being a good neighbour (without the capitals). If we purport to value the relationships of the informal sector in their own right, if, as one volunteer Organiser has put it, the ideal of neighbourhood care is that the care a community needs should be provided within and by that community, with voluntary and professional agencies contributing no more than 'backup' support and resources, then the promotion of neighbourhood care is going to be a delicate, protracted and certainly an untidy business. It would be much easier to decide that neighbourhood care is about *substituting* formal for informal caring relationships than to decide to support informal care.

To extend an argument advanced by Collins and Pancoast in their study of *Natural Helping Networks* (1976), one might say that dilemma facing the Neighbourhood Care movement is this: is the objective to enhance natural helping networks, or is it rather to plant artificial networks in settings in which natural networks have failed to emerge? And if it is the latter, is there any hope that the artificial networks could in due course be naturalised in those settings? Once again, the answer is of course not either/or but both. It is not a matter of making a choice but of seeing that neighbourhood care is engaged in doing two quite different things – and of keeping them both clearly and separately in mind in the practical organisation of Neighbourhood projects. That seems to be where the real difficulties arise.

A peculiar problem for neighbourhood care lies in the fact that while Neighbourhood Care projects build on the evocation of sentiments of local attachment and neighbourly concern (and are to that extent at one with the main sources of informal care), they are in other necessary respects unavoidably dependent on formal organisation and the commitment of individuals to narrowly defined roles and tasks (and are to that degree firmly part of the formal system). To put it bluntly: in the informal sector people *care* for people they care-*for*; but the members of Neighbourhood Care projects are committed to giving care to people neither they nor possibly anyone else will care-for. The informal sector is built on affect; the Neighbourhood Care movement, if it is to do more than simply mirror the inadequate informal system, must be built on something else. The whole point is to extend care beyond the reach of affect. But what is there to build on other than either market incentives or bureaucratic control?

This brings us to a fundamental dilemma for social policy. Is neighbourhood care to be an invasion and takeover of the area of need that the informal sector currently fails to meet, justified in terms of that failure and conducted under the banner of an essentially spurious appeal to local attachment and to the desire for a renewal of informal caring relationships? Or is it to be an authentic regeneration of informal care through the provision of background support, toleration of a great deal of administrative untidiness and a deliberate restriction of the boundaries of the welfare state?

Both possibilities are open. The principal obstacles to personal involvement in neighbourhood care appear to be lack of time, lack of skills and lack of confidence. These obstacles can quite easily be overcome by suitably modest processes of induction. Once they are overcome, the capacity of volunteers to discover the satisfactions of reciprocity within the provision of care seem to be considerable. The provision of care can quite realistically take one of two forms. We can *supplant* informal care by the formally organised delivery of services. Or we can cultivate and *sustain* informal care by facilitating reciprocal relationships within extensive networks of helpers and the helped – never being quite sure in the end which is which. The voluntary provision of neighbourhood care may straddle uncomfortably both options.

Much of the apparent consensus about the general desirability of more neighbourhood care that exists today exists only because those who think that neighbourhood care means more localised formal services and those who think it means stronger informal systems have not yet appreciated the degree to which they are talking about different (and possibly incompatible) things. Neighbourhood care is a term which can refer either to (1) the achievement of intensive and extensive neighbourliness within localities or to (2) the provision of formal social services 'in the community' with no necessary reference to neighbourliness at all. Most of the recent promotion of neighbourhood care has hopefully, not to say blandly, assumed that these two distinct ideals can somehow be reconciled in practice even if they do appear to be at odds in principle. But can they?

In practice most Neighbourhood Care projects find themselves in the peculiar position of trying to realise both types of neighbourhood care at once. Specifically, they find themselves trying to use formal means, an agency or organisation, to promote informal social relationships, neighbourliness and reciprocal care. And most of their immediate practical problems revolve around the difficulties of holding a balance between the formal and the informal worlds – what level of payment to Good Neighbours will ensure their reliability as helpers without subverting their identity as neighbours? What measure of contact with, or subsidy from, the Social Services Department will give one the information, resources and access to clients that one needs without branding one as just another official agency, just another bit of 'the welfare'? Rather depressingly, in the event most projects tend to opt for stronger links with the formal welfare world ("if only we had a paid Organiser") rather than to persist in what they typically experience as a

Neighbourhood care as a form of organised care

frustrating struggle to activate indigenous neighbourliness. The theoretical ambiguity in the idea of neighbourhood care is very definitely also re-enacted as a practical difficulty in social policy.

The discussion may be taken further by considering the sort of relationship that might exist between public caring authorities and the Neighbourhood Care movement. Three types of relationship may be discerned: colonisation, conflict and coexistence. Of these only the last, coexistence, seems seriously appropriate to the development of neighbourhood care in the sense of neighbourliness; but the first, colonisation, may well be the best suited – at least in the short run – to neighbourhood care in the sense of service delivery. If that is right, a fairly acute moral dilemma, a choice of values, obviously faces those who are currently responsible for the formation and implementation of policy in the field of the personal social services.

Colonisation encompasses a wide range of practical relationships in all of which the social networks of the neighbourhood are seized by statutory or voluntary service agencies and subordinated to their ends. Such exercises may be dressed in a more or less elaborate rhetoric of 'neighbourhood care' or similar benevolent symbolic legitimations. They are typically oriented to both care – service delivery – and control – coverage, accountability and direct access to 'trouble spots' however those are defined. Their common strategy is to create dependency. The striking, and perhaps worrying thing about colonisation is, however, that it does often seem to be a rather effective way of delivering services to localities – if that is all one wants to do.

Colonisation itself can take different forms. The simplest may be termed Domination. Here statutory or voluntary agencies merely impose their own preferred hierarchies of control on local social systems. The most obvious example is the strategy of boundaries – of marking out and enforcing distinct spheres of action, competence and responsibility. The workings of such a strategy are plainly revealed in a study such as Holmes and Maizels's *Social Workers and Volunteers* (1979). What such research conveys is above all a forcible sense of the extent to which social workers (in this case), for reasons not wholly unconnected with the insecurity of their own claims to professional expertise, effectively delimited the activity of volunteers, excluding them from virtually all types of case work and assigning them an approved, but subordinate, role in 'befriending' and in doing practical chores for the elderly and the physically handicapped and generally in working with those client groups with whom social workers least like to work themselves. There is ample evidence that just this sort of ordering of roles is applied by both statutory and voluntary agencies in established relations with care-givers in the informal sector as well. And all down the line many less powerful participants have been content if not happy to accept the spheres of action assigned to them in this way – after all they are being given *some* sort of socially endorsed role. Nevertheless, the relationship at the heart of such processes is unavoidably disabling as well as enabling. While the boundary strategy serves to recruit people to the subordinate roles approved for them by the powerful it quite clearly also deters many others from more active participation in the giving of care. If the British Association of Social Workers (BASW) is the champion of Domination in the world of the statutory agencies, perhaps the WRVS could be singled out as the most adept practitioner of this type of relationship among voluntary organisations. But the propensity to Domination seems to lurk among the organisers of virtually all care projects operating at the neighbourhood level or on the boundaries of the formal and informal systems. How necessary and how desirable is that sort of relationship? It produces results, but at what sort of price?

The second main form of Colonisation might be called Appropriation. This is a somewhat more subtle as well as a considerably more all-encompassing relationship. In this case boundaries are not just drawn but drawn in such a way as to *redefine* previous perceptions of the formal and informal sectors; usually forcibly including, for whatever good reasons, that which was once informal in an expanded area of the formal. The movement to register child-minders is a conspicuous recent example of this sort of colonisation. The recommendation of Collins and Pancoast (1976:117) that statutory and voluntary agencies should seek out the 'central figures' in local networks of neighbouring with a view to maximising their effectiveness and simultaneously using them as the crucial gate-keepers between the formal and informal systems is made in the light of the very clear recognition that in the past that sort of strategy has usually ended up by transferring the best care-givers of the informal system to the formal system with a consequent more or less drastic impoverishment of the former. Many Good Neighbour schemes, as understood by their organisers, at least, are in effect also largely exercises in appropriation – attempts to redefine in organisational terms caring activities already taking place in the locality. And those Social Services Departments which are beginning to worry about the 'terms and conditions of work' of Good Neighbours and thinking, for example, of possibly placing Good Neighbours under the administrative umbrella of the Home Help Service – or of getting them signed up as members of the National Union of Public Employees (NUPE) or the National and Local Government Officers' Association (NALGO) – are plainly on the brink of a massive piece of appropriation the implications of which for the informal system are also worrying them.

The advantages of appropriation are the advantages of bureaucratic tidying up and control. Unfortunately, despite a good deal of official and academic optimism the administrative gain is in practice usually also the informal sector's loss. Mrs Wilkinson now plays her part as a Good Neighbour by keeping up the impeccable filing system expected of her by the Volunteer Liaison Officer from whom she sometimes gets referrals. Unfortunately, as a result, she is now too busy to go on visiting arthritic old Mr Graham next door as she used to do. Anyway, someone else is supposed to do that now – if only they could be found. This is *not* an unusual dénouement of the drama of appropriation. The challenge to voluntary and statutory agencies is to find the gate-keepers of the informal sector and settle for relating to them *as such*. Why is it that as in more conventional forms of colonisation the journey of exploration so frequently ends in an act of appropriation – with the gate-keepers turned into client princes?

The third main form of colonisation is Incorporation. This can be seen either

Neighbourhood care as a form of organised care

as a more extreme and comprehensive form of appropriation or as strategy which in some ambiguous ways goes beyond colonisation and looks towards a more authentic coexistence of formal and informal systems at the neighbourhood level, a recognition of the irreducible element of politics which the new neighbourhoodism has injected into local social networks. The immediately visible difference between incorporation and appropriation is that some serious attempt is made by the more powerful (formal) parties not just to respect the untidy integrity of the less powerful but actually to build some measure of informality into their own procedures. An interesting example is provided by the Cumbria gossip 'monitoring' policy. The philosophy of the Cumbria Social Services Department explicitly favours a more informal approach to social care than that involved in the promotion of Good Neighbour schemes. Instead of encouraging such schemes they have set out to 'map' the communities for which they are responsible with a view to building 'a system of communication between us' rooted in the informal networks of gossip and running up to and through all relevant service-providing agencies.

At the neighbourhood level such a project involves the discovery of people willing to function as 'watch-dogs' for specified small local areas – in that respect the system could be thought to look not unlike the more conventional Street Warden arrangement; indeed, the fact that the Cumbria watch-dogs are allowed to call themselves Street Wardens is one sign that the system is in the end an exercise in colonisation rather than in coexistence. However, the distinctive features of the plan are the seriousness with which the search for informal networks and their 'central figures' is conducted, the conscious resistance to formalisation of the networks the search reveals and the readiness of the authority to be extremely flexible in the way it negotiates working relationships locally. The attempt is to draw the informal sector into an over-all system of care with the least possible disturbance of its existing internal relationships. The results are untidy but seem where they have been studied in any detail (in Barrow for example) to have included a measurable strengthening of localised informal care. At the very least, informal local information and intelligence systems have been turned into resources within the formal sector that enable statutory and voluntary bodies to deliver their various services with improved effectiveness.

In one way or another Colonisation seems to be the common destiny of most Neighbourhood Care projects and the usual fate of attempts to bridge the boundaries of the formal and the informal systems. Often (as in the early history of the British Empire) what happens seems to reflect the hypnotic fascination of the powerful for the powerless at least as much as any positive greed for territory on the part of the powerful. Our own study of Good Neighbour schemes (Abrams *et al.* 1981a) for example, points to an almost reckless enthusiasm among the (admittedly middle class) organisers of the vast majority of schemes to surrender their fragile projects to the superior managerial powers and resources of established statutory and voluntary agencies. The commonest and almost ubiquitous 'need' of the schemes reported to us by their organisers is for an injection of paid, professional management. So much for informal neighbourhood care. Formalisation is the order of the day – preferably through rather loose and discrete links, but nevertheless the problem is to get organised: rather a well-run colony than a mere tribe. What is sad about such tendencies to succumb to colonisation is that there do seem to be more positive alternatives.

One possibility is Conflict. It is here that the modern informal sector, the new neighbourhoodism and its distinctive networks could be so important. Vast numbers of neighbourhood projects including many Good Neighbour schemes come to life not only as a medium for the construction of new informal networks and the provision of this or that service but more specifically as instruments of political struggle. Their value and interest lies in that *combination* of ends: care and sociability (networks) and politics. In historical perspective the most dramatic and significant innovation of the present phase of the life of the welfare state will probably turn out to be the shift from administration to conflict. The new neighbourhoodism is at once a reflection of that shift and an attempt to build new networks of social attachment through political action. In the 1930s, organisations of unemployed workers could be treated as a transient perversion of the normal flow of a fairly smoothly administered welfare world. By the 1970s Claimants' Unions and a host of militant welfare rights groups had redefined the normal existence of the welfare state as something very much more turbulent. It has been made clear today that the organisation and distribution of welfare is controversial and an unavoidable, indeed proper, occasion for dispute.

In that context the appearance of a multitude of groups that combine the translation of need into demand (rather than the acceptance of care) with the construction of strong informal networks of friendship is an event of considerable importance. Certainly, as many of the projects studied suggest, there are profound tensions and ambiguities within such groups – above all a fateful readiness to believe that absorption into the official world might be a tactically shrewd way of pursuing radical objectives. Few, however, of even the most bureaucratic minded organisers of the schemes studied go that far. Rather, a substantial minority of the ventures brought to light appear to be committed to the principle that the organisation of protest might be the best way of maintaining the integrity and renewing the energy of the informal social system. Disasters as the Community Development Projects may have been from the point of view of Home Office control or conventional academic knowledge, they did without exception demonstrate the possibility of intensifying the solidarity and effectiveness of informal neighbourhood networks through conflict. That lesson cannot be ignored in any serious discussion of neighbourhood care or of the proper or desirable relationship between the formal and informal sectors of our social system.

Nevertheless, unless conflict leads somewhere it is in the end a sterile and demoralising prospect. One destination to which it could lead is of course conquest. So far as informal localised care is concerned, such an outcome is inconceivable. What is conceivable is some sort of coexistence, a sufficient strengthening of the informal sector to enable it to deal intimately but on equal terms with agencies in the formal system. Coexistence would differ from Incorporation not in the extent to which informal and formal social care were

Neighbourhood care as a form of organised care

closely meshed together but in the fact that in a relationship of coexistence the values, norms and relationships of the informal sector would be brought forward and sustained as a basis for social policy in their own right and not re-made to suit the administrative or other purposes of the formal system.

These ideas about the relationship between the informal and formal systems of care will be pursued further in chapter 11. They give some indication of the way in which Philip Abrams's ideas about neighbourhood care in general were developing, and how neighbourhood care fitted into the pattern of existing statutory, voluntary and informal social care. These ideas also helped to shape, but were in turn influenced by, the ten case studies of Neighbourhood Care schemes reported in the next three chapters.

8 Ten Neighbourhood Care schemes

The growth of interest in neighbourhood care may in its modern form, be traced back to the Seebohm Report of 1968, which called for 'a community-based and family-oriented service' that would 'enable the greatest possible number of individuals to act reciprocally, giving and receiving service for the well-being of the whole community'. The Durham team, as described in the first chapter, became interested in efforts made by a number of voluntary and statutory agencies to foster systems of neighbourhood care in a more structured way than the informal, next-door neighbouring studied during the first phase of the project. They conducted the study of Good Neighbour schemes (Abrams et al. 1981a) by posing the question of whether, and to what extent, existing statutory and voluntary organisations 'made room' for Good Neighbouring within an established pattern of care; raising the issue of how to balance help and need, suggesting that help was more forthcoming in areas where it was less needed, and less forthcoming where it was more needed, and highlighting the paradox that although Good Neighbouring was primarily concerned with encouraging informal caring relationships, to succeed it needed carefully thought-out formal relationships. These are issues highlighted again in this and the two succeeding chapters.

The main stage of the second phase of the research was carried out by Sheila Abrams, Robin Humphrey and Ray Snaith, under the direction of Philip Abrams. This chapter and the two which follow are based upon a condensation of their Report to DHSS (1981). A full analysis of monograph length which goes beyond the material presented here appears in Abrams, Abrams, Humphrey and Snaith (forthcoming). The aim of the second phase was to examine as closely as possible a small number of Neighbourhood Care projects selected on the basis of significant criteria of type of locality, type of organisation and type of immediate welfare environment. The studies were to document the ways in which a series of analytically distinct types of Neighbourhood Care ventures worked, the characteristics of their members and clients, and the pattern of support (or lack of support) provided by local statutory and voluntary agencies, and to draw comparisons between those involved in the projects and indicative samples of local residents not involved in them. More fundamentally, they were to elucidate the two-way *relationship* between the projects' own aims, activities, characteristics, organisational forms, achievements and difficulties and, on the one hand, their environment of informal social care, and, on the other hand, their environment of formal welfare provision. In other words the idea that organised Neighbourhood Care

Ten Neighbourhood Care schemes

projects are crucial experiments in opening up the frontier between formal and informal care was the heart of the study.

Some of the specific questions addressed included the following:

(1) What is the range of activities involved in the various grass-roots caring enterprises broadly identified as Good Neighbour schemes? Do such ventures constitute a distinct type of social care?
(2) How widespread are such ventures? Are they more common in some areas than in others? And if so, why? Is it the case, for example, that they are most easily established in areas where informal caring networks are already strong and where statutory provision of services is generous – that is, where they are least needed?
(3) What are the main differences between such projects in terms of aims, organisation, finance and local involvement? Are there significant differences between, say, schemes operated by churches and those operated by official bodies or local residents? Or between those in which helpers or organisers are paid and those in which they are unpaid?
(4) Can the universe of projects be broken down in terms of any useful classification of types? If so, is any particular type of scheme particularly associated with any particular type of policy, organisational arrangements or local social conditions?
(5) What are the motives, characteristics and values of those recruited to help in Neighbourhood Care projects? Are they significantly unlike those who do not join in any identifiable ways?
(6) How can we identify and assess the success or failure of Neighbourhood Care projects? In what ways can their success or failure be related to variations in organisational format, local social conditions, welfare environment and so forth?

The case studies were also intended to answer two questions thrown up by previous research. The first related to processes of social selection of clients:

(7) Who are the Clients of neighbourhood care? How far do those served by such projects constitute a category of people with distinct characteristics within the population of their locality? How did they come to be Clients? How far and why do other people in the same locality and with similar needs fail to become Clients? In what ways do projects meet the needs of Clients? How significant is the care they give in relation to other care the Clients receive and in relation to Clients' own perceptions of their needs?

Earlier research had highlighted the apparent importance of reciprocity, as distinct from altruism, as a 'dispositional' base for neighbourhood care of an informal kind. In looking at projects operating across the frontier of formal and informal care:

(8) What is the role of reciprocity in shaping and sustaining the relationship between the Helpers in Neighbourhood Care projects and those they help? How far was the earlier 'conclusion' about the central place of reciprocity in neighbourhood care (and about the diversity of forms reciprocity can take) supported or modified by closer study of the relationship between local Helpers and Clients on the one hand and local residents who are neither Helpers nor Clients on the other?

These questions had considerable general relevance for both social policy and social analysis. It was hoped that they would provide a substantial sense not only of the extent and range of localised social care in our society, and of the extent to which further informal sources of such care could be mobilised and effectively linked to the resources of voluntary and statutory provision, but also of the fundamental nature of the social relationships within which such care does or does not flourish.

The design of the research, in particular the selection of localities and Neighbourhood Care projects for study, was guided by the earlier work discussed in previous chapters. In particular, the selection was guided by the team's views about (1) the nature of the 'informal' system, (2) the range of normal relationships between the informal and formal systems of care, (3) the general factors conducive to high levels of neighbourhood care and (4) the social sources of reciprocity.

The coexistence of an attenuated traditional system of informal neighbourhood relations and an emergent modern system seemed to give Neighbourhood Care projects – whether they were seeking to mobilise informal resources or to deliver formal services – a quite distinctive array of targets. These included on the one hand kin relationships actually or potentially carrying significant measures of informal care, and the capacity of co-residents to monitor one another's circumstances with a high degree of accuracy and understanding; and on the other hand the presence of certain categories of people, children, young mothers, the retired, newcomers and various sorts of activists who were in the market for local social involvements. The research was weighted towards giving special attention to the capacity of Neighbourhood Care projects to activate this set of traditional and modern resources.

In considering the sorts of relationships that might exist between the formal and the informal systems of social care, and the possible role of Neighbourhood Care projects in building such relationships, it seemed sensible to the team to begin with some sense of the actual nature of those relationships. There were in fact two sets of relationships to consider: those between Neighbourhood Care projects and surrounding statutory and voluntary welfare agencies; and those between the projects and their local pool of resources for informal care. They tried on the basis of existing literature and their own earlier research to identify in advance a number of main types of each of these relationships. On the formal side (the relation of welfare agencies to Neighbourhood Care projects) it seemed that the common patterns were those of *colonisation*, *conflict* or *coexistence*. And so far as the informal side was concerned (the relationship of projects to the informal fabric of care in their localities) it seemed that the best-documented patterns could well be characterised as a matter of *patronage*, *redundancy* or *isolation*.

General factors conducive to high levels of neighbourhood care were cultural resources, structural facilities and personal capacities. The field inquiries were organised to permit an examination of these three levels of general conditioning. Trust, knowledge and predictability would be good examples of cultural resources especially conducive to strong patterns of neighbourhood care – a base of information, understandings and dispositions

Ten Neighbourhood Care schemes 137

in terms of which caring activities could be seen to 'make sense'. Efficient means of communication between those with needs and those able to help them, comprehensive monitoring networks, visible, convenient and accessible location of care-givers or coordinators exemplified structural facilities for neighbourhood care. And time, skills, knowledge of how to help and a modest personal prosperity were characteristic instances of relevant personal capacities.

The importance of reciprocity as a source of informal care was emphasised in chapter 6. Philip Abrams was impressed by the extent to which a pattern of 'life cycle' and heterodox reciprocity seemed to obtain: that is to say, a pattern of people repaying much later on and to third parties debts of care they had incurred earlier on or elsewhere. It is not just that caring parents seem to produce caring children but that caring neighbours seem quite commonly to have experienced caring neighbouring themselves in other places and at other times. So the main project aimed to explore the extent to which these impressions of long-range reciprocity were justified; to see, for example, whether the idea that local residents who cared for their neighbours were indeed distinguished from other residents by personal experiences of having received or known neighbourhood care would stand up to scrutiny. More generally the aim was simply to see how far neighbourhood care was indeed embedded in reciprocity and insofar as it was how far such patterns of reciprocity were short-run or deferred and extended. If the limits of reciprocity were reached, what were the nature and origins of norms of beneficence, ingrained moral standards on the strength of which some people behaved altruistically?

This, then, formed the intellectual backdrop to the main phase of the research. A pilot study undertaken in North London (described in the Report to DHSS (1981)) highlighted the significance of social class factors (both in the composition of the neighbourhood and of the members of the Neighbourhood Care project), of the institutional origins of projects (as between residents, voluntary organisations and statutory agencies), of certain organisational features of projects (such as the payment or non-payment of Helpers and coordinators) and particularly the general posture of local welfare authorities towards the whole issue of neighbourhood care. Given that the study was to be restricted to ten cases, systematic comparison of all the variables already identified as analytically important could not be incorporated within the general framework.

> On most matters the study was going to have to be simply, even naively exploratory. The essentially interpretative issues identified in the way we understood the two informal systems, the relationships between formal and informal care, the general factors conducive to neighbourhood care, the functions of reciprocity and perhaps of beneficence, were not matters that could be specified firmly enough in advance to provide guidelines for sampling cases. They were insights (we hoped) to refine in the course of investigation. The initial sampling of cases had to proceed on firmer ground. And the ground we chose was that provided by our pilot study – especially insofar as its importance had been confirmed by our earlier study of Good Neighbour Schemes. In effect, our sampling was organised in terms of three major variables each of which we felt we had some *a priori* reason to consider likely to be

of major significance in determining patterns of neighbourhood care and for each of which we felt we could ascertain 'weights' for any given case with reasonable confidence before commencing detailed local investigations. These three variables were social composition of the neighbourhood, key organisational attributes of the Neighbourhood Care project, and the general posture of the relevant statutory agencies towards neighbourhood care. (Report to DHSS, 1981).

The policy stance of statutory agencies was ranged along a continuum of eleven types of orientation. The extremes of the continuum were postulated to be – as hypothetical ideal types – complete statutory domination at one end and complete statutory neglect at the other. In between, three broad patterns were distinguished – the high profile, statutory-led mix, the partnership or springboard relationship and the low profile or safety-net pattern – each of which could at least in principle be further sub-divided into three principal variants which might be called need-oriented, task-oriented and cost-oriented. Each of these ideal-typical positions seemed to represent a possible distinct actual posture which actual statutory bodies might conceivably adopt – with distinct actual consequences – in practice. The major sampling decision was to try to find Neighbourhood Care projects which could be identified as operating in the context of a spread of ascertainable variants within this range of ideological and political dispositions towards neighbourhood care.

Towards the extremes, it was possible to find exemplifying cases without such difficulty: Stonegate was plainly blessed, or burdened, with an authority committed to the statutory-led, need-oriented pattern, just as Easethorpe enjoyed (or suffered) a welfare environment in which the cost-oriented safety-net orientation prevailed. The more central (partnership) patterns were harder to identify in advance. Nevertheless, as the schematic allocation of cases to types in table 8.1 shows, the team did in the end feel that they had been able to select studies fairly systematically, albeit not comprehensively, in relation to the continuum of type of welfare authority stance.

In choosing localities in terms of social composition and location, simple criteria were used: working class, middle class and socially mixed on the one hand; urban, suburban and rural on the other. The survey of Good Neighbour schemes indicated that the largest single concentration of such schemes was to be found in socially mixed urban localities and that they were least likely to be found in solidly working class neighbourhoods and thoroughly rural milieux respectively. The team decided, however, to skew sampling towards types of theoretical interest, rather than simply to reflect numerical incidence. Four of the localities studies were indeed urban and socially mixed, but of the rest two were urban and working class, three were suburban (one middle class, one mixed and one working class) and one was rural and socially mixed.

A final set of sampling criteria concerned the origins of projects and the payment or non-payment of their key personnel. So far as origins were concerned, a distinction was made between initiation by statutory agencies, by churches, by lay voluntary bodies and by *ad hoc* groups of local residents. Earlier research indicated that the commonest source of initiation was the churches, followed by voluntary bodies, local residents and, a poor fourth,

Table 8.1 *The continuum of type of welfare authority stance towards neighbourhood care*

Authority policy	The continuum	Examples from the case studies
	Complete statutory domination	
High profile	Statutory-led need-oriented	Stonegate; Brandling
	Statutory-led task-oriented	Skeffington
	Statutory-led cost-oriented	
Springboard	Partnership need-oriented	Tattworth; Grantley
	Partnership task-oriented	Bradbury
	Partnership cost-oriented	Trimdon
Low profile	Safety-net need-oriented	Parsons Green
	Safety-net task-oriented	Southfield Park
	Safety-net cost-oriented	Easethorpe
	Complete statutory neglect	

statutory agencies. But here again it was decided to sample on the basis of theoretical interest. Because of interest in the prospects of forays into neighbourhood care from within the statutory sector, five of the projects studied were ones that had been initiated by statutory agencies. A further two were built from the grassroots, and two others – because of their ubiquity and proclaimed relative success – from those started by church groups.

So far as payment was concerned four main patterns were examined: the payment of full wages to all concerned, the payment of token honoraria, selective payment of certain personnel, the complete absence of payment. As the last of these was both the most common and the most controversial in the whole field of neighbourhood care (and a feature which is often held to maintain the link between organised neighbourhood care and informal care), five projects in which no payments were involved were chosen. Of the other five, two had paid Organisers, two made token payments to their Helpers and one paid full wages to all concerned.

To study the full range of patterns of neighbourhood care permitted even by the team's limited array of fairly crude variables would have required some 250 case studies. In choosing ten, they could only restrict themselves to a small range of variations which they took to be of particular analytical interest. The characteristics of the ten cases studied are shown in table 8.2. The research was intended to be an exploratory study, not to provide a definitive analysis. The comparative data in particular must be understood as referring only to the specific contrasts permitted by the case studies, not across the whole range of possible differences. On the other hand, having selected ten instances from the universe of possible patterns, the team believed that the terms of analysis they had developed would allow them both to examine the structure and dynamics of those particular patterns quite thoroughly and subsequently to venture

Table 8.2 *The characteristics of the ten case studies*

Place	Social composition	Initiation	Payment	Welfare environment
Stonegate	Urban Working class	Statutory	Wage-work	Statutory-led Need-oriented
Brandling	Urban Mixed (mainly working class)	Residents	Paid Organiser	Statutory-led Need-oriented
Skeffington	Urban Mixed	Statutory	Token payments	Statutory-led Task-oriented
Grantley	Urban Mixed	Statutory	Paid Organiser	Partnership Need-oriented
Tattworth	Urban Working class	Statutory	Unpaid	Partnership Need-oriented
Bradbury	Suburban Working class	Church	Unpaid	Partnership Task-oriented
Trimdon	Urban Mixed	Statutory	Unpaid	Partnership Cost-oriented
Parsons Green	Suburban Mixed	Residents	Unpaid	Safety-net Need-oriented
Southfield Park	Suburban Middle class	Church	Unpaid	Safety-net Task-oriented
Easethorpe	Rural Mixed	Residents	Unpaid	Safety-net Cost-oriented

some reasonably strong inferences about the conditions for neighbourhood care in general.

The ten localities studied will now be briefly described. This is an abbreviated description. Fuller accounts are available elsewhere (Report to DHSS 1981; Abrams, Abrams, Humphrey and Snaith 1985a; 1985b; forthcoming). Each locality is anonymised, but the description gives a general indication of its main characteristics. All are in different parts of England.

1. Stonegate: Hunting Valley

The welfare environment of Stonegate is statutory-led. Stonegate is a steel town, a great manufacturing city with a long-established skilled population. Although much of the city's nineteenth-century fabric remains, especially a central commercial and residential area of finely-proportioned stone buildings, it has expanded rapidly into the surrounding countryside during the last 30 years. The local authority has been Labour-controlled for half a century and has proudly and aggressively set high standards in housing, public transport services and welfare provision. The research in Stonegate was particularly focussed upon its Warden service. Although this covers the whole city, its workings in only one area, Hunting Valley, were studied. This working class suburb was situated on both sides of a steep valley running out from the city, covered with modern council-housing developments built since the war and planned and landscaped to a high standard of design. In the valley were four distinct housing types: semi-detached and terraced housing, two- or three-storey blocks of flats, maisonette complexes and twelve-storey blocks of flats. The particular street we chose for the Residents' interviews was situated high on the west side of the valley with views across most of the development.

In this road, there were three reasonably distinct social worlds: two areas of terraced houses at each end of the road and an area of low-rise flats, mainly one-bedroomed and mainly inhabited by elderly couples or single people, facing a group of family houses in the central stretch. Each section had a distinct atmosphere. The first was almost universally described as a very neighbourly place and contained at least one generally acknowledged 'Good Neighbour', a nurse who was well known and trusted as a provider of informal help and care among her neighbours. This area seemed to be inhabited mainly by couples in their early middle age with young families. The extent to which these people liked and helped their neighbours and had close friends living nearby was striking; there were extensive informal social networks here that sustained a strong sense of belonging to a well-liked neighbourhood. At the other end of the street, physically identical as it was, the social atmosphere was entirely different. Here pleasure at living in the area did not spill over into any enthusiasm for fellow residents. Rather, distrust and privatisation were rampant. "I will tell you what I think of my neighbours, then – they are rubbish ... they all are round here" – that from a man who said that a really nice neighbourly place would be the ideal environment for bringing up children. Those who had attempted sociable activity in the neighbourhood at large seemed for the most part to have withdrawn from it disillusioned – one woman on the revealing ground that "they all seemed to come from the other end of the street". This case supported the finding that there is no easy way in which neighbourhood relations can be directly inferred either from built form or social class.

The Stonegate Warden service described on p. 122, started in 1963 with 20 wardens and at the time of the research had 187. It was a statutory paid venture in neighbourhood care. The idea for such a service was developed when it became apparent that the Home Help service was not providing adequate cover for elderly isolated or mentally handicapped clients. A need was identified between the existing statutory provision and the frontiers of voluntary and informal provision and the authority, in line with its general policy of direct statutory response to need, invented the new service to meet it. The service was fully incorporated into the working of the Authority's Family and Community Service under the overall charge of a specially appointed Chief Assistant for Domiciliary Services. In a sense, therefore the relevant welfare setting for the Warden service was not that of the Department of which it was itself a part but rather the non-statutory complex of neighbourhood care in Stonegate alongside which the Warden service operated.

Non-statutory formalised neighbourhood care was rather firmly in the hands of old-established voluntary and ecclesiastical organisations rather than those of *ad hoc* local projects, most prominently via the Stonegate Council of Churches. Their Council for Community Care was an elaborate alliance of all the main Christian churches, Social Services, Probation, and the Area Health Authority (AHA), drawn together to support a wide range of local neighbourhood care. Three schemes attempted to provide voluntary care to supplement statutory provision. A Good Neighbour scheme was in operation, there was a corps of Community Care volunteers, and a liaison scheme to link referrals from statutory and voluntary agencies to local Helpers. Though these schemes were firmly established, the system was weakest where needs were greatest. The projects flourished where church congregations and middle class residents were most numerous, and had much less impact in solidly working class areas. There were practical limits to such efforts, and it was to meeting need beyond these limits that the statutory project was directed.

The research team concluded, on the basis of their study of Hunting Valley, that in Stonegate a formula for integrating a statutory-led comprehensive response to social need with the human qualities of neighbourhood care had been impressively worked out. There were of course many problems unresolved in the working of the Home Warden service which a fuller study would have to explore. One particularly striking finding, however, was that, insofar as the statutory appropriation of neighbourhood care was indeed successful both as efficient management and as sensitive care, it seemed to leave little room for conventional voluntary efforts. Several people associated with the Home Warden service said that they didn't really see how anything comparable could be provided by volunteers – that, for example, however stringent the cuts, they would think it essential to preserve the Home Warden service on its present basis rather than reconstitute it using volunteers if the needs of clients were really going to be met. Perhaps they were right. But if they were, where does that leave all that voluntary action?

2. Brandling Good Neighbour scheme

Brandling is one of the inner London boroughs overwhelmingly working class in composition. The borough has high population density, poor housing stock, high unemployment especially among black youth, much vandalism and little open space. The area as a whole is one eloquent of the worst forms of urban change: neglect of the public fabric of the environment, high population turnover – especially among the middle class minority – a general sense of a hard, insecure existence in a place that just happens to be there. And yet such impressions are misleading in some important respects. There are in fact still many people in Brandling who have lived there all their lives and have family and long-standing friends living nearby.

The local authority responsible for Brandling is one with a long-standing tradition of radicalism and devotion to the needs and interests of the working class. It has a proud record of pioneering action in many fields of social reform and welfare provision. Since Seebohm, the borough as a whole has developed

Ten Neighbourhood Care schemes

a policy of encouraging and funding community and voluntary initiatives and projects as well as supporting community-based work by the Social Services Department. Brandling Good Neighbour scheme received substantial financial support from the council, as well as help and advice from local neighbourhood and community workers. Several statutory agencies made referrals to the scheme. The pattern was plainly statutory-led, but domination and colonisation were minimised by the principled willingness of the statutory authority to transfer funds to local groups on the basis of a high level of trust in the groups' own accounts of their social usefulness. They themselves were not direct agents, as in Stonegate.

A lay visiting group from local churches in Brandling had been active in the large council estates of the area for some years and it was from this in 1972 that a specific concern about loneliness, isolation and immobility, particularly among the elderly, emerged. Lilac Estate, a large local authority development, was in its earlier stages at this time and the group members called on homes there to provide some kind of welcome to the area and to ask if there were any problems they would like help with or information about. The experience of the church visiting group highlighted what was believed to be a serious need for a more formally organised way of bringing helpers and need, especially the needs of the isolated elderly, together. The area office of the Social Services Department was approached and immediately welcomed the idea.

From this grew the Good Neighbour scheme. At first the core group of workers, exclusively middle class, lacked usable informal links with the overwhelmingly working class and non-church-going population of the urban neighbourhood. However, by dint of effective organising, a modest grant from a charitable trust for a paid part-time coordinator, and a central office provided by a local church, the scheme became better known. From 1973 it was funded by the council, and by the late 1970s this met almost all its budget, which paid for a full-time organiser.

The success of the scheme in building up trust and friendship in its relations with the local residents is indicated by the fact that by far the greatest proportion of its referrals come from local people approaching the scheme directly and in person for help (875 out of a total of 1049 in the year 1979–80). Those from neighbours and relatives and local voluntary bodies of one kind or another account for as many as those from statutory care agencies (Social Services Department, Health Services, Home Helps and the Probation Service). The Social Services Department's requests were in any event mainly for transport.

An analysis of referrals in 1979–80 showed that over two-thirds were for transport and another one-fifth for advice. The transport involved in the main taking elderly people from their homes to Day Centres or to Old People's Clubs. The advice function was not one that was advertised, but emerged from local contacts with the scheme. Although a visiting service had been an objective of the scheme from the start, less than three per cent of referrals in 1979–80 involved visiting. Though the coordinator devoted a great deal of time to arranging visits, the scheme failed to promote them, apparently for two

144   *Organised neighbourhood care*

reasons, lack of time in an area where many women worked or were single parents, and the distance between social classes, which was difficult to bridge. "People are too busy surviving themselves" was the succinct way the co-ordinator put it.

The Good Neighbour scheme has also fostered self-help groups, setting up projects such as summer play schemes to the point when they become self-sustaining. It established a second-hand shop on a profit-making basis, providing a reason for local people to drop in to the scheme's premises.

The extent and range of the scheme's activities at the time of the research indicated how over the years it had built on and changed its original basis; from the traditional pattern with strong church connections, an emphasis on seeking 'volunteers', formal linking, the matching of individuals, 'doing things for others', it had moved to one which increasingly stressed informal contacts, reciprocity, self-confidence, self-help groups and the building of wider community links. One clear quantitative indicator of the effects of these changes was available: in addition to the predominantly middle class core of around 70 volunteers, mostly providing transport, there were about 300 predominantly working class contacts, from whom the scheme got help or on whom it could call for help, advice and support. They were involved in different ways and to different degrees; they did not see themselves as 'volunteers' and many of them received help, advice or support from the scheme as well as contributing to it.

3. Skeffington Visiting service

Skeffington is one of England's great commercial and industrial cities with a population of about half a million, one in six of whom are over the age of 65. The overall Social Services budget for the city in 1979 was £28m. Skeffington City Authority is one of nine local authorities which together make up the Skeffington conurbation. The Visiting service studied covered the whole of the area of Skeffington City. It was not confined to any one neighbourhood and lacked a defined local setting. It was nevertheless worth studying because it was confined to occupants of private housing (other provision being made for council tenants) and because it involved token payments to its helpers. Though most of the clients lived in old artisan terraces rather than bourgeois suburbs, half of them were middle class.

Faced with a large population of dependent and isolated elderly, Skeffington Social Services Department had devised a double-barrelled policy involving a paid Warden service for council tenants and a Visiting service identified as 'Neighbourhood Mums' for everyone else. The project was initiated on the strength of a familiar rhetoric (not necessarily the less sincere for being familiar) of providing 'a friendly, caring service' for the isolated elderly, with a preventive as well as therapeutic role. It was stressed that elderly people themselves would be free to decide for themselves whether they felt like having 'a friendly visitor' and that the scheme would not therefore 'impinge on their privacy'. The officials most closely involved also hoped that it would in some way help to combat the disintegration of neighbourhood and perhaps restore some 'of the community spirit that was everywhere in the past', an admirable but possibly utopian proposal in view of the general dismantling of Skeffington's old inner-city communities through urban renewal and rehousing on peripheral estates.

The official aims of the Visiting service were to be: (1) To provide weekly feedback for social workers about the elderly. (2) To encourage the elderly to be interested in themselves and others. (3) To involve the local community in caring for the elderly in the area – by, for example, arranging outings and social activities or visiting on a neighbourly basis. It was the last of these purposes that made it seem that the project could be taken as falling within the terms of our definition of neighbourhood care.

The scheme was established in the early 1970s. Potential Visitors were recruited in the localities where they would be active by posters in shops, libraries and doctors' surgeries. Applicants were interviewed and references taken up. On appointment, Visitors were then introduced to 15–20 people on their round as well as to key social services and health staff locally. Visitors were paid a nominal amount and provided with free telephones. Applicants varied in their age and stage in the life cycle. The aim of payment was to allow all people, regardless of social status, to do voluntary work, and to try to break its middle class monopoly.

The first phase of the history of the Visiting service was one of positive incorporation based on the enthusiasm of the Visitors and the flexibility of the Organiser in the Social Services Department, though the project was ostensibly initiated, organised and sustained (on a loose link basis) by the statutory authorities. However, the people who came forward as Visitors were people for the most part already deeply caught up in informal neighbourhood care, and drawing often on long-standing traditions of caring, with strong local attachments and involvements, who responded to the invitation to support the project because they saw it as a natural extension of caring relationships in which they were already engaged. Both the helpers and the residents we sampled in Skeffington proved to be exceptionally (by the standards of our other samples) disposed towards neighbourliness and informal care.

In 1974 the service was transferred from the Community Development team to the Domiciliary Services Division of the Social Services Department, which also supervised the Warden scheme for council tenants. This structural shift rapidly led to a clash and confusion of issues concerning the fundamental nature of the project. Previously the project was significantly separate from the Social Services Department, leaving the Visitors a real measure of collective independence and personal responsibility. It now became an integral part of the official domiciliary services apparatus and subject to the heavy procedures of routine control. One immediate effect was that the Visitors were now formally assigned to area offices. Instead of meeting together centrally as a distinct group they were required to attend area meetings along with the full-time wardens. Simultaneously, various efforts were made to enhance their accountability and competence. The coherent collective entity was rather quickly dissolved into a number of pockets of isolated and highly confused individuals. There were also problems of paid Wardens and Visitors paid a pittance working side by side. The Wardens were NUPE members, and questions of dilution and threats to job security arose.

By 1979–80 the Visiting service was being slowly and deliberately killed off by those administratively responsible for it in the Social Services Department. This had little to do with availability of helpers or the quality of the care provided, and everything to do with administrative efficiency and rationality as officials interpreted it. The local authority was firmly oriented to efficient, business-like administration and the optimally cost-effective execution of necessary and rationally-defined tasks. From that point of view the confusions within the provision of domiciliary care for the elderly created by Wardens and Visitors working side by side were self-evidently troublesome. The Visiting scheme existed in a no-man's-land between volunteers and paid employment, not fully within the control of the Division. The Department concluded that the territory in question should be taken over by one side (the voluntary sector) or the other (the statutory sector).

> It was partly a problem almost of tidiness: 'they provide a useful service of limited value; they may spend more time with their client than a warden, but their days are unstructured and disorganised'. Farewell, informal care one is tempted to add. (DHSS Report)

The solution found by the Social Services Department was not to replace Visitors as they dropped out of the scheme, though this was not announced to those who remained.

The dilemma was a serious one. On the one hand a category of need had plainly fallen through the net of the statutory welfare system, and token payments had served to recruit a large number of people who were willing to attend to that need and to do so in ways that did seem to precipitate more general neighbourhood involvement. On the other hand the initial exclusion of occupants of private housing from statutory welfare services provided by waged staff was highly dubious. And the subsequent discrepancy between paying Visitors a pittance for 20 hours' work caring for these people while paying others ten times as much to work 35 hours caring for the occupants of council housing was even more dubious. One can see why an authority committed to a statutory-led solution to the problems of neighbourhood care and working on a firmly task-oriented basis would be bound to end up running down an anomaly such as the Visiting service. In the process, however, something valuable, an important and distinctive contribution to neighbourhood care, was being lost.

4. Grantley Neighbourhood project

Grantley is a small residential area consisting of about 750 low-rise, privately owned or rented dwellings, mostly terraced. As a whole, this district of the city of Barhampton is predominantly middle class, close enough to the city centre to have been residentially 'desirable' for many years. However, some years ago Grantley itself was transformed by the building on its very edge of a high-rise block of flats which now completely dominates the neighbourhood. The block, Dene House, was built by the local authority and consists of 137 flats on 27 floors. Originally the building was intended to house couples and small families especially those affected by clearance in the central areas of the city. However, the policy of the Housing Department is not to accommodate children under 16 in tower blocks and by the time of the research it had become very largely occupied by old people.

The immediate initiative for the Grantley Neighbourhood project was provided by a survey of Dene House by two social workers and a long-standing sense of social division in the neighbourhood between the inhabitants of the House and those of the rest of Grantley.

The survey of the Dene House inhabitants showed a relatively high degree of satisfaction, but feelings of isolation. 56% suffered from an illness or disability that affected their mobility; 14% were unable to manage housework; 24% were unable to do their own shopping; and 8% were unable to prepare their own meals. 21% said that they were actually unable to leave their flats. In addition to all this there was a manifest dearth of social life in and around the building: 7% of the tenants attended a Luncheon Club each week and 8% attended an Over 60s Club. Apart from that 'there appears to be no ... expression of communal social activity'.

Various political initiatives in Barhampton for local action led after several vicissitudes to the crystallisation of a proposal for the appointment of a neighbourhood worker for Grantley based in Dene House. When appointed, the residents of Dene House objected to the use of a flat as a base, and the worker moved to church premises among the low-rise dwellings. The salary of the neighbourhood worker, Sean Strachey, was paid by the Social Services Department, but he was responsible to the local management committee of the project which included local residents.

In fact this committee was very divided as to appropriate courses of action for the neighbourhood workers. Torn between strong advocacy of a structured Visiting service for the elderly (from the Age Concern representative not least) and keen enthusiasm for 'the social side' from the Grantley Residents' Association representatives, Sean Strachey himself tended to compromise. He himself was not attracted by the idea of a Visiting service, which he saw as abstracted and formalistic. Furthermore, his own experience of Dene House convinced him that there was a good deal less isolation, immobility and serious need for care there, and a good deal more general sociability, than the Dene House survey had suggested. His own hope was to build up a network of contacts and relationships within the neighbourhood as a whole that would survive his own departure and serve as a strong framework for informal care and for the mobilisation of formal care as and when needed. Thus although he did try to develop a Visiting service, and recruited both Helpers and Clients to it, he never saw that as the main concern. Rather,

> "we have tried to achieve a community identity of spirit which will bring down some of the barriers that prevent people caring for each other. We have done this by the very existence of the project, by saying that this is an identifiable area, by creating social activities in the area on the basis of its being an area. We would, to some extent, be succeeding whatever we did because we are making a statement about the area, saying that it is a community, reinforcing people's attitudes to it."

And from that point of view developments such as the '12 o'clock Club' (a Saturday morning film show for children), a variety of social events, and even the regular meetings and fairly wide membership of the Neighbourhood Project Committee, seemed to him to be in themselves positive steps taken.

Sean Strachey's account of the visiting service provided a nice illustration of the ideals, the confusions and the limitations of the project.

> "I didn't feel that it was what I wanted. I wanted an *egalitarian* system of helping, achieved by placing demands on the old people that are visited and asking favours of them. But the people who helped and were helped had this traditional view of voluntary work ... because I'm a social worker, a part of the welfare, and people expect to be helped, and if I introduce a person to a 'client' then they expect to help, it hasn't worked. As soon as you enter into the game of voluntary visiting you seem to be bound by conventional rules."

He made considerable efforts to blur the distinctions between Helper and Client by, for example, telling the people in need that there were others in the area who might benefit from knowing them; but, as he conceded, "I don't think I convinced them." After a year in post he had persuaded a total of five Grantley residents to become regular Visitors – hardly a formidable closing of gaps between the two sections of the community nor, if the estimates of need in the Dene House survey were at all accurate, a very substantial contribution to adequate neighbourhood care. Nevertheless, it may well have been the best that could be done in the circumstances. The combination of cross-purpose political pressure, professional indifference and community antagonisms was hardly something an inexperienced even if enthusiastic solitary worker could be expected to reduce to a coherent and effective pattern of neighbourhood care within a year.

One key figure was Joanna Graham, the local Conservative councillor for Grantley who chaired the area team and favoured community activities. The Age Concern representative thought that the idea of generating a self-sustaining network of neighbourhood care was utopian and that it would have been possible to move towards the generation of informal neighbourhood care through the construction of a formally structured Visiting service. In this respect he saw what was actually attempted as simply unrealistic. Some months after the neighbourhood worker's appointment had expired, the management committee continued to meet, the '12 o'clock Club' flourished, and another Grantley Festival, which Sean had organised, was in prospect. The Visiting scheme had collapsed, and if any of the elderly residents of Dene House were in need of visiting, the Grantley Neighbourhood project did nothing for them. On the other hand, the morale and community spirit of the Grantley area as a whole had been enhanced, as had Joanna Graham's chances of being re-elected.

5. Tattworth: the East Kinley Neighbourhood Network scheme

East Kinley is an urban area of a large Midlands city. Most of the area covered by the Network project consists of terraced houses. There is a small inter-war council estate of houses with gardens. Some of the old streets have been demolished though most have been replaced by local authority houses and bungalows. There are 1,400 houses in the area of the scheme; it is a small and compact area with a school and leisure centre nearby and a church where the East Kinley Neighbourhood and Advice Centres are based. Generally, the social character of the area can be classified as working class. It is culturally mixed, having a large population of Asian origin.

The general policy of the local authority towards voluntary organisations was to encourage them and use them. The voluntary sector was seen as a means of providing complementary and additional services rather than as a means of keeping its own statutory and financial commitments to a minimum. In addition to encouraging and grant-aiding voluntary and local organisations and groups, the department established a paid part-time Warden service to visit elderly people regularly, and provide some help with the housekeeping, shopping and so on. A Home-from-Hospital service had been implemented, jointly funded with the Health Authority, providing some free home help service for someone who has just come out of hospital.

The Neighbourhood Network schemes, which were partnership-based, had their origin in the history of statutory intervention by professional workers in East Kinley as well as in the specific contributions of certain community workers. What became the East Kinley Neighbourhood Centre began in 1973 as a Family Advice Centre, staffed by social workers helping with problems consequent upon urban redevelopment. By 1977, these problems had receded and the centre became a Neighbourhood Centre staffed by community workers. In 1978–9, workers at the centre decided to focus their efforts in small areas within East Kinley and to create Neighbourhood Network schemes as a bridge between the formal and informal sectors. Two of these schemes were studied. One was located on the Vulcans Lane estate, a predominantly white area with a large number of old people. A local social worker considered that the estate had a history of being unneighbourly, people choosing to emphasise their privacy. The other centred on Grey Street, a terraced road with a predominantly Asian population and a tendency of people to keep themselves to themselves and mix on a family basis.

The aim of the schemes was to promote neighbourliness and sociability, breaking down barriers between people, especially between ethnic groups and between young families and children and the old residents. The broader aim was to create a more caring community by keeping an eye on people, and obtaining or providing help and support for those who need it. This was done through 'contacts', local residents who distributed leaflets from the scheme to the houses they were responsible for, were therefore known to neighbours as a means of obtaining help and advice, and attended the bi-monthly group meetings run by the community worker. At these meetings a number of issues related to environment, traffic and repair of houses were discussed. A day trip and a multi-racial social evening were organised.

The Neighbourhood Network schemes were not effective, however, in arranging care of a more personal kind. Indeed, no cases of help between neighbours being provided as a result of the two schemes were found. This was not a primary objective. It appeared from the two areas studied that the scheme performed other functions. In addition to providing a means of airing 'environmental' issues and organising social events – enhancing life and creating greater community involvement – about a third of the contacts stated that they joined the scheme in order to get to "make friends and get to know people locally". This was especially true for the widows in Vulcans Lane and to some extent for the Grey Street scheme, where there was a tendency for people to keep themselves to themselves and restrict their lives to their immediate families. Some of the Grey Street contacts also referred to the need to bring white and Asian people closer together. One old woman spoke for others in Vulcans Lane when she said, "I like going to meetings, it takes you out of the house and you mix"; while another contact told us that "it does make you sit and think more – you do chat with other neighbours more than you would otherwise". In Grey Street one contact said, "I enjoy going to the meetings, it's a night out. I enjoy taking the letters around and they'll get to know me when I go and collect the forms."

In terms of their actual delivery of personal care, the achievement was small in terms of numbers helped. It could be argued that the networks provided a potential enabling basis for future care and support, but this was impossible to evaluate. As a local officer of the Social Services Department put it, "the contribution of such schemes is a drop in the ocean as far as referrals to the department are concerned". The orientation of the community workers involved did not in any case place the fostering of personal help and care by neighbours as a top priority, and the scheme's greatest effects were in breaking down some of the reserve between families and between racial groups which characterised both areas.

6. Bradbury Christian Council Care scheme

Bradbury was at one time a village, but is now part of a large conurbation in the north of England. The district has a suburban character, with housing ranging from old terraces to tower blocks, with standard housing estates preponderant. Socially it is overwhelmingly working class. In 1971 the local authority had established a Community Services Division within its new Social Services Department. It had introduced a modest Street Warden scheme, with some 20 people provided with a telephone and paid a small amount weekly to 'act as the eyes and ears of the department'. Historically there was a weak tradition of formal voluntary schemes of a directly caring kind.

The Care scheme began in 1977 as a result of an initiative from Bradbury Christian Council (BCC). It had a dual function: bringing local Christians and their churches closer together, and providing a caring service for local people in need. With advice from the Social Services department, it was decided that a Visiting service for the elderly and housebound would be initiated. Social Services were asked to provide the names of people in the area who could benefit from such a service. All those identified were visited first by the chairman of the scheme, then by the Visitor, who reported back monthly in writing to the scheme secretary. The scheme has provided a consistent and continuing Visiting service on a small scale. At the time of the study, fifteen people visited seventeen housebound or lonely old people regularly. The Visiting service Organiser said that the regularity of the visits depends on "how they find them and whether they are visiting more than one person, but it is at least once a fortnight and usually once a week if the helper is only visiting one person. It can be more than once a week at times or involve shopping and odd jobs if the visitor wants." This Visiting service continued after the old person had been transferred to a residential home or to a long-term hospital ward. Most of the helpers who undertook such long-term visiting were women; five were men. The visiting was done without any payment, even towards expenses. The visiting secretary stated that it was very difficult to find more Helpers to provide visits, but there were no problems in providing a continuing and reliable service with the Helpers that they had.

The Care scheme also fostered other activities. It held occasional social evenings and provided transport to them. It began a holiday scheme for 'deprived children'. Through the Inner City Partnership, funding was obtained for a peripatetic craft instructor for the disabled and housebound elderly. In conjunction with Age Concern, the Christian Council helped to staff a day club for the physically handicapped. It also had revived the local Disabled Association.

The number of people participating in the BCC Neighbourhood Care scheme was quite small, despite the large congregational base in the Church of England and Catholic Church in Bradbury. In part this reflected the working class character of the area and the unpaid character of the visiting work. Though all the Visitors were working class, they were marked out by their Christian commitment. The mixture of ecumenicalism and care gave participants a powerful rationale for what they did:

> a combination of normative compulsion and religious identification produce(d) strong feelings of personal satisfaction which in a sense is a kind of care of the care-givers. (DHSS Report)

As a formalised caring initiative the scheme has a firm and steady organisational basis; it also has a marked tendency to stolid stagnation. The participants had a strong and effective commitment but did not really want to expand the number of Visitors since those involved derived satisfaction from the cohesiveness of the existing group. One committee member put the matter bluntly:

> "We are not aiming to service the whole of Bradbury. We do not want to be a massive organization helping everybody. We want to work together as Christians and do a bit of good for people in need in our area. I believe we have successfully done that."

A number of observers praised the excellent liaison maintained between the Care scheme and the local Social Services Department. Each was aware of what could and could not be done. The overall policy of the Department, aware that there was not an untapped vein of volunteers in Bradbury, had moved to a recognition that to guarantee reliable help for elderly and housebound people then weekly honorarium payments, Street Wardens as

152 Organised neighbourhood care

'eyes and ears of the departments', and a new community care scheme involving a flexible range of help and negotiated payments were the crucial service layers additional to professional resources, rather than volunteers. The difficulties and limitations of Bradbury Christian Council were indicative of the state of volunteering in this urban district as a whole. Its example served to show that volunteers and such voluntary care schemes were a useful addition to, and not a substitute for, care based on different kinds of paid employment.

7. Trimdon Street Warden scheme

The studies in Trimdon, a large industrial and commercial city in the south of England, were a comparative study of independent Street Warden schemes in different parts of the city, Darnton and Bream, and Strathburn. Most of Darnton consists of old, small terraced houses and narrow streets built at the end of the last century. The streets in Bream are wider, and its housing dates from the early to middle twentieth century. Darnton is working class, Bream more mixed with some middle class enclaves. The population is well established. Strathburn is a large council housing estate on a 'greenfield' site on the outskirts ranging from tower blocks, through low-rise flats to conventional houses, which predominate. Built during the 1950s, its population numbers about 21,000. The estate is homogeneously working class, many having moved there as a result of inner city redevelopment.

The origin of the Street Warden scheme in the city lay in The Link, a centralised voluntary liaison office in the city whose central aim is to foster communication between statutory and voluntary services. By 1972 it had five full-time staff, funded by the local authority. The catalyst for the emergence of the Street Warden service was the fuel crisis of 1972, which led the Link Liaison Officer to create the first of some 40 schemes throughout the city, with 400 District Organisers and 3,000 Wardens. The Darnton and Bream scheme was set up by a local Health Visitor who was giving up full-time work to have a baby. With the support of the Liaison Officer, the Darnton and Bream Neighbourhood Service was started. In Strathburn, a 'Fish' Voluntary Care scheme, with church backing, had emerged and then faded away. In the mid-1970s, the Liaison Officer responded to local interest in creating a Street Warden scheme and helped to get one off the ground.

The schemes began as a source of emergency help, but gradually broadened their scope to neighbourly help more generally. The main categories of active help provided were visiting, shopping and collecting prescriptions. The Darnton scheme provided a limited amount of transport. The Strathburn Helpers have involved themselves in fund-raising and arranging outings for the elderly and physically handicapped, collecting blankets and coal for distribution to a few homes at Christmas and also organising lunch in their own homes for the isolated and housebound elderly. One difficulty in evaluating the scheme was that in nearly all cases the Street Wardens could be described as 'good neighbours' and were quite well known as such before the scheme existed. Much of the help provided by the scheme's volunteers could

Ten Neighbourhood Care schemes

be attributed to the informal system of care; it is highly likely it would have been given had the scheme not existed.

In each scheme, only a few volunteers undertook long-term visiting. All the District Organisers had difficulty in meeting requests for the service from the Link office. In Strathburn, visiting was largely carried on by a core of eight helpers which has remained unchanged over time and who were involved in the church-based 'Fish' scheme.

In the city, the Street Warden service was most successfully established in the solidly middle class areas in the north. Darnton and Bream was not one of these, but its scheme was strongly organised and well established. One of its main problems was a surfeit of volunteers. It appeared that 25–30 of the 80 Street Wardens had never been called upon for their services. In part this reflected the emergency, waiting, watchful warden side of the service and also to some extent the general characteristics of the area – relatively stable population, 'self sufficient' family households, and (district or city) kinship ties. In Strathburn, on the other hand, there were only a few volunteers – all well used – and a very weakly organised scheme. There were in the area none of the middle class housewives who provided the backbone of the service elsewhere (including Darnton and Bream). A large proportion of the women on the estate had paid, usually part-time, employment. There was also a higher proportion of single-parent families than in the city as a whole. Objective conditions partly accounted for the outcome.

Those involved in the scheme in Strathburn, however, themselves also preferred to have as little organisation as possible amongst themselves. There was a preference for informality in Strathburn generally. Neighbours provided each other with help in any case, and Street Wardens were seen as part of that informal network. Indeed the Street Wardens were part of that large proportion of the Strathburn population which was well established, stable and with strong local kinship ties. All of the Street Wardens except one had family or relatives, usually children, in Trimdon, nine of them in Strathburn itself. What is critical with regard to the potential for the development of Neighbourhood Care schemes was their antipathy towards formal organisation and responsibilities which they appeared to share with many of the Strathburn residents. As one of the Wardens said: "Other people around here especially the older ones do quite a lot for neighbours anyway. But they don't want to help as part of a scheme. They want to do it in their own way and time."

In the Darnton and Bream scheme, there was little involvement by the local Social Services department, other than through the central organisation. Local social workers in the area were predominantly concerned with families and children on a nearby large council estate. As one put it, "They [Street Wardens] are concerned with quality of life; we are concerned with life and limb." They operated at a higher level of need than general good neighbourliness. On the Strathburn estate there was more contact, partly because Social Services had more clients, and an office, on the estate, and partly because of a stronger community work orientation among local social workers. Although they provided some support for Wardens, however, the division of task was clear. As a local social worker put it, Street Wardens were:

> "community-based people to whom people in need of local non-professional help could be referred. They should feel that they can refer back to us for our help. They are essentially a substitute neighbour: we do not see them as taking away our responsibility. Visiting for purposes of befriending, companionship and keeping an eye on people is not basically seen as a social worker's role. If their Visiting services were not forthcoming, they would not be provided by us."

Social Services involvement, however, was sharply reduced following cuts in expenditure, loss of jobs and concentration exclusively on statutory case loads, from 1979 onwards.

The study of these two Street Warden schemes showed that resources and organisational support from some source are crucial to the development and provision of neighbourhood services. Money, facilities, equipment, administrative personnel, advice, particular skills and support all played an essential part in the not very extensive care provided by these two Trimdon schemes. If the sort of partnership between the statutory and voluntary sectors, which was the intended goal of The Link and its subsequent initiation of the Street Warden service, is to be a reality then the local authorities and their official agencies have to take the point of that lesson.

8. Parsons Green Neighbourhood Group

Parsons Green is a suburban area five miles south-east of the centre of Casterley, in East Anglia. It has a population of approximately 7,000 people. The original village developed, largely since 1945, into a suburban overspill with planned streets, avenues and cul-de-sacs. Across the High Street from the church is a new community centre which has been built to cope with the fairly recent rise in population and the increased number of young families in the area. The community centre provides a focus for a wide range of local activity including some of the functions of the Parsons Green Neighbourhood Group. The housing in the village itself is mixed, combining council with owner-occupied estates.

Interviews with residents in two parts of Parsons Green did not suggest it was a neighbourly place. None of them went regularly into the houses of their closest neighbours, and few found a strong sense of community in the area. One feature that might account for the relative withdrawal from neighbours was the relatively strong involvement with families and relatives. Whether or not the residents interviewed were representative of Parsons Green as a whole, they were certainly very unlike residents interviewed in other areas, and unlike the Helpers in the Parsons Green Neighbourhood Group in the closeness of their family ties. Over 90% of them described their families as "very close knit" (compared to 53% in our samples of residents generally and 45% of the Parsons Green Helpers). 64% of the council estate residents we interviewed and 47% of the private estate residents had relatives living in the neighbourhood and almost as many saw relatives outside their immediate family at least once a week.

Casterley clearly fell in the low profile, safety-net, statutory environment for neighbourhood care. Both in the country and city, relatively limited efforts had been made to cultivate localised service provision on an *ad hoc* basis. The statutory authorities in city and county appeared to be interested in voluntary neighbourhood action without actively developing clearly defined policies of support and development.

A striking feature of the Parsons Green Neighbourhood Group when first studied was its combination of a rather strong sense of territorial, neighbourhood, boundaries with a remarkably unrestricted sense of the boundaries of its caring activities. "The group operates in part of Parsons Green only – as far as the cross roads at the Green Man public house and part of Plumpley Road." The overall sense of the project was very highly localised. By contrast, the Group had an exceptionally open sense of its functional boundaries. There appeared to be hardly any need which the Group would not try to meet if appropriate local resources were available. Formal organisation was minimal. There was a coordinator and her deputy. Financial contributions were made by the coordinator and funds were raised by coffee mornings and jumble sales. No grant was received from Social Services.

A key role was played by the coordinator, who devoted more than thirty hours a week, seven days a week, to the Group. The point of the Group for her was not so much to organise people into doing things they would not otherwise do as to build up *connections* to enable people to help one another more effectively: "I believe that people who are doing things should keep together; the link is important, vital." The Parsons Green Neighbourhood Group implemented its aims through a Visiting service, an Information service, and a variety of specialised groups handling different problems, needs or interests. The Visiting service was the heart of the whole thing – both in terms of the value of the Group in the eyes of statutory and voluntary agencies and local residents and of what it had done for its own members. The Visiting service, overseen by the coordinator, was a basis for 'befriending'. It involved about 30 volunteers allocated on a one-to-one basis. Detailed advice on 'how to befriend' was given to the volunteers and arrangements were also made for them to discuss their visits regularly with the coordinator. Great effort was put both into assessing the needs of clients and into assigning helpers to cases appropriately and maintaining their morale thereafter. The advice and 'training' that the coordinator provided – including written notes for 'befrienders' – were of unusually high quality among the schemes studied.

In addition to an information function, the neighbourhood group ran a babysitting circle, a clinic group, open house for young and expectant mothers, a music afternoon for long-stay hospital patients, and a social and mutual support group for People On Their Own (not a success due to reluctance to be identified in this way).

Helpers in Parsons Green placed more emphasis on friendship than in any other scheme studied. This reflected a greater equality of condition among those involved. Four-fifths of Helpers were under 40 (a third under 30), many had young children themselves, a greater proportion were working class than in any other project studied, and they put in more time working for the scheme. Half of the Helpers claimed to have become friends of the people they helped. Several people interviewed as Helpers turned out to have first come into contact with the group as referrals. The distinction between the two roles was not all that sharp. In general, moreover, visiting was seen as doing something for the visitor as well as the visited. The coordinator herself acknowledged that the basis of the visiting was "reciprocity – I hate that word, but it's true. I give them things and they give things to me. I feel at home when I go to see them. We're not just dealing with straightforward referrals there." At least from the point of view of Helpers, the Group had been a way of turning care into friendships.

The success of the scheme appeared to be reflected in Parsons Green, which had a village-like atmosphere and where a community of interest had been built around the activities of the Group. The role of the coordinator was crucial, through her success in matching Helpers and Clients, and the careful guidance and friendliness fostered. The coordinator, despite the amount of work she did, was not paid, nor did she wish to be. She saw her involvement as tied closely to her more general social ideals. "I believe that people should help one another – something to do with the development of people." And perhaps more specifically: "I feel women have for many years seen themselves as second class citizens; they can be powerful in encouraging people to give themselves to the community." By the same token, the scheme was over-dependent upon her. If she withdrew, it would be likely to collapse. It owed nothing to statutory support. Social Services evinced benign interest and eschewed financial involvement.

9. Southfield Park Community Link

Southfield Park is a prosperous little community, on the very edge of the Greater London conurbation, in one of the richest counties in England. It combines proximity to London, a pleasant environment and many quasi-rural amenities. Although hard to distinguish visually or ecologically from adjacent, similar, communities, Southfield Park has a population of roughly 4,000 people residing in some 1,500 houses. Its character is set by handsomely suburban villas, which dominate both the surviving terraced houses of the old village and the streets and estates of more modest pre- and post-war development, including a spattering of council housing. It is a heterogeneous area composed of internally homogeneous streets, but the tone of the whole is somehow firmly set by the comfortable suburban respectability of streets such as Prince Edward Drive, where the residents' interviews were carried out. The Drive was broad and spacious, almost as if designed to allow broad-bodied cars to glide effortlessly past one another, and its detached houses were set within their own grounds, universally obscured by banks of ferns and high hedges – one's immediate impression is that people here must have considerable difficulty in even seeing their neighbours. A second impression was that asking residents to discuss questions of neighbourliness and neighbourhood care affronted deeply held convictions about both privacy and individualism.

The district is socially mixed in terms of class and age. Newcomers

Ten Neighbourhood Care schemes

outnumber established residents and there is considerable turnover. Old-established institutions like the parish church therefore provide an important point of reference. Community Link grew out of the church and most if not all of its original members were regular church-goers. Although many of the more recent members, particularly the younger ones, are not members of the congregation they still benefit, in terms of social integration, from being involved with a group that has such strong connections and such central standing in the 'village' as a whole.

Statutory social services in Southfield Park were a safety-net. The Assistant Social Work Director for Breezing, of which Southfield Park is one of twelve divisions, explained the position to us quite simply: "When people need help they should try first to get it from their family or neighbours, then they should try Voluntary care groups and use the Social Services only as a last resort. We act as a sort of safety-net when they cannot cope." The county used volunteers very extensively and supported voluntary organisations generously. Certain forms of need (for example, services to the blind) had been transferred *en bloc* to the voluntary sector. Joint management committees were common for other services. Coordination with existing voluntary bodies combined with encouragement and limited practical help for emerging and small local groups. The pattern was one of devolution to high-level voluntary agencies combined with discreet administrative colonisation of weaker ventures.

Community Link was launched in 1970 by the rector of the parish church. The original aim of the project was to function as a 'semi-emergency' service and volunteers were sought for such activities as driving, visiting, shopping and babysitting. To begin with local response was poor; it seems to have been difficult to convince people that their services were really needed. Accordingly, a more positive approach was sought, that would serve as a means of bringing people together and through that help to create a climate of self-help. In the revised conception of the project, the provision of caring services was set in the context of, almost treated as a pretext for, wider purposes; caring, diagnostic, supportive and preventive roles and finally and most important – involvement. This sense of ulterior purposes behind and within caring activity was one of the distinctive features of this particular project. The Helpers tend to see their participation in Community Link in terms of "caring" (rather than, say, "neighbouring" or "befriending") and as a matter of "doing things for others" (rather than, say, "making friends locally" or even "making Southfield Park more neighbourly"). And the most usual form of their participation was the provision of transport. This included lifts to hospitals and clinics, shopping, trips to day centres and taking the housebound out for a drive once a month.

The project had little in the way of formal administration. There was no central office and the effective structure of the project as seen from outside was provided by a list of telephone numbers, particular volunteers being responsible for particular tasks. It was an interesting compromise between the immediacy of a Street Warden arrangement on the one hand and a central office on the other. The arrangement was sufficiently formal to be acceptable to and manageable by the statutory authorities; on the other hand it was felt that "people are frequently diffident about asking a next-door neighbour for help, or even a friend, if the request involves much time, but are happy to do so if the request goes to a third party". The method was also felt to protect the Helpers from exploitation and, perhaps most valuably, to allow The Link "to work as a team – jobs that would be a burden to one are no problem for a group". The scheme had few financial problems, since the area and the participants were prosperous, and some who were unable to give time gave money instead.

One of the benefits of taking part in the scheme was the value of social contacts between Helpers (see chapter 10). Yet even among those most involved in the project a striking ambivalence about the whole issue of the cohesion of the neighbourhood often lay very near the surface. People used to impersonality and relative social independence could find the presence of flourishing, and intrusive, neighbourhood networks somewhat daunting, even while they themselves welcome the existence of those networks as proof that they are not living in just another anonymous suburb. In particular, one street that was almost entirely populated by young married couples with children, which provided many of the Helpers for the Community Link project and in which a network of informal help and care that blossomed into frequent social gatherings and activities had been constructed, provided us with some striking examples of just such ambivalence. Two of the Helpers we interviewed in the street said quite frankly that the constant sociability was all too much for them and that they were seriously thinking of moving on that account.

10. Easethorpe Village Help scheme

Easethorpe is a rural area near Lushing in the heart of the South Downs. The Village Help scheme covers three adjoining hamlets (Easethorpe, Pastures and Verdant) of approximately 400 houses in all. Beyond the original housing, there are a number of newer houses and bungalows where the bulk of the retired men and women who make up the Village Help scheme live. In this rural setting the community activities were centred around the church and the village hall. And the most active group of people were the middle aged to elderly couples who had moved to Easethorpe after retiring from their professions (electrical engineers, accountants, pharmacists, teachers, small businessmen). Few of the helpers were working class, despite 60 council houses in the village. The most predominant interest in common among Helpers was the church, followed by the local amenity society.

As in Boswell in Cumbria (chapter 4) there was a good deal of informal neighbourliness, though some evidence of social cleavages between three groups within the local population, the moneyed, the retired and the (working) council-house tenants. The Village Help scheme, initiated by a retired social worker, developed at first within the local amenity society. After consultation with the local Social Services Department, whose budget for volunteer schemes was very small, it was decided to form a

> rural Care Group of socially minded volunteers so as to stimulate local inhabitants into thinking about the philosophy of self-help and, perhaps more

importantly so as to establish support for the elderly, the handicapped and families at risk in the local community. (Original Village Help plan)

Set up in 1975, by 1980 it had over 40 volunteers out of 400 houses in the area. Its modest funds derive from gifts and fund raising activities of its own.

Every year each house in the village is circularised. The aim of the Easethorpe Village Help scheme is to help where necessary by visiting the aged or lonely, reading to the blind, sitting for a while with old folk or the handicapped who cannot be left, to relieve the hardworked relative, doing light handymen jobs, assisting with completion of forms and correspondence, and fetching pensions, shopping, etc. In an emergency, it provides cooking of meals, *emergency* help in the home, caring for infants, and providing transport. Referrals come from people themselves, from their neighbours and from Social Services. But the organiser was careful not to offer help if it was not asked for, nor to take on tasks which should properly be borne by Social Services. The emergency nature of the scheme was stressed. It did not include taking people out for a drive for pleasure.

The special feature of this particular scheme was that neither the Organiser nor the Helpers were quite sure where the dividing line was between the 'formal' and the 'informal' aspect of care in the areas of the scheme. As the Organiser herself told us:

> "This is supplementing, but certainly not taking over from formal voluntary groups and local authority – supplement but not usurp – or through good neighbourliness – prefer that if possible; because I think that's the natural thing ... I would love ordinary neighbourliness to take over – I think it is increasing neighbourliness in the area – many people go back to people who have been helped and been helped by them. There might be some confusion over where to draw the line between the Village Help scheme and good neighbourliness – and does it matter anyway?"

Out of the ten schemes which we studied it was not surprising that the Helpers in Easethorpe had the highest percentage of people who saw themselves as 'neighbours' (29%) when participating in the scheme.

It would seem that one way or another – either informal or formal – the village of Easethorpe and surrounding villages were covered in most 'caring' ways, though contact was weakest with the council estate. The community had done a very good job in helping to solve the problems of local transport. Financially the costs of running the scheme were negligible, so long as the volunteers were willing to give time and energy generously. It was a matter of the middle class looking after each other to a large extent.

Conclusion

This brief overview of the ten schemes highlights the characteristics of the schemes shown earlier in table 8.2 (p. 140). It provides a descriptive backdrop for the more analytical discussion of the scope, achievement and potential of Good Neighbour schemes in the two following chapters, which draw upon the Report to DHSS (1981). A full analysis of the neighbourhood care studies is presented in Abrams, Abrams, Humphrey and Snaith (forthcoming).

9 Ventures in neighbourhood care: the perspectives of Helpers and Clients

The descriptive sketches in the previous chapter of the ten localities studied provide no more than a skeleton. Now some flesh and clothes need to be put on. A balance has to be drawn between the local context and the overall picture. The first part of this chapter presents some aggregate data about Helpers and Clients in the ten schemes, derived from formal interviews in each locality by members of the Durham team. The nature of these data should be borne in mind in interpreting the results. (For fuller details and analysis, see Abrams, Abrams, Humphrey and Snaith, forthcoming).

The localities were chosen in terms of a theoretical rationale set out at the beginning of the last chapter. The aggregate data presented are compiled from ten separate samples of Helpers and of Clients, and do not represent statistical universes of each. The generalisability of this data, in a statistical sense, is severely limited. In interpreting the results, due allowance has to be made for the specific nature of the various social milieux in which the projects studied existed, and the particular range of relationships with the wider welfare environment that shaped their composition and nature. Nevertheless, even though the data have to be classed as contextual rather than representative, certain qualified generalisations, tentative inferences and statements of relationship can be advanced with some confidence.

Some 253 Helpers were interviewed in the course of the research. They were distributed as follows: Stonegate, 31; Brandling, 28; Skeffington, 27; Grantley, 5; Tattworth, 26; Bradbury, 18; Trimdon, 32; Parsons Green, 33; Southfield Park, 25; Easethorpe, 28. Seven-eights of the Helpers were women, a striking confirmation of the preponderant involvement of women in neighbourhood care (and indeed care generally). Many projects had the dual aim both of providing caring services and trying to develop a more 'neighbourly' society – and neighbouring, again, is widely understood as peculiarly the business of women rather than of men.

There was little difference between the Helpers interviewed and the general population in terms of marital status. Of the Helpers, almost two-thirds had dependent children. 5% had an adult dependant, and 30% had no dependants. Clearly the situation differed between stages of the life cycle, but age-for-age, the absence of children from the household was a factor in its own right positively associated with being a Neighbourhood Care Helper.

In age, four-fifths of Helpers were over 30 and under 70, with a clustering in the 30–39 and 50–59 age groups, which each included a quarter of all Helpers. Among the 253 Helpers, just over half were classified as middle class and just under half as working class. This distribution is contrary to findings of class participation rates in voluntary social service activity, and needs to be understood in the context of the particular case studies. Under certain circumstances, working class people evidently do participate substantially in neighbourhood care. The age ranges within the classes showed that almost twice as many Helpers in their thirties were middle class as were working class; and, conversely, an almost complete reversal of that pattern among Helpers in their fifties, of whom three-fifths were working class. Indeed working class Helpers outnumbered middle class Helpers in all age ranges except 30–39 and 70–79. An obvious further question is how far payment can be shown to influence class patterns of participation. 59 of the Helpers interviewed were paid; all of them were women; and 51 of them were working class. The few paid middle class Helpers were distributed evenly over the whole age range, whereas paid working class Helpers were strikingly concentrated in the 50–59 age category – being distinguished in that respect both from paid middle class Helpers and from unpaid working class Helpers. Looking at the relationship between age, social class and payment, two clusters in particular stood out: in the 30–39 age group, seven-eighths of the Helpers were voluntary and two-thirds were middle class, perhaps reflecting limited family commitments and limited economic pressure. In the 50–59 age group, nearly two-thirds were working class and over half were paid, reflecting a pattern of minimal family commitments but high economic pressure. There were also marked educational differences. Half of those aged 30–39 had left education at 18 or later; four-fifths of those age 50–59 had left school aged 16 or earlier.

Of the Helpers as a whole, just under half were in full-time work, and just over half were housewives, retired, unemployed or in part-time employment. Of the 142 Helpers in the latter group, half were housewives, nearly a quarter retired, 3% unemployed, and a quarter in part-time work (all but one women). A significant minority of the Helpers in full-time employment were in fact working as Helpers. This group apart, neighbourhood care presupposes a pool of Helpers who are neither in full-time work nor weighed down by family commitments.

One of the most striking regularities to emerge was in answer to a question whether the Helpers would describe themselves as religious people. This preponderance of religious attachment – in a society supposedly characterised by advanced secularisation – was the more surprising when it is appreciated that only two of the ten projects (Bradbury and Southfield Park) had any overt religious connection. Some support for the secularisation thesis could, arguably, be found in the fact that Helpers were less likely to be religious the younger they were: 43% defined themselves as religious in the age group 20–29, compared to 83% in the age group 60–69. However, this pattern could equally well be interpreted as evidence of the life cycle organisation of religiosity. And in any event the figures should not be treated as directly indicating the motivations inducing Helpers to participate in neighbourhood care. Only one quarter of the Helpers interviewed agreed that their "decision to get involved was influenced by religious considerations". Nevertheless, the data do suggest, however unselfconsciously, that background ideologies

Table 9.1 *Differences between Neighbourhood Care schemes: ranking of Helpers on different variables*

	Sex	Age	Social class	Availability	Religiosity
Stonegate	1	8	1	10	1
Brandling	7	2	7	7	5
Skeffington	1	9	4	1	8
Grantley	1	3	8	9	2
Tattworth	8	7	2	6	7
Bradbury	10	6	3	5	10
Trimdon	6	5	5	2	4
Parsons Green	4	1	6	8	3
Southfield Park	5	4	9	3	6
Easethorpe	9	10	10	4	9

Notes: Variables are ranked as follows:
Sex: 1 = most females, 10 = least females
Age: 1 = predominantly young, 10 = predominantly elderly
Social class: 1 = predominantly working class, 10 = predominantly middle class
Availability: 1 = least in full-time employment, 10 = most in full-time employment
Religiosity: 1 = fewest religious, 10 = most religious.

identifying altruism as a moral absolute are one important factor explaining participation in neighbourhood care of an organised sort.

A summary of the characteristics of the Helpers in different areas is shown in table 9.1. This permits some comparisons to be made. The ten areas all had a predominance of female Helpers. In Stonegate, Grantley and Skeffington they were all women. The only project with less than three-quarters of its Helpers female was Bradbury, where two-fifths were men. The age distribution was more varied. At one extreme, four-fifths of the Helpers in Parsons Green were under 40; in Stonegate four-fifths of the Helpers were aged 40–59; and in Easethorpe over four-fifths were over 50.

In terms of social class, most of the projects were in fact sharply polarised in class terms. Stonegate was the most extreme example – all of its Helpers being clearly working class. Similarly, East Kinley (85%), Bradbury (83%) and Skeffington (74%) were all projects dominated by working class Helpers. Trimdon and Parsons Green were the projects with the most evenly mixed class composition – the former's Helpers being mostly working class (63%) and those of the latter being mostly middle class (64%). The remaining four projects were all middle class: 71% of the Helpers in Brandling, 80% in Grantley, 84% in Southfield Park and 86% in Easethorpe.

Treating the Skeffington Helpers as volunteers, this project had no members in full-time employment and the highest proportion of housewives (70%). At the other extreme, four-fifths of the Helpers in Grantley and all the Helpers in

Table 9.2 *Number of activities undertaken by Helpers in the scheme*

Activity	Stonegate	Brandling	Skeffington	Grantley	Tattworth	Bradbury	Trimdon	Parsons Green	Southfield Park	Easethorpe
Visiting	28	6	27	3	6	17	24	23	9	8
Referrals	17	—	23	—	1	2	23	—	2	—
Transport	2	14	4	2	—	2	3	—	15	17
Odd-jobs	29	4	17	—	1	5	5	1	1	2
Child-minding	—	1	—	—	—	—	3	6	2	2
Shopping	31	2	24	2	2	4	17	9	9	4
Collecting prescriptions	30	—	19	1	1	2	11	3	1	2
Other	28	17	20	1	25	5	22	16	9	11
Total number of respondents	31	28	27	5	26	18	32	33	25	28

Note: Table based on responses to Q.22 on p. 261: 'What sort of things do people do in the scheme?' Respondents were able to give multiple responses.

Stonegate were in full-time employment, in the latter as the staff of the project itself. By contrast, Stonegate had the lowest proportion of Helpers viewing themselves as religious (52%). Grantley (with 60%) and Parsons Green (with 61%) were the only other projects which came at all close to having an equal ratio of religious to non-religious Helpers. In all the other projects sizeable majorities of the Helpers saw themselves as religious: Trimdon (69%), Brandling (71%), Southfield Park (72%), East Kinley (73%), Skeffington (78%) and Easethorpe (79%). Bradbury with 94% of its Helpers identifying themselves as religious plainly led this particular field – but hardly surprisingly since it was organised on a direct ecclesiastical basis.

The activities undertaken by Helpers in the ten schemes included visiting (mentioned 151 times), shopping (104), collecting prescriptions (70), odd jobs (65), transport (59), referrals to other organisations (56), child-minding (14), and other tasks (154). There was, however, considerable variation between different projects, as table 9.2 shows. Skeffington, Bradbury and Stonegate were all primarily visiting projects offering limited transport services and not undertaking child-minding, for example, at all. Trimdon and Parsons Green had more diversified patterns of activity – with the relatively high proportion of 18% of Helpers' activity going to child-minding in the latter. A quite different pattern is represented by Southfield Park, Easethorpe and Bradbury with their emphasis on the provision of transport; and yet another by Tattworth where the distribution of information as a basis for collective neighbourhood action was the single most prominent activity of the Helpers. These general characteristics should not be pushed too far. In Easethorpe, for example, the transport service was the focus for a large number of informal caring relationships.

The number of hours per week given to the projects by Helpers varied considerably. Half the Helpers (including those who had not been called upon) were spending on average an hour a week or less at the time of interview. Another one-quarter spent between two and five hours per week. A small minority of one in eight spent more than 25 hours per week. There was considerable variation between the projects in the number of hours worked, and one finding was that there appeared to be two kinds of Helper: the larger number of casual Helpers and a smaller core of potential semi-professionals (whether paid or not).

As well as spending very modest amounts of time on their projects, most Neighbourhood Care Helpers gave help to a very limited number of people. The distribution is shown in table 9.3. There was again considerable variation between projects. Reflecting their 'emergency' role, as many as half of the Helpers in Tattworth had not actually helped anyone and a further quarter had helped no more than one person – further evidence that this is one of those projects based on a small core of activists. Almost all of the Easethorpe Helpers gave help to two people or less a week. Parsons Green, with its stress on group activities, had eight Helpers who worked a total of 29 hours a week helping individuals, but 30% who took no part in one-to-one helping. Trimdon had four-fifths of its Helpers helping only one person but two Helpers who helped 5 people a week and one who helped 20. Southfield Park and Bradbury

Table 9.3 *Number of people helped per week*

	Number of people								
	0	1	2	3	4	5	6–10	11–20	21+
Number of Helpers	38 (15%)	110 (44%)	17 (7%)	12 (5%)	3 (1%)	8 (3%)	31 (12%)	29 (11%)	5 (2%)

were the only two fully voluntary projects that involved all their Helpers in helping at least one person a week and both of these projects had sizeable minorities helping two or more. Although most of the Helpers in Brandling fell into the usual pattern of helping one or less than one person a week, the two paid workers each helped between 11 and 20 people a week. The two projects that offered payments to their Helpers had quite different patterns – each also related to the mode of payment. The Helpers in Skeffington who received token payments mostly helped between five and ten people each week, and the fully paid Helpers of Stonegate normally helped over 11 people, 16% helping over 21 people.

Turning from the Helpers in the ten schemes to the Clients, 145 Clients were interviewed distributed as follows: Stonegate (17), Brandling (11), Skeffington (18), Grantley (7), Tattworth (9), Bradbury (18), Trimdon (19), Parsons Green (18), Southfield Park (18), and Easethorpe (10). Stonegate, Brandling, Southfield Park, Skeffington and Trimdon were all samples from a complete list of clients; in the other projects, all current clients were interviewed. It should be noted that these Clients represent only the most easily visible side of the activity of the projects, reflecting their specific visiting and domiciliary functions. Many of the projects achieved their most important results in the generation of informal relationships or of relationships in which the Helper–Client distinction was deliberately and thoroughly blurred, rendering the formal categories meaningless – all of that was ignored in the sampling of Clients. Those projects which (successfully) pursued the cultivation of community links and self-help activities and collective neighbourhood action would certainly repudiate any suggestion that their contribution to neighbourhood care could be captured at all adequately in any study involving the category 'Clients'. Nevertheless, all the projects studied organised their work around that categorisation – if only to justify their existence to and obtain grants from statutory and voluntary bodies. Neighbourhood Care projects, one could almost say, have to have 'Clients' before they can do anything else.

Four-fifths of the Clients interviewed were women. Of all Clients, one in eight were single, one in five were married, one in twelve separated or divorced, and three out of five were widows. By age, only one in eight of Clients were under 60. One-third were over the age of 80. Clients were predominantly working class, only 18% being classified as middle class. Within the working class group, more than half were unskilled manual workers or their wives. Two-thirds of the Clients were living alone. These data point clearly to who the typical Client of a Good Neighbour scheme was likely to be. Neighbourhood Care schemes are, in the main, a matter of help given by women to women; for the most part by women in families to women living on their own; and the core of Clients was made up of working class women living alone.

Unlike the Helpers, there was much less variation between projects in the characteristics of Clients. Comparisons are therefore needed only where there is deviation from the norm. Most of the schemes' Clients were female. Tattworth was the only scheme not to have a majority of female clients, largely because its Clients tended to be married couples; and Easethorpe had the highest proportion of male Clients (30%). Parsons Green had easily the 'youngest' population of Clients, with only 28% over 70 and 44% under 40. Easethorpe was the only other scheme to have less than half its Clients aged over 70 (30%). All the other projects had most of their Clients aged over 70, Bradbury (95%), Skeffington (89%), Stonegate (88%) and Grantley (86%) having almost all of their Clients in the range 70–89 and Trimdon, Tattworth and Southfield Park all having one in ten of their Clients over the age of 90.

Only three schemes had a substantial proportion of middle class Clients – Parsons Green (67%), Easethorpe (50%) and Southfield Park (28%). Bradbury (83%) and Brandling (73%) had the highest proportions of unskilled working class Clients. Parsons Green (11%) had the fewest unskilled working class Clients. Only three schemes had a majority of their Clients living with others – Easethorpe (67% not living alone), Trimdon (58%) and Parsons Green (53%). All the schemes had Clients living in solitary situations, especially Southfield Park (86%) and Bradbury, Stonegate and Brandling who all had between two-thirds and four-fifths of their Clients living alone. It is hardly surprising that all of the Clients in the Skeffington scheme lived alone as it was organised from the Social Services Department who allocated Clients to the scheme for that reason.

An attempt was made to find out what social contacts Clients had with children, other relatives, neighbours and friends. The information related only to contacts, not the extent of care or help provided, and was important in assessing the degree of social isolation of a Client, and hence the value to her or him of Good Neighbour visiting. Of the 99 Clients who had children not living with them, 43 were "living nearby". Only 4 of those 99 Clients did not have any contact with them at all and 77 Clients said that they saw their children regularly. However, there were 38 Clients who lived alone and either did not have children or never saw them and a further 2 Clients in the same situation who only rarely saw them. Furthermore, only about half of the Clients aged over 50 saw their children regularly, and of the 25 clients in their seventies who never saw or did not have any children 22 lived alone. 11 of the 15 Clients in their 80s who did not have any children lived on their own. 'Childlessness', whether actual or in effect, was in itself a crucial source of isolation and of the resulting need for neighbourhood care.

The extended family is often said to play an important role in providing informal care. 72 of our Clients (50%) had some contact with their relatives while 53 (37%) had relatives living nearby. 40 Clients (28%) saw their relatives regularly and two-thirds of those 40 Clients were either in their seventies (13 Clients) or their eighties (12 Clients). However, 31 Clients between 70 and 79 and 21 Clients between 80 and 89 never saw relatives, and 23 of the former and 13 of the latter age range lived on their own. 15 Clients (9%) lived completely without any kind of family contact or support, living on their own and never seeing children or relatives. 11 of these Clients were in their seventies, and 3 in their eighties.

The measure of contact with neighbours was whether neighbours called to see the Client, rather than just passing the time of day in the street. Of the 15 Clients without family contact, 8 were not called on either by neighbours. Although 106 Clients (73%) said that they had "friendly relations" with their neighbours, half of the Clients reported that their neighbours did not call on them, and of these two-fifths lived on their own. Broken down by age, 4 of the 9 Clients in their sixties whose neighbours did not call on them lived alone, as did 18 of the 23 Clients in their seventies, 7 of 11 in their eighties and 1 of the 3 in their nineties. Isolation appeared in many ways to be a self-aggravating social condition.

This was confirmed by answers to a question about friends. Only 28 Clients (19%) said that they saw a friend or friends regularly. Of the 79 Clients (54%) who did not see their friends, 13 were in their sixties, 28 in their seventies, 26 in their eighties and 5 in their nineties. And, here again, the cumulative isolation was maintained.

Taken together, these data suggest that in the ten localities, the world of the Clients of Neighbourhood Care was not at all a world of densely woven informal relationships with Neighbourhood Care Helpers simply added on to social contact with family, friends and neighbours. Though the most significant contacts were with other members of the family, it was distinctively a world of significant isolation from informal care.

Differences between projects were examined by constituting an 'isolation score'. This is shown in table 9.4. The method of construction for the ranking of schemes was to allocate scores for different answers to each question – 1 point for seeing a child, relative, neighbour or friend rarely, 2 points for occasionally and 3 points for regularly. The sum of these scores was then divided by the total number of Clients for that scheme leaving the scheme's mean score. The schemes were then ranked from 1 (the highest mean and hence the least isolated) to 20 (the lowest mean and therefore the most isolated). Friends were omitted, since only a minority had contact with them.

One of the main impressions left by the table is of the inconsistencies between different forms of contact and isolation; thus Grantley's Clients had the lowest score for contact with their children and the second highest score for contact with their relatives and their neighbours. Stonegate, Parsons Green, Southfield Park and Skeffington all scored high on some measures of isolation and low on others. The areas with the highest isolation scores, Skeffington, Brandling, Bradbury and Stonegate, included two solidly working class areas where informal ties were traditionally strong, but apparently no longer effective. Great variability was the norm. Very few schemes had Clients who had equally frequent contact with a range of informal contacts.

Table 9.4 *Isolation scores*

	Social contact with:			Aggregate score	Overall rank
	Children	Relatives	Neighbours		
Stonegate	4	10	6	20	7
Brandling	8	4	10	22	10
Skeffington	9	3	9	21	8
Grantley	10	2	2	14	3
Tattworth	1	6	5	12	2
Bradbury	6	7	8	21	8
Trimdon	7	8	4	19	6
Parsons Green	2	5	7	14	3
Southfield Park	3	9	3	15	5
Easethorpe	5	1	1	7	1

Note: For explanation of scores, see text.
Overall rank: 10 = most isolated; 1 = least isolated.

The Durham team also interviewed a sample of Residents in the seven of the ten areas not in receipt of care or assistance from Good Neighbour schemes. The results of these interviews, since they bear less directly on the main theme, are not reported here but may be studied in the full report (Report to DHSS 1981, pp. 253–75; Abrams, Abrams, Humphrey and Snaith, forthcoming). Some results incorporating data for residents are referred to later in this chapter and in the next chapter.

Help and care may come from a number of directions. Apart from formal agencies, three primary groups are of overriding importance: the family (including the extended family), friends and neighbours. As noted earlier, the Durham team was interested in the extent to which such primary groups had been broken down by the processes of differentiation and bureaucratisation characteristic of modern industrial society. To find out how reliant people were on the family, friends and neighbours, compared to statutory sources of help, all those Residents and Helpers interviewed in the ten areas were asked: "If you were ill, housebound or in need of help for some other reason, have you got three people who you could turn to for help?" Out of 426 respondents, only 19 (4%) said they could not think of three people they could turn to. Not all respondents named three people (the mean number mentioned was 1.9 people).

Of the persons named, 339 were family members, 231 were neighbours, 172 were friends, 7 were members of their church, 7 volunteers or voluntary organisation members, 6 the person's doctor and 5 people from Social Services. The family was still seen as the most immediate source of help for the vast majority of respondents. Moreover, one-quarter said that all three people who they could turn to for help were family members. Another quarter mentioned a combination of family and friends or family and neighbours. Some 159 respondents said that they would count on their family even though they did not live in the area. Interview responses suggested that there were no limits on the type of help that could be sought from the family; from social visiting, house maintenance and decorating, odd jobs and errands to financial matters and help in times of personal crisis.

Nevertheless, the figures for neighbours and friends showed how important these groups also were to substantial numbers of respondents. 21 respondents said that all their three people were neighbours; only 9 people said they would turn only to friends. The number of respondents mentioning neighbours was particularly high and indicated a reliance on neighbours over and above casual acquaintance. Only 47 respondents (11%) divided their three people equally between family, friends and neighbours. This reinforces the earlier point that primary groups and the 'informal sector' is not a seamless web but rather a fractured mosaic. Different people rely on particular groups to varying extents.

The interviews with Residents and Helpers probed further into what people thought appropriate to and sought from relationships with their neighbours. One question touched on the moral imperatives of neighbouring: 'Do you think there are any sorts of help for which people *ought* to be able to count on their neighbours?' Over four-fifths replied that they did. The sorts of help that were mentioned fall almost exclusively into the category of things that need quick attention, half referring to tasks of a simple nature – "Borrowing things", "Shopping and paying bills for people who are ill", "Babysitting and popping in and helping out", "If need someone in a desperate hurry, being friendly with neighbours can turn to them quickly, it is a good thing", "Only odd messages and the like" – and half specifying emergency help – "illness, death", "If ill, run for doctor", "In an emergency – like at the moment my neighbours gave my daughter her dinner yesterday when I cut my finger and had to go to the hospital". One-fifth mentioned both the simple service type of task and the provision of emergency help. One in ten of the respondents included sentiments concerning "keeping an eye on those at risk" and one in seven specified the elderly as a group that neighbours should especially look after.

The next question asked sought to explore the opposite end of the spectrum: what people did not want their neighbours to be involved in. The question was "Do you think there are any sorts of help for which people *should not* turn to their neighbours?" 60% said that there were, as against 31% who thought there were not. The answers clearly showed that people wanted their neighbours to be kept at a social distance and would not like relationships to develop into anything too intimate. Two-fifths mentioned that financial concerns should be excluded from the concern of their neighbours. Neighbourly relations were still very much based on a sort of bartering system where goods and services were exchanged rather than bought and sold. It was quite permissible to borrow a cup of sugar but not the price of one. One in seven said that personal matters should not be shared with neighbours and one in ten mentioned matrimonial concerns as being private. Nearly all of those respondents added that these were strictly a family affair.

Two areas emerged from the interview data as the particular preserve of neighbours. Firstly there were those needs that arose quickly, required quick alleviation and were not dependent upon specific technical occupational skills. A short list from many similar replies exemplified the sort of tasks that fall into this category: "We just borrow from each other when we're short", "We do gardens, post letters, collect papers – that sort of thing"; "Babysitting, lending tools, helping dig out drains, transport to the supermarket", "We knit for the neighbours and lend them tools, keep an eye on old people and the wife visits them for company"; "We have a neighbour's child from school when she has to work in the afternoons"; "We take in the post and keep a key when they're not there – sometimes take the milk in"; "I always have a key for next door and opposite when they go away on holiday – I go in to see if the houseplants are alright." These tasks were not only simple but also sufficiently urgent that neighbours were turned to for help out of desperation due to speed of reaction rather than appropriateness. These sorts of emergencies, where time is of the essence, can range from the comparatively trivial such as "if it's raining we take in the washing" to catastrophes, an example being "I helped my neighbour next door when her husband died and the woman next door when she was ill." Form and Nosow (1958) have estimated that as high as 75% of people connected with major natural disasters may be rescued during the first few hours by neighbours or kin living nearby.

The second category of neighbourly activities derived from territoriality. Services provided both publicly and privately affect all the residents of an area. Similarly local political and social issues were primarily of concern to people living in the relevant neighbourhood. The following extracts show the diversity of needs that were important to people living in close proximity with each other: "We pay their rents"; "I belong to the Tenants' Association"; "I started the 'village centre' – hired a hall once a week and grannies played with the kids whilst mothers chatted amongst themselves"; "I'm trying to get a petition up about the lorries going down this road – they go too fast and it's too narrow. It's dangerous and the houses are taking a constant hammering with all the shaking that goes on."

The two kinds of help are not mutually exclusive. An obvious case of overlap was when people look after their neighbours' houses when they are away. Many respondents said that they involved themselves in doing this, some mentioning specific tasks such as "watering the plants" and "looking after the pets" whereas others were plainly protecting property by "keeping an eye on the place" and "switching a light on at night and closing the curtains to look as though they're at home". Indeed the common protection of property was a major type of neighbourly help amongst middle class respondents.

In a few cases, involvement went further, with people offering long-term and continuous care to their neighbours. The following quotes speak for themselves, "I look on my neighbour as a daughter . . . and she probably thinks of me as a mother"; "We have helped an elderly couple next door for years – we make sure they're alright. We pay their milk bill and exchange papers and I go shopping for them. My husband also put a bell in their house that rings in our place which they can use if ever they need us", and "We go and visit an old

Ventures in neighbourhood care

lady in Coronation Street – she lives in one of the old houses opposite the school." These people had lived in their area for a considerable period of time, and were the exceptions to the general rule of behaviour between next-door neighbours.

The replies quoted, with these exceptions, pointed to a dividing line between what was, and was not, admissible within neighbourly as opposed to kin or friendship relations. In one sense, neighbourly relations may be defined as living in close geographical proximity without the level of personal attachment characteristic of friendship. Even neighbours on unfriendly terms would be likely to help each other out in emergencies or with local problems of a communal nature. But the long-term, arduous, time-consuming work of continuous care of an elderly or disabled person would be most unlikely to be undertaken by a neighbour unless there was added to neighbourliness some additional element such as friendship. These issues are of considerable relevance to policies to promote community care through neighbourliness. To what extent is it realistic to hope that neighbours will become something like friends or surrogate members of a family and therefore adopt a more catholic attitude towards the areas of help that they are willing to undertake?

Friends tend to be the weakest structurally of all primary group ties in that they lack the permanence of the family and the frequent face to face contact of neighbours. This is particularly true when geographical mobility separates friendship groups. The relative weakness of friendship ties was born out in the interview data. With a few notable exceptions, people regarded the family as the primary source of help with personal and matrimonial problems. Furthermore, the absence of family need not mean that friends adopted the functions normally associated with the family. An elderly man who had no family was interviewed. He would not ask his lifelong friend to help him with a complicated financial problem (that did not involve the borrowing of money) because he thought "that it wasn't proper to burden him with problems like this".

Included in the interview schedule for Residents were questions which asked how respondents envisaged the alleviation of their own needs, and how they thought the needs of neighbours, in a hypothetical situation, should be met. These were designed to tap people's perception about the appropriate sources of help from different primary groups. In relation to their own needs, respondents were asked:

(1) "Suppose that you had to go away unexpectedly for a day or two and needed someone to keep an eye on a sick member of the family"; with the suffix common to all these three questions of "To whom would you be able to turn to for help or do you think that you would have to cope as best you could on your own?"
(2) "Suppose you were laid up for a couple of weeks after an operation and needed help with meals, shopping, cleaning and so on." (suffix)
(3) "Suppose you were really ill and bedridden for a long time with some chronic illness and needed a lot of looking after." (suffix)

The pattern of responses is shown in table 9.5 and was quite striking. Although respondents were invited to name as many as they wished of self/family and

Table 9.5 *Sources of help to meet hypothetical needs of the respondent*

	Family	Friends	Neighbours	Social Services
Keep eye on sick member of family	73%	7%	18%	1%
Needed help for couple of weeks	79%	9%	20%	7%
Needed lot of looking after for long time	75%	6%	7%	30%

Note: Rows do not total 100% because of multiple responses.

relatives/friends/neighbours/Social Services/volunteers or voluntary organisation/church/other, the predominance of family was quite overriding. Whether looking for short- or medium-term emergency help or for longer-term help, people would look to their family in preference to anyone else. This varied somewhat according to proximity, but family was still preeminent for those whose family did not live nearby.

Friends appear to play an extremely marginal role. Neighbours were somewhat more important but the scores for both categories were surprisingly low considering the high percentages they had both obtained in the earlier general question quoted above (p. 168). It is clear that although people think of neighbours and friends as people that they can turn to in a general sense, their functional roles in specific helping circumstances are almost insignificant in comparison to the importance of the family.

In relation to the needs of a hypothetical neighbour, respondents were asked:

(4) "Suppose you learned that one of your neighbours was ill and there was no one in the house to look after things for a couple of days"; suffixed by "Who do you think should help or do you think that they should cope as best they could on their own?"

(5) "Suppose you learned that a neighbour had a chronic illness and needed company from time to time." (suffix)

(6) "Suppose you learned that a neighbour was bedridden and needed regular help with cooking and odd jobs." (suffix)

The range of responses was the same as for the previous questions, with "on own" added. The pattern of response is shown in table 9.6. It was clear that people had very different views about how their own needs could be met as opposed to how their neighbour's needs should be met. The perceived importance of the role of neighbours as well as the family, friends and Social Services was apparent. The 'self' category showed that most respondents were at least in principle willing to help their neighbours, particularly with short-term or social needs.

The remarkable disparity between how little the interviewees felt their neighbours *could* do for them themselves (table 9.5) and what they felt neighbours *should* do for each other (table 9.6) can be explained in two ways. Firstly, there has been much sociological work that shows that people do not always do what they say they will do. The differential that exists between

Table 9.6 *Sources of help to meet hypothetical needs of the respondent's neighbour*

	Self	Family	Friends	Neighbours	Social Services
Ill and look after things for couple days	77%	55%	5%	66%	13%
Needed company from time to time	77%	66%	15%	71%	7%
Bedridden, need regular help, cooking, odd jobs	40%	56%	7%	29%	69%

Note: Rows do not total 100% because of multiple responses.

norms and their practical applications is well known. However, this explanation is inadequate to explain such drastic differences between the two sets of answers. A more fruitful explanation would be that the disparity occurred because informal networks by means of which needs could be identified and alleviation sought (and a willingness to help be translated into practical neighbourly activities) had either disintegrated or were never there in the first place.

The role of the Social Services was also perceived to be considerably more applicable to neighbours than to respondents themselves, particularly in relation to long-term help. That the state should accept responsibility for that type of need, typically the sorts of work done by the domiciliary services, did not seem to be widely questioned. However, that acceptance was rooted in a general awareness that some people do need to receive help from the state, rather than the realisation that the respondent might be in that situation herself. It is however a relevant finding in relation to the question of where people think social care for others should come from.

The categories 'church' and 'volunteers or voluntary organisations' do not appear in tables 9.5 and 9.6 because they were so rarely mentioned by respondents. This finding was particularly poignant, and significant, in relation to the study of Good Neighbour schemes. After excluding Stonegate because it was fully paid, half of the respondents in the Residents' sample said that they had heard of the Good Neighbour scheme in question and therefore would presumably have the concept of volunteers and voluntary organisations somewhere within their terms of reference. Yet *not one* respondent thought that they themselves would resort to them when in need. Only one or two thought, in relation to the needs of neighbours, that volunteers would be suitable for most of the tasks, and a handful said that they could help their neighbours if they needed company from time to time. It seemed that the idea of alleviating either one's own or other's needs by turning to volunteers or voluntary organisations simply did not occur to people. This finding has critical policy implications. No matter how efficient a Neighbourhood Care scheme is in terms of the delivery of care, problems still have to be identified before the process can begin. In the study of Good Neighbour schemes nationally (Abrams *et al.* 1981a), out of the 483 schemes who admitted that they had major problems, 15% said that one of these problems was a shortage of clients. In this study, one quarter of the Helpers interviewed thought that a problem for their scheme was "the degree of willingness of people in need of help to seek or accept it". Most schemes relied heavily on referrals from social workers, doctors, health visitors and other professionals, for their clients. Although the schemes must serve a useful function in supplementing the work of these professionals, their prime aim is arguably to recruit clients directly from their localities. The impact of services provided by Neighbourhood Care schemes depends not only on considerable public awareness of their aims but also on local residents accepting the scheme's role as a legitimate source of care. These results suggest that volunteers and their organisations have hardly started along their journey for popular recognition and acceptance of their work.

Class differences were also apparent in the responses to both sets of questions. In the set about the respondents' own needs, there was little difference about family help between professional and managerial respondents on the one hand and semi- and unskilled manual workers on the other. There was a marked difference in the propensity to look to neighbours (and to a less extent friends), those in the highest social classes being much more willing to contemplate them as a source of aid. A third to half of respondents would consider this, compared to less than one-fifth among the manual workers, if help was needed for a couple of weeks. This lack of informal help among the semi- and unskilled working class was not counteracted by a willingness to turn instead to the Social Services. The pattern of care amongst these two groups was clearly characterised by a relatively strong reliance on family with weak functional lines with neighbours and friends.

In the set of questions about meeting a neighbour's needs, there was greater reliance upon both friends and neighbours among middle class respondents. The most striking difference, however, was in respect of the unskilled working class group, less than half of whom thought the family would be a source of help. Friends were seen as of negligible importance. Neighbours were thought as important as the family if one were ill or needed company, Social Services more important than the family if one were bedridden. These findings suggest the need for further exploration of the failings of the family as a source of support for the most disadvantaged, a hint of which was picked up in the Street Study of Fielding Close in chapter 4.

A different perspective was provided by a question asked of the sample of Clients, what was their most important social contact. One-third named their children (a majority mentioning their daughter), one in seven mentioned other relatives, one in seven the home help, one in ten a visitor from the Good Neighbour scheme being studied, another one in ten a next-door neighbour, and one in twenty a friend. This modifies slightly the picture provided by the Residents' sample. Those who named the home help tended to be those without family or relatives, or who saw them only rarely, although a few who saw their children regularly still regarded their home help as the most important social contact. Bearing in mind that just over half the Clients interviewed were receiving a visit from a volunteer, the one in ten who mentioned the project visitor rises to one in five in cases where voluntary visiting was taking place. This suggests that such volunteers may be effective in combating isolation by visiting and socialising, even if the general perception (in the Residents' sample) was that this was not a very salient form of help.

The social context of who helps and why

The results of the Helpers' survey show clearly that determining factors in who became involved in Neighbourhood Care schemes were gender, social class, values and availability. Women completely dominated the schemes, becoming involved in them to the extent permitted by responsibilities in the home, rearing children and in employment. If the care scheme where the helpers were full-time employees of the local authority is excluded, then the availability of women through their non-entry into the labour market was of paramount importance: two-thirds of the remaining volunteers were not in full-time employment, a third of those being housewives and only a quarter of them being in part-time work. To a considerable extent our overall findings underestimate the general predominance of middle class helpers in local care-based schemes, a result out of line with that of other research such as the National Opinion Poll (NOP) survey commissioned by the Wolfenden Committee. This was because the case study schemes were not chosen as a random sample of all schemes, but on the basis of analytical relevance which included an emphasis on working class settings. Nevertheless if we compare the schemes where some form of payment was given to helpers (full-time wage and token payment) with those where helpers received no payment, the former schemes were made up of helpers who were 87% working class while those in the latter group comprised 56% middle class helpers. The availability of time derived from relative affluence was significant.

Personal values also clearly played a determinant part. Two-thirds of Helpers described themselves as 'religious' and half of them were active members of organised religions. However, only a quarter of them stated that they had become involved in schemes because of religious convictions as such. On the other hand two-fifths of all Helpers said that "general ideals about society" were consciously part of the reasons for their getting involved. While middle class and working class Helpers were almost identical in their positive response to being 'religious', two-thirds of middle class Helpers were members of an organised religion compared to only two-fifths of the working class. Almost twice as many middle class as working class Helpers said that general ideals were involved in their taking part in their local scheme (56% compared with 29%), working class Helpers not having knowingly formalised their participation in this way.

The factors predisposing to participation in Neighbourhood Care schemes were interconnected. They found a specific expression in the availability of women for local care in terms of their free time, family and home commitments, need to take paid employment or get involved in the community and their particular socialisation.

The distinction between 'traditional' and 'modern' neighbouring, discussed in chapter 5, was explored by comparing Helpers and Residents in terms of a number of characteristics. The difference between them was found not so much in amount of contact with family and neighbours as in the quality, intensity and, particularly, the degrees of commitment involved. The overall different quality of Helpers' neighbouring was indicated by their greater likelihood to develop very close relationships with their immediate neighbours. Participants in local care schemes were also highly likely to be involved in intensive as well as extensive informal neighbourly help often of a highly committed and concerned kind, such as the daily care of an old person who was ill, or regularly calling on someone who was isolated. In contrast the overall tendency of Residents was to be involved with neighbours on the basis of emergency, convenience, necessity or service exchange, all within a framework of politeness and acknowledgement of varying degrees of pleasantness. The only clear exception was mothers with young children who were not in the labour market. Elsewhere the general trend was that of casual or more calculated helping without serious involvement. Recurrent typical examples were borrowing of tools, keeping an eye on the house, taking in parcels or paying the rent for households where husband and wife both went out to work, mutual helping with car repairs or home improvements, use of telephone when someone was taken ill and assistance when someone was locked out or away from home. Of the Residents, 72% said that people "keep themselves to themselves" in their area, a further 15% said this was partly the case. When asked their perception of the general level of neighbourliness only 9% stated their neighbourhood was "very neighbourly". For the great majority of residents the general state of neighbouring in which they lived was distinctively "modern". People were prepared to be helpful but without getting too involved or too close. Emotional and social distance was a desired state of affairs in this privatised world, centred around the nuclear family, where close kin-based help is likely to be the preferred choice in times of need.

Many Helpers emerged as part of a tenuous, beleaguered and ambiguous world, a kind of traditional survival within the modern social universe. Nearly a third of participants stated that it was only partly true that people "kept themselves to themselves" in their local area, though half of them said this was the case without qualification, and third of Helpers described their neighbourhood as "very neighbourly". For most, this more positive perception of local neighbouring reflected their own neighbourly niche. Yet the broad trend was confirmed: most of the Neighbourhood Care scheme participants were aware of the modern nature of the neighbourly context of their local area generally. A substantial number of others were more discriminating in their views but the contrast with the Residents' markedly less positive opinions of neighbouring serves to underline these broad differences. Though there was no significant difference in how long each group had lived in their area, in answer to a question about their desire to remain in the area, four-fifths of Helpers said they would choose to stay in the area but only half of the Residents' sample said they would do so. Those taking part in schemes were much more likely to identify with the traditional characteristics of being settled, or "having roots", while non-participants identified much more with the modern pattern of being geographically mobile or having aspirations to be so.

The most striking difference between Helpers and Residents concerned membership of voluntary organisations and groups. While only a small minority of Residents reported taking part in formal voluntary groups, 60% of those taking part in organised Neighbourhood Care had *other* voluntary commitments. These included the Womens' Institute, Townswomens' Guild, Save the Children Fund, and Rotary Club, as well as church-based groups such as the Brownies/Guides, Mothers' Union or Union of Catholic Mothers. The difference was particularly marked in the working class. Half of working class Helpers had such membership, compared to 10% of working class Residents. Such high voluntary involvement should be seen in relation to the argument developed above, that participants followed social patterns more akin to the traditional neighbourly communities. Helpers had higher representation in both informal and formal systems of care and support. This immediately poses the question whether the Neighbourhood Care schemes simply recruited those who were already 'good neighbours' and/or 'volunteers'.

When class differences between Helpers and Residents were examined more closely, the extent to which the picture of traditional neighbourliness needed to be modified was clear. Working class Helpers were more different from working class Residents than their middle class counterparts. In comparison with working class participants, middle class participants reported a greater likelihood to take part in formal organisations and markedly greater formalised reasons for joining the scheme, but somewhat paradoxically, in view of the class basis of the traditional neighbourly community, more of them categorised their local areas as being "very neighbourly".

A striking underlying feature of these patterns was that working class areas were more likely to be 'social deserts' in terms of neighbourliness. Both working class Helpers and Residents were markedly more likely to describe their locality as one where people kept themselves to themselves; no less than three-quarters of working class Helpers said this was the case. Within that social world, working class Helpers tended to be 'odd' in two apparently contradictory ways, one more 'ideal typically' working class and the other more middle class. They were less privatised and more *informally* involved with neighbours as well as family and kin who did not live with them. But they also had markedly more involvement in *formal* voluntary organisations. Although sharing a positive view of their district (two-thirds believed they had a lot in common with others in the area), they also were involved in modern, organised, neighbourhoodism. This has implications for recruitment to Neighbourhood Care schemes. To what extent are they tending to recruit or draw in people who are already key informal or formal carers? If they are, the result could be the formalisation of what is already going on rather than the mobilisation of new Helpers and the generation of additional local help and support.

With middle class respondents, participation in formal voluntary association activity was much higher, as one would expect from other studies, and there was not a marked difference between Helpers and Residents in the proportion (two-thirds compared to half) who were involved. What requires explanation is why some middle class people become involved in Neighbourhood Care type voluntary activity and others do not.

One possible explanation may be in terms of the involvement of middle class women in informal local helping networks. Only one-third of the middle class Helpers had kin living in their locality. Given the dominance of housewives and young mothers in the middle class group of Helpers, this may explain their more neighbourly characteristics compared to Residents. Middle class women with the time to get involved and/or the need to do something worthwhile, or the need to overcome the isolation of bringing up children with little or no outside family support, may have been a vital social basis for the mobilisation of Neighbourhood Care volunteers in a social context which facilitated such formal organisational involvement, given the traditional middle class preference for privatisation and varying degrees of formality in relation to people living in their locality. This relates to one problem found in some middle class areas of a surplus of Helpers over Clients, and the suggestion (cf. Abrams *et al.* 1981a) that Neighbourhood Care schemes can become instruments for the mutual aid and support of the Helpers themselves.

The comparison of social classes suggests an inversion of the traditional sociological stereotypes of the close-knit, highly integrated working class community and the atomised, privatised domestic world of the middle classes. The study provides evidence of the demise of traditional neighbourly working class communities and of increasing privatisation. It is now in working class neighbourhoods that people are more likely to keep themselves to themselves. This reflects social changes resulting from urban redevelopment and rehousing, women entering the labour force to a greater extent, and a more home-centred pattern of leisure. There is more evidence of organised neighbourliness in middle class areas, albeit somewhat more formalised but nevertheless, particularly among those with young children and other housewives, a potentially important source of social contact. From a policy point of view, establishing projects in such areas poses less of a problem. It is working class localities, where modern conditions of neighbouring prevail, and where there is a weak tradition of formal voluntary care organisation, which present the main challenge to Neighbourhood Care mobilisation.

To conclude this discussion, a little more attention will be paid to variations between the ten schemes, particularly in respect of participation in other voluntary organisations and whether Helpers were paid or unpaid. One revealing question asked of Helpers was whether they had encountered obstacles to becoming involved in their scheme. The responses are shown in table 9.7. The schemes with the fewest obstacles were those using paid Helpers, while those with the higher obstacle score were schemes based on traditional voluntary service delivery. This is consonant with the finding that the key difference between paid and unpaid Helpers was in their relative experience of and affinity with formal organisations and formal normative justifications for joining. A similar pattern was found when comparing Helpers

Table 9.7 *Were there any obstacles to your becoming involved?*

	Yes %		Yes %
Stonegate	10	Brandling	29
Skeffington	7	Bradbury	22
Tattworth	11.5	Trimdon	25
Parsons Green	15	Southfield Park	44
Easethorpe	29		

Table 9.8 *Membership of other voluntary organisations*

	Yes %		Yes %
Stonegate	26	Brandling	75
Skeffington	44	Bradbury	78
Tattworth	50	Trimdon	84
Parsons Green	33	Southfield Park	84
Easethorpe	79		

Table 9.9 *Proportion of Helpers who had other voluntary group membership, by social class and payment*

	Social class	
	Middle class	Working class
Paid Helpers	71%	29%
Unpaid Helpers	69%	66%

on different schemes in terms of their membership of other voluntary organisations. This is shown in table 9.8. The gradient in part reflects the class composition of scheme Helpers, but also whether they were paid or not. The importance of payment and its influence upon scheme Helpers is shown in table 9.9. The class difference overall between middle and working class concealed the fact that middle class paid Helpers were as likely as unpaid Helpers to belong to other voluntary organisations; that working class unpaid Helpers were scarcely less likely than their middle class counterparts to belong; but that working class paid Helpers were very significantly less likely to belong to other voluntary organisations. The involvement of unpaid working class Helpers was partly accounted for by church membership, approximating more closely to the conventional middle class pattern. The general middle class preference for formal local and voluntary care was not evident among paid working class Helpers.

The contrast can be highlighted by comparing two schemes, Southfield Park and Stonegate. Southfield Park was a conventional Voluntary Care scheme located in the most affluent area of the ten studied. Its participants were strong on religious identification and participation, and the project in which general ideals were the strongest influence of any. Membership of other voluntary organisations was the highest of any project. Half the women participating were housewives, and fewer than 1 in 20 had part-time work. Stonegate, on the other hand, was an area where paid employment was a standard and necessary activity for adult women as well as men, unlike middle class Southfield Park; only 1 in 8 Residents interviewed were housewives, 6 out of 10 respondents were in full-time jobs of a generally working class nature with a further 1 in 10 in part-time work, statistics with a crucial bearing on the availability of a pool of 'volunteers'. Yet 1 in 10 of the Stonegate Residents were retired, potentially at least in need of neighbourhood care.

It was not surprising that such a homogeneously working class area lacked a cultural tradition of formal voluntary groups and these were not the (quite widespread) middle class choices of Southfield Park. They were an Old Peoples' Club committee at the community centre, the Young Women's Christian Association (YWCA) and a Tenants' Group, all with an emphasis on mutuality and informality rather than voluntary care. And most of the extra 'voluntary' activity of the Helpers turned out on closer inspection to be social and working men's clubs! The Stonegate scheme combined informal caring and caring based on paid work. Stonegate's paid carers were all middle aged and over, mostly from old inner city areas so that they had experienced traditional neighbourliness while in general they had felt that being a Warden or a home help was something they knew about, could do and would like, but payment was necessary to generate and harness their neighbourly talents because of their need to take a job. Without care as paid work the breadth, depth and direction of help and support to the most needy would have been lost.

The participation of local women in the Warden scheme was not normatively based in a formal or conscious way. These Helpers had the lowest incidence of religious participation of any group and the lowest level of influence of 'general ideals' on their joining the care scheme. Neighbourhood care as paid work of 'ordinary' local women 'fitted' this social setting and was accepted by Clients and Residents. For the Wardens it was the extension of a way of life, of cultural experiences and traditions and of the need for paid work. They wanted a job and cared about people, the wage was important as was the job's worthwhile nature and the personal competence they felt, which in turn was related to their social class, gender and availability in a particular social and cultural setting with definite traditions and contemporary interrelations of informal and formal bases of help, advice and support.

So to conclude: Who helps? – generally local women. Answering the question Why is not so straightforward. Religiously-based altruism and normative obligation or duty are minority feelings, reciprocity being the vital link between schemes and actual or potential Helpers. To put the matter bluntly, unless people do or feel they will get something out of their involvement they will not continue for long or not join at all. The return could be a payment or be a specific kind of help, which was obviously the case where the Neighbourhood scheme was based on mutual aid as in Parsons Green; or it could be more general, taking the form of, for example, emotional satisfaction from doing one's duty, putting others first, as in voluntary service schemes like Bradbury and Trimdon, or also the diverse and diffused possibilities of more 'politically' or community development orientated projects as in Tattworth. What a scheme has to offer and the return it promises is only one determinant of who participates. This is also facilitated or constricted by availability and cultural tradition and in turn related to social class, gender and the particular local setting as a way of life and a social milieu. A fuller analysis of the material in this chapter is presented in Abrams, Abrams, Humphrey and Snaith (forthcoming).

10 Limitations of neighbourhood care

The study of neighbourhood care in the two preceding chapters was based upon a series of comparisons. The heart of the matter was a three-way comparison between types of social setting, types of welfare environment and types of project organisation (cf. table 8.2, p. 140). The use of such a framework was intended to generate some distinct types or patterns of neighbourhood care, each characterised by distinct forms of action, limitations, prospects of success and styles of caring. In this chapter, particular attention is paid to the quality of the work and relationships generated by these different types and the limitations associated with each type.

In the scheme presented early in chapter 8, particular emphasis was placed on the way in which schemes were initiated, and on the extent to which those working for them received payment. The case studies showed that payment was of vital importance, but that what mattered was less who started a project than what sort of relationship had been worked out between formal (statutory and voluntary) and informal personnel and resources. The organisational feature which, alongside but not unrelated to payment, emerged from the data as decisively differentiating Neighbourhood Care projects was that of the extent to which a project operated autonomously on the basis of statutory, voluntary or local action or on the basis of one of a number of possible patterns of partnership between them.

Six distinct organisational patterns were found: (1) the autonomous statutory pattern represented by Stonegate and Skeffington; (2) the autonomous voluntary pattern represented by Bradbury; (3) the autonomous local action pattern represented by Easethorpe and Parsons Green; (4) the pattern of statutory–voluntary partnership as found in Trimdon; (5) the pattern of voluntary–local action partnership represented in Southfield Park; and (6) the pattern of statutory–local action partnership found in different ways in Brandling, Tattworth and Grantley. The missing pattern, the combined partnership of all three elements (which many would presumably consider the ideal basis for effective neighbourhood care), was not one that had been realised in any of our chosen cases although several were edging towards it and the Brandling project had perhaps come closest.

The distinctive limitations of the projects and their distinctive patterns of caring were quite closely related to this pattern of organisational differences. The data did not permit any definitive testing of such a relationship, if only because other hypothetical key variations, in welfare environment and social setting, had to be allowed for. Once that was done, the range of relevant

Table 10.1 Questionnaire to Helpers

Question 44: What sort of things would help the scheme to be more successful? (i) These are some of the things which other schemes have experienced as problems. Have you any of them been so in your scheme?

	Stonegate	Brandling	Skeffington	Grantley	Tattworth	Bradbury	Trimdon	Parsons Green	Southfield Park	Easethorpe
Too few Helpers	52%	61%	44%	40%	11%	61%	66%	30%	72%	4%
Too many Helpers	—	—	—	—	—	—	—	3%	4%	—
Lack of commitment of Helpers	3%	25%	11%	20%	8%	6%	3%	3%	—	—
Too much contact with local SSD	—	—	—	—	—	—	3%	—	—	—
Not enough contact with local SSD	13%	4%	33%	—	4%	17%	31%	3%	8%	—
Contact with other organisations or individuals outside the scheme	7%	—	4%	—	4%	11%	28%	3%	4%	—
Lack of finance	29%	54%	48%	20%	46%	17%	22%	30%	4%	4%
Degree of willingness of people in need of help to seek/accept it	42%	21%	30%	20%	12%	17%	50%	6%	24%	7%
More publicity	16%	36%	15%	20%	27%	22%	75%	9%	48%	14%
Better transport arrangements	13%	43%	30%	—	23%	17%	53%	—	20%	7%
Premises	—	14%	7%	20%	4%	11%	6%	3%	4%	—
Other	—	3%	—	—	23%	17%	—	12%	24%	4%

comparison, even within the highly simplified framework used, far exceeded what the research team had resources to explore. The tentative conclusions offered here about the relationship between organisation and action are not intended to overlook the enormous complexity of variation in the real world of neighbourhood care.

The limitations of Neighbourhood Care projects were approached by asking Organisers, Helpers and officials a straightforward question about the main problems experienced. The responses to Question 44 on p. 264 are shown in table 10.1. It is worth comparing these results to the data obtained from the national survey of 1,000 Good Neighbour schemes. These are shown in table 10.2.

There were some striking differences in the aggregate level of discontent from project to project. Respondents were allowed to mention as many problems as they wished so that the maximum possible discontent rating for each project under our system of coding would have been 1,200. The actual totals achieved by each project thus indicate both that the overall level of dissatisfaction with the way any of the projects works was not very high (even though 58% of respondents said that their own project was affected by a serious problem of some sort), and that there are quite dramatic contrasts between some types of scheme and others. Those associated with the Easethorpe project, for example, with a global discontent rating of 40, might well be thought to be satisfied to the point of complacency, while at the other (relative) extreme the Trimdon Helpers, with a score of 339, were plainly fairly heavily burdened with a sense of the limitations to their own effectiveness. Nevertheless, the general picture to emerge is one which suggests that those (few) people who have been drawn into neighbourhood care of any organisational type were reasonably happy with the project with which they were involved even though a majority of them could also think of at least one serious limitation which, if overcome, would appreciably increase their effectiveness. By comparison with the generality of Good Neighbour schemes those of our case studies which were emphatically dependent upon voluntary service delivery and monitoring in their distinctive activities (Bradbury, Brandling, Southfield Park and Trimdon) were all strikingly likely to report a shortage of Helpers as a significant problem. By contrast, Parsons Green, Tattworth and quite spectacularly, Easethorpe, where the business of neighbourhood care was conceived in very different terms (as collective self-help) were all relatively unaffected by that particular difficulty. And those three projects were also the least likely to report that their efforts had been hampered by the reluctance of people in need to seek or accept help; and the least likely to feel the need for the sort of institutional base provided by special premises. Interestingly, the three projects with statutory support and/or some element of paid work but falling short of full-time wage-work (Tattworth, Skeffington and Brandling) all substantially reported lack of financial support as a significant limitation and were well ahead of the field in that respect. The Stonegate (full-time, paid) Helpers also expressed that concern to a considerable degree, but it is not clear whether they were thinking of the level of their own wages or of the general restriction of funding throughout the statutory Social Services:

Table 10.2 *The major problems of 1,000 Good Neighbour schemes*

Major problem cited	% of schemes
Shortage of Helpers	43%
Inappropriate Helpers	21%
Transport difficulties	20%
Organisation/administration	19%
Inadequate contact with external agencies (Social Services, etc.)	19%
Shortage of Clients	14%
Other	29%

Source: Abrams *et al.* (1981a:39)

their supplementary comments on the question suggest, however, that they were referring to ancillary services ("more meals on wheels", "part-time Wardens to take over when we're sick or on holiday", "spare bed-linen for emergencies") which the Social Services might in principle have provided if money had been available. By contrast, the projects most strongly committed to an ideology (or principle) of voluntarism (Bradbury, Easethorpe, Southfield Park, and Trimdon) were markedly less likely to see lack of finance as a serious problem.

The Helpers' evidence creates a difficulty. There is a natural inclination for people involved in any venture to which they personally are deeply committed to over-estimate its value and success if they possibly can. The question of the limitations of Neighbourhood Care projects could not, therefore, be adequately assessed on the basis of Helpers' perceptions alone – their personal involvement could so easily lead to both over-estimates of the projects' achievements and under-estimates of their real limitations. Some independent measure was essential. Accordingly the Residents in seven of the project areas were asked what they knew of the project we were studying. Clients were also asked for an appraisal of the project in the overall pattern of the care they were receiving. The proportion of Residents who had heard of their local scheme varied from four-fifths in Easethorpe, Southfield Park and Grantley, through two-thirds in Stonegate, half in Brandling, to one-fifth in Parsons Green and one-eighth in Bradbury. But what emerged was very little relationship between what the Helpers thought they were achieving and what was perceived by those living in the neighbourhood or in need of care within it. There was no success-story. In Easethorpe, where the Helpers reported fewest problems, the highest number of Residents were aware of the project. The projects in Southfield Park, Grantley and Stonegate were also undeniably well-known to local Residents. But those in Bradbury and Parsons Green had made hardly any general impact – notwithstanding the general enthusiasm and high morale of the Helpers. And in Brandling, where a major effort to be known had been made, half of the Residents did not know that the project existed.

The basic contrast to emerge was between projects oriented to an ideal of voluntary service, projects firmly tied to the statutory services' conceptions of priorities and responsibilities in social care, and projects built up on the basis of a notion of the mutual involvement of local Residents with one another. And powerfully cutting across that dimension of variation was, once again, the dimension of social class. The case studies very rarely provided pure examples of distinct theoretical types (although here as elsewhere Stonegate and Easethorpe came very close to doing so), but here as elsewhere despite the actual mix of tendencies in most actual projects some broad tendencies could be discerned.

Consider first the case of Trimdon. Despite its statutory origins this was a project which had been left almost entirely in the hands of volunteers operating on the basis of a fairly traditional model of voluntary service delivery and monitoring. Yet the volunteers knew that they were supposed to have statutory backing – that the organisational basis of the project was that sort of partnership – and their sense of the limitations of the project revolved very explicitly around their belief that the expected partnership had not materialised. They saw themselves as needing more effective statutory support. Thus: "There's been a complete breakdown in communication between whoever is in charge and me – I just don't know what I'm supposed to be doing." Or, "We need more advice and referrals down the line from the Social Services Department to District Organisers to us – and back again, more contact with official bodies, more referrals, and also to make it more trustworthy." Again, "Of course there are limits to what we can do ... what's the point of finding out that people need help if the official follow-up isn't there?" What stood behind the very strong sense of inadequate contact with official agencies (both Social Service and medical) in this project was an appreciation that voluntary activity of the Street Warden type was and perhaps could be no more than a task of liaison – and that to do even that limited work well presupposed both vigorous support from the official caring services and firm trust from the prospective recipients of care in the local community.

And unfortunately this project, like so many others of its type, had been unable to evoke either. Relatively well-organised as it was, it had neither managed to get itself used by social workers, doctors, district nurses and other 'officials', nor contrived to convince local people that it was the appropriate local medium through which help and care might be sought rather than anything less or more formal. The challenge to a venture of this sort was to establish its reliability and value in an extended flow of service provision in the eyes of the responsible statutory agencies and at the same time to establish its value and reliability as a genuinely local force doing something more for local people than they could do for themselves in the eyes of the community of prospective Clients and Helpers. One side of the challenge required official organisation, structures, titles, badges, formal hierarchies and lines of responsibility; the other required a certain social invisibility, a capacity to be there as neighbours rather than to intrude officiously, as volunteers. The trouble of course was that pursuing either objective militated against realisation of the other. Helpers in projects such as the Trimdon Link ended up confused, demoralised and isolated, unable to persuade those they knew to be in need to let them help them, unable to convert helpful neighbours into organised Helpers, unable to persuade the official agencies to take them seriously as a distinct agency of social care.

The crux of the problem was hidden beneath the surface of the complaint that such projects were primarily hampered by a shortage of Helpers. It was precisely (to refer back to table 10.1, p. 183) the projects organised in terms of a conventional voluntary model of service delivery that reported this difficulty most emphatically (Bradbury, Brandling, Southfield Park and Trimdon). And although there were significant shades of difference, the shared sense of their inability to discover the pool of potential volunteers 'out there', waiting to be mobilised, which some contemporary mythologies of social care favour, provided the key to a general and rooted limitation of that approach to social care which must be taken very seriously. To put it brutally, when serious questions of trust were being raised the voluntary model could not convince either responsible professionals or natural good neighbours. The effects were obvious. On the one hand, "people do help one another quite a bit round here but you can't get them to meetings or to register as Street Wardens". On the other hand, as the Trimdon case study makes very clear, the failure of the scheme to penetrate or mobilise the world of informal care is seen as justifying a progressive restriction of statutory support: "I cannot see the scheme expanding if the impetus has to come from us." Caught between these two perceptions what should have been a bridge became an island. Projects of this type either settled for a restricted role and access, delivering less than vital minor services to an admittedly limited section of those in need, perhaps remaining largely unknown in the community as a whole and more or less reconciled to a permanent inability to recruit adequate numbers of Helpers (which was the pattern exemplified by the Bradbury project and by the Darnton and Bream version of the Trimdon project), or they achieved some major reconstitution of their organisation and functions which generated the vitality and growth which the voluntary service model of neighbourhood care on its own could not sustain (as in Brandling and more enigmatically in Southfield Park and the Strathburn version of the Trimdon project).

In this context at least the Bradbury project provided a base line for the limitations of this approach to neighbourhood care. Over four-fifths of the Bradbury Residents had never heard of the project; a similar proportion of its Clients judged the work it did less than vital; of all the projects we studied its Helpers were the least likely to think that their own scheme was the best way of meeting local needs for neighbourhood care, the most likely to say that it was not. It was also the most solidly working class of any of the areas we studied and had the highest concentration of unskilled manual workers among its Residents. It was the area whose Residents were most likely to say that their neighbourhood did not have a strong sense of community and least likely to admit to doing anything for their neighbours on a regular basis. On the other hand, if the Residents of Bradbury were the least likely of all our groups of Residents to identify their neighbours as the people they would turn to for help they were, by contrast, the most likely to be in close and supportive contact with kin, the most likely to have family living in the area, reporting a very high level of family contact and intra-family helping. There was plainly a distinctive and class-based social world here. And even though it was one that contained a high level of need for neighbourhood care, and even though the Bradbury Helpers were themselves predominantly working class, the voluntary service model of neighbourhood care obviously had great difficulties in penetrating it. Bradbury had the highest proportion of Residents (96%) who had had no personal experience of involvement with voluntary organisations and only 8% of them thought of voluntary organisations of any sort as an appropriate source of help for themselves (as compared to 72% and 68% in our two most middle class areas). Outside the narrow compass of the church, voluntary service was simply an alien social form. The constant cry for "more Helpers" was one that that sort of social milieu was not going to answer. Given, however, the essentially limited commitment of individual Helpers in this model (the fact that both the form and the amount of help offered were normally highly resistricted), more Helpers were indeed the indispensable condition for success.

In Southfield Park and Brandling the same problem was evident but it had to some extent been solved or side-stepped by varying either the functions or the form of organisation of the projects. In Southfield Park the structural and geographic alignment of the project with the class system had allowed it to develop an interesting duality of function capable of sustaining the morale of the Helpers even in the face of their limited access to the world of the Clients. Put crudely, in Southfield Park middle class Helpers helped themselves to sociability by delivering services to working class Clients. On that basis, the project managed to operate as a useful, albeit modest, form of social service and monitoring for the isolated (mainly elderly working class) in areas adjacent to rather than immediately part of the streets inhabited by the Helpers, while also acting as an effective device for building neighbourliness within the middle class world of the Helpers themselves. The enthusiasm generated by the successful performance of the latter function carried, and yet depended on, the continued (but for any one Helper again quite limited) performance of the former.

There was of course a problem about which of the functions mattered most. From the point of view of Age Concern (to whom the project was primarily responsible) and the Social Services Department in Southfield Park, the value of the scheme plainly lay in its specific services to the elderly; its main limitation was the resistance of the members to any suggestion to extend the scope or professionalism of that work. But to get anything of that sort done at all by the project depended on the external agencies tolerating and supporting the 'neighbourly' restriction of effort to which the Helpers were attached. From the point of view of the Helpers (and, incidentally, the Residents who were exceptionally well-informed about the existence of the project, nearly two-thirds having actually considered joining it), the value of the scheme lay no less plainly in its linking and sociable functions, its sense of spontaneity and its highly local autonomy. Yet the necessary condition for all that was, within the limits of personal spare time and petrol costs, the provision of some ascertainable measure of voluntary service to others. The two functions existed, in other words, in symbiosis – a delicate balance underpinning both the successes and the limitation of the project. The successes were from some points of view very considerable – not least in that, the resources of the Helpers and their principled attachment to the idea of voluntarism being what they are, the project represented no financial drain on the resources of the statutory sector at all. The main limitation (over and above the limitations of type of care, extent of personal effort, accountability and so forth associated with all projects of this type) was that once moved outside the peculiar setting of places such as Southfield Park to consider the country as a whole, there were simply not enough clusters of economically comfortable, non-working and at least mildly religious housewives to get anywhere near to meeting the needs for social care that were known to exist, following the Southfield Park model or anything like it. The conditions necessary to the peculiar local success of that project were unfortunately also peculiarly local.

What had happened in Brandling was perhaps a little more encouraging. Here, the move away from a traditional 'charity' model of voluntary service had been rather more emphatic. As in Southfield Park the project began primarily as a visiting service and, as the difficulties of bridging the gulfs of social class were discovered, moved from that to a concentration on transport services (see table 9.2, p. 163). The obstacles to effective one-to-one, cross-class care in Brandling were a great deal more formidable than they were in Southfield Park: there was no predominant middle class territory here from which to sally forth to do good; the Clients of care were to be found not in small isolated pockets of a suburban village but in great tracts of council development rendered almost impenetrable by lurking teenage gangs and endemic fear of muggings behind locked doors and walls of mistrust. But the Brandling project did not simply retreat to the provision of transport. Instead, it was largely reconstituted in terms of advice, self-help initiatives and *ad hoc* services provided through and around the medium of a shop. While voluntary Visitors were an alien agency in such settings, shops were entirely natural. And after five years the shop had proved a focus for the generation of a wide range of very specific forms of care: a little (highly valued) visiting for the very isolated, a good deal of transport, a great deal of advice and information, a club, diverse community-development ventures. Of course one must not exaggerate the success of the Brandling project: half of the Residents we interviewed had not heard of the scheme. Of those who had, three-quarters had never thought of doing anything with it. Four-fifths of the Residents had had no experience of involvement with any sort of voluntary organisation and there was a quite extraordinary consensus among them that the appropriate source of help apart from relatives and neighbours would be the statutory services not voluntary agencies – in part at least reflecting the fact that, as one Client put it: "Brandling Council is top of the bill for the disabled" (as for many other client groups). This indicated, too, that the welfare state, like shops and families and clubs, was recognised to play a part in this particular type of social world in a way that formal voluntary service could not hope to do.

Such success as the project had achieved was associated, by Helpers,

Clients, knowledgeable Residents and Officials alike, not just with the shift to the (effectively) informal mechanism of the shop but even more with the presence at the heart of all the scheme's activities of a paid Organiser, and, backing that up, paid staff for the shop. Constant testimony was paid to the specific personal qualities of the Organiser. Her enthusiasm, organisational talent and personal warmth plainly were crucial factors. But they would not have been available to the project had it not been possible to put the central coordinating tasks on a properly paid basis. There are no doubt many people with the personal qualities of the Brandling Organiser living in the many other areas of the country like Brandling, who could be drawn into neighbourhood care as waged work and who like her and for perfectly good reasons could not be drawn into it as volunteers. And in the case of Brandling at least, proper funding had in the long run to mean statutory funding. The Brandling Helpers had learned the vital advantages of proper financing; that was why of all our groups of Helpers they were, ironically, most insistent on the need for more finance (table 10.1).

What projects rooted in the voluntary service model of social care could do at a neighbourhood level was, then, severely constrained both by the relations they had with the larger environment of welfare agencies and by the way they fitted or failed to fit into the local class structure. At best they could monitor need and provide company for the very isolated and specific caring services for others on something less than a comprehensive basis. To break the nexus of limitations that stood behind their common problems of "too few Helpers" (which is really a problem of limited commitment and restricted access) they needed to move, one way or another toward quite different bases of action. What of projects initially rooted in such different bases? Apart from Trimdon and Brandling, four of the projects we studied had a significant statutory pivot of organisation: Tattworth, Grantley, Stonegate and Skeffington. The last two of these were unambiguously located within the statutory sector and Stonegate was, as it were, fully statutory. To turn next to that extreme instance of an alternative model is to realise the full extent to which the statutory system can, if it chooses, constitute an utterly different world of social care. Stonegate was the project whose Helpers helped most people and did the most work for those they helped. It was the only one of the projects we studied of whose Clients a majority (three-quarters) considered the work of the project "vital" to their own well-being. The only other area where more than a third of the Clients saw the work of the project in such terms was the one with the only other firmly statutory project, Skeffington (two-fifths). Both were projects operating in just the sort of strongly working class social milieu which our voluntary model projects had, to the extent that they clung to the model, so notably failed to penetrate.

These findings considerably amplify the findings of the early national survey of Good Neighbours. This identified the following as factors which would make Good Neighbour schemes more successful (Abrams *et al*. 1981a:40): more Helpers (44% of 590 respondents), different Helpers (28%), more finance (19%), better contact with Social Services (14%), a paid organiser (11%), more Clients (11%) and "other" (54%). The sizeable number men-

Limitations of neighbourhood care

tioning "different Helpers" was interpreted as an indication of the problems that many schemes faced in matching the help they could offer to the need for social care existing in particular localities.

The limitations of Neighbourhood Care schemes were quite clearly related to the type and mix of activities undertaken. A broad distinction may be made between three different types of effort: monitoring the state of well-being of near neighbours; performing specific caring tasks such as cleaning, gardening, shopping, reading or driving; and organising public activities of various sorts in the locality which would attract Residents and indirectly foster neighbourliness. The ten case studies showed quite clearly that in different schemes there was a quite different focus of effort (table 9.2). In some schemes the visiting service was the core, in others there seemed to be evidence that middle class Helpers could find visiting working class clients "boring", and even that there was some client resistance to being the object of attention in this way. On the other hand, activities like providing transport, running a day centre, or helping the disabled, were in some schemes both valued as ends in themselves and as a means of social contact among the Helpers.

To assess the significance of the variation between schemes, the interviews with Helpers and Clients probed the way in which each defined what their Neighbourhood Care scheme provided. What could be said about the quality of the work and relationships generated by the Neighbourhood Care projects studied? A number of questions covered the ways in which caring relationships were experienced and understood by those involved and the Helpers were also asked to describe their initial hopes and aims on becoming Helpers and also to say how they now saw themselves. The general pattern of answers to these questions is presented in tables 10.3 to 10.6. There were striking differences in all three respects – aims, self-images and relationships – between the different projects and areas, and the discussion which follows is concerned to elaborate and account for those differences by drawing on a good deal of further, qualitative, material from the interviews.

The tables point to variations which immediately invite comment: why should the Helpers in Stonegate and Skeffington choose so frequently to define their relationship with those they helped as "caring", while those in Parsons Green and Bradbury spoke almost as emphatically of "befriending" and why should "doing things for others" have been a particularly important basis for initial participation in neighbourhood care in Easethorpe and Stonegate or "making the locality more neighbourly" in Brandling? Part of the problem was that the codes used in the questionnaire were not discriminating enough: "making friends locally" turned out to have quite different meanings in Tattworth and in Grantley, although the general theme was stressed by the Helpers in both places. But at a deeper level, if one compared the whole pattern of answers locality by locality and related that in turn to the qualitative comments and interpretations of respondents, the relational core and experience of neighbourhood care did vary substantially from setting to setting. These variations had a good deal to do with the social composition of the locality and the organisational form of the Neighbourhood Care project. And once again the significant differences seemed to be bound up with social class

Table 10.3 *Questionnaire to Helpers*
Question 30: Before you started, what was the most important thing which you saw yourself personally as being able to achieve in the scheme?

	Stonegate	Brandling	Skeffington	Grantley	Tattworth	Bradbury	Trimdon	Parsons Green	Southfield Park	Easethorpe
Doing things for others	61%	28%	48%	40%	31%	56%	47%	42%	48%	64%
Making friends locally	6%	21%	11%	40%	27%	6%	19%	18%	16%	14%
Encouraging others to help themselves	23%	11%	22%	—	8%	—	3%	15%	—	7%
Making your locality neighbourly	3%	36%	7%	20%	31%	33%	31%	18%	36%	11%

Table 10.4 *Questionnaire to Helpers*
Question 36: How would you describe your relationship with those that you help?

	Stonegate	Brandling	Skeffington	Grantley	Tattworth	Bradbury	Trimdon	Parsons Green	Southfield Park	Easethorpe
Neighbouring	—	21%	4%	40%	31%	11%	19%	9%	20%	29%
Befriending	23%	18%	26%	20%	15%	50%	16%	70%	24%	21%
Caring	74%	36%	70%	40%	31%	33%	56%	18%	48%	43%
Social work	—	4%	—	—	3%	—	3%	—	—	—
Duty	3%	11%	—	—	11%	—	—	—	4%	—
Other	—	4%	—	—	—	—	—	4%	—	4%

Question 36(ii): Have any become friends?

	Stonegate	Brandling	Skeffington	Grantley	Tattworth	Bradbury	Trimdon	Parsons Green	Southfield Park	Easethorpe
Yes	52%	36%	78%	100%	23%	39%	53%	48%	48%	14%
No	13%	46%	22%	—	69%	6%	41%	21%	52%	39%

Table 10.6 *Questionnaire to Helpers*
Question 39: Which of the following comes nearest to the way that you see yourself as a participant in the scheme?

	Stonegate	Brandling	Skeffington	Grantley	Tattworth	Bradbury	Trimdon	Parsons Green	Southfield Park	Easethorpe
Neighbour	—	14%	4%	20%	11%	—	25%	6%	16%	29%
Helper	61%	32%	15%	20%	50%	22%	28%	18%	52%	21%
Counsellor	—	—	4%	—	—	—	6%	—	4%	—
Friend	35%	11%	67%	60%	31%	61%	19%	61%	16%	29%
Voluntary worker	—	21%	11%	—	8%	11%	19%	10%	8%	14%
Other, don't know etc.	3%	22%	—	—	—	—	3%	6%	4%	4%

193

on the one hand and with the contrasts between statutory and voluntary organisation on the other.

Certain distinct patterns of caring were apparent in the clustering of responses and projects. These patterns were not always sharply differentiated from one another and tended to be a matter of implicit balances of character or disposition suggested by the quantitative data when read in conjunction with the qualitative material generated by the open-ended questions. There were, for example, several suggestive ways in which the projects with a substantial statutory base seemed to differ from all the others even though they also differed from one another in some respects. In both Stonegate and Skeffington, neighbourhood care was highly unlikely to be seen as a matter of neighbouring and extremely likely to be defined as caring – as a relatively formal service in other words. At the same time, in both places Helpers were particularly likely to have become personal friends of those they helped and/or of others in the project, emphatically so in Skeffington where two-thirds of the Helpers were willing to define their participation in the project as a matter of friendship and four-fifths said that they had become friends with those they helped. These (it will be remembered) are the only two projects in which extensive helping, helping more than six people a week or helping for more than ten hours a week, was the normal pattern of activity; they were the only projects in which Helpers were paid (a wage in Stonegate, a token payment for part-time work in Skeffington); they had the oldest Helpers and the Helpers most likely to have finished education early. Perhaps particularly interesting is the fact that they also proved to be the projects whose Helpers were least likely to belong to any voluntary organisations or projects other than the Neighbourhood Care scheme itself (table 9.8, p. 179). Tattworth, the third project with a substantial formal statutory input (the organisation provided by the community workers) had a quite different pattern of motivation and perception among its Helpers. This was only to be expected, given the very different purposes for which it was brought into being. Nevertheless, the emphasis on friendship was again evident – in the form of an aspiration to make friends locally and on a substantial sense among the Helpers of participating as friends even though the majority here, as in Stonegate, saw themselves as Helpers rather than anything else. And in Tattworth, too, there was a high proportion of Helpers who left school early and who belonged to no organised groups apart from the Neighbourhood Care project. In terms of the occupations of their Helpers (or Helpers' spouses) these three projects were the most working class of all those studied. From an organisational point of view they were the ones most closely bound to the apparatus of the welfare state. It is not surprising that distinct styles and conceptions of caring should stand behind their Helpers' accounts of their involvement. Each of these projects had its own particular character, yet viewed together they suggested powerfully the existence of an approach to caring firmly and specifically rooted in working class experience. Payment and organisation, far from being inimical to that approach, may well be the necessary conditions for giving it life.

The first thing to stand out in this approach was the degree to which caring was seen as both natural and enjoyable. The caring tasks assigned to the

Helpers were, as it were, sociable occasions that came easily in the taken-for-granted texture of long-established ways of life. Thus:

> "I get a lot of enjoyment out of helping the elderly"; "My husband keeps telling me to give it up, but I enjoy it"; "The payment is just a little incentive, we argue about it but we all go on doing it, we enjoy doing it, enjoy the satisfaction"; "Once you start you get to know all the people, it gets friendly, it's just a question of being friendly"; "I get a lot of pleasure; if they stopped my wages I'd still go – a lot of them look on me more as a relative than a Neighbourhood Visitor, I really enjoy it"; "I wouldn't do it if I didn't like it"; "I've always been neighbourly"; "We're all friendly here"; "I've always been like this – in and out helping each other"; "There's nothing finer than people, nothing nicer than being amongst people"; "I enjoy watching people enjoy themselves; I like people"; "These people you visit – you have nice conversations and hear stories and what's happened to them and their life history – like when I was a kid"; "I just really like being involved with old people, my mother was just the same"; "As kids we could have walked into anybody's house – there were old people in the yard, we used to help them, people helped each other"; "I've always been friendly with old people"; "I used to be a home help but I wanted to do more caring than cleaning – it seemed more natural somehow"; "The old ones appreciate it and that makes me feel good, it's like my family used to be"; "I just like old people, I always have, talking and listening, that's it."

In all three samples the sense of everyday enjoyment of caring, as a matter of talking, mixing, sharing experience, helping out, doing things one would do anyway, was very strong. And it was set in the context of high and long-standing levels of contact, involvement and mutual help with both kin and neighbours. The tiredest clichés about working class community seem at one level to be the active reality of these Helpers: "You've only got to stand at your door and somebody will come along to chat"; "We've got a little shop where you meet everybody"; "I wouldn't like to move, I've got good neighbours, friends, a nice house, I'm within walking distance of my family"; "Everyone in the Close is very friendly, I'd trust any of them." But at a rather deeper level these perceptions of community and the engrained ideal of community that are bound up with them are seen, in all three settings, to be in jeopardy. A part of the Helpers' reasons for engaging in neighbourhood care might almost be a matter of fighting back against forces seen as threatening an established neighbourly social order. The threat to community was seen in different ways in different places. It may come as architects and planners: "They've split the community; it used to be a mining community – knocked the terraces down and put flats there, I think flats are like prisons"; "In the old courtyards everyone used to neighbour; when my mother was expecting they were all more or less expecting and they all used to help each other – the flats have destroyed that"; "They've made it less neighbourly than when I was a child; unless you're hanging washing out you don't talk"; "They didn't need Home Wardens once, but you've got to have them to keep an eye on the old people in a place like this." Or it may be the social concomitants of inner city blight – strikingly, half of the Helpers in Skeffington would have liked to move from the area where they lived for that sort of reason: "It's deteriorated so much over the years, come down in the world, bad people have moved in"; "I don't like it any more or the people, they're rough and scruffy"; "It's all the wild dogs and the badly behaved children – making hell on earth for elderly people"; "We've had four break-ins, it's affecting my health – the City feeling's gone"; "It's just that I've got really bad neighbours – but if I left I'd have to come back to see the old people." Or it may be a matter of facing the challenge of ethnic mix: "Asians don't mix with Jamaicans, whites don't mix with coloureds – you can't go on like that"; "It's becoming a very unfriendly place, people don't talk to each other, can't sometimes; we had to do something to get people to mix in again"; "People have become frightened to get help, frightened to let people in – bringing people together, airing difficulties, talking to one another, it all helps make us more friendly"; "Lots of things need doing round here; we need to get together; I hope we'll have a neighbourhood"; "Get people mixing – they find they enjoy it"; "In the scheme the Indians, English and West Indians get together; we demanded a better water supply; we get to know each other and do something for the neighbourhood." In whatever form it occurs the feeling was of a social fabric threatened and worth defending – and of sociability expressed as care, as a renewal of social cohesion, as a suitable form of defence: "People ought to mix and be friendly; well, you can't just sit in your house can you?"; "It makes you more friendly and neighbourly."

At the same time, the threats to such patterns of solidarity were real. Physical and social isolation, economic and domestic insecurity, inner city decay and multi-racial co-residence were all really there. It was clear that nostalgia and goodwill would not make them go away or construct community in the face of them. The problem of social cohesion had to be worked at and the work had to be organised. Working class people simply did not have space in their lives for the sort of work and organisation that was necessary unless it was itself constituted as work. The housewives and retired people would do their best but everyone's first need was for a job. The importance of the Stonegate project was the way it demonstrated that, far from being incompatible with paid work, a distinctively working class pattern of care was dependent on it and could flourish on the basis of it. The contradiction between the impersonal world of bureaucratically organised wage work and the warm humanity of voluntary caring, so entrenched in the literature of social care, simply did not apply here. The whole point of this pattern of care, rather, is that it is a pattern of unalienated work. The Stonegate Helpers were quite explicit about this: "I've got to work anyway, but it's the perfect job"; "I've always liked housework and helping people, I might as well be paid for it, I need the money"; "I do it for the wage really, but it's doing more of what I'd do anyway, what I'm good at"; "We all go to work, we have to, it's good money and I like doing it"; "You could say the money is a necessity, but it's what I want to do"; "I had a chance to go back to [a local factory] with the young people but I turned it down; this is just right for me – the money's fair and I like meeting the old people, doing things for them, they trust me"; "I'd do it voluntary if I had lots of money."

One other possible basis for unleashing this particular pattern of care is hinted at in the experience of the Tattworth project. Here it was not individual effort made possible by wage work but collective effort in pursuit of shared interests that was the distinctive mode of action: interpersonal caring – "the coloured woman next door looks in to see I'm O.K.". It involved intergroup politics, a joint struggle to defend and improve the amenities and services of a shared territory. The history of the Labour movement in this country and the history of Black protest in the United States both suggest that neighbourhood politics of this sort, neighbourhoodism, could in time prove a very effective vehicle for the first pattern of caring, the pattern of *Care as Working Class Community*. But at least in the case of Tattworth it was too soon, when the research was done, to be sure. What was more certain was that the pattern could not be sustained by the type of organisation developed in Skeffington. The system of token payments may have ensured the reliability and accountability sought by the statutory authorities but it had no impact on the realities of the labour market. The Helpers who came forward did so on the basis of understanding, hopes and intentions characteristic of the whole pattern of caring in question – but they were recruited only from that small fraction of working class women who either could afford to stay out of the labour market or could not find a way into it. The pattern of care was tapped but could not be fully mobilised. This pattern of care was latent, a potentiality of working class life which was neither merely an artefact of certain externally created forms of organisation nor something that, within the existing conditions of working class life, working class people could sustain extensively without appropriate forms of organisation, whether they be economic or political. The issue is discussed further in chapter 12.

The fact that the basis of the pattern did lie ultimately in class experience and culture rather than anything else was confirmed if one looked across all of the projects studied to separate working class Helpers from non working class Helpers. What then emerged as the distinguishing characteristics of this type of caring were indeed defining features of the involvement of working class Helpers wherever they were found, even though they could only become the predominant features of whole projects in places such as Skeffington, Tattworth and Stonegate and in forms of organisation which recognised the economic and political realities of working class life. Expressed in qualitative terms, it was a pattern in which care was embedded in what were seen to be natural, enjoyable, obvious, sociable relationships (however hard they may be to achieve in the actual contemporary world), relations of "empathy more than sympathy" as one Tattworth Helper put it. In practice the options for building such relationships seemed to be caring as wage-work and neighbourhood politics.

A second, distinct, pattern of care among the projects studied was *Care as doing Good*. This was exemplified in pure form in Southfield Park – an example of projects which are extremely common nationally – and in mixed form in Bradbury and Brandling, largely because of a strong working class presence. In this pattern it is sympathy not empathy that matters. The Helpers may but usually did not feel themselves to be the same sort of people as the Client. But they had a strong sense of their obligation to help – and to do so, in many cases, just because the helped were so different, whether in terms of class, race, religion or more elusively simply of 'fortune'. The Helpers in these projects were in an odd way moral or cultural strangers in their own neighbourhoods; involvement in neighbourhood care was for them particularly likely to be a way of making themselves more at home in those neighbourhoods – not by changing their own identity but by establishing for themselves a morally laudable, useful, good, responsible or progressive function within a differentiated community. Thus, it was the Helpers in these three projects who were most likely to say that "making the locality more neighbourly" was the motivational origin of their participation in neighbourhood care. And the glosses they provided of those answers emphasised the degree to which they were speaking to their own estrangement – "if one's lucky enough to have all this ... house ... car and so on, one should do something about it"; "I felt I had a lot of advantages which others didn't have"; "It's a matter of social conscience; the world is a mess"; "There are so many people in need here, it just seemed my duty to help them"; "I've been very fortunate – I wanted to offer something"; "I don't want to lead a purely selfish life"; "I wanted to be part of the community." At the same time these Helpers were, among the long-established projects, the least likely to have made friends with those they helped and the most likely to be either religious or middle class or both. Their "desire to be helpful" was firmly anchored in those specific social distances from those they saw as needing help.

In several ways the three projects were very different from one another and they revealed interesting variations on the common theme. Whereas Brandling and Southfield Park both had high proportions of middle class Helpers, reflecting the awkward social mix of the former and the dominant structuring of the latter, Bradbury was one of the most homogeneously working class areas studied, and the differentiation of the Helpers from the area as a whole was in that case religious. Essentially the Bradbury project was an ecumenical venture concerned to bring denominational activists together in Christian unity – neighbourhood care was a way of expressing a common interest in something which separated them from the community but gave them a shared orientation towards it. Caring was not just a matter of "doing God's work" or "religious convictions" or "faith and idealism". Nor was it just a matter of creating the sort of identity within the locality implicit in such statements as: "I like to see people happy, they look up to me because of my faith, people tend to cling to me because of my faith." Such statements must seriously affect the way in which the claim of the Bradbury Helpers that they see themselves as "befriending" those they help is interpreted. The fact was that these people, like their secular counterparts in Southfield Park and Brandling, saw neighbourhood care as a way of changing the neighbourhood, of making it more the sort of place they would like it to be rather than of defending or consolidating what they took it to be already. The perspective was active but distanced, benevolent no doubt but also intrusive.

The parallel sentiments in Brandling – at least among the 53% of middle class Helpers almost all of whom do not live in the locality in which the project finds its Clients – centred on the social responsibilities of the socially privi-

Limitations of neighbourhood care

leged: "This is a very mixed area socially, most of the people in the scheme are quite privileged, we feel it's important to help others." Almost uniquely among the projects, this scheme produced a significant number of Helpers who saw their relationship with those they helped as a matter of "duty" or of "social work". The question unavoidably posed by these responses was the extent to which neighbourhood care in this pattern was anything more than an expression of simple social guilt: "The scheme exists to help people and to make sure that our neighbourhood is a caring one; there's a lot of contrast in this area, a lot of very privileged people and a lot of underprivileged – why should I have a house like this?" This is not to deny that the result of the Helpers' involvement was a great deal of positively useful and supportive activity; a high proportion of them were highly educated and firmly committed to making the locality what they call "more neighbourly" – but what they actually had in mind was, nevertheless, best described as resistance to what the other residents of the area would create if left to themselves: "There's a lot of anti-social behaviour and vandalism here – the black woman next door's a prostitute – it all stems from a lack of community, we need to get people back into their community." And even when it was not a question of resistance there was the peculiarly middle class, and alienated, problem of embarrassment: "I like being treasurer of the scheme, I think it employs my talent usefully to help others, and I couldn't bear to go visiting people in dreadful conditions – I'd have dreadful feelings about my own privilege." Being good seemed to be a matter of taking action to defy the realities of a fractured social system: "Just because we're professional people, it doesn't mean we can't be part of the community."

In the more tranquil environment of Southfield Park the same pattern – "I'm lucky, and should share it a bit" – recurred but here the tone was much more relaxed and at the same time its sociable meaning for the Helpers more pronounced; not (as in the first pattern) a matter of implementing the sociability of the community as a whole but just the opposite, a way of escaping from the community's natural tendencies towards privatisation. It was as though doing good was on the one hand a little better than doing nothing, and on the other hand one of the very few things that these particular people could legitimately do to escape from the domestic isolation which was the normal condition of life in their neighbourhood – Southfield Park Helpers were the least likely of all our groups of Helpers to have very close relationships with their own immediate neighbours and the least likely to have been engaged in neighbourly activities before becoming involved in an organised project. And in sharp contrast to the situation in, say, Stonegate or Skeffington, most of them had not become friends with the people they helped; their image of themselves as "caring" and "doing things for others" included a clear sense of the ways in which the others were not like themselves; friendship was not on their agenda. Thus:

> "I was fed up, stuck at home with little kids, I wanted something to do"; "I was approached by somebody and I did have spare time – I was pleased to do something"; "I did have a car and time"; "There seemed to be needs to be met, I thought, why not, I like to be helpful if I can"; "I didn't really think about it – I'd got the time, I was here, it's very good to help people, and a bit of

society, too"; "I like to help if I can and I had time on my hands"; "If people need help and you have spare time why not do it?"; "It was a chance to know people – they seemed a fairly interesting group – I didn't see it as onerous"; "I quite enjoy meeting old people, I had a car and I was at home all day, I wanted to be useful"; "It seemed like a good idea"; "My husband thought I should do something".

On the one hand, then, "it's a good thing to help", "if one is able to do things one should try and help", "it's bad to lead a purely selfish life", but on the other hand the neighbourhood was unneighbourly and on the whole that was how it should be: "We like to think of ourselves as a bit exclusive, like to lead our own lives; people don't want others to know their affairs, they don't want 'togetherness'." There was an edge of definite non-involvement in this type of caring. It was not often expressed as bluntly as this, but was widely diffused in subtler ways through projects in which this pattern was dominant. Thus, in Southfield Park the Helpers were well aware that "trying to create a climate of self-help" was the main general purpose of the project – "even the elderly should live independently . . . it's up to everybody to do things for themselves, there's a lot more they can do, they can get out . . ." – and this in itself seemed to distance them from those they helped, adding to the sense of caring, tasks performed conscientiously and effectively but without much warmth, which seemed to be the crux of the pattern of Doing Good.

The data suggested a third major pattern of caring, *Care as Trouble Shared*. It was not wholly present in some projects and wholly absent from others, but in one or two cases nevertheless created a dominant tone. A Trouble Shared is, thus, the mode of caring that distinguished Parsons Green and Easethorpe, in particular, from the other projects studied. The marked tendency for the Helpers in these projects to see themselves participating as neighbours or friends rather than as Helpers provided a first key to the common pattern of caring created within what were in other ways two very different projects. As distinct from the solidarities of interest and empathy that marked the first pattern and the individualistic moralities that pervaded the second, this was a pattern of more immediate interpersonal reciprocity. In different ways the Helpers in both these projects were keenly aware of the ways in which helping was a question of doing things for one another. In Easethorpe there was a very high level of general neighbourliness, and the Neighbourhood Care project floated, to a considerable extent, on the surface of that; and on the modest prosperity of its largely retired middle class population, largely engaged in caring for one another in an informal way. Thus:

> "There's a lot of neighbourliness that isn't connected with the scheme; like last year, for example, I had on one occasion to get my next door neighbour in the middle of the night – because of my husband – and she didn't mind at all; that's the kind of understanding we have"; "I pop in next door to see the chap of 86 every day – and I know that my neighbours keep an eye on me. We have little scraps but we get over them – like a family do"; "If someone's not well I go in and do shopping; the neighbours are friends – I visit twice a week regularly; I have both side keys and I look after their pets; they help me in return, if I'm not well they make my meals, shop, keep an eye on me."

Limitations of neighbourhood care

Relatively isolated in their small country village, sharing the common predicaments of old age, but with at least a modest platform of economic security beneath them, these inhabitants of Easethorpe developed patterns of mutual help which their Neighbourhood Care project only formalised. These Helpers were the oldest and the most middle class of any studied; they were also by far the most likely to believe that the area in which they lived had a strong sense of community – and to be able to supply detailed evidence of good neighbouring to support their belief.

Nevertheless, from the point of view of social policy, Parsons Green was a more interesting case, just because there comparable forms of mutual involvement had been created in the face of much less promising social circumstances. Doubtless the strong sense of the Parsons Green Helpers that what they were doing was "befriending" rather than caring in part reflected the determination of the Organiser that the project should be defined and constructed in those terms. But the extent to which a network of such friendships, friendships rooted in the organisation of mutual help, had been built up in a locality divided on class lines, not perceived as particularly neighbourly, by people without much previous experience of neighbourly helping and conspicuously unlikely to have very close relationships with their neighbours, was still very impressive. And the key to the project's success did seem to lie in its conception of caring as a reciprocal process, an exchange of need as well as of help:

> "The volunteer and the subject – it evens out – she's my friend and now I'm hers"; "It goes from being an artificial situation to being a natural one – you realise how much you're getting out of it"; "Everyone was wary to begin with, but now we're all friends, help each other"; "When I joined I was a very lonely person, I thought of it as voluntary work to keep me busy, but now it's so much more than that, a real group of friends"; "We all help each other – not to be lonely, to make the community spirit."

Quite persistently the caring relationship was seen as giving as much as it demanded; the need that was met for the Helpers was an almost universal need to be freed from the loneliness which they experienced as the normal condition of life in Parsons Green prior to the creation of the Neighbourhood Group. Of course, that pattern was also apparent in Southfield Park but unlike the ideology of Doing Good, with its emphasis on specific caring tasks aimed at a goal of self-help, the pattern of a Trouble Shared generated firm relationships which did make possible the sort of escape into society which the Helpers (in both places, but more seriously in Parsons Green) felt they wanted.

The quality of caring in Easethorpe and Parsons Green was, then, remarkably similar and remarkably unlike that prevailing in any of the other projects. Yet in Easethorpe it was something that grew almost naturally out of the pre-existent circumstances and disposition and relationships of the residents, whereas in Parsons Green it was an artefact of a determined effort to construct neighbourhood care. In Easethorpe the movement had been from mutual help towards organised neighbourhood care as a means of consolidating and tying up the loose ends of relationships that were already there. In Parsons Green it was exactly the opposite; organised neighbourhood care focussed on the idea of befriending, on the idea that "we are all in the same position, a helper one day and then helped the next, volunteers are not a race apart, we all need friends", came first and was the necessary precondition for turning a soulless suburban tract into a community perceived now by the Helpers and Clients as indeed enjoying a strong sense of community. "Befriending" is an embarrassing, unnatural sort of word; yet organising neighbourhood care to pursue it in Parsons Green had clearly smashed the prison of loneliness for many people as well as delivering to others the caring services with which social policy must rightly be mainly concerned. Three-quarters of the Parsons Green Helpers were under the age of 40, which made them conspicuously the youngest caring population encountered; and they were almost evenly recruited from working class and middle class occupations, which was also unique; in both respects they could be regarded as a portent for social policy. There was little doubt that their successful recruitment had a great deal to do with the fact that the project in which they were involved had found a way of generating the Trouble Sharing approach to social care which grew naturally in places like Easethorpe.

The evidence thus suggested the existence of three distinct patterns of neighbourhood care. There was no strict or complete matching of these types to particular locations or forms of organisation. Some of the projects studied, Trimdon for example, displayed no clearly dominant pattern at all. Nevertheless there was a certain degree of fit between patterns of caring and both neighbourhood social composition and project organisation: certain patterns plainly flourished best in certain types of setting and on the basis of certain types of project design. Each of the three patterns of caring could be an effective context and medium for the delivery of caring services under appropriate social and organisational conditions. The policy maker is not left free simply to choose the pattern he or she happens to prefer. The task, rather, is to work out which pattern of caring will deliver most care in the light of the social conditions and organisational resources actually available in any given neighbourhood. But that in turn involves understanding the very different meanings that care can have for different people in different social situations and different caring projects.

The theoretical distinctions with which the Patterns of Neighbourhood Care project began (discussed at the beginning of chapter 8) highlighted important dimensions of difference among the ten schemes. The typology of Care as Working Class Community: Care as Doing Good; and Care as Trouble Shared did bear some relation – but not a one-to-one relation – to the distinction between high profile, low profile and springboard policies by local authorities, and to statutory-led, safety-net and partnership modes of organising neighbourhood care. The salience of social class as an influence was confirmed. The degree and mode of involvement of people living in rural and urban areas was also important. As in the Street study of the Cumberland village, the village of Easethorpe seemed to have much more natural neighbourliness than any of the urban or suburban areas studied.

It was clear, however, that the initial distinctions were not a straightjacket into which the data were forced. The main conclusions modified the emphasis on partnership or safety-net care. The salience of the mode of interaction between Helper and Client, as much as the form of collaboration between the scheme and the local Social Service Department, came to assume greater significance. Hence although Parsons Green was originally classified as a low profile safety-net need-oriented scheme, the feature which assumed most importance was the way in which Helpers became friends and neighbours, reciprocity developed and care became trouble shared, in contast to the social distance evident in Southfield Park, Brandling and Bradbury, where the Helpers were 'doing good'.

To draw the discussion in the last three chapters to a conclusion, two issues need particular attention. One is the relationship between formal and informal care, to be discussed further in chapter 11. The other is the most effective form of neighbourhood care in terms of adequacy and reliability of service provision. The issues are related, as they are to the appropriate mix of statutory, voluntary and informal forms of care and of wage payment.

The central question that surrounds the debate over the formal and informal systems is whether the former type of care can generate the latter. Or, to put it into practical terms, can Neighbourhood Care schemes actually encourage ordinary neighbourliness? Several different methods were tried in the course of the research in an effort to construct an objective measure that would indicate a rise or fall in neighbourliness due to the intervention of a scheme. The questions devised proved, however, to be by nature too problematic to reliably ascertain the formative constitution of neighbourly relations. Furthermore, and more fundamentally, the research team realised that the question was inextricably related to both the organisational framework of the particular scheme and the social context in which it existed. They therefore decided to abandon the aim of generating quantitative data and instead to locate the problem of the generation of informal care within a wider discussion.

There was, of course, no definitive model of a scheme that was bound to make localities more neighbourly, but rather a series of different types of scheme with differing aims which when related to the social composition of their areas could be assessed in terms of their appropriateness for this activity. Thus the Bradbury scheme, a formal voluntary organisation existing in a working class suburb which was comparatively badly off in terms of familial and neighbourly help, could not be said to have stimulated ordinary neighbourliness, although it is true that the organisers were more concerned with ecumenical than neighbourly relations. In Grantley, the scheme was initially proposed in response to perceived problems in a tower block full of elderly working class people. It then underwent a change in direction towards trying to bring the residents of that tower block into contact with the other predominantly middle class inhabitants of the area, and ended up by making the latter group a more cohesive social entity but doing very little for the elderly. In Stonegate the myth of formal structures and paid Helpers crushing informal associations was exploded by observational evidence. This suggests that relationships between the Helper and the helped had extended both emotionally and practically far beyond the official terms of reference *and* that the work of the Wardens had substantially reinforced the informal care received by their Clients from their neighbours and in particular from their family.

The most recurrent example of informal care which stemmed from the schemes was that which the Helpers gave to each other. Neighbourly and friendly relations were established amongst the Helpers in no less than four schemes, each for quite different reasons. In Parsons Green, middle class and working class housewives became friendly largely as a result of the careful matching process operated by the organiser, Mrs Smythe. The young middle class housewives of Southfield Park created extensive, perhaps rather too extensive, informal links with each other after initially making contact through the Care scheme. The shop in Brandling provided an ideal setting whereby the working class members of the Good Neighbour scheme could get to know each other. And the structure of the Tattworth project which identified their members as contacts and residents rather than Helpers, facilitated a certain amount of self-generating neighbourliness amongst them, many having said that they had never spoken to each other before they joined the scheme.

It was in Easethorpe that the most interesting relationship between the formal and informal was discovered. The scheme seemed to be both an extension of the informal networks already existing in the area but also it fed into and extended those networks by its activities. So, at one and the same time it was created by, and helped to create, ordinary neighbourliness. Three factors external to the scheme itself – modestly affluent retired couples, the village itself as a context and the church as a focal point to the social life there – helped to create a highly favourable setting for voluntary care. Such conditions were untypical of those in which most of the elderly live in Britain, particularly those most in need of neighbourhood care.

Statements about the generation of informal relationships should be grounded in an assessment of their practical value to extract meaningful implications for social policy. To what extent can voluntary Neighbourhood Care schemes be relied upon to deliver social care adequately even if they are reasonably proficient in terms of service delivery and comparatively successful in encouraging neighbourly acts within the locality? Both the limitations of neighbourly relationships and voluntary schemes have been discussed in detail in earlier chapters, and the aim here is to highlight the policy implications.

A major conclusion was that a commitment to reliable neighbourly care cannot rely solely on voluntary effort. *Action for Care* (1981) observed that 'the incidence of Good Neighbour schemes does not so much reflect the level of need in a given environment but rather the availability of Helpers and organisers, as for example in areas where there is a large supply of people (mainly women) who do not do full-time work and can afford to meet the costs involved in being a good neighbour'. This mismatch between Good Neighbour schemes and need suggested that although the ten schemes might differ in aims from the traditional voluntary service approach, they were populated by very much the same sort of people – the middle class housewife. Voluntary Good Neighbour schemes were therefore on the whole for certain types of people, in certain types of places, and offering only certain types of help, in that they established links between isolated neighbours, but in essence only offered the sorts of neighbourly help that might have been previously missing. Apart from the need to have a sufficient number of available Helpers, Good Neighbour schemes also needed resources for the payment of Organisers and incidental expenses, and required extensive statutory back-up services to cover the service areas where they were inherently weak.

The main conclusion stemming from the research was that the traditional voluntary service approach was simply inadequate for most of Britain. The new Neighbourhood Care strategy based on community development offered exciting possibilities, discussed earlier in the case studies of Tattworth and Brandling. One of the clearest messages coming from the research was that neighbourhood care could only be organised by carefully taking into account the social composition and way of life of the relevant locality. In some, usually middle class, areas voluntary schemes could be relatively effective providers of care. This was so particularly if a subtle 'Trouble Sharing' strategy was adopted that cemented relationships by means of the ethos of reciprocity. However, in areas that lacked the relevant social characteristics to make that sort of scheme work, that was not possible. These were homgeneous working class areas where the economic need to work influenced the woman just as much as the man. It was in these areas, where social isolation could be coupled with economic hardship, that the issue of payment of indigenous workers, or neighbours, became vitally important for any serious attempt to alleviate local problems. The study of Stonegate illustrated how payment could harness neighbourly resources, which through force of circumstances would otherwise have not been available, and also generate more informal help in that it encouraged kin and neighbours to offer support in addition to the formal help being given. The possibility of having a scheme of this sort was in turn dependent upon a Local Authority that was 'need-based' It metaphorically viewed its role in the provision of care as a 'springboard', providing a reliable base from which voluntary and informal care could be propelled into the areas where they were most needed and offered the sorts of help that they could realistically perform. It was this, rather than a 'safety-net' catching those who toppled off the tightrope of over-stretched non-statutory sources.

The viability of payment of indigenous residents as an effective means of providing neighbourhood care is shown by its universality – payment is *always* a possibility and in some types of social milieux essential, whereas voluntary schemes can only be important where the local social circumstances create a large supply of potential Helpers. The serious provision of social care on a localised basis would require the recruitment of local residents into a paid army of non-professional neighbourhood workers, each carrying out a variety of tasks, or performing different tasks from each other, according to the needs and wishes of the local community.

11 The relationship between informal and formal care

To the extent that the ten case studies provided a test of the forms of relationship set out in chapter 7, they pointed not to colonisation, conflict or coexistence, but to widespread confusion. Indeed, several years of advocacy of neighbourhood care (beginning in 1976) combined with the uncertainty and contradiction of policy objectives which that advocacy had contained and obscured, and with the political, administrative, financial and practical difficulties of actually doing anything about neighbourhood care, had reduced most authorities to a state of confusion ranging from mild muddle to more or less uncontrolled panic. Among the case studies, Grantley was a conspicuous site of confusion. The characteristic relationshiup that resulted was *ad hoc*, patchy and unpredictable. Different arms of the same service proclaimed different policies, initiatives were launched enthusiastically and then abruptly abandoned, the commitments of individuals took the place of settled institutional arrangements – so that when a key individual left, whole policies and relationships were likely to collapse. There was a general sense of trying to do the best one could, without having either to define policy firmly or seriously commit resources. All concerned were uneasily aware of the contrary pull of the resources of the formal system and the values of the informal system and not at all sure what to do about it. Yes, we would like to be part of the regular referral system of the Social Services Department and to receive a grant from them. And yes, we are trying to strengthen and extend informal care in relationships governed by affect as an alternative to service care through formally bounded relationships. And no, we don't know what to do about the problems of accountability, reliability and ethics that constantly arise in the effort to straddle the two worlds. How does one organise to promote lack of organisation?

Many welfare authorities adopted what could be called a 'low profile' posture in relation to neighbourhood care. This might reflect on the one hand a rather positive *laissez-faire* conception, in which authorities did nothing deliberately in order to leave room for the local and the informal and the voluntary to flourish – a 'safety-net' view of the welfare state in which the object of policy was to minimise the reach of formal provision; among the ten studies, the situation in Southfield Park came very close to this mode. Or it might reflect a more active sense of the irrelevance, unreliability and ineffectiveness of Neighbourhood Care ventures in relation to the major policy commitments and objectives of the welfare agencies in question – a more or less considered decision that involvement in neighbourhood care was not

Informal and formal care

worth the time, money and effort it would require: and the Parsons Green study would seem to exemplify that situation. In either case, however, the essence of the neglect relationship was that welfare authorities do little or nothing to encourage bridge-building between the formal and informal systems of care in the form of Neighbourhood projects. The problem of neighbourhood care would be seen either as one properly to be left to the locals themselves, or as one to be met, for reasons of accountability, economy and efficiency, by way of conventional service delivery on the part of properly qualified staff.

Those welfare authorities and agencies which eschewed neglect and contrived to avoid confusion most often did so on the basis of some form of colonisation. Colonisation (see chapter 7 and Abrams 1984b) encompassed a wide range of relationships in which the neighbourhood was, in effect, either directly invaded by statutory or voluntary services or indirectly dominated by them. Either way, informal resources were tapped and bound to the purposes of the colonisers. A bridge was built but the traffic across it was almost entirely one way. Such exercises might be covered by a more or less benevolent rhetoric of 'care' and 'participation', but their distinctive feature in practical terms was the way in which they combined the provision of care with the establishment of control. Control might of course be established quite blandly – client princes might as it were, be found in the locality to 'orchestrate' neighbourhood care activities. Or it might be established quite bluntly through, for example, a system of paid and accountable workers.

The common effect, however, was to create a relationship in which the price of care was dependency. There is not much doubt that colonising the informal sector – as compared to the postures of confusion or neglect – was a noticeably effective way of promoting neighbourhood care, even if at the expense of the informal system itself. In some respects Stonegate was a striking demonstration of the paradox – a strongly need-oriented authority had developed comprehensive and effective Neighbourhood Care services, but at palpable cost to the energy and scope of local grass-roots caring projects.

Colonisation may be seen in different forms ranged along a continuum of control from a direct imposition of the values and objectives of the formal authorities to a complex (but still ultimately authority-based) dialogue in which significant concessions were made to the integrity and essentially different nature of informal caring relationships. At the 'soft' end of the continuum there were plenty of examples to indicate that welfare authorities that wished to do so could cultivate forms of neighbourhood care in which the awkward untidiness of the informal world of social care was appreciably allowed for even within the framework of overall formal domination (the Trimdon and Brandling studies were cases in point). It seems, therefore, that while the 'welfare environment' of neighbourhood care would be a decisive determinant of local patterns of care and the viability of any attempted bridge-building, it would be a mistake to assume that the colonising instincts of purposeful welfare authorities necessarily precluded the possibility of an authentic integration of formal and informal care.

There is also the important question of the relationships between localised caring projects and actual and potential givers of informal care in their localities. Some of the most vigorous and well-established Neighbourhood Care projects seemed, on investigation, to be rooted in relationships of social patronage; relationships in which, characteristically, middle class people offered services to working class people out of a more or less well-defined sense of class duty. In effect such projects carried the process of colonisation into the heartlands of the informal world. They were often highly 'successful' in delivering various types of service and in monitoring various types of need. Whether they did anything at all to activate or regenerate informal caring relationships among the colonised population was more obscure. At the other extreme a relationship of redundancy was also quite well documented (for example, in some features of the situation in Southfield Park). In these cases organised neighbourhood care was widely perceived as simply formalising patterns that existed in the locality anyway; an otiose, often glory-seeking dressing-up of the ordinary informal, taken-for-granted informal life of the community: "We're all good neighbours here anyway." There was no doubt that many Neighbourhood Care projects came to see themselves, and to be seen by residents, as unnecessary in this sense. What was harder to establish was whether such projects were always really redundant – whether formalisation had really had no generative or supportive effects. And the third well-documented pattern was one of isolation; a state of affairs in which a project simply failed to expand beyond its initial circle of supporters and effectively penetrate the universe of local residents. For want of Helpers, or Clients, or both, such projects languished as ineffectual enclaves of good-will within their localities. Moreover, the isolation effect seemed quite often to be linked to a developed sense of social division within the locality, a sense of 'them and us', to a refusal of some to be patronised by others, in effect.

These conclusions pointed to the need to think through more carefully the relationship between informal and formal care. The sociological studies in Part 1 also pointed in the same direction. Neighbourhood care can be provided on the basis of limited commitment by statutory Social Services or by voluntary organisations. It is occasionally provided on the basis of unlimited commitment in relations of neighbourliness. Certain very low-level forms of care, information and monitoring can no doubt also be provided through the normal networks of neighbouring or by injecting cash payments or other extrinsic rewards into the pattern of neighbourhood life. But we no longer live in the sort of society in which neighbouring grows easily into neighbourliness. Social policy, insofar as its proper concern is the delivery of services – or the stimulation of demand – should abandon the attempt to cultivate neighbourliness and turn instead to a consideration of the ways in which actual patterns of neighbouring might be effectively articulated with statutory and voluntary interventions into neighbourhood life.

Philip Abrams was concerned throughout the research on neighbours and neighbouring with the extent to which informal and formal care articulated with each other. Some consider that they are complementary, and speak of 'interweaving' them, others suggest they are more often in conflict. The evolution of Philip Abrams's ideas on this interrelationship is of interest, not only in itself but

Informal and formal care

in relation to more general debates about how to combine formal with informal care. Near the outset of the research, he saw a possible contradiction between the formal and informal sectors and asked whether interweaving was a realistic possibility.

> The drastic separation of community care from other forms of social care allows one to seize on the notion – so forcibly indicated by the general sociological literature – of an antithesis between community care and social care as a whole. Might it not be that we are faced with a profound normative conflict here between two radically opposed modes of social organisation, bureaucratic and communal? And that the growth of the bureaucratic forms of social care has therefore to be seen as a structural obstacle to community care rather than as a natural framework for it? (Abrams 1978a:79–80)

A lecture on neighbourhood care to the Volunteer Centre in 1978 was devoted almost entirely to suggesting that the world of informal neighbourliness and the world of formal care through the welfare state, far from being complementary, were deeply at odds with one another, founded on incompatible principles, even mutually exclusive.

> Consideration of the problems of social care has tended to assume the existence of a 'continuum' of forms of care running from the informal extreme of private two-person relationships to a formal extreme of large-scale public administration; a continuum from the family and the neighbours to the Department of Health and Social Security, with voluntary organisations and social work agencies ranged appropriately along it. From the point of view of understanding neighbourhood care this notion of a continuum of caring relationships is in fact misleading and dangerous, and we ought instead to start out by envisaging a discontinuity, a principled antithesis almost, between the formal and the informal. (Abrams 1978b:2)

In a paper written in 1979 and published in 1980 he pursued the idea of a frontier between them within neighbourhood care:

> Neighbourhood care can plainly mean two quite different things; it can mean the efficient delivery of bureaucratically administered welfare services to neighbourhoods, the welfare state reaching out more vigorously and comprehensively to the places where those in need reside. Or it can mean, as an alternative to the extension of the welfare state, the cultivation of effective informal caring activities within neighbourhoods *by* local residents themselves – discovering, unleashing, supporting and relying upon indigenous caring agents and locally-rooted helping networks. Clearly these two conceptions of what neighbourhood care might be are not necessarily compatible with one another. Personally, I would be inclined to argue that attempts to realise either one are likely to militate directly against the realisation of the other – that they are in principle incompatible. (Abrams 1980:12–13)

Yet Philip Abrams's views of the potential for inter-relating formal and informal care seemed to be undergoing change. Late in 1979, he gave four seminars on neighbourhood care at the Volunteer centre. Directed to an audience working primarily in the voluntary sector, the sharp antithesis between the formal and informal sectors was softened without being altogether abandoned.

> [I]n an earlier paper [Abrams 1978b], it was argued that ambiguity might well conceal a deep-seated antagonism of mutually exclusive policy options – that delivering services and evoking neighbourliness might well turn out to be alternative rather than complementary objectives. Such a view is also the implication of the orthodox sociological understanding of the nature and dynamics of local communities (cf. Nisbet 1969; Minar and Greer 1969). And it is sharply highlighted as a dilemma for social policy by Collins and Pancoast (1976). However, a year later I am not sure about this. Research by Michael Bayley (1973) and by Michael Power (1980), and increasingly our own research too, is suggesting that one can, at least in some circumstances, have it both ways; that the intrusion of artificial helping networks (whether voluntary or statutory) into a neighbourhood does not have to occur at the expense of natural helping networks. Indeed, there is some evidence that the former can positively stimulate and help to sustain the latter (Gerson *et al*. 1977). In other words, the ambiguous goals of Neighbourhood Care policies and projects now seem to me to point towards tension rather than towards contradiction. That is encouraging, but it does not of course remove the basic dilemma – which is that neighbourhood care as service delivery does not *have* to have anything to do with neighbourhood care as neighbourliness, or vice versa. Indeed, these two types of neighbourhood care could perfectly well be thought of as irrelevant to one another. Accordingly, if neighbourliness care of type (a) – neighbourliness – is thought desirable in its own right as an objective of policy, neighbourhood care in sense (b) – service delivery – will have to be designed and implemented in specific appropriate ways, which could prove an expensive, even inefficient, business. Neither type of neighbourhood care is going automatically to achieve the other. If we want both, we must develop policies specifically tailored to that double purpose. Left to themselves Neighbourhood Care policies of type (b) do not do the sorts of things that would cultivate neighbourhood care of type (a) – that is perhaps the heart of our problem. The method of formal organisation, our distinctive mode of service delivery, may not actually subvert informal care but neither is it an easy or sure way to promote it. The balance of research evidence thus leaves the dilemma of ambiguity intact.

In 1979, too, writing to E. M. Goldberg at the Policy Studies Institute, then preparing her review of research on social care of the elderly (Goldberg and Connelly 1982), he played down the antithesis for a different reason.

> On the opposition/complement debate about the relationship between formal and informal care, I have really modified my own views since writing the rather strong statements you quoted. Not that I don't still think there would be opposition if a strong informal system existed, but that I am now pretty certain that no such system does exist (at least insofar as neighbourhood is concerned) and that therefore in practice the problem does not arise. The formal agencies can to a large extent go ahead and provide whatever care they can without worrying about their side effects on natural helping networks.

As the research on Good Neighbourhood schemes progressed in the years between 1978 and 1981, Philip Abrams's scepticism about the possibilities of linking formal and informal care diminished. This change of view came about partly as a result of the national survey of Good Neighbour schemes. The Durham team found that both scheme organisers and Social Services officials

Informal and formal care

thought that there was a need to respect the boundaries between the informal and formal sectors. Open communication and contact, particularly a flow of referrals, should be encouraged between the official agency and the schemes, while at the same time the formal agency recognised the reality of less structured groups using natural local care. Formal and informal sectors should be linked, but neither should be allowed to incorporate the other. Considerable emphasis was given to the need for dialogue without control.

The overwhelming opinion within the schemes was against a policy of administrative incorporation and rationalisation by formal agencies, and in favour of dialogue.

> The trouble is that . . . [while] in order to realise their special objectives [Good Neighbour schemes] must be seen as distinct from organised social welfare, they are at the same time aware that, in certain practical respects, *organised welfare holds the key to their own survival* [emphasis in original]. Those keys are information, cases and above all, cash. (Abrams *et al.* 1981a:49)

The Durham team drew attention to the tension between the cultivation of neighbourliness and the provision of social care. In practice they could easily become separated and the latter pursued at the expense of the former. Schemes had no easy recipe for building in the rewards of neighbourliness, and in response to immediate pressure to provide caring services, tended to move toward a more traditional voluntary service type of activity and organisation. The scheme, however, which made most impact upon Philip Abrams's thinking was of a rather different kind, the Stonegate Home Warden scheme. This was of decisive importance in breaking down his scepticism about the potential for interweaving statutory and informal care.

The scheme is described in more detail in chapters 7 and 8 but the general conclusions which Philip Abrams drew were unambiguous. Stonegate could be regarded as having solved, at least in principle, the problem of combining neighbourhood care with the encouragement of neighbourliness. The daily routine of the Wardens – working within a few minutes of their own homes and thus genuine neighbours, sharing the same local social world – appeared to provide a firm base for the growth of personal and sincere caring relationships. The 'gleam of caring qualities' had often transformed their work into a form of neighbourly care based on local knowledge. The Warden's regular visits, and the simple tasks they carried out, had led to solid friendships and involvements.

The Durham team pointed out that the success of the scheme left little room for voluntary care.

> [A] formula for integrating a statutory-led comprehensive response to social need with the human qualities of neighbourhood care has been impressively worked-out. There are of course many problems unresolved . . . One that particularly struck us was that, insofar as the statutory appropriation of neighbourhood care is indeed successful both as efficient management and as sensitive care, it seems to leave little room for conventional voluntary efforts. We were not really surprised to be told by several people associated with the Home Warden service that they didn't really see how anything comparable could be provided by volunteers . . . Perhaps they were right. But if they were where does that leave all that voluntary action?

212   Organised neighbourhood care

Another, rather different, Street Warden scheme, run by volunteers, was studied in Trimdon. On the basis of this they concluded that resources and statutory professional or other organisational support are crucial to the development and provision of neighbourhood services. Money, facilities, equipment, administrative personnel, advice, particular skills and support all played an essential part in the not very extensive care provided by these two Trimdon schemes. If the sort of partnership between the statutory and voluntary sectors, which was the intended goal of The Link and its subsequent initiation of the Street Warden service, is to be a reality, then the local authorities and their official agencies have to take the point of that lesson.

The Neighbourhood Care research identified several ways in which projects with a substantial statutory base, particularly the Stonegate scheme, differed from the others studied. In Stonegate, neighbourhood care was most unlikely to be seen as a matter of neighbouring and very likely to be defined in formal terms as caring. At the same time, Helpers were particularly likely to have become personal friends of those they help ("I don't call her 'Home Warden' or 'Mrs', I call her Alice and she's my angel"). Helpers were paid, the scheme had the oldest Helpers and those who had left school earliest, and the Helpers were least likely to belong to any voluntary organisation or project other than the scheme itself. The Stonegate scheme was the project whose Helpers helped most people and did the most work for those they helped. It was the only project studied of whose Clients a majority considered the work of the project 'vital' to their own well-being. It was, moreover, a project operating in just the sort of working class milieu into which voluntary model projects had failed to penetrate.

Philip Abrams placed particular emphasis upon the fact that the Stonegate Home Wardens were paid. The scheme's importance was to demonstrate that far from being incompatible with paid work, a distinctively working class pattern of care was in fact dependent on it and could flourish on the basis of it. The contradiction between the impersonal world of bureaucratically organised wage work and the warm humanity of voluntary caring, so entrenched in the literature on social care, simply did not apply here. The whole point of this pattern of care, rather was that it was a pattern of unalienated work.

The type of care involved was characterised in chapter 10 as Care as Working Class Community. The basis of this pattern lay ultimately in class experience and culture rather than in anything else.

> Expressed in qualitative terms, it is a pattern in which care is embedded in what are seen to be natural, enjoyable, obvious, sociable relationships (however hard they may be to achieve in the actual contemporary world), relations of "empathy more than sympathy" ... In practice, the options for building such relationships seem to be caring as wage-work and neighbourhood politics. (Chapter 10, p. 197)

The Stonegate case showed how payment could harness neighbourly resources that through force of circumstances would not otherwise have been available, while also generating more informal help to the extent that it encouraged kin and neighbours to offer support to the formal help being given. It depended on a Local Authority which saw the statutory provision of care not

Informal and formal care

statically as a 'safety-net', but dynamically as a 'springboard' to provide a reliable base from which to propel voluntary and informal care into areas where they are most needed and offer the sorts of help they can realistically perform. Philip Abrams maintained that if the makers of social policy were really serious about the provision of care on a localised basis, then they should look toward the recruitment of local residents into a fully-paid army of non-professional, neighbourhood workers each carrying out a variety of tasks. The argument that neighbourhood care cannot be provided on the cheap is discussed further in the concluding chapter.

Philip Abrams's developing ideas on the relationship between formal and informal care reflected a good deal of more general uncertainty about how, if at all, the two could fit together. The debate has gone on for more than a decade, fuelled by government policies favouring 'community care' without specifying clearly what is meant by the term. An influential early formulation was that of Michael Bayley.

> The simile of the interweaving of the informal help and caring process active throughout society, and the contribution of the social services, is a sound one. It takes one beyond the stage of care *in* the community at home but living in isolation from those round about. It takes one beyond care *in* the community *in* institutions, even small ones which have little involvement or share in the community. It takes one beyond care *by* the community, if by that one is suggesting that members of the community, untrained and unaided, should be left to get on with it. It takes one to the point where a partnership of the community at large and the social services is seen as essential by both. The caring done by families, friends, neighbours or larger, more organised groups of people is seen, recognised and acknowledged. An attempt is made to see both particular needs and the strengths and limitations of the informal resources available. The social services seek to interweave their help so as to use and strengthen the help already given, make good the limitations and meet the needs. It is not a question of the social services plugging the gaps but rather of their working with society to enable society to close the gaps. (Bayley 1973:343)

Several common principles have been identified as part of the aim of 'interweaving' formal and informal care. These include the realisation that clients of statutory services have strengths and resources as well as problems and needs. To meet the shortfall between an individual's needs and their own resources, the value and importance of informal helping within an enduring social network is acknowledged. The existence of different conceptions of helping, varying with cultural norms and the particular relationship, should be recognised. Though professional and informal carers will make different contributions to care, there should be equal status, shared decision-making, mutual respect and collegiality in partnerships between professional staff and informal carers. The ultimate objective is shared responsibility for care, balancing the roles and responsibilities of each partner (Froland *et al.* 1980).

The relationship between statutory and informal sources of care has been expressed more formally by Litwak and Meyer (1966) in terms of a balance theory of coordination between bureaucratic organisations and community primary groups. Recognising that bureaucratic structures and informal groups differ markedly, social scientists have tended to emphasise the insulation and incompatibilities between the two. At one extreme is the Weberian ideal type of bureaucracy, at the other the warmth and intimacy of the family. Litwak and Meyer suggest that this antithesis has been exaggerated, and that there are in fact distinct complementarities between the two. If they are too isolated, they are likely to interfere with each other and reduce the contribution of one or the other in achieving a social goal. If they are brought too close together, their antithetical ethos is likely to disrupt one or both. If, however, coordinating mechanisms can be developed which balance their relationships at a midpoint of social distance where formal and informal care are not too intimate and not too isolated from each other, an optimum situation can be achieved. This, in essence, is the 'balance' theory.

Though this is a useful statement of the problem in more general terms, it is an abstract model. What of the reality? Philip Abrams in his earlier papers placed the main emphasis upon the discontinuities which undoubtedly exist, and several sources suggest that there are a number of different considerations which militate against straightforward 'interweaving'

One obvious one is the different roles which formal and informal carers play. Being employed to provide care establishes certain expectations, including the notion of fixed duration – hours of work or a shift – while informal care, particularly in the family, has no beginning or end unless relief is available. (For one example, see Flew 1980.) Good Neighbour schemes varied in the commitment expected, but in general they involved limited liability on the part of the care-giver (cf. Leat 1979). Professional roles and the roles of informal care-givers are different, and there exist considerable problems in attempting to integrate the two. It cannot be assumed that the two will happily co-exist side by side.

A second obstacle is status. Status and class differences were a significant factor in several of the Good Neighbour and Neighbourhood Care schemes studied, but they enter into dealings between formal and informal carers more directly. The expertise of the professional or bureaucrat often translates into a judgement of superior knowledge; problems and solutions come increasingly to be defined in terms drawn from formal care; informal care-givers are seen as needing training to acquire some degree of professional skill; and as a result, supervision of informal by formal care-givers results, rather than collaboration. The relativity of culture and local norms takes second place to professional norms and standards (Froland 1980:580).

These differences in role and status are inseparable from different kinds of knowledge which formal and informal carers value. Professionals are trained in technical skills and possess specialised information, while informal care is based on personal knowledge, whether through experience, background or culture. Informal ties are typically particularistic and ascriptive (in terms of Parsons's pattern variables). Intense patterns of local neighbouring, for example, have had their origin in what Max Weber called traditional action, whereas local Social Services and Health staff are thoroughly imbued with an orientation to rational action. 'The references for professionals are formal training, other professionals, career aspirations and the immediate working environment, while references for the informal helper centre on shared needs, experiences, and traditions within a

Informal and formal care

set of relationships with others' (Froland 1980:580). Moreover, professional knowledge is not necessarily superior. Skilled workers, for example, may lack the skills necessary to promote interweaving. They may be unable, for example, to judge when the stress of informal caring is building up. A study by Sainsbury and de Alarçon (1974) showed that even visiting psychiatrists were better at detecting demented or antisocial elderly people than they were at identifying those with neurotic tendencies or personality disorders who could be just as wearing upon their families.

Philip Abrams quoted with approval Parsons's distinction between affective and affectively-neutral action. One most important difference between formal and informal care lies in its emotional content and loading. As Roy Parker has pointed out,

> 'sharing' [care] has an attractive sound to it, it is commendable. That does not mean to say that it is easily realised. It may be hard to achieve emotionally and, practically, it may be exceedingly complicated to organise. We know, for instance, how difficult it is for the parent of the child in care to share that child's care in any meaningful fashion with residential care staff or with foster parents. Sharing care may mean sharing love or sharing anguish and pain. Not least, adults who have experienced independence may be reluctant to share their self-care with others. In fact, if one looks carefully at how tending is organised, the succession of responsibility is much more common than genuine sharing. (Parker 1981:24)

This gap between emotional involvement and detachment is not one that can easily be bridged. A number of different types of Good Neighbour scheme attempted to achieve this, but were nearer to the pole of emotional detachment than involvement. This subject of the emotional tone of care has not received enough attention in discussions of interweaving.

Different ideological outlooks also influence outcome. Too little attention is generally paid to the recipients of care, without whom no giving or provision would be possible. On what kinds of terms are they prepared to accept help? As Roy Parker has suggested (1981:24),

> [i]t may prove much more difficult than we imagine to create helpful networks for old people at the point when they are required, not least because such new arrangements may prove to be unacceptable to them. They will have no experience of an earlier mutual aid relationship to offset the potential stigma of dependence upon the gifts of virtual strangers.

Different models of the relation between formal and informal care also reflect ideological differences. Philip Abrams distinguished between coexistence, conflict and colonisation, the latter subdivided into domination, appropriation and incorporation. A similar though slightly different classification distinguished between conflict, competition, cooptation, coexistence and collaboration (Froland 1980:577–9). Such classifications reflect not just differences in practical outcome, but different evaluations of the desirable goals of the formal and informal caring sectors and the proper relationship between them. This in turn is grounded in beliefs about what each can usefully contribute to a national policy for care.

Political and professional interests are involved. To the extent that political parties favour either statutory provision or self-help, policies for relating formal to informal care will be affected. For example, traditionally the Labour Party has been profoundly distrustful of voluntary organisations as 'an odious oppression of social dignity' (Crossman 1973). The Durham team detected resistance to Good Neighbour efforts in the mining village of Sunniside on the grounds that provision for care, it was felt, should be either informal or statutory – there was no middle way. Currently, much emphasis is placed by the present Conservative government upon the virtues of self-help, though it is not entirely clear how far this is meant to extend in the social service field, nor what should be the precise role of the voluntary sector.

Various ethical dilemmas also hinder efforts to interweave formal and informal care. Professional workers have their own ethical codes and norms, but these are usually premised upon a boundary of confidence between fellow-professionals and outsiders. When it is necessary to share private information about a client with a neighbourhood care-giver who is part of a local network, entirely new problems are created. Robert Pinker pointed this out in his dissent to the Barclay Report (1982:254–6), where he referred to 'today's secular welfare evangelicals, who wish to advertise their services in every pub, pulpit and private residence in the country' without any attempt to assess the privacy implications. Darvill has raised similar questions about the attempt to mobilise neighbours and other local residents as carers. (See also Bulmer 1985b.) Will interweaving

> provide the different forms of the public world, including neighbourhood groups, with channels for spreading their tentacles into the privacy of family life further than is acceptable? Will we be forced to be active, forbidden to be lazy? Will grandma and her granddaughter ever be allowed to be free of each other? (Darvill 1983:258)

More general social trends may run counter to promotion of a policy of interweaving. "No one else could cope with my mother" is a familiar phrase to would-be volunteers, but the sociological foundations of such suspicion and the tendency to privatise family problems are poorly understood. Are these tendencies similar to those which lead to the most dependent old people in residential homes being the ones who least welcome visits and help from outside volunteers (Parker 1981:24)? Does inadequacy seek to hide its head rather than share the pain and anguish?

Administratively, channels of accountability pose a formidable obstacle to interweaving different types of care. Social workers, in particular, are part of a local government structure in which they are subordinate to managers who themselves are answerable to the chief executive and committees of elected representatives. Though in practice they have quite a high degree of professional autonomy, this represents quite a major obstacle to experiments with money or people. It is perhaps significant that some of the attempts to interweave formal and informal care have been concerned far more with the elderly, with whom social workers are much less involved, than with children, where they are involved. Indeed, apart from self-help in caring among mothers with young children, the main form of intervention with children is statutory, within tightly-

Informal and formal care

drawn legal limits and within highly formalised procedures. Where the informal sector is involved, this is either (like the Street Wardens) on a payment basis, as with fostering, or responsibility is completely transferred over a period of time, as with adoption.

Accountability also serves as a powerful barrier, even within the formal sector, between personal Social Services and Health services. One of the objects of 'patch' or locally-based systems of Social Service delivery appears to be not just to try to bring formal provision closer to the recipients, but to break down some of these bureaucratic obstacles between different services. Indeed, to do so may be a more important practical achievement of such experiments than the institution of general interweaving, though it is too early to judge.

Even within a particular service, there may be barriers which are an important hindrance to the merging of formal and informal sectors (Offer 1984). The role of welfare assistants is one example. These are attached to area officers of Social Service Departments, doing routine but useful work such as checking facts or escorting the elderly to hospital. But why is it necessary for such functions to be handled centrally and bureaucratically, rather than locally in the area where the clients live?

In the Stonegate case, the Durham team found that Street Wardens had little contact with local social workers and did not find them very effective when they did. The first stage of the Dinnington research (Bayley *et al.* 1984) showed that home helps and Wardens, though playing an important role at the local level, had slight contact with other field workers such as social workers, health visitors, etc. Other professionals did not exploit the position of Warden and home help to best advantage, leaving the workers, especially the Wardens, feeling isolated (Bayley 1982:194–5).

Fiscal policy has played a part too in hindering the interweaving of formal and informal sectors. In particular, the tax and social security position of informal carers is in many ways disadvantageous. Married women who give up work to look after invalid relatives are particularly penalised, both in terms of the tax burden on the family and in not being entitled to Invalid Care Allowance. Additionally, their pensions suffer. Underlying these policies is a difference of political outlook, not corresponding to party lines, between those who welcome paying taxes and local rates in order to be relieved of responsibility for awkward people and to be freed of extended family ties, and on the other hand those who desire *not* to spend too much on public services, especially for the poor, dislike large local government bureaucracy and favour volunteer and informal forms of care.

Philip Abrams was therefore justified in his early papers in emphasising the obstacles which there were to bringing formal and informal care together. There existed and exist a considerable number of quite powerful difficulties in the way of interweaving the two, which he was right to bring out. As he became more involved in the Durham research, however, the barriers came to seem rather less salient, and the scope for collaboration more promising. Part of the pressure for interweaving has come from social trends indicating greater need and demand. Though the elderly population is not growing as a percentage of the whole population, dramatic changes are taking place in the structure of the elderly population itself with a rapid increase in the proportion of 'very old' (over 75).

Another important factor has been the continuing willingness of carers to assume responsibility for care. A high proportion of the elderly, for example, are cared for by members of their families. Research in rural Wales has shown that approximately one-quarter of the elderly receive help with routine chores and household maintenance. Most of this help comes from the family, but subgroups who do not have kin nearby depend to a larger degree on friends and neighbours. These include the single, the childless, those who live alone or with elderly relatives, and those who have no close relations. Only a small proportion of the elderly (less than 5%) need help with personal care, and for them most help comes from another member of the household, usually a spouse. Though the family is the main support, friends and neighbours are an important source of borrowing things and transport (Grant and Wenger 1983:41–2).

Other factors favouring interweaving have been cutbacks in public spending, a desire to combine the best of statutory provision with local community mobilisation, and criticism of the quality of care provided in formal institutions such as hospitals, residential homes and homes for the mentally handicapped (Darvill 1983:251–5). At its most optimistic, interweaving was seen as a form of total community care. Formal authorities would have an enabling role *vis-à-vis* informal care through fiscal measures and the provision of support services.

> Let us spell out clearly ... what interweaving is not. Interweaving is not about shifting responsibility from statutory services onto informal providers. Neither is it about co-opting and colonizing informal systems or about superimposing existing packages of care on the community. If interweaving is to work well, it must start from the perspective of the community or locality as a caregiving system by seeking to reinforce and optimise existing resources and creating resources to fill gaps in provision. It therefore requires familiarity with family and neighbourhood networks; consultation with network members as well as clients, development of partnerships with other social services, such as doctors' practices, schools, churches and voluntary organisations; and ... a requirement to view the whole community as both needing and offering support. (Grant and Wenger 1983:48)

For interweaving to work effectively, a shift in focus from the authority of statutory services to the resources inherent in the locality has to be achieved (Wenger 1984:189). Different models have been proposed – 'patch' social work by Hadley and McGrath (1980, 1984), the use of volunteers (Harbert and Rogers 1983), the mobilisation of informal helping networks by the Barclay Report (1982) – but a common element is the aim of achieving less reliance upon services imposed from above and greater reliance on informal local inputs. Philip Abrams fully appreciated that this involved questions of local power and accountability. This was embodied in his model of colonisation–conflict–cooperation, and in ideas about the mobilisation of neighbourhoods discussed in the next chapter. His analysis of the relationship between informal and formal care was not, however, uncontested. His most explicit critic, Michael Bayley (1981), argued that Abrams's model of colonisation was too undirectional. In addition to the possibility of the formal colonising the informal, there was the possibility of the informal colonising the formal. It was positively

Informal and formal care

unhelpful to posit a 'principled antithesis' when what one was trying to develop was a sensitive understanding of the relationship between the two.

In conclusion, it would be quite inappropriate to regard Philip Abrams as having had the last word on the relationship between formal and informal care. If in his early papers he somewhat overstated the antithesis, he revised his views in the light of empirical evidence produced by the Neighbourhood Care project. At his death his ideas were still evolving, in a field where ideology and value-preference still tend to take precedence over well-grounded research conclusions. But at least his work was not open to the criticism of glossing over sociological realities to achieve a particular policy objective, as the Barclay Report has been criticised (Allan 1983; Timms 1983; Bulmer 1985b). His sociological approach to social policy was detached and unsentimental, with a continuing insistence on recognising the limits of choice in a society which imposed real constraints on policy-makers.

His work was not definitive because the shifting boundary between formal and informal care remains one of the most keenly debated in the politics, policy and professional practice of social care. Wenger (1984:191) posits a pendulum effect in social service provision in many European countries between centralism and localism. The proper boundary between statutory and family care is of keen interest to Conservative governments in several countries. Welfare evangelicals of various hues proclaim the merits of locally-based services and interweaving. The two great virtues of Philip Abrams's approach were to provide a conceptual analysis of the relationship between informal and formal care, grounded in sociological theory, not personal beliefs or rhetoric, and to insist that the issues needed to be resolved through empirical research. As Goldberg and Connelly have observed in the course of their research review, 'the suggestion that statutory, voluntary and semi-voluntary neighbourhood services can mesh with each other still does not answer the question ... where the one ends and the other begins' (1982:169). What is in no doubt is that further work is needed on this important and contentious area.

Conclusion

12 Neighbours and neighbourhood care: a forward look

Philip Abrams's work on neighbours and neighbourhood care blended social philosophy, sociology and social policy in a rich mixture. The account of his work here is necessarily incomplete, since it breaks off with his death, but is by no means static. Indeed, one of his foremost characteristics was his delight in intellectual exploration, sometimes pushing alternative interpretations to the point of paradox. In this final chapter, some of his general reflections are presented and the implications of his work for the future study of informal social ties and for social care policy brought out. In doing so, the fertility of the blend which he achieved between philosophy, sociology, social policy and other lines of thought is worth emphasising. In an age when observance of conventional academic boundaries is the rule, he was an exception who was not content to be confined by a single discipline. Not only did he seek to link creatively the study of social policy to sociology, but drew on the work of economists, anthropologists and historians to strengthen the analyses put forward.

This fertility is apparent in his reflections upon the philosophy of social care. In the study of social policy and administration in Britain there has been a strain – for some too strong and overt a strain – of moral philosophy. In Philip Abrams's work it was self-effacing and unobtrusive, a sceptical rational humanism without illusions about the perfectibility of human beings. Not for nothing was there a picture of the title page of Hobbes's *Leviathan* in the corridor outside his Durham office.

Unusually, in a seminar given at The Volunteer Centre in the autumn of 1979, he examined the place of values in the study of neighbourhood care. He emphasised at the outset that no single view was adequate. Moralities were one-sided onslaughts on the complexities of life, but since life was many-sided, no morality had a unique claim to correctness. Neighbourhood care was a case in point. It was an essentially contested concept, in Gallie's term (1956).

The inner complicity of the achievement signified by the concept often seems to amount to nothing less than a unity of moral contradictions. The idea of neighbourhood care accredits a fusion of the formal and informal, of egoism and altruism, of reciprocity and patronage, of autonomy and social control, of tradition and innovation, of self-help and dependency. Such a package of antitheses is bound to be riddled with moral ambiguity and a rich mine of evaluative conflict. In particular, the dominant role of altruism must be questioned. From the Charity Organisation Society to Richard Titmuss's *The Gift Relationship* (1970) there was a fragile practical consensus that caring was a primarily altruistic activity and as such morally and socially desirable. Debate centred on the problem of whether or not altruism was merely an option in human relationships or could be shown to be a transcendent duty, a natural imperative or even, as Titmuss proposed, a fundamental individual right. But another body of criticism was developing which challenged drastically the claims made for altruism as an unambiguous and one-dimensional basis for moral action. 'One of the commonest ways of being self-centred is to put other people in your debt by doing things for them' (Macmurray 1935:156–7). Psychologists proclaimed the largely self-seeking nature of much seemingly altruistic behaviour (Schwartz 1967). Radical social critics of both left and right denounced the ways in which the altruistic acts of donors violated the autonomy of recipients (Illich *et al.* 1977; Simpkin 1979). Anthropologists documented the extent to which gifts had to be understood as tools for the creation of either dependency or debt (Mauss 1925; Malinowski 1922; Bailey 1971). Political theorists such as Mill, Hobhouse and Oakeshott advanced the claims of both equality and personal freedom against the patronising or colonising intrusions of the altruist. In the strong colours of other bands of the moral spectrum the altruistic justification for care began to appear increasingly blurred, murky and dubious. Helping could be seen as a complicated form of controlling; giving as a complicated way of taking; altruism as reciprocity.

Care can be seen as both natural and contrived, as at once needed and imposed, as simultaneously enhancing and impoverishing the lives both of those who receive and of those who give. When we introduce the additional element of the neighbourhood the problem becomes even worse. Richard Titmuss attempted a distinction between gifts as tools and gifts as gifts, recognising the potentially coercive nature of giving and, most oddly, insisting on the importance of anonymity and distance in social care as a means of eliminating the self-oriented side-effects of altruism (people should be free to give but not to decide to whom they give; the recipients of care should be 'strangers').

One strain of radical criticism of altruism holds that it is intellectually fraudulent and socially pernicious. Historians have repeatedly demonstrated the ways in which progressives and reformers of all kinds have expected childishness from the 'dependent' as the price of care; the violation or surrender of rights being justified through the unexamined application of the equation: need = dependency = non-competence. Sociologists of caring institutions and agencies have identified category upon category of caring agents as little more than a sort of moral secret police. A great deal of social care can be seen as a 'coerced waiver of rights' on the back of economic inequity, as an alternative to recognising the latter as the real problem (Glasser 1978; Illich *et al.* 1977; Gaylin 1978).

In a sustained attack on the 'pathology of caring' Simpkin (1979) argues that all attempts to legitimate social policy in terms of care must be seen as masking efforts to inflate the roles and power of those designated as care-givers by deepening the dependency and powerlessness of the cared-for. The more personalised the provision of care becomes, the more the beneficiary is brought face to face with this segregation and the more effectively impersonal social control is enforced. The strength of Simpkin's analysis is that it does

Neighbours and neighbourhood: a forward look

reveal the full extent to which care and control are inextricably connected. Its weakness – and it is a crippling one to my mind – is that his alternative, to substitute the concept of radical social work for that of care, totally fails to break the connection. Radicalising the clients is no less an exercise in colonisation than the more conventional relationships. It is only spuriously more client-oriented. In effect it, too, proposes to use the weak for the purposes of the strong.

Granting that we cannot hope to find a single value, harmonious cluster of values or moral first principle in terms of which neighbourhood care should be definitively assessed, there is no need to despair of the possibility of evaluation. Neither amoralism nor situation ethics are forced upon us by the empirical and conceptual contradictoriness of neighbourhood care. Admittedly, the concept accredits an achievement which presupposes a synthesis of antagonistic values. That does not make it incomprehensible. Nor does it leave practical attempts at neighbourhood care beyond the scope of moral judgement in everyday life. What it does is (a) to force one to recognise that any moral appraisals of neighbourhood care that one advances will be or may be (quite properly) contested, and (b) to encourage one, therefore, to recognise the sense of adopting at least some measure of moral pluralism in making such appraisals. Rather than insisting on the right to altruism or to autonomy, rather than championing the 'natural' reciprocities of informal neighbourhood life (which are of course not natural at all) or public responsibilities for the reliable and accountable satisfaction of this or that need, the sensible course is to allow that any achievement of neighbourhood care is going to be based not on the unequivocal pursuit of this or that value or morality but on an accommodation of values, a more or less uneasy coexistence of moralities.

Those of us who believe in neighbourhood care are stuck with the task of defending an enterprise which devotees of simple moralities will assail from all sides. We can do so in my view only by asserting strenuously the pragmatic *desirability* of contradiction, the morality of trying to have your cake and eat it – that is, of working at both care *and* autonomy, both the informal *and* the formal, both spontaneity and accountability, both *Gemeinschaft and Gesellschaft*. We can degrade people by caring for them; and we can degrade them by not caring for them (Marcus 1978). We must encourage life to defy the simplicities of moral philosophy.

So we must learn to live where we are. One requirement for that is to possess some sort of moral compass, some sense of the multiplicity of directions from which value arguments, the winds of morality, can blow. It is at this point, rather than in the wrangles about care versus autonomy, formal versus informal social action, egoism versus altruism that we enter a worthwhile field of debate, an area where the empirical and the evaluative could hope for a fruitful meeting. Following Durkheim and Weber, in the mainstream of sociological theory, there are four primary directions of morality, four lodestones of practical moral life in terms of which social action is organised and in terms of which it may properly be evaluated. They are Custom, Altruism, Reciprocity and Egoism. All social action, and especially the social action embodied in 'caring', could usefully be analysed in terms of some such conception of the fundamental tendencies of morality and it would not be absurd to argue that relationships which held all four tendencies in balance in a manner satisfactory to all parties concerned could be judged 'good' relationships.

Where did Philip Abrams see the sociological study of neighbours and neighbouring leading? At the most abstract level, his philosophical and sociological ideas overlapped. The considerable emphasis which he placed upon reciprocity, and the need to develop a theory of neighbouring as social exchange, ran through his writing from the beginning of the first phase onwards. The transactional element in social relations between neighbours had not been given enough attention in the sociological literature, and, drawing on economics and anthropology, he placed it centre stage. His analysis of reciprocity, however, was a subtle one, recognising that it could take different forms and be deferred for long periods of time. The material in chapter 6 will continue to provoke sociologists to further clarify the basis of informal social relationships.

Local social ties of an informal kind, he was clear, had nowadays to be studied in terms of social networks rather than either individuals or institutions, while he fought shy of reifications such as the 'community' or even 'neighbourhood'. Neighbourhoods in their modern form were social constructions (cf. Suttles 1972) rather than passive geographical entities. The transition from traditional to modern neighbourhoodism (see pages 91–5) had swept away the archetypal form of *Gemeinschaft*. It was being replaced by other bases. Friendship was one (see pp. 95–9), but the political element was especially salient. It is arguable that Philip Abrams overdrew the contrast between traditional and modern neighbourhoodism, or at least that the evidence for the view that traditional neighbourhoodism was lost needed much fuller documentation, and indeed is a proposition which requires testing in further research. Nevertheless, he clearly believed modern neighbourhoodism had a strong political element.

Attempts to revive traditional local social networks are largely misguided if it is hoped thereby to secure patterns of neighbourliness which will provide care with anything like the measures of coverage and reliability possibly achieved by the most tightly-knit versions of such networks in the past. One cannot and should not want to re-create the conditions for that sort of neighbourliness. What *is* possible is to accept that the so-called 'informal' system of social care – except as a system of care between kin – is irretrievably lost, but that an adequate substitute for it can be found in the formal projects and schemes of the new neighbourhoodism. This means recognising that the networks generated by the new neighbourhoodism are essentially and necessarily political in nature; their energy and effectiveness are tied to the fact that they are making *demands*. This in turn means that instead of patronising or colonising the local community, as envisaged by the original conception of neighbourhood care, the existing statutory and voluntary agencies are going to have to learn to live with it as an equal. Whether or not one goes as far as some American city governments, some serious surrender of powers is unavoidable if one really wants any significant measure of social care to be provided within neighbourhood social networks (Abrams 1980:23).

> Modern neighbourhoodism in its purest form is an attempt by newcomers (and in principle we are all newcomers now) to *create* a local social world through political or quasi-political action. Great organisational skills and ingenious organisational devices are often used in attempts to mobilise old and new residents alike in order to protect amentities, enhance resources and, to a greater or lesser degree, wrench control of the local *milieu* from outside authorities and vest it in strictly local hands. Much of the driving force and most of the success of the enormous diversity of Neighbourhood Care projects up and down the country springs from these sources.
>
> Admittedly the movement is not nearly as developed in this country yet as it is in, say, the United States, where neighbourhood associations have become formal members of the 'urban partnership' embodied in the President's programme for the cities, where a national Neighbourhoods' Commission has deliberated (National Commission on Neighbourhoods, 1979), and where many cities – Atlanta, Washington, Pittsburgh, for example – have granted legal recognition to neighbourhood councils which exercise varying degrees of autonomy over planning and service delivery for their respective areas. Nevertheless, the elements of the movement already exist here and are becoming increasingly self-conscious (for one example see Gibson 1984). Neighbourhood associations are arguing that they can deliver services to local residents more efficiently (and more humanely) than bureaucracies administered by the city, county or state (cf. Hallman 1984).
>
> The problem of neighbourhood care is not one of propping up or renewing the traditional type of neighbourhood network. It is a problem of coexisting with troublesome, demanding and often extremely hostile formal organisations which, for all that, can and do develop and sustain networks of sociability and care within localities in ways public bureaucracies and their staffs plainly cannot. Neighbourhood care is a real possibility in our sort of society. But not on the basis of reinforcing or renewing the traditional informal networks as the Seebohm and Wolfenden Committees seem to have imagined. Those networks are dying and should be allowed to die. Today, neighbourhood care means working out a constructive relationship between the state, nationally and locally, and neighbourhoodism, the politicised voice of local attachment. (Abrams 1980:18–19)

This interest in the mobilisation of local residents was reflected in the plans for the third phase of the research on the Caring Capacity of the Community. A vigorous, grass-roots, neighbourhood organisation seeking, among other things, to protect its territory from the encroachment of outside authorities, was seen as an essential element. One major element in the third phase was a study entitled 'Mobilising Community Involvement', subsequently carried out after Philip Abrams's death by Ray Snaith (see Snaith 1985).

He studied two disadvantaged inner city areas on Tyneside as a microcosm of the working out of alternative strategies for community involvement, both by local residents and by the state. These were two 'hard to let' estates, in Newcastle and Gateshead, identified as priority areas within the Inner City Partnership authorities. Different forms of involvement studied included juvenile jazz bands, mothers' and toddlers' groups, luncheon clubs, tenants' groups, community centre management committees, and women's and unemployed support groups. From the point of view of residents, involvement is a matter of breaking out of the private world of the family, friends and neighbours, and of reassessing individualistic solutions to social problems and common needs. There is a range of options for public participation from traditional recreational and social groups (such as the sports club or working-men's club) through self-help or caring for others to agency-linked volunteers, official cooptation of activists or independently organised political protest. Action may be initiated by statutory bodies, by the organised voluntary sector, or at the grass-roots.

Snaith's study (1985) considered the nature and impact of intensive, area-based, urban management, critically examined the charge of apathy in disadvantaged urban neighbourhoods and investigated the varied character of community involvement in practice using semi-structured interviews and participant observation. The focus was on the relation between formal provision and informal involvement, and the scope for sharing power with citizens in the meeting of need, the possibilities of decentralising services, and the scope for encouraging and funding a non-statutory sector of groups and projects of various kinds to mobilise community involvement.

The research grant application stated the research focus thus: It is clear both in this country and much more dramatically in the United States that under certain conditions vigorous community involvement in social policy is a practical possibility. Such involvement is most likely to occur and most likely to spill over into improved community care (both 'in' and 'by' the community) when it is mobilised by way of fairly high politicised neighbourhood movements and organisations – groups which see themselves as battling rather than collaborating with existing institutional authorities.

Ray Snaith has suggested in a personal communication that the idea of neighbourhood care in the context of locality needs further refinement. In principle the pursuit of political aims which bring people together can be a necessary condition for fostering informal, friendly or caring contacts, but they are not sufficient in practice. Philip Abrams did not specify the sufficient conditions for turning localised political mobilisation into longer term self-generating relationships of a different, non-political kind based on sociability and helpful exchange. Nor did he adequately reference his argument to consideration of the theory of the state.

Philip Abrams was not able to fulfil his aim of visiting the United States to study the Neighbourhood movement there. The much livelier American scene, with active neighbourhood organisations and a strong 'local control' movement, reflects both a different system of central and local government, and the much greater degree of urban blight than in Britain. How far American experience can be translated to the British context directly must be open to doubt. However, it provides and raises general issues that deserve fuller consideration from a sociological standpoint.

Take, for example, the claim, with echoes of the Greek city state, that

> there is special virtue of politics based on a small space, in which some people can, by and large, know one another and share some sense of the place in which they live – and consequently share civic interests. Politics in a space of human scale permits face-to-face citizenship. (Morris and Hess 1975:9)

Neighbours and neighbourhood: a forward look

The National Commission on Neighbourhoods suggested (1979:234–5) that:

> neighbourhoods serve as important mediating structures between individuals in their private lives and the larger institutions of public life. Neighbourhoods are the settings within which human scale organizations operate – the churches, schools, civic associations, and small businesses that serve to bring the individual into the social fabric of the community. By using the mediating structure of the neighbourhood and its local institutions as channels for human services, they can be organized and delivered in ways that more adequately meet the needs of individuals. At the same time, residents can contribute their own strengths to the community by participating in the development of services.

The concept of 'mediating structures', introduced in chapter 1, is a fruitful way of generalising Philip Abrams's sociological approach to the neighbourhood. It has echoes of the 'corporation' or occupational association of Durkheim (whom he much admired), but on a different basis. Reflecting on the American debates about local control, Janowitz and Suttles suggest that the locality provides a milieu in which the civic ideals of democracy can be given some meaning in face to face encounters.

> The survival of parliamentary democracies depends heavily upon how nearly its separate, local parts – its more intimate circles – relate to and interpret the larger movements of the wider society. Here, the local community seems to have a central, if not unique, role. Where the family, the peer group, and the church congregation tend to be very homogeneous and to have very narrow interests, the local community creates a potential interface between diverse interests and the opportunity to debate, sort, sift and balance each against the other. This potential is of extraordinary importance, for while it is the habit of sociologists and most contrived groups to speak of narrowly defined interests, real individuals are the repository of an aggregate of interests, most of them poorly represented by the formal groups that currently have an acknowledged role in the political process. It is in the local community that individuals have the opportunity – by no means always realised – both to internalise and aggregate the diverse gains and costs of public policy. (1978:84–5)

Philip Abrams then, in writing of the scope for political mobilisation within neighbourhoods, was tapping into a rich sociological vein, and one moreover with considerable relevance for public policy. For example, Lord Scarman, in his report on the Brixton disorders of 1981, urged greater consultation between local authorities and community groups over resource allocation, and observed that 'inner cities are not human deserts; they possess a wealth of voluntary effort and goodwill' (1982:159–60). Philip Abrams's ideas on how mobilisation might occur, and on what basis neighbourhoods could be organised, were not spelled out, but he had begun to develop a fruitful line of sociological speculation.

This discussion of neighbourhood mobilisation, 'local control' and mediating structures, is a good example of how difficult it is to draw a sharp line between the sociological and social policy elements in Philip Abrams's work. This is true also of his typological analysis of the forms of relationship between neighbourhood groups and the larger world of statutory and voluntary agencies – neglect, colonisation, conflict and coexistence (see pages 129–33). For this was both a sociological analysis of power relations and a typology for the study of the interweaving of formal and informal care. Philip Abrams did not live to read the Barclay Report (1982). Had he done so he would have endorsed the sociological critique of it offered by Graham Allan (1983) (whose earlier work (1977; 1979) Philip Abrams referred to constantly), pointing out the unreality of many of the sociological assumptions about informal networks and their mobilisation on which it rested (see also Bulmer 1985b). The relationship between formal and informal care remains of central interest in social policy, and needs to continue to be studied sociologically as a phenomenon of power and organisation. For example, one hypothesis to explore, derived from Roberto Michels, is that organisation is both a vital condition for mobilising involvement and antithetical to its persistence. Instances of self-liquidating organisations become of particular interest in that context.

Crossing fully the line from sociology to social policy, Philip Abrams's work had a number of general themes of continuing significance. One important distinction he maintained throughout, and indeed it is reflected in the bifurcated structure of this book. There was an antithesis between neighbourhood care as sociability and neighbourhood care as service delivery. The former involved informal social contact and exchange through 'natural' localised social networks, the paradigm case being next-door neighbours helping one another; the latter entailed the more organised provision of 'care', whether transport, shopping, or other necessary social services. To some extent his argument about the frontier between formal and informal care rested on this distinction. Neighbourhood care he saw as becoming a meeting ground for the informal values of reciprocity, mutual defence, proximity exclusion and internal social control and the formal values of provision, coverage, distance, accountability and external social control.

At one extreme, represented by Boswell village, informal values were totally predominant. But this was the exception rather than the rule. The usual problem was how to tap caring capabilities in other contexts. The tradition of caring was itself rooted in a special sort of reciprocity and therefore could be renewed through social policy if means were found of giving people opportunities to engage in caring relationships. There was no evidence that society was running out of caring mothers (cf. Nodding 1984). That being so, the problem was to find ways of enabling people to renew their involvement in caring relationships despite the mobility and uncertainty of their personal careers, their distance from their own kin and the probable strangeness of the social environments in which at any moment in their lives they were likely to find themselves. Robin Humphrey's research at the third phase explicitly addressed the issue of how formal organisations might foster informal networks (1984).

He made a case study of an attempt by a voluntary organisation, Age Concern, to combat isolation by instigating informal networks in a town where the proportion of elderly people was rising rapidly as the young migrated in search of jobs. This was weakening informal support systems. Age Concern's strategy was to draw old people into a popular event that would provide a suitable setting for the development of friendships and the reinforcing of neighbourly ties. Although the participants in this event were indeed found to benefit socially by

Neighbours and neighbourhood: a forward look

their participation (they were significantly more involved in friendship networks than a control sample of other local elderly people), it had only a limited impact on the social life of the elderly in the town as a whole. The event was successful in attracting only a highly specific group of elderly people; they were all women and over half were widowed. In addition, many of these women were found to fashion their social lives through participating regularly in a number of voluntary activities. This was, in part, a response to the deep divide that exists between the social lives of elderly men and women in such a homogeneous working class ex-mining town. Women, independently from men, were virtually excluded from the traditional formal social facilities available in the town. For similar cultural reasons, men did not engage in the voluntary activities seen as the domain of women. The possibilities for the successful promotion of informal networks by formal organisations were therefore limited by the surrounding social environment.

The possible tensions between the informal and formal sides of care were evident even in the Stonegate Street Warden scheme, where the morale of Wardens had to be bolstered against other local residents (who were not clients) who complained that they also should receive the service. Such feelings could well be reinforced and disseminated by neighbourhood social networks so that a particular Warden could find herself viewed as a source of trouble among her neighbours rather than as a provider of help. In extreme cases such reactions could even reach out to affect the clients, increasing their isolation from the rest of the neighbourhood rather than reducing it.

The conditions favouring each type of care were becoming more apparent. As he told the Volunteer Centre seminar in 1979: Reciprocity and engrained, usually religious, norms of beneficence favour neighbourliness; as do social closure and insecurity of certain kinds; and information, time, trust and competence. On the other hand, cash and material facilities for transport, contact and monitoring favour localised service provision; as do patch, Street Warden and out-work forms of organisation and a relative autonomy of volunteers and social work assistants *vis-à-vis* professionals and statutory agencies. There is no necessary fit or compatibility between these two types of care. Moreover, the first form of neighbourhood care, 'natural' neighbourhood care, is not going to flourish 'naturally' in our sort of society on a significant scale. Even where it *appears* to flourish, it is the relationships of kinship (above all) and of friendship that usually turn out to be the real bonds, not those of neighbouring. On the other hand we know that about 0.5% of the population (say, 300,000 people) are fairly actively engaged in organised voluntary efforts to promote the cultivation of neighbourhood care in the second sense, the sense of grafting service delivery into localities.

None of the various efforts to foster neighbourhood care have found a recipe for consummating the marriage of the two kinds of neighbourhood care with the measure of success (in terms of reliability, continuity, skill, coverage and responsibility) that would make it possible for neighbourhood care to replace other forms of care. The only realistic expectation about the relationship between neighbourhood care, in either sense, and other forms of care is one cast in terms of balance, coexistence and complementarity – good neighbours

232   Conclusion

as nursing-aids perhaps, but not as substitute nurses. And at that level we know that most actual versions of such relationships are currently – to the extent that they flourish at all – fairly authoritarian or fairly conflict-laden forms of colonisation and of response to colonisation rather than forms of coexistence and mutual support. Meanwhile, on the ground, politics rather than neighbouring would seem to be the most important relationship for the cultivation of neighbourhood care in either sense; above all if one wants to cultivate it simultaneously in both senses. Organisational and political themes rather than the evocation of natural helping networks or latent norms of neighbourliness play a decisive part.

He thought that if neighbourhood care was treated as a project or an ideal, rather than a description of the world, then there was no reason why one should not aim both to pursue neighbourliness and to maximise localised service delivery. Acknowledging that it was an ethical and political programme, Philip Abrams discussed the possibilities for future action in terms of voluntary action for neighbourhood involvement and voluntary action for informal care. (These are developed more fully in Abrams 1985.) The theme of voluntary action for neighbourhood involvement was pursued explicitly in Robin Humphrey's research in the third phase of the research (Humphrey 1984).

Philip Abrams began the discussion of voluntary action for neighbourhood involvement by distinguishing six types of voluntary work: direct service-giving of a philanthropic kind; helping to run a voluntary organisation; financial assistance; public service (e.g. membership of a local authority); participation in self-help groups for people with common problems; and pressure group activity (Jones, Brown and Bradshaw 1978:80). He was concerned with action falling into the last two types, self-help or pressure group activity. Voluntary organisations interested in neighbourhood involvement needed to combine an activist, self-liquidating image of organisation with a populist theory of politics. They should cultivate the 'intimate-enemy' relationship with public authority and external agencies rather than the more service orientations of the 'harem' or 'call-girl'. Relevant examples of effective practice would be found in the area between the twelve Community Development projects on the one hand and the fifteen hundred or so amenity societies on the other, rather than in the experience of the familiar charitable and service-delivery organisations.

Neighbourhood involvement, in his view, was increasingly political, a matter of recruitment to social movements rather than the receipt of social services. Voluntary groups would have to proceed as champions and advocates rather than as patrons and providers – perhaps even as trouble-makers rather than trouble-shooters. He recognised, however, the obstacles that lay in its way. Such a strategy required that local residents tried to shape the destiny of their neighbourhood for themselves. A strong and authentic local base was needed – but this ran counter to the trend for leading voluntary organisations to become 'national' rather than 'local' in orientation. The determination to wrest power from a range of statutory authorities ran counter to the ethos of collaboration, liaison and dependency characteristic of voluntary–statutory relations. And action needed an image of community that local residents could identify with, not the alien image often imparted by the middle class leadership of such organisations (for example, middle class newcomers to rural villages, cf. Newby 1979). Organisations, moreover, created their own problems. At the neighbourhood level there was a tendency for organisations to become redundant in the eyes of residents. Either the job for which they were created had been done and they were seen as increasingly pointless, or incapable of promoting the issue for which they were created and so progressively less worthwhile. Yet the sheer apparatus of organisation and its rewards for those staffing it allowed organisations to persist long after they 'lost' their issues. The crisis in the late 1970s in the National Federation of Community Associations was a striking example. There often came a point when 'the logic of organisation' got in the way of issues and of local involvement.

Voluntary action for informal care, on the other hand, was a different world – one of relations, reciprocity and religion.

Something like nine-tenths of the care given to those who in various ways cannot fend for themselves in our society is given by spouses, parents, children and other kin. If any policy for informal social care is to be relevant to the actualities of need and provision it must begin with relations and the problems and possibilities of supporting the bonds of kinship. The two principal motivational bases of informal care, altruism and reciprocity, develop most strongly – some would say uniquely – within the world of kinship. The ideal of domiciliary care proclaimed by the vast majority of those actually and prospectively in need of care is in effect a blunt preference for the family. Most of the work of neighbours, friends and members of voluntary agencies (including Good Neighbour schemes), and indeed of many statutory employees, can reasonably be viewed as either supplementing and supporting the work of relations or filling the gap in the lives of those in need who for one reason or another have no relations. The fact that quite large numbers of people are in this last predicament (say, between 5 and 10% of the population of an average neighbourhood), does not seriously qualify the case for regarding kinship, and the provision of surrogate kin, as the crux of the system, and of the problem of informal care. The task is essentially one of evoking and sustaining commitment. It begins unthinkingly, exploiting the 'natural', that is, socialised, commitment of close relations to one another and proceeds increasingly deliberately and overtly to seek ways of deepening and reinforcing that commitment and of building functional equivalents to it among non-kin.

A vital precondition for this commitment is competence. Readiness to help in principle is blocked in practice by a disabling fear of the risks. Conversely, it is found again and again that those who do volunteer to give care informally are recruited decisively from those who have given care previously or for other reasons see themselves as knowing how the job should be done. Fortunately, competence can be learned – either through direct experience or through a wide range of more formal educational methods.

Over and above competence, informal care thrives on reciprocity. If carers are characteristically recruited from those who have given care or been taught how to give care in the past, they are no less typically recruited from those who are aware of themselves as having previously received care. And although one can hardly envisage training people for reciprocity as easily as one might think of training them for competence, there are practical possibilities for enhancing the perception of reciprocal involvement with others which really ought to be considered. It is a matter of creating contexts for reciprocity. Many voluntary organisations, and especially many Good Neighbour schemes, seem in practice to work in just that way. It is the key to the often spectacular success of so many so-called 'self-help' organisations: self-help is mutual help. Conversely, helping others can be self-help; for a substantial majority of those who give help informally to people other than their kin, it certainly *is* self-help. The important thing is not to run away from, or be embarrassed by, the selfish implications of helping other people. Many of the most successful voluntary projects which seek to recruit helpers and carers for the informal system (such as Good Neighbour schemes) understand this very well. The array of devices by which organisers lead volunteers to an appreciation of 'what's in it for them' is extensive and well known. It is not only the relationship with clients but the social milieu of the project itself which can be used in this way. Reciprocity is not a dirty word. An extension of that principle which could be more controversial but which is nevertheless used successfully by many projects is actually to seek to recruit informal carers from among those who themselves need or could benefit from informal care.

The third major basis of informal social care is religion. About three-fifths of Good Neighbour schemes could equally well be described as Good Christian schemes and across the whole range of informal caring, from nursing dependent relatives at home to visiting and doing odd jobs for strangers, people with a strong sense of religious commitment are disproportionately active. Perhaps what is needed here is more research. From a practical point of view it would be very useful to know what if anything stands behind the norm of altruism which religious carers invoke. Why, for example, should that norm appear to work as a source of informal care so much more strongly among working class Catholics than among most other religious groups? Because it is peculiarly a 'community' religion? Because of the peculiar policies of that particular church in relation to birth control? Because of the relative social segregation of the social milieux in which working class Catholics live? One could list a host of possibilities to explain the differential involvement of particular religious groups in informal care and all of them would point behind the norm of altruism to fairly complicated origins and concomitants of informal care mediated by religious belief rather than fully determined by it. Again, religion is obviously an important 'enabling' factor in informal care – an alternative perhaps to practical competence in providing a basis of legitimacy and confidence from which to act. But, again, why should some religious groups, middle class Protestants for example, seem to be so much more blessed in this respect than others? In other words the definite correlation of religion and informal care does not lead me to propose a policy of more vigorous religious education. Instead it suggests the need for closer investigation of the varieties of social experience with which religion is associated and of the ways in which different religions mediate different varieties of social experience to produce varying patterns of involvement in informal social care.

The relationship between formal and informal care remained a continuing

Neighbours and neighbourhood: a forward look 235

preoccupation. In this respect, the study of the Stonegate Good Neighbour scheme, with its statutory-led use of Street Wardens, had made a particular impact. At quite an early stage of the research, in 1977, Fred Robinson prepared a paper on 'The Home Help Service: an example of organised altruism'. This described the scale of home help provision in England and Wales and the nature of the service. (For an up-to-date account, see Dexter and Harbert 1983.) He drew on the Government Social Survey study of home helps (Hunt 1970). He concluded that:

> the Home Help Service fits into the broad themes with which we are concerned: social and community care, patterns of helping, altruistic relationships and, possibly, reciprocity ... we might wish to probe more deeply the relationship between Home Help and client. Existing evidence points encouragingly towards an altruistic element and perhaps even a reciprocal one (Home Helps obtaining satisfaction from providing a useful social service, for instance). It is especially interesting that real friendship so often develops out of an employee–client relationship; the fact that payment is made and specific jobs have to be done does not seem to counter this. In the debate on informal care versus formalised, state-provided service, the Home Help Service may demonstrate a stable, successful compromise. (Robinson 1977:1, 8)

Three years later, the research grant application to SSRC for the third phase on 'The Caring Capacity of the Community' made a strong statement of the merits of the Stonegate type of approach. Having studied informal care in six contrasting localities and examined the problems, difficulties and achievements of 850 Good Neighbour schemes we are inclined to conclude that an optimum recipe for community care would be one that combined a well-financed and administered statutory service using paid home-wardens working on a small patch basis with a vigorous grass-roots neighbourhood organisation seeking, among other things, to protect its territory against encroachments of outside authorities.

This does not by any means exhaust the policy relevance of Philip Abrams's ideas, but it draws attention to the salient general points.

It would be misleading to leave the impression that Philip Abrams's work was of unique importance or that he was working in isolation on the theme of neighbours and informal care. This was not the case. A number of research projects in the late 1970s and early 1980s dealt with closely related issues in one way or another (see Johnson and Cooper 1984, Parker et al. 1984). Diana Leat's work on neighbours (1979, 1983) has already been mentioned. Knight and Hayes's study of *Self-Help in the Inner City* (1981) painted a gloomy picture of the possibilities of urban neighbourhood action, Hedley (1984) a more hopeful one. Clare Wenger's monograph (1984) arising from the Social Services in Rural Areas Project at the University College of North Wales, Bangor, thoroughly analyses the different forms of informal support available to the elderly. Complementary data are available from the Northumbrian study of social networks in care (Johnson and Macdonald 1983), directed by Noel Timms as part of the SSRC initiative on the caring capacity of the community. Studies of care of the elderly are under way by Michael Power in Bristol (Power 1980, Power et al. 1983) and Alan Walker and Hazel Qureshi in Sheffield. Field and Hedges

(1984) provide survey evidence on the relatively small numbers of people involved in informal care and neighbouring. The motivations of informal carers were investigated as part of the Kent Community Care scheme (Qureshi et al. 1979, 1983), while the main project investigated new strategies of support for the elderly at risk of institutional admission. This policy worked through decentralised social work case management which encouraged case managers to use resources flexibly in the best way to meet their clients' needs (Challis and Davies 1980; Personal Social Services Research Unit (PSSRU) 1983). Further studies along these lines are under way in North Wales and Gateshead. A different line of inquiry, focussing more on decentralisation of statutory services to the local level have been pursued in two Yorkshire localities, Dinnington and Normanton. At Dinnington, Michael Bayley, Rosalind Seyd and Alan Tennant have studied an experiment in local management of coordinated Health and Social Services (1984), while in Normanton Roger Hadley and Morag McGrath have investigated 'patch' social work (1980, 1984). Hadley, Dale and Sills (1984) have also studied locally-based teams in East Sussex. The overlap with the work done by Philip Abrams was partial and in some cases (for example, the Normanton work) slight. However, almost all of these projects have been concerned with activities spanning the boundary between formal and informal care.

The same is true of activities outside the social care field *in strictu senso* based on the neighbourhood or community. Schemes such as 'Neighbourhood Watch' or neighbourhood crime prevention (National Association for the Care and Resettlement of Offenders (NACRO) 1984) are exercises in 'self-policing' in which local informal initiatives are intended to complement the formal responsibility of the police. (For a complementary sociological analysis, see Taub, Taylor and Dunham (1984).) At the community level, the scope or potential scope for locally-based activities related to social policy is very wide (Willmott 1984). There is, however, ambiguity about what 'community' refers to, and in particular a common failure to distinguish different geographical levels or areal units, for example, the street from a group of streets from a district from the town as a whole. The continuing failure to distinguish clearly between 'community' as rhetoric or ideology from actual patterns of social relationships at these different levels needs urgent exploration through more research, not least in the field of social care.

What pointers to the future does Philip Abrams's work offer? He threw out so many ideas, not all of them fully developed, that there is an embarrassment of riches to choose from. The material in earlier chapters defies useful summary here, so instead two ways forward from his work will be considered, more academic topics for further theoretical reflection and empirical research, and practical courses of action which might be followed to promote neighbourhood care.

Many of the problematic academic issues are implicit in earlier discussions and will be dealt with very briefly. One substantive aspect of neighbouring and neighbourhood care which requires more attention is the relationship between residential proximity and inter-ethnic cooperation and conflict. Tattworth was a racially-mixed area, but the research as a whole may give the impression that whereas social class, age, sex and religious affiliation are sociologically significant criteria, race or ethnicity are not. Clearly, if this impression is given it would be misleading, and more research is needed. Similarly, differentiation within the working class would repay further study. There are hints at several points that the respectable/rough distinction still operates, and may be particularly significant for interaction between neighbours. This is a matter for further inquiry.

More work is needed also on social support networks, to identify more clearly and precisely the ways in which informal support enables social care to be made more effective. Particular policy interest focusses upon enabling dependent minorities to live in the community, whether the infirm elderly who might otherwise be institutionalised, or the mentally-handicapped or mentally-ill whose institutions have been closed. Other groups, however, merit attention, including the less infirm elderly, single parents and mothers with young children, who are not dependent but still need help, and on the other hand those who live in institutions but could still benefit from neighbourly support. Such studies in turn require greater scientific precision, to move beyond the metaphor of a network to an adequate method which can capture the complexity of the real world without becoming lost in esoteric mathematics and computing procedures. Price (1981) is critical of the latter tendency, while Barnes and Harary (1983) provide a defence. Some of the difficulties are reviewed in Bulmer (1985a). The role of 'key figures' and 'sociometric stars' needs pursuing in the context of local neighbourhoods.

More evidence is needed about who actually provides care and of what kind in what circumstances. This in turn requires finer distinctions about types of care (cf. Parker 1981), and distinctions between physical care and psychological support. What role is played by relatives and friends in informal care of the elderly, for instance, and how does this relate to their social isolation or feelings of loneliness (cf. Bulmer 1984c)? Linked to this, who cares for the carers? What kinds of help and support do they require and how can the considerable burdens of looking after a dependent relative at home be lightened? Recent studies which throw considerable light on these questions have been carried out at the National Institute of Social Work. Enid Levin, Ian Sinclair and Peter Gorbach investigated the supporters of confused elderly persons at home (1983, 1986). A group led by Ian Sinclair has made a detailed study of informal care, services and social work for the elderly clients living alone in a London borough (Sinclair *et al.* 1984, forthcoming). More studies of this type are needed.

Local mobilisation is a broad topic which touches on issues of decentralisation and community politics. Philip Abrams cut through much of the rhetoric of community care but failed to establish precisely how neighbourhood mobilisation would promote neighbourhood care. More work is needed upon these connections. Questions need to be asked about the extent to which the locality can provide certain types of care, by comparison, for example, with self-help groups composed of people in a similar condition (rather than living in the same place), such as one-parent families or parents of the mentally handicapped. Moving to the macrosociological level, the role of mediating structures requires further thought and inquiry. To what extent can the locality in industrial society by a meaningful focus for people's activities? To what extent does sociological scepticism about the importance of locality underemphasise the role of informal ties in the social structure and ignore the whole issue of social care and support? These questions include among them some which Philip Abrams would certainly have gone on to investigate had he lived.

Turning to practical action, he did not hesitate to put forward practical recommendations for the promotion of neighbourhood care. To the Volunteer Centre seminar in 1979 he made two general points and a number of specific suggestions. Those responsible for fostering neighbourhood care must recognise the highly arbitrarily and often inconveniently bounded nature of neighbourhoods. Wilful territorial bounding was so plainly important in accounting for the success of so many of the more successful Good Neighbour schemes. For example, the Parsons Green scheme operated in a narrowly delimited local area and would not go over those boundaries. Moreover territorial bounding is determined subjectively, not by administrative maps and plans but by all sorts of mundane practical experiences. And these can differ sharply from household to household. My effective neighbourhood may be quite different from that of my next-door neighbour. It will depend on such things as where we both work, shop, send the children to school, what buses or trains we catch, what pubs or clubs we use, where our friends and relations live. So that the pattern of neighbourhood care in which I might be caught up would not necessarily fit neatly on a map with that of my neighbour. And it seems to be important to build neighbourhood care on actual neighbourhoods in this subjective sense rather than on neighbourhood objectively defined from without. In practical terms this means structuring care in terms of agencies felt to be local by the recipients and mediators alike rather than by formal administrative agencies. Fortunately there are plenty of such agencies; schools, churches, sometimes shops or pubs, almost always general medical practices – and almost always not County Halls and Social Service Department offices. In this respect the present move away from local authority based district nursing towards surgery based community nursing is an encouraging step towards meaningful neighbourhood care.

Secondly, and as importantly, those formulating policy must recognise that the boundaries in administrative and organisational practice between informal and formal care are not as sharp and clear cut as those working in formal organisations might wish. Relationships between informal and formal care tend to worry everyone involved in them. On the one hand the right relationship is one that is both close and permissive. On the other hand, the division of labour between formal and informal care needs to be at once much more precise and very much more complex than it normally is at the moment. The informal carer needs to be 'covered' by the authority of formal carers without being swamped by it, while at the same time most case loads or caring tasks need to be divided up between formal and informal carers in detailed, considered and subtle ways. There is great scope and need for practical experimentation to test out different ways of setting up the relationship.

The specific suggestions arose in relation to the earlier discussion of voluntary action for informal care. In addition to a broad policy perspective, there were certain fairly specific practicalities which agencies interested in promoting or supporting informal care would have to face. One particular

Neighbours and neighbourhood: a forward look

suggestion concerned the competence of informal carers. More thought needed to be given to how people could be taught some of the caring skills. Competence-training is an essential but as yet badly neglected step towards effective informal care – both in reinforcing the work of kin and in recruiting non-kin (neighbours or not) to such work. Shyness is not a fact of life. People who have taken ski courses usually then go skiing; perhaps people who had taken care courses would then ...? After all, one of the main reasons nurses and social workers are reluctant to share their responsibilities with their clients' relations or neighbours is because so many of the relevant tasks really are skilled. Certifying the competence of kin and neighbours would remove obstacles to informal care on both sides. The Durham team were particularly impressed by one or two examples from Neighbourhood Care schemes, for example, where the Organiser in Parsons Green had provided detailed notes of guidance for volunteer visitors, covering how to approach the person visited, what rules to follow, when to contact the coordinator, the need to keep out of family quarrels, to avoid judgements of the person being visited, and to avoid gossip with others about the person visited. In Stonegate, Street Wardens were given a week-long course after 6 months, followed by a 16-week day release course, organised by the authority's Further Education service. All Wardens interviewed testified to the great value of this training in consolidating both competence and commitment.

It might also be possible to offset the decline in negative sources of neighbourliness by an independent increase in the positive sources. Factors such as skills should, from a policy point of view, be thought of as autonomous variables. Hitherto, neighbourliness has been largely a product of the prohibitive costs of other kinds of attachment and forms of support. The rewards rather than the costs of neighbourliness would seem to invite attention in future research.

Many of the practicalities had to do with cash. However cost-effective informal and community care may be when compared to formal and institutional care the overt and concealed costs of adequate informal care are themselves high and a first essential step is to present the true bill to both national and local government. The perennial conclusion of innumerable voluntary care projects that things would have gone well if only one had had a paid Organiser or coordinator is realistic rather than pathetic. Running a fully effective Good Neighbour scheme for a population of 20,000 can be and should be a full-time job. And back-up cash resources are needed too, whether to produce news-letters, provide transport, or cover the incidental expenses of carers. Should not kin who devote substantial parts of their lives, even all their lives for long periods, to giving care informally have all the relevant resources of the formal sector brought to their doors? Should not they also have something like the income they might have had if they'd simply dumped granny in a hospital and taken a job? Once one begins to think about the costs involved in facilitating informal care so that it could hope to match the standards of provision and reliability expected from formal care, the list of prospective charges spins out endlessly. It is clear that one is advocating something very expensive indeed. A first set of practical measures, therefore, would be to produce realistic estimates, set them in detail against the costs of other forms of care and conduct a few experiments – carefully monitoring properly funded alternatives – to see whether pound for pound it really is the case that informal care can do the same job as formal care in more desirable ways and with more human effects. Or more constructively to show just what it would cost to give informal care of this or that sort effectively, and to argue for it on that basis rather than to continue to lurk behind the dangerously tattered fig-leaf of a cheap alternative to the welfare state.

Two weeks before his death, speaking to an Age Concern conference in Durham, Philip Abrams trenchantly criticised the idea that voluntary care could be a low-cost alternative to statutory provision.

> Governments have been pushing what they call the informal system of care, and they have got it wrong. They will need to spend money to provide back-up services. If we want to go into neighbourhood care in a big way in urban areas, the evidence we have points to the conclusion that caring must be turned into a proper job with paid wages, and we cannot rely on volunteer housewives who simply don't have the time or sufficient numbers to do the work. (Quoted in *The Guardian*, 18 October 1981)

Neighbourhood care is not just a form of service delivery to 'save the council money' or 'relieve overstretched social services'. A commitment to a broader vision of neighbourhood care is needed, which is most likely to be compatible with welfare environments that are high-profile and statutorily-led, and which understand the limitations as well as the advantages of neighbourhood care.

Others studying informal care have concluded that the effective provision of care requires additional resources. Keeping the frail elderly at home is not a cheap option, and local authorities face increasing costs in providing support (Tinker 1984). Wenger (1984:193–4) suggests that financial inducements may be used to recruit and maintain carers not already involved in caring. Nominal payments need not be costly, but can make it possible for neighbours to accept caring responsibilities in lieu of other part-time employment (cf. also Islington 1977; Leat 1979).

This in turn raises the question of what level of payment is appropriate: a wage as in the case of the Stonegate Street Wardens, or a nominal payment as in the case of the Kent Community Care scheme (Challis and Davies 1980)? The latter is open to the charge of bringing in cheap labour; the former to that of unreasonable expense. It partly depends on what is the aim. If the aim is to accord the helper some recognition and overcome worries about interference by both helper and client, then nominal payment may be adequate. If it is to make the worker accountable to an organisation, then the wage rate would seem more appropriate (Goldberg and Connelly 1982:169–72). Such dilemmas lie at the heart of the attempt to link formal and informal care.

Cash alone, however, was not enough. Information and information networks within the world of informal carers and between that world and formal agencies needed to be developed. (At the time of his death, Philip Abrams was planning an action research project jointly with the Volunteer Centre on this topic.)

Informal carers, whether kin or surrogate kin or quite casual and occasional helpers, typically exist in a deep fog of ignorance: ignorance about where care is needed, ignorance about how to give it, ignorance about where to find it if they themselves cannot cope. In all these respects informal care could be made very much more effective by quite simple efforts to spread the knowledge (often possessively) possessed by many voluntary and statutory agencies. There isn't really a dearth of people to care for; it is, to say the least, wasteful that so many would-be informal carers should think that there is. There isn't really a dearth of specialist services; it is well-nigh criminal that so many actual informal carers should feel locked in a closed world with their dependent relatives for the want of such services.

And the question of who was to care for the carers – the most serious of all – had to be faced. A close appraisal was required of the needs of carers, especially caring kin. Any substantial move toward community care meant the creation of a host of new needs for ancillary support on the part of the kin, neighbours and volunteers who became the main agents of care (cf. Wenger 1984:189). Their emotional and relational needs set limits to the care that could be provided. What informal carers themselves seemed to feel they need in order to see through the tasks taken on were (1) occasional relief from their solitary responsibilities for others, (2) insurance against the consequences of the possible mistakes they might make, (3) affirmation of the value of what they are doing, (4) information (again) about how to do what they are doing more safely, thoroughly and economically, (5) attention to their own problems and (6) company. Their research suggested that there were economies of scale in this area. Relatively large and diversified projects such as Alphaville and Parsons Green seemed better equipped to supply care for carers than did single-task schemes.

In the third phase of the research, Sheila Abrams's project studied daughters whose mothers suffered restricted mobility and were cared for by their daughters at home. The grant application recognised that many such daughters ended up needing care themselves, or at best seriously disenchanted and demoralised. In order to assess the emotional, relational and physical costs of community care to the informal carers themselves, Sheila Abrams (with the help of Dennis Marden) interviewed a sample of 38 married women living with their elderly mothers (aged 75 or over) in the same households in Durham and Cambridge. The mother–daughter relationship was chosen because of its archetypal nature, its greater frequency and its continuing interest to sociologists. The daughters were asked about their mothers' health and disabilities, and information was collected about what kinds of tasks had to be undertaken for the mothers and who performed them. The study looked also at the extra financial costs of care (including loss of potential earnings) and the psychological and social strains experienced by the daughters, in terms of their personal feelings towards their mothers and the impact of care on their marriages, their families and friendships.

As in other studies, care was found to be provided almost exclusively by the daughters, and the statutory and voluntary services gave little relief. The daughters' attitudes towards caring varied in ways which were not directly related to the burden of care, and an attempt was made to see whether this could be understood in terms of the models discussed by Philip Abrams in his work on altruism and reciprocity. Thus, the daughters had come to care via different routes, not always from a deliberate choice. Some mothers had arrived early when they were still young and active and able to help to look after the daughters' children, while others had arrived late when they were already old and unable to care for themselves. The study asked whether attitudes towards caring could be understood as a direct exchange of services, as a return of services rendered by the mother at some earlier stage of the relationship, or as the daughter demonstrating to her children the kind of care she would herself like to receive in the future. (For a full account, see S. Abrams and Marsden (1985).) The subjective experience of caring also deserves to be highlighted more (see Briggs and Oliver 1985). Taken together with other recent studies like *Who Care for the Carers?* (Equal Opportunities Commission (EOC) 1982), it is clear that this subject requires much further attention both from the points of view of practice and research.

Philip Abrams concluded that action research projects were required to test out some of the alternatives. More systematic attempts needed to be made to assess the financial, emotional and relational costs of community care compared to more formal systems. Meticulously designed and evaluated experiments, rather than definitive policy proposals, seem to be the crucial next step for informal care at this stage of our knowledge (and ignorance). In addition to more experiments with various kinds of payment and financial support and various forms of organisation (especially Street Warden and patch arrangements), we need to introduce experiments on a whole range of other measures theoretically conducive to more effective informal care: on various ways of relaxing and redefining the boundaries of formal and informal care; on various ways of keeping care-givers informed; and on ways and means of providing appropriate forms of care for carers themselves. The distinction between a programme of experiments and a programme of substantive policy measures is of course a fine one; experiments are also measures, so perhaps these suggestions are not as modest as they appear. The Wolfenden Committee (1978) offered the following conception of the relationship between voluntary action and informal social care:

> In relation to the informal system of caring the special contribution of the voluntary sector consists of filling or bridging the gaps between the individual and the statutory services through the medium of organised arrangements for mutual aid and ... care and by transmitting from one side to the other knowledge about unmet needs and available resources.

If implemented, the sort of experiments outlined would go a significant way towards putting flesh on such bones.

Appendix

The methodology of studying six streets and ten Neighbourhood Care schemes

This appendix describes how the Street studies reported in chapter 4 and the study of Neighbourhood Care schemes in chapters 8 and 9 were conducted, provides some detail about each (including copies of interview schedules used) and presents the rationale for the particular blend of methods used by the Durham team. This account is necessarily compressed, but is largely based on Philip Abrams's own writings.

The empirical research conducted in the first and second phases of the research was very much a team effort. Philip Abrams inspired the work, formulated the problem, developed ideas and posed questions to be investigated, and throughout discussed their field work experiences with other team members. He did not, himself, however, undertake any field work, which was done by the other members of the team. As one team member put it: "He wasn't one for going out and collecting the information himself. That didn't appeal to him at all." However, he played a most active role in directing and bringing together the research. There were regular team meetings at which the plans and results of the work were reviewed. Draft papers reporting the results of research in the field were prepared by team members and revised by Philip; others were written jointly by different members led by Philip; while a majority were written by Philip. He took a most active role at the writing up stage. As one team member put it,

> "What Philip did and what was his great forte was that he was able to see through the empirical detail. He was very perceptive. He was able to see through to themes and draw them out. His style was very much a synthetic one, pulling bits and pieces from all over the place and bringing them to bear on whatever was the centre of his attention at the time."

The Street studies

The Street studies are described in chapter 4 and material from them appears elsewhere in the book. The rationale for the type of street chosen for study was discussed on pp. 46–7. This section briefly considers the approach and chronology of the research, and in more detail the rationale of the particular use of intensive interviewing adopted.

The choice of particular 'streets' for study was to some extent fortuitous. One of the research team lived in Etherege Terrace, another of the research team had lived in Congreve Hall and had a sister living in Austen Avenue. A third member had lived in Carlisle, and had friends living near Boswell village. The County

Table A1 *Localities where the Street studies were carried out*

Place	Pseudonyms	Studied by	Period of fieldwork	Number of households interviewed	Number of occupied houses in street
Yorkshire woollen town	Austen Avenue (Balaclava Road)	Sheila Abrams	October 1976–April 1977	28	41
Leeds	Dryden Square	Janice Davinson	September–October 1977	37	46
County Durham	Fielding Close (Hutton Crescent)	Fred Robinson Janice Davinson	Spring and Summer 1977; follow-up February 1978	15	20
Cumbria	Boswell village	Janice Davinson	February and March 1977	31	32
Durham	Etherege Terrace (Prospect Terrace)	Fred Robinson	October 1976–February 1977	18	22
Cambridge	Congreve Hall (Manor Court)	Sheila Abrams, Janice Davinson	August and October 1977	36	85

Methodology

Durham New Town was the site of one of the team's PhD research. Nevertheless, the particular localities selected differed in terms of class and stability, presenting an interesting contrast in different styles of neighbouring.

The localities, fieldworkers and dates of fieldwork are shown in table A1. The names of localities are pseudonyms to preserve confidentiality. The first two streets studied were Austen Avenue and Etherege Terrace. For this purpose a comprehensive check list of items of information was prepared, under five general headings: General information on the area; The houses and their occupants; Neighbouring; Attitudes to neighbours; Beyond the neighbours. Neighbours were defined as all those who lived in the street, but neighbouring as a type of relationship based on regular contact and mutual benevolence which might or might not involve neighbours and might or might not be confined to the neighbourhood. "Our task is to see to what extent relations with neighbours are neighbourly."

Members of the research team were asked to try to interview a member of every household living in the street, and a high response rate was achieved. The greatest number of refusals or no contacts was in the middle class area, Congreve Hall. Respondents were interviewed informally in their own homes, usually without others being present. An interview schedule with a series of open-ended questions was used (table A2). The questionnaire was not, however, used in a rigid way but rather as a guide to the conversation. The interviewer took brief notes at the time and wrote up a full account immediately afterwards.

Each researcher then wrote a draft analysis of the material, some of which has been incorporated in chapter 4. This analysis was predominantly qualitative, though some frequency distributions were produced to look for straightforward associations – for example, between length of residence and extent of neighbourly help. Philip Abrams also drew extensively upon the material in published papers that he wrote at the time (e.g. Abrams 1978b; Abrams *et al.* 1979; Abrams 1980). In 1980, he wrote the following account of how the Street studies research had proceeded.

The problem of access

Armed with a framework for observation supplied by our categories and definitions we now felt ready to meet the world. But would the world agree to a meeting? There was reason to suppose that neighbouring was one of those sensitive topics especially resistant to research. Just to the extent that neighbouring was a valued form of interaction we would have to expect it to be screened from the eyes of outsiders, protected by the norm of 'not-gossiping'. At an early stage we discussed our research plans with some veterans of earlier locality studies and the comments we received in this respect were depressingly uniform. Thus:

> "I flatter myself that I'm reasonable at a fair range of interviewing, yet I seem to have retired hurt from four or five attempts to do studies of neighbouring. My chief recollection . . . is of an uneasiness in the personal relationships of a kind which I don't recall having in many other studies. People just didn't know what I was 'after', I think. Probably some of this uneasiness stemmed from my

Table A2 *Street Studies: interview schedule*

1	General information on the area – as on check list
2	General description of each house:
2(a)	Type of tenure
2(b)	Who lives in the house?
2(c)	Occupations: who works at what and where?
2(d)	Anyone housebound or attending clinics on a regular basis: any disability of any kind?
2(e)	Leisure activities – anything involving a large block of time away from home?
2(f)	Good times/bad times – not a detailed life history but some sense of prominent life experiences – especially of hardship, unemployment, etc.
2(g)	Telephone
2(h)	Car
2(i)	Television
2(j)	Public transport

and pattern of use of these resources.

3	*Neighbouring*
	How many people do you know in the street? With which other people in the street are you on good terms, bad terms, no terms? Description of these relationships – greeting, visiting, or what?
3(a)	What is the basis of *neighbourly* relationships with neighbours, possibly to be followed up with the basis of *un-neighbourly* relationships, for e.g. proximity, help, common interest or what?
3(b)	With whom else are you on 'neighbourly' terms – that is, people not living in the street? Descriptions of these relationships. Where do they occur – at work, through leisure activities, or what?
3(c)	*Family*. Where do they live? How often are they seen? What sort of contact? Any key members?
4	*Attitudes to neighbouring*
	What makes a 'good neighbour' or a 'bad neighbour'? *Ask about real situations and what happened*, for e.g., at a time of stress, loneliness, bereavement, running out of tea, etc? Who would you turn to?
4(a)	How do these experiences relate to *other places, other times* and how do these relate to the present place and time?
4(b)	How would a 'good neighbour' behave in specific situations: illness, loneliness (try to get reaction to stories of old people dying alone and no one knowing for days), various kind of troubles?
5	*Beyond the neighbours*
	Are there organisations, the church, the club, the welfare – or specific services – meals on wheels, visiting library, Round Table – to which you would look to for help or general support?
5(a)	How far does/should formal service replace informal neighbouring?
5(b)	Are organisations felt to be reliable?
5(c)	Where do relations fit in to the overall pattern of giving and receiving help; are there specific kinds of help 'reserved' to *family relations*. (Relate information of this sort to information on family background.) Are these relationships felt to be 'reliable'?
5(d)	Have you ever helped others on an organised basis – 'Good Neighbour schemes' for example? If so, how and why? If not, why not?
5(e)	Have you ever received help from such a group?

own unresolved questions about what I was looking for, but I don't think it was all ... my fault. It was the topic, and the attempt to do a blanket coverage of a whole street asking people about the neighbours, which seems to have broken ... taboos." (Dennis Marsden, personal communication)

Proximity enables one's neighbours to know things about one which one might much prefer not to have known, and which are perhaps carefully guarded from others: "Our bedroom is right next door to theirs – you should hear the way he snores." It can force one to share with the neighbours 'back-stage' areas of life which one would dearly like to have to oneself. For such reasons alone confidentiality is likely to be the cornerstone of neighbourliness, and mutual respect for privacy the basis of tolerable neighbouring. Conversely, research on neighbouring can appear as a direct assault on the very heart of the relationship. Mrs Smithers in Fielding Close said to us, "Old Mr Coleman now, I could tell you things about him ..." But she didn't. And old Mr Coleman for his part observed: "There's some right bitches round here – mind you, I'm naming no names." And he didn't. Could we really hope to get further than that? Sometimes the obstacle was explained to us in helpfully direct and explicit terms. For example, Mr and Mrs Bell in Etherege Terrace wrote us a note to say, "We don't want our neighbours talking about us so we're sorry but we won't talk to you about them." Occasionally, the refusal of research was aggressive and opaque – as in the case of Colonel Sanders of the Congreve Hall estate who said, "No, you may not interview me; there's too many sociologists and do-gooders going around poking their noses in where they're not wanted." Actually, the only strident and comprehensive hositility to research that we encountered came from middle and upper middle class people. But in every one of our six streets a majority of the residents indicated some anxiety and concern about the delicacy of the ground we wanted to explore. Whatever they felt about their neighbours, whatever their own practical involvements in neighbouring and whatever their general ideas and beliefs about neighbourliness, they seemed inhibited by an instinctive feeling that the less said about the whole topic the better. It appears that discretion is the better part of neighbouring.

We knew of no formula of research method that would enable us to surmount such a barrier. Very intense ethnography involving prolonged residence and perhaps eventual absorption into the networks of gossip, the secrets and routines of each street was the obvious answer. When it came to studying neighbouring, however, we were not entirely happy about that solution. If we were right to think that confidentiality was one of the vital moral conditions for neighbourliness, any access we might gain to neighbourly relations as a result of being genuine neighbours ourselves would presumably place us in a difficult ethical dilemma. In presenting our findings we would in effect be breaking the taboos to which we had in effect subscribed in order to make the findings in the first place. Unless we gave the impression of subscribing to the taboos of neighbourly discretion we could hardly expect to be treated as neighbours. If we did give that impression and thereby contrived to enter the networks of neighbouring what sort of neighbours would we be if we then gossipped in print? It seemed that the sociologist was professionally trapped into being a pretty nasty human being. Was it a coincidence that our relationships with our own neighbours seemed to become a little more guarded once it was known that we were studying neighbouring? Could we get to know more about the veiled world of Mrs Smithers and old Mr Coleman without getting ourselves entangled in the very veils of discretion in which from the point of view of the outsider that world was swathed?

On the other hand, did it matter? Was anything going on behind the veils that we needed to know about? Had we any reason to suppose that, from the point of view of wanting to understand the social sources of neighbourliness, the intimate knowledge of the insider included secrets that were in any way relevant? Might not the backstage world of neighbouring consist of endless trivialities immensely important to the self-esteem of individuals but of little sociological concern except insofar as, *collectively*, they constituted a backstage world? The important thing to know about neighbouring might be that it had a backstage area rather than what went on there. Yet what went on on particular backstages could be *just* what determined whether neighbourliness did or did not flourish between particular neighbours. Whatever our assumptions about its significance, or even its existence, the possibility of a significant 'invisible' world of neighbouring was not something we could ignore. Our ethical scruples notwithstanding, an effort to get behind the veils of discretion, even if only to discover whether they were really there, had to be made. And having reached that decision we found it helpful to distinguish between two types of confidentiality. There is the insider confidentiality accorded to persons, and the outsider confidentiality accorded to researchers. The former is won as a recognition of membership; it is detailed and comprehensive, resting on the assumption that one can be trusted with much information because one will divulge little to outsiders. The latter is negotiated as a contract mediating divergent interests; it restricts what may be known, preserving the integrity of a backstage world, but allows that something may be known *and divulged* under stated conditions. The researcher who is frankly an outsider faces the problem of negotiating a contract as favourable as possible to the interests of research, of winning enough confidence to make the terms of the contract relatively comprehensive and unconditional. The researcher who proceeds as an insider faces a quite different problem. Insofar as one succeeds in really being an insider, one has then to unmask the researcher beneath the skin. If one is conscientious about that one will negotiate rights to divulge the secrets to which one has been privy. If not one will simply betray a multitude of confidences. Many researchers have managed to conceal the discomforts and moral hazards of this process from themselves by studying groups among whom they had no intention of living once the research was finished and whose members were distinctly unlikely to read the research reports about themselves written for quite separate audiences. In studying neighbouring in one's own society, that sort of evasion of the implications of membership is not readily available.

A final reason for being sceptical about the merits of participant observation in studying neighbouring in one's own society seemed to be implicit in a good deal of general theorising about social networks. The message of a considerable and impressive body of anthropological research seemed to be that the very networks with the highest levels of solidarity – and from our point of view, neighbourliness – could be expected to be the hardest to get to know from within. Paradoxically, it appeared that the information relevant to our purposes about such networks might well be more easily obtained by investigators who were very plainly not themselves members of the networks in question. The crucial relationship is the relationship postulated between density and communication in social networks. The ideal-type of the neighbourly milieu, whether specified as the traditional working class community or in some other way, envisages networks of considerable density – that is, a milieu in which a very high proportion of the social links which could possibly exist do actually exist, in which most of the people who interact with any given individual also interact with one another independently of that individual. Density in turn, as Boissevain has pointed out (1974), is a measure of potential communication within a network; whether or not all those people actually do talk to one another about a given topic.

And to the extent that they are not prepared to take risks, neighbouring in high density networks could be expected to be less accessible to the researcher-as-insider than neighbouring anywhere else. The other side of the finding that people in Woodford are more friendly, in the sense of having casual and open relationships with their neighbours, than people in Bethnal Green, could be that the world of neighbouring in Bethnal Green and places like it is, just because of its density, much more closed and inaccessible to any particular insider, including the insider researcher. The denser the network the more good relations within it may depend on strategic silences. And as a corollary to that really knowing such a network from the point of view of any one insider could entail one in being such a bad risk that one would be quite systematically denied the opportunity to know it from the point of view of others.

Since the problem of access seemed to point in such different directions we decided to compromise. One of our six streets, in the event it was Etherege Terrace, was to be studied from the inside on the basis of participant observation by one of us enjoying the identity of long-term resident and authentic neighbour. One of the others, Fielding Close, was to be investigated no less exclusively from without, by way of formal questionnaires administered by strangers. In the other four cases we attempted to combine elements of both approaches: short-term residence (three months was devoted to each street), plus interviews with members of every household, plus observation (rather an extraordinary amount of time spent in local shops, pubs, clubs and on pavements, greens and public benches). The element of uniformity was simply that in all six cases we would at the end of the day have discussed a standard list of topics and asked a minimum list of identical questions in every household. The context and form in which that would happen was deliberately varied: very oblique in Etherege Terrace, very direct in Fielding Close, casual but explicit elsewhere. Our hope of course was that this variety of styles would give us some insight into the strengths and weaknesses of each – rather than simply enabling us to reap the disadvantages of all three.

Reliability and complexity

Meanwhile, some preliminary pilot interviews quickly suggested that the real problem we would face might not be access as such – in the sense of persuading people to talk about the topics in which we were interested – but rather, reliability. It seemed that our major challenge might not be to gather information but to interpret it. From the outset, we found that the great majority of people were entirely willing to give us the accounts of neighbouring for which we asked. But we found, too, that those accounts were alarmingly likely to be flatly contradicted by the accounts we received from their neighbours. Sometimes their accounts were also contradicted by our own observations of their practical activities. Often the discrepancies seemed at first sight to be no more than a matter of points of detail or shades of emphasis. But typically such details – whether or not Miss Brothers was *always* popping in to see Mr Crewe, just *how* cruel Mr Vincent was to his cat – proved to be highly significant touches in an elaborately painted picture of neighbouring as a whole, a picture finely composed of a mass of such touches. On rare occasions the gulf between accounts was so wide, the contradiction so major and direct that it was impossible to see where or how interpretation could begin. While almost everyone appeared to construct images of neighbouring in ways that were in some measure partial, in some degree a self-oriented selection from the available evidence, a few people in every street presented us with images totally at odds with those presented by their neighbours. When, for example, we first asked Mr Shrimpton in Austen Avenue whether he had time to talk to us he replied simply, "No, I bloody well haven't"; but he then went on to give us one of the blackest accounts of neighbouring we were to hear anywhere. General misanthropy and particular animosities pervaded everything he said; he was familiar with virtually all the misfortunes that had overtaken the inhabitants of Austen Avenue in recent years; any individual about whom he was asked was judged unfriendly, indifferent or hostile; local people in general he found cold, unhappy or hypocritical: "they pray on Sunday and they're buggers on Monday"; for himself he insisted that he saw no one, spoke to no one, was spoken to by no one, was an isolate in a fragmented world. Later we visited Mr and Mrs Bryant who lived next door. We were to say the least surprised when Mrs Bryant told us, "We've always been very lucky with our neighbours; Mr Shrimpton has always been good" and again when she was giving us her idea of a "good neighbour" and said, "Someone you could go to if you needed help ... like Mr Shrimpton." It turned out, too, that for all Mr Shrimpton's professions of isolation he saw quite a lot of the Bryants: "I go in most days to see if he's alright. I have a key in case he's ill and I can let myself in."

It occurred to us of course that Mr Shrimpton, or indeed Mrs Bryant, had been putting us on. But our further observations and conversations suggested that things were more complicated than that. Mr Shrimpton was indeed widely thought to be unfriendly and solitary by the inhabitants of Austen Avenue. And he did indeed have a strong relationship of neighbourliness with the Bryants who were themselves widely seen as outgoing and neighbourly people.

Methodology

One respect in which Mr Shrimpton differed from most people was that he had not allowed one neighbourly relationship to colour his understanding of neighbours and the locality in general. There were of course other reasons why his view of neighbours in general was so jaundiced. But eventually we were to conclude that the Shrimpton–Bryant relationship was one of the most important we had come across from the point of view of understanding the social sources of neighbourliness. This example emphasises the complexities of interpretation (as distinct from the difficulties of access) which the study of neighbouring seems to us to present. The task resembles that of assembling a mosaic from a vast number of pieces apparently almost wholly lacking in continuities of colour and design. Specifically, we were daunted by the discovery of the extent to which people living next door to each other seemed to inhabit not only different houses but different worlds of neighbouring.

At this point we had already moved a long way from our original notion of a study based on 'mere' observation. Although the point we had reached could hardly be called sophisticated it was at least fairly complicated. We had moved from a proposal simply to look at the world to a theory-derived selection of certain forms of the world as particularly worth looking at. We had identified empirical indicators of those forms themselves presupposing independent theoretical justification. We had elaborated ideal-typical models (definitions) of the interactions and relationships we wished to investigate as a heuristic instrument of access to everyday life. And we had offered to interpret the intimations of reality we could assemble not at all directly but in terms of those models. We had withdrawn from any conception of simple observation to a complex, albeit compromised, strategy of observation involving multiple and diverse efforts to know other people's lives. And we had recognised that our problem was at bottom not one of knowing the world but of interpreting it – that the best we could hope to do was to achieve a credible account of how people constructed neighbouring, not an account of what neighbouring 'really is'.

The study of Good Neighbour schemes

With the beginning of the national survey of Good Neighbour schemes in 1977 (see chapter 1 and Abrams *et al*. 1981a:15–58) the research changed gear somewhat. The national survey yielded data on 1,026 local schemes, which were systematically analysed to discern significant regularities. The national survey was combined with six cases studies which, like the Street studies, looked at particular local areas in depth and analysed the resulting data predominantly in qualitative terms (Abrams *et al*. 1981a:59–98). In a paper about the methodology of this Good Neighbour research (1984c), Philip Abrams discussed the problems of measuring informal care by means of such 'soft' data, and of generalising more broadly from such studies. He admitted the uncertainties of taking the necessary step from empirical detail to morphology and classification. Open-ended interviews provided a preliminary orientation, but given a degree of analytic concentration, they could lead to a classification of types of relationship or variation which in turn could lead to the derivation of hypotheses for testing.

Appendix

Throughout both phases of the research, his primary interest lay in this direction rather than in the precise quantification of the number, frequency or weight of contacts between neighbours, or achieving greater precision in the analysis of networks. Nor did he attempt a cost-benefit analysis of Neighbourhood Care schemes.

The study of ten Neighbourhood Care schemes

This rationale for the case-study held good for the ten case studies of Neighbourhood Care schemes selected according to criteria explained in chapter 8. These differed from the Street Studies in using a broader range of research methods, including interviewing with a precoded and structured schedule. Despite greater quantification of data, however, the use of the case-study as an in-depth means of studying neighbourhood care was similar. In 1981, Philip Abrams wrote the following account of the methodology. The ten schemes studied are summarised in table A3.

The research involved four distinct methods of work: formal, structured interviews using questionnaires; informal interviews and conversations; non-participant observation; and the study of documentary records, reports and files. Without becoming involved in the general advocacy of methodological pluralism or 'triangulation', we are fairly certain that for the purposes of our particular project a plurality of methods was indispensable, if only because each case study involved the investigation of an organisation, four distinct populations associated with it and the relationships between them. In each case, we could expect to find some kernel of documentary evidence mapping the overt history and structure of the project and to build around it data obtained from (a) those who organised the project and undertook the various caring activities it sponsored (Helpers), (b) those who received care as a result of the activities of the project (Clients), (c) those living in the locality within which the project worked (Residents) and (d) agents of the official and voluntary bodies making up the welfare environment of the project (Officials). And finally we expected to complete our understanding of each project by way of close, day-to-day observation of its practical workings.

So far as Helpers and Residents were concerned it seemed sensible to make formal questionnaires our basic instrument of research. It was among these populations in particular that we wished to explore our various hypotheses about the conditions of neighbourhood care and for that reason alone standardised, formal procedures appeared unavoidable. Clients and Officials were a different matter. Having attempted to use formal methods with equivalent populations in earlier research it was obvious to us that many Clients, being perforce frail, elderly, anxious, insecure, possibly confused and so forth, would find it difficult or disagreeable to have to cope with a formal interrogation. Informal conversation, structured on the basis of a check-list of our own concerns, seemed to be the necessary method in this instance. And a similar procedure seemed appropriate when talking to Officials, not because of their psychological condition but because we rapidly realised that their various involvements with neighbourhood care were likely to be so *very* various, so *ad*

Table A3 *The ten Neighbourhood Care schemes studied*

Pseudonym	Characteristics of area	Studied by	Helpers	Clients	Residents
Stonegate	Hunting Valley, a district of a great steel city	Sheila Abrams, Robin Humphrey and Ray Snaith	31	17	22
Brandling	An Inner London borough, overwhelmingly working class	Robin Humphrey and Ray Snaith	28	11	20
Skeffington	A commercial and industrial city of half a million	Robin Humphrey and Ray Snaith	27	18	—
Grantley	A mixed area on the edge of a middle class district of Barhampton, a northern city	Robin Humphrey and Ray Snaith	5	7	24
Tattworth	East Kinley, a working class racially-mixed area of a midlands city	Robin Humphrey and Ray Snaith	26	9	—
Bradbury	A suburban working class district of a northern city	Sheila Abrams, Robin Humphrey and Ray Snaith	18	18	26
Trimdon	A large industrial and commercial city in the south of England	Robin Humphrey and Ray Snaith	32	19	—
Parsons Green	A suburban area of 18,000 people on the outskirts of an East Anglian town	Sheila Abrams, Robin Humphrey and Ray Snaith	33	18	24
Southfield Park	A prosperous suburban area on the very edge of the Greater London conurbation	Robin Humphrey and Ray Snaith	25	18	20
Easethorpe	A village in a rural area in the heart of the South Downs	Sheila Abrams, Robin Humphrey and Ray Snaith	28	10	20
		Total	253	145	156

hoc and particularistic, that it would be impossible to devise a standardised questionnaire for them as a category which would catch the all-important subtleties, nuances and particularities of detailed policy and action which we took to be essential for an understanding of the ways in which the welfare environments of neighbourhood care were constituted.

Accordingly, our pilot study proceeded on the basis of two questionnaires and two check lists. The questionnaires were drafted in sections reflecting our analytical assumptions and employing mainly open-ended questions. The check lists took the form of inventories of points to serve as *aides-mémoire* for conversations which we hoped to develop in a relatively responsive manner without our imposing a pre-ordained sequence. In the event the pilot study indicated a number of methodological difficulties which we had not anticipated, but also pointed to some opportunities for more disciplined interviewing than we had initially thought would be possible. The questionnaires for Helpers and Residents were both changed quite dramatically following the pilot study. Although we saw no need to reconstitute our framework of analysis or the basic thematic design of the questionnaires, we did feel it necessary to modify, extend and sometimes abandon many particular questions within each section of the questionnaires. Conversely the questionnaires as a whole became a good deal more purposefully structured. The interview schedule finally used for Helpers is reproduced as table A4 to give a flavour of the approach. To save space, it has been compressed. Fixed choice pre-codes are indicated thus: Yes/No; Middle class/Working class/Other.

The Clients' interview underwent a radical but quite different change in form. We decided to add a short formal questionnaire to our check list. In effect the Clients in the pilot study proved a good deal more resilient and capable of handling formal interviews than our initial stereotypes had led us to expect. Instead of trying to slip various routine questions into a diffuse conversation with a view to producing a set of merely qualitative individual vignettes, we therefore decided that we could manage to standardise a good deal of demographic and situational data for Clients even within the framework of a discussion ostensibly concerned with subjective experiences, memories and personal impressions. This measure of standardisation meant that we could make comparisons and draw inferences within this particular body of data with a good deal more confidence than we had originally hoped. By contrast, the interviews with Officials had to be made even more qualitative, *ad hoc*, respondent-oriented than we had expected.

Having revised our procedures in this way we then had to face the more directly operational issue of finding appropriate samples of respondents in each of our chosen categories. There was little difficulty so far as the Helpers and Clients were concerned. Once the relevant populations had been carefully generated – and for that we were inevitably dependent upon the organisers of our Neighbourhood Care projects – we simply looked at the numbers case by case and decided whether we could manage to interview the whole category or whether we would need to sample. Previous experience had indicated that in the time available to us we could probably manage to interview about 30 Helpers and a similar number of Clients. If a particular project had substantially more than 30 people in either category we would have to sample – always aiming to end up with approximately 30 respondents per category per study. Sampling, where necessary, was random on the basis of an alphabetical listing of the relevant population. In this respect our research methods were highly conventional.

The choice of populations of Residents was rather more problematic. Initially, we had thought in terms of sampling the whole area as defined by each Neighbourhood Care project. In principle this would have been the most appropriate way of satisfying one of the main aims of the research – namely to test the impact of the project on the neighbourhood. However, there were many important analytical aspects of the research that would have suffered badly had we proceeded in that way. The pilot study indicated that a random sample, again numbering 30, taken from a heterogeneous population was likely to be so fragmented that much of the data collected would be superficial to the point of meaninglessness. Not being able to secure adequate representative samples of whole areas we concentrated instead on fairly close studies of carefully selected 'indicative' streets or sub-sections. These concentrated studies would not allow us to claim that our Residents represented the whole population of the neighbourhoods in question, but they would plainly have a solid 'bench-mark' value – they would provide us with usable information on the involvement or non-involvement in neighbourhood care of at least one characteristic sub-set of the population of Residents within the total area of each project. This enabled us to make some assessment of the impact of the project in question and to estimate the extent of informal care and the norms and values surrounding it with firm reference to at least one clearly defined local social context. The criterion for choosing the 'street' in each locality was therefore that it should in some definite way (housing type, class composition or whatever) be characteristic of a major facet of the make-up of the area as a whole. Once the street (or streets) for each locality had been chosen we sampled randomly from households.

Finding appropriate samples of Officials was still more problematic and finally defeated our efforts to be scientific. The problem was that the cluster of agents relevant to the working of Neighbourhood Care projects was likely to be constituted in ways that varied dramatically from project to project and from locality to locality. Precisely because neighbourhood care is a relatively new and obscure field of action for statutory and voluntary agencies alike there is no standard hierarchy of management, responsibility or policy-making. In every case we could be sure that some tangle of politicians, officials of statutory and voluntary organisations and welfare professionals would constitute a significant environment for the project in which we were interested. But in each case it was likely to be a different tangle. It seemed sensible to begin in each case at something like the appropriate Assistant Director level in each relevant Social Services Department area office. But it was never possible to establish a standard universe from which to sample and we simply had to follow whatever leads we were given in whatever direction they led. We had to adopt a snowball sampling procedure case by case ensuring as best we could that we gathered snow wherever it was available. It should be said that, rather to our surprise, the Officials, once we had found them, proved the easiest of all our categories of respondent to interview. From Directors of Social Services and Chairpersons of Social Services Committees through the whole rambling apparatus of welfare administration, social work and voluntary service the people we wanted to interview were almost without exception quite willing to be interviewed and remarkably forthcoming as well. A certain defensiveness on matters of policy – often no doubt reflecting a genuine uncertainty as to what policy was – was sometimes evident, but we encountered very little hostility and, on procedural and practical matters, a great readiness to give us all the information we wanted. As a whole the Officials seemed as keen as we ourselves were to know what neighbourhood care was.

Our other samples were, in fact, less easy to reach. We chose to make our initial approach by way of an introductory letter outlining the credentials and purposes of the study, guaranteeing confidentiality and proposing suitable arrangements for an interview. The advance warning seemed to justify itself – and indeed to contribute to the research to the extent that in some localities we found that by the time we arrived on certain doorsteps informal networks of discussion had been used to establish a (usually) favourable disposition towards the research. It was among the Residents (not surprisingly as they were bound to have the least direct interest in the ostensible topic of the research, the local Neighbourhood Care project), that we had the worst problems of refusal and non-response; perhaps an overall non-response rate of 40%. To some extent, but unfortunately not fully, we had allowed for this by initial surplus sampling or compensated for it afterwards by re-sampling. But a significant disparity nevertheless remains between the response rates of our Residents and those of our other three sets of respondents.

The observational side of the research tended to grow out of the initial contacts with the key personnel of each project. (The fieldworker for each case study is shown in table A3). We began with a tendency to observe the neighbourhood and the project alike through the eyes of the project's organisers. And in every case we found that by the end of our period of fieldwork we had moved to a significantly broader, more complicated, point of view. We had allowed for a period of up to one month to be spent living in each of the localities in which our chosen projects operated. In each case we began by touring the area fairly thoroughly on foot and by examining as much documentary material about it as we could obtain through the local library, Social Services Department and so forth. After initial discussions with the organisers we tended to begin our formal programme with interviews with the Helpers, going on to Clients and Residents and saving the Officials until the end – so that by the time we came to them we had built up a fairly firm sense of the neighbourhood and the project for ourselves and could discuss both in a reasonably 'informed' manner.

Although we were not in any sense involved in 'participant' observation we found that simply by being around on a day to day basis, by watching bits of the projects in action, by listening to multifarious accounts of it and to the complaints and enthusiasm of those who were involved with it, we quickly formed a fairly well-grounded sense of both place and project which was

Methodology

distinctly more rounded than that of any one of our informants. At the same time we found that we could rapidly begin to draw on the perceptions and assumptions of both those participating in the project and local residents to refine and sharpen the more qualitative aspects of our own inquiries. And, finally, we also found that we were frequently drawn into informal relationships with people involved in the projects we were studying which seemed to be both mutually rewarding (and in some cases long-standing beyond the confines of the research) and an important means of breaking down our own special identity as researchers and obtaining a manifestly more immediate access to the subjective realities of the projects we were seeking to study. Provided one can negotiate the ethical and relational traumas involved in thus being simultaneously a researcher and a human being there would seem to be very considerable advantages (for both researchers and human beings) in this type of observational everyday proximity to one's 'objects' of investigation.

Table A4 *Good Neighbour schemes: schedule for interviews with Helpers*
Note: To save space the full schedule of 23 pages has been compressed by the omission of precodes (indicated by /) and alteration of the layout.

A: Classification data:
First of all I'd like to talk to you about yourself
1. (i) Name
   (ii) Address
   (iii) Age
   (iv) Marital status: Married/Single/Other
   (v) Occupation/or Former occupation
       If married:
       (a) Spouse's occupation: Middle class/Working class/Other
   (vi) What age did you leave full time education? Before 16/16/18/later
   (vii) Would you describe yourself as a religious person?   Yes/No
       If Yes:
       (a) Do you belong to any organised religion?   Yes/No
       (b) Which one? C of E/RC/Methodist/Other

B. Now I would like to ask you about your family:
2. How many brothers and sisters do/did you have?
3. What members of your family do you have living at home? Children/Spouse/Adult dependant
4. How often on average do you see members of your family who do not live with you? At least once a week/Once or twice a month/Less
   (i) Do any of them live in the area?   Yes/No
5. What sort of contact is it that you have with those relatives?
6. Would you describe your family as a close one? Very close/Fairly close/Tend to go our own way/Not close to each other at all
7. Would you say that your parents are particularly neighbourly people?   Yes/No
8. Would you say that your parents have influenced your own feelings about neighbours?   Yes/No/Not at all

Table 4 (*cont.*)

C. I'd like to talk to you about the places you live in or have lived in and the area of the scheme:
9. Do you live in the area of the scheme? Yes/No
10. How long have you lived where you are living now? Less than a year/1–5 years/More/All your life
11. How would you describe the place where you live now? Would you say that it is: Very neighbourly/Fairly neighbourly/Not very neighbourly/Definitely unneighbourly/Mixed – no clear impressions
    If neighbourly:
    (i) In what ways is it neighbourly?
    (ii) Is that area Working class/Middle class/Mixed
12. I would like you to tell me about the neighbourhood where you spent your life, or most of it, as a child; would you say that it was:
    (i) Working class/Middle class/Mixed
    (ii) Council housing/Private housing/Mixed
    (iii) City/Town/Suburban/Rural
    (iv) Very neighbourly/Reasonably neighbourly/Not very neighbourly/Definitely unneighbourly/Mixed/No clear impression

D. I'd like to ask you now about your experience of neighbouring:
13. Do you (or any member of your family) do anything for your neighbours apart from involvement in the scheme? Yes/No
    If Yes:
    (i) What is that?
    (ii) How often? More than once a week/Once a week/Occasionally/Rarely/Never
14. Do any of your neighbours do anything for you (or your family)? Yes/No
    If Yes:
    (i) What is that?
    (ii) How often? More than once a week/Once a week/Occasionally/Rarely/Never
15. Have you any experience of needing help from your neighbours and not feeling able to ask for it? Yes/No
    If Yes:
    (i) What was that situation?
    (ii) Why did you not ask for it?
16. Have you any experience of needing help from neighbours, asking for it from them and not getting it? Yes/No
    If Yes:
    (i) What was that situation?
    (ii) Why do you think the help was not forthcoming?
17. If you were ill, housebound, or in need of help for some other reasons, have you got three people who you could turn to for help? Yes/No
    If Yes:
    (i) Who? Family (specify)/Relatives (specify)/Friends/Neighbours/Social Services/Doctor/Health Visitor/Church/Volunteers/Voluntary Organisations/Other
    (ii) Why would you turn to those people?
    (iii) Would you turn to the same people in an emergency? Yes/No
    If No to (iii)

Table 4 (cont.)

(a) Who would you turn to? Family (specify)/Relatives (specify)/Friends/Neighbours/Social Services/Doctor/Health Visitor/Church/Volunteers/Voluntary Organisations/Other
(b) Why would you turn to these people?

E. What about your experience of any activity or group similar to that of the scheme:

18. Are you a member of, or have you ever belonged to any voluntary organised groups or clubs, apart from this scheme? Yes/No
    If Yes:
    (i) Which group or club?
    (ii) What sort of activity have you taken part in through this/these organisation(s)?

F. Now I'd like to find out more about your involvement in the Good Neighbour scheme:

19. On average how many hours a week does your participation in the scheme take up?
    (i) Does this vary from week to week? Yes/No
    If Yes to (i)
    (a) Why does it vary?
20. Do you receive a payment for this? Yes/No
    (i) *If Yes:* How much is that a week?
21. On average how many people do you help per week?
22. What sort of things do you do in the scheme? Visiting/Referrals to other organisations/Transport/Odd jobs (specify)/Child-minding/Shopping/Collecting prescriptions/Other (specify)
23. How long have you been involved in the scheme? 0-½ year/½-1 year/1-2 year/2-3 year/3-4 year/4-5 year/over 5 years
24. In your case were there any particular obstacles to your becoming involved? Yes/No
25. What were the personal considerations which led to your becoming a Good Neighbour in this scheme?
    Probe if not mentioned:
    (i) Would you say that your own experience of neighbouring affected your decision to become a Good Neighbour in the scheme? Yes/No
    Specify:
    (ii) Did your getting involved have anything to do with any general ideals about society which you may have? Yes/No
    Specify:
    (iii) Was your decision to get involved influenced by any religious convictions? Yes/No
    (iv) Do you think that your decision to get involved was in any way influenced by your experiences of the place where you lived as a child? Yes/No
    Specify
26. How did you get to know of the scheme? Knew people in scheme/Publicity in library/Publicity in shopwindow/Doctor's surgery/Work/Literature through door/Word of mouth/Community Centre
27. Did you know anyone connected with the scheme before you joined? Yes/No
    (i) Did any of these people influence your decision to join the scheme? Yes/No
    If Yes:
    (a) Who was that?
    (b) Would you say that was an important or a slight influence? Important/Slight

Table 4 (*cont.*)

28. What contact do you have with the other helpers in the scheme?
    (i) Have you become really friendly with anyone in the scheme apart from the people you help? No one/1 or 2/Quite a few (3-6)/Many (over 6)
29. Before you joined the scheme, were you doing the same sort of neighbourly things as you are now? Yes/No
30. Before you started, what was the most important thing which you saw yourself personally as being able to achieve in the scheme? (Show card.) Doing things for others/Making friends and getting to know people locally/Encouraging others to help themselves/Making your locality a more neighbourly place to live in/Other
31. Has your experience of being a Good Neighbour in the scheme led you to change those expectations? Yes/No
    If Yes:
    (i) In what ways have your expectations changed?
    (ii) What reasons do you have for changing them?
32. What would you say you as an individual Good Neighbour in the scheme get out of taking part?
33. What is it that keeps you involved in the scheme?
    If answer to 20 is Yes:
    (i) Is the fact that you receive some payment for your services important in your deciding to continue your work in the scheme? Yes/No
    If answer to 20 is No:
    (ii) Would receipt of some payment for your services be important in your deciding to give a longer term commitment to the scheme? Yes/No
34. As a result of your work in the scheme do you have contact with any of the following organisations or particular individuals? (Show card.) Tenants/Residents' Associations/Community Associations/Local Councillors/Local GPs/Local Trades Unions/Vicar/Priest/Church group/Other Voluntary groups (specify)/Other
    If contact with any:
    (i) Is this link up good or bad for the running of the scheme?
        (a) Why do you say that?
    (ii) Looking at the list do you feel that the scheme would be more successful if you had contact with more of these other bodies or individuals? (Show card.) Yes/No
        If Yes to (ii)
        (a) Which ones? Tenants/Residents' Associations/Community Associations/Local Councillors/Local GPs/Local Trades Unions/Vicar/Priest/Church group/Other Voluntary groups (specify)/Other
        (b) Why those?
        If No to (ii)
        (a) Why not?
    If no contact with any:
    (iii) Looking at the list do you feel that there are any organisations or individuals with whom the scheme would benefit from having contact? (Show card.) Yes/No
        If Yes to (iii)
        (a) Which particular ones? Tenants/Residents' Associations/Community Associations/Local Councillors/Local GPs/Local Trades Unions/Vicar/Priest/Church group/Other Voluntary groups (specify)/Other
        (b) Why did you choose those?

Methodology

Table 4 (*cont.*)

If No to (iii)
Why did you say that?

35. Do you think that you would be doing the same sort of neighbourly things even if the scheme ceased to exist?   Yes/No

G. I now want to ask you some questions about your involvement with those you help through the scheme

36. How would you describe your relationship with those that you help? (Show card.) Neighbourly/Befriending/Caring/Social work/Duty/Other (Please choose the label that best defines that relationship)
    (i) Has that relationship changed over time?   Yes/No
    If Yes: (a) How?
    (ii) Have any become friends?   Yes/No
    (iii) Have you ever refused any job or stopped seeing any person that you have helped for any reason?   Yes/No
    If Yes: (a) Why?

37. Thinking of the people that you have helped, do you ever think that they are to blame for the situations that they find themselves in?   Yes/No/DK
    If Yes: (i) Can you give examples?
    If Yes or No:
    (ii) In your opinion what other reasons are there for the situation which the people needing help find themselves in?
    (a) *Probe*: Do you think that they could in any way be victims of an unjust society?   Yes/No/DK
    (b) Why do you say that?

38. It is sometimes said that what is really necessary nowadays is for people to do more for themselves. Would you say that you: Strongly agree/Tend to agree/Strongly disagree/Tend to disagree/DK/Have no definite view
    If strongly agree or tend to agree:
    (i) How do you think people can do that?

39. Which of the following comes nearest to the way that you see yourself as a participant in the scheme? (Show card.) Neighbour/Helper/Counsellor/Friend/Voluntary worker/Other/Not matter/DK

40. Has your work in the scheme included getting people who you have helped to think about the reasons why they are in the situation that they find themselves in?   Yes/No
    If Yes: (i) What sort of things do you say?

H. Now I would like to talk to you about the scheme itself:

41. What do you think are the general aims of the scheme?

42. Thinking of the main sorts of help or care most needed by people in your area, could you tell me what you see these as being?
    (i) How could these needs be met?
    (ii) What sorts of needs do you think a Good Neighbour scheme can meet?
    (iii) Do you think that a Good Neighbour scheme, rather than anything else is the *best* way of meeting these needs?   Yes/No/DK/No clear view
    If No: (a) What sort of things do you think would be better?

43. Do you believe that *this* scheme is successful in providing the help needed?   Yes/No

Table 4 (cont.)

If Yes:
(i) What do you think are the main reasons for its success?
(a) *Probe*: There are some of the things which other schemes have experienced as being important. Has any of these been important in your scheme? (Show card.) Number of helpers/Commitment of Helpers/Contact with local Social Services Department that you have had/Contact with other organisations or individuals outside the scheme that you have had/Adequate financial resources/Degree of willingness of people in need of help to seek/accept it/Having a full-time or paid organiser/premises/Other

44. What sort of things would help the scheme to be more successful?
    (i) *Probe*: These are some of the things which other schemes have experienced as problems. Have any of them been so in your scheme? (Show card.) Too few helpers/Too many helpers/Lack of commitment of helpers/Too much contact with local Social Services Department/Not enough contact with local Social Services Department/Contact with other organisations or individuals outside the scheme/Lack of finance/Degree of willingness of people in need of help to seek/accept it/More publicity/Better transport arrangements/Premises/Other
    (ii) Do you think it is possible that the problems or difficulties that you have mentioned can be overcome? Yes/No/Dk
    If Yes:
    (a) What sort of action do you think is necessary in order to get the problems tackled?
    If No:
    (b) Why do you say that?

45. Is your scheme organised or supported in any way by the Social Services Department of the local Council, or any other Council Officials? Yes/No/DK
    If Yes:
    (i) What form does that take? Initiated/Organised/Referrals/Grants/Other
    (ii) Does it help or hinder the operation of the scheme in your opinion? Help/Hinder
    (a) Why do you say that?
    If No:
    (iv) If the local Social Services Department were involved would you still have joined the scheme? Yes/No/DK
      (a) Why do you say that?
      If Paid:

46. Do you think that there would be any need for you to join a union in your capacity as a Helper in the Good Neighbour scheme? Yes/No/DK
    If Yes: (i) Why?
    If No: (ii) Why not?

47. It is sometimes said that volunteers should give help when public sector employees like ambulance drivers, hospital staff or social workers are on strike. Do you agree with that? Yes/No/DK
    If Yes: (i) Why?
    If No: (ii) Why not?

48. It is sometimes said that it is important for helpers to live next door or very near to those being helped. How far do you agree?
    Strongly agree/Tend to agree/Tend to disagree/Strongly disagree/DK/No definite opinion
    If other than DK:
    (i) Why are you of that opinion?

Table 4 (cont.)

49. There are all sorts of helping schemes in existence these days, yours is called a .... Is that important to you? Yes/No
    If Yes: (i) Why is that important to you?

50. Do you think there are differences between an organised Good Neighbour scheme and ordinary neighbouring that is not organised? Yes/No
    If Yes:
    (i) What are these differences?
    (ii) Do you think that the work of your scheme has increased ordinary neighbourliness in your area? Yes/No
    If Yes to (ii):
    (a) Do you think that your organised scheme could eventually be replaced by ordinary unorganised neighbourliness in your area? Yes/No
    (b) What reasons have you got for saying that?
    If No:
    (ii) Do you think that this is possible in the future? Yes/No
    (a) What reasons have you got for saying that?
    (b) How do you view that prospect? Do you think it is for the best? Yes/No/Doesn't matter/DK
    If other than DK for (b):
    (c) Why do you say that?

I. Now I would like to ask you some questions about general neighbouring:

51. Are there any sorts of help that people should receive from neighbours rather than from other people? Yes/No
    If Yes: (i) What sorts of help?
    If No: (ii) Why do you say that?

52. Would you say that neighbourly activities are especially suitable for women rather than men? Yes/No
    (i) Why do you say that?

53. Are there certain kinds of neighbourly activities that are especially suitable for women rather than men? Yes/No
    If Yes?
    (i) What are they?
    (ii) Why do you say that?

54. It is often said that "neighbouring isn't what it used to be". Would you say that this area is less neighbourly than it used to be? Yes/No/DK
    If Yes or No:
    (i) Can you say more about that and the reasons why you say that?
    (ii) *Probe*: Some people say that people are very isolated today. Do you agree? Yes/No/Partly/DK
    If Yes or No to (ii):
    (a) What reasons do you have for saying that?
    (iii) It is said that people "keep themselves to themselves" today. Do you agree? Yes/No/Partly/DK/No definite view.
    (iv) It is said that there is a lot of 'keeping up with the Joneses' among neighbours these days. Do you agree? Yes/No/Partly/DK/No definite view
    (v) It is often said that people today are too concerned with 'looking after number 1' to

bother about helping their neighbours, do you agree with that? Yes/No/Partly/DK/No definite view

J. Community
55. Would you say that this area (the area of the scheme) has a strong sense of community? Yes/No/Partly/DK/No definite view
 If other than DK:
 (i) Why do you think that?
 (ii) If you had a choice, would you still live in this area? Yes/No/DK
 If Yes or No to (ii): (a) Why do you say that?
56. When the term 'community' is used what does that mean to you personally?
57. How would you describe your relationship with your immediate neighbours? Very close/Fairly close/Indifferent/Neutral/Fairly distant/Very distant
 (i) Why do you say that?
58. Thinking of your own situation, would you say that you have a lot in common with the people in this area? Yes/No/DK
 If Yes: (i) (Why do you say that?) What sort of things have you got in common?
59. Thinking now of the people who live in this area, would you say that they have a lot in common with each other? Yes/No/DK
 If Yes: (i) What sort of things do you think they have in common?
60. If you had a choice, would you choose to remain living in this area? Yes/No/DK
 If other than that:
 (i) Why do you say that?
 (ii) What sort of area would you like to move to?
61. Finally, though we hear a lot of talk about the need for good neighbours nowadays, people tend to have different ideas about what a 'good neighbour' is. Could you say what you personally understand by the term 'a good neighbour'?

Bibliography

Abrams, P. (1962) 'Democracy, technology and the retired British Officer', in S. P. Huntingdon (ed.), *Changing Patterns of Military Politics* (Glencoe, Ill.: Free Press), pp. 150–89.
Abrams, P. (ed.) (1963) *John Locke: Two Tracts on Government* (Cambridge: Cambridge University Press).
Abrams, P. (1965) 'The late profession of arms: ambiguous goals and deteriorating means in Britain', *Archives européens de sociologie* 6(2):238–61.
Abrams, P. (1968) *The Origins of British Sociology 1834–1914* (Chicago: University of Chicago Press).
Abrams, P. (1970) 'Armed forces and society: problems of alienation', in J. N. Wolfe and J. Erickson (eds), *The Armed Services and Society: alienation, management and integration* (Edinburgh: Edinburgh University Press), pp. 24–43.
Abrams, P. (1972) *Being and Becoming in Sociology: an inaugural lecture* (Durham: University of Durham).
Abrams, P. (1977) 'Community care: some research problems and priorities', *Policy & Politics* 6(2):125–51.
Abrams, P. (1978a) 'Community care: some research problems and priorities', in J. Barnes and N. Connelly (eds), *Social Care Research* (London: Policy Studies Institute and Bedford Square Press), pp. 78–99.
Abrams, P. (1978b) *Neighbourhood Care and Social Policy: a research perspective* (Berkhamsted, Herts.: The Volunteer Centre).
Abrams, P. (ed.) (1978c) *Work, Urbanism and Inequality* (London: Weidenfeld and Nicolson).
Abrams, P. (1978d) 'Towns and economic growth: some theories and problems', in Wrigley and Abrams (eds) (1978), pp. 9–33.
Abrams, P. (1980) 'Social change, social networks and neighbourhood care', *Social Work Service* 22, February, pp. 12–23.
Abrams, P. (1982) *Historical Sociology* (Shepton Mallet, Somerset: Open Books).
Abrams, P. (1984a) 'The uses of British sociology, 1831–1981', in Bulmer (ed.) (1984), pp. 181–205.
Abrams, P. (1984b) 'Realities of neighbourhood care: the interactions between statutory, voluntary and informal care', *Policy & Politics*, 12(4) (October):413–29.
Abrams, P. (1984c) 'Evaluating soft findings: some problems of measuring informal care', *Research, Policy and Planning* 2(2):1–8.
Abrams, P. (1985) 'Policies to promote informal social care: some reflections on voluntary action, neighbourhood involvement and neighbourhood care', *Ageing and Society* 5(1) (March):1–18.
Abrams, P., Abrams, S., and Davinson, J. (1979) *Patterns of Neighbourhood Care: a preliminary report* (London: Association for Research in Voluntary Action and Community Involvement (ARVAC) Occasional Paper No. 1).

Bibliography

Abrams, P., Abrams, S., Humphrey, R. and Snaith, R. (1981a), *Action for Care: a review of Good Neighbour schemes in England* (Berkhamsted, Herts.: The Volunteer Centre).

Abrams, P., Abrams, S., Humphrey, R. and Snaith, R. (1982) *A Handbook of Good Neighbour Schemes in England* (Berkhamsted, Herts.: The Volunteer Centre).

Abrams, P., Abrams, S., Humphrey, R. and Snaith, R. (1985a) *Patterns of Neighbourhood Care: case studies in their social context* (Durham University Department of Sociology and Social Policy, Rowntree Research Unit Working Paper).

Abrams, P., Abrams, S., Humphrey, R. and Snaith, R., edited for Neighbourhood Care Organisers by Leat, D. (1985b) *Creating Care in the Neighbourhood* (London: Advice and Development for Volunteering and Neighbourhood Care in London (ADVANCE)).

Abrams, P., Abrams, S., Humphrey, R. and Snaith, R. (forthcoming) *Neighbourhood Care and social Policy* (London: HMSO).

Abrams, P., Deem, R., Finch, J. and Rock, P. (eds) (1981b) *Practice and Progress: British Sociology 1950–1980* (London: Allen and Unwin).

Abrams, P. and McCulloch, A. (1976) *Communes, Sociology and Society* (Cambridge: Cambridge University Press).

Abrams, S. and Marsden, D. (1985) *The Costs of Community Care: a survey of daughters caring for mothers* (Goldsmiths College, University of London, Department of Social Science and Administration, mimeo).

Allan, G. A. (1977) 'Class variation in friendship patterns', *British Journal of Sociology* 28:389–93.

Allan, G. A. (1979) *A Sociology of Friendship and Kinship* (London: Allen and Unwin).

Allan, G. A. (1983) 'Informal networks of care: issues raised by Barclay', *British Journal of Social Work* 13:417–33.

Anderson, M. (1971) *Family Structure in Nineteenth Century Lancashire* (Cambridge: Cambridge University Press).

Arensberg, C. M. and Kimball, S. T. (1940) *Family and Community in Ireland* (Cambridge, Mass.: Harvard University).

Bailey, F. G. (ed.) (1971) *Gifts and Poison: the politics of reputation* (Oxford: Blackwell).

Baldock, P. (1974) *Community Work and Social Work* (London: Routledge and Kegan Paul).

Banfield, E. C. (1958) *The Moral Basis of a Backward Society* (New York: Free Press).

Barber, B. (1983) *The Logic and Limits of Trust* (Rutgers, N. J.: Rutgers University Press).

Barclay Report (1982) *Social Workers: their roles and tasks* (London: Bedford Square Press).

Barnes, J. A. (1954) 'Class and committees in a Norwegian island parish', *Human Relations* 7:39–58.

Barnes, J. A. (1969) 'Networks and political process', in Mitchell (ed.) (1969b), pp. 51–76.

Barnes, J. A. and Harary, F. (1983) 'Graph theory in network analysis', *Social Networks* 5:235–44.

Barton, A. H. (1969) *Communities in Disaster: a sociological analysis of collective stress situations* (Garden City, N.Y.: Doubleday).

Bates, A. (1964) 'Privacy – a useful concept?' *Social Forces* 42:429–34.

Bayley, M. J. (1973) *Mental Handicap and Community Care* (London: Routledge and Kegan Paul).

Bibliography

Bayley, M. J. (1981) 'Neighbourhood care and community care: a response to Philip Abrams', *Social Work Service* 26, May, pp. 4–9.

Bayley, M. J. (1982) 'Helping care to happen in the community', in Walker (ed) (1982), pp. 179–96.

Bayley, M. J. et al. (1984) *Neighbourhood Services Project: Dinnington: Working Papers* (Sheffield: University of Sheffield Department of Sociological Studies).

Becker, G. S. (1980) *Altruism in the Family and Selfishness in the Marketplace* (London: London School of Economics, Centre for Labour Economics Discussion Paper No. 73).

Bell, C. and McKee, L. (1984) 'His unemployment, her problem' (University of Aston, Birmingham, mimeo).

Bell, C. and Newby, H. (1971) *Community Studies* (London: Allen and Unwin).

Berger, B. (1960) *Working Class Suburb* (Berkeley: University of California Press).

Berger, P. L. (1977) 'In praise of particularity: the concept of mediating structures', in P. L. Berger, *Facing up to Modernity: excursions in society, politics and religion* (New York: Basic Books), pp. 130–41.

Berger, P. L. and Neuhaus, R. J. (1980) *To Empower People: the role of mediating structures in public policy* (Washington D.C.: American Enterprise Institute).

Blau, P. (1964) *Exchange and Power in Social Life* (New York: Wiley).

Bloch, M. (1962) *Feudal Society* (London: Routledge and Kegan Paul).

Boissevain, J. (1974) *Friends of Friends: networks, manipulators and coalitions* (Oxford: Blackwell).

Boissevain, J. and Mitchell, J. C. (eds) (1973) *Network Analysis: studies in human interaction* (The Hague: Mouton).

Bott, E. (1957) (1971) *Family and Social Network* (London: Tavistock) (revised edition with new Introduction, 1971).

Bracey, H. E. (1964) *Neighbours: on new estates and subdivisions in England and the U.S.A.* (London: Routledge and Kegan Paul).

Bramson, L. (1961) *The Political Context of Sociology* (Princeton: Princeton University Press).

Briggs, A. and Oliver, J. (1985) *Caring* (London: Routledge and Kegan Paul).

British Sociological Association (BSA) (1982) 'Obituary: Philip Abrams', *Network: the newsletter of the B.S.A.*, No. 22, January, p. 2.

Brown, R. K. (1982), 'Philip Abrams, 1933–1981', *Sociology* 16(1):i–iii.

Bulmer, M. (ed.) (1977) *Mining and Social Change: Durham County in the Twentieth Century* (London: Croom Helm).

Bulmer, M. (ed.) (1984a) *Essays on the History of British Sociological Research* (Cambridge: Cambridge University Press).

Bulmer, M. (ed.) (1984b) *Sociological Research Methods* (London: Macmillan) (second edition).

Bulmer, M. (1984c) 'Local inequality: sociability, isolation and loneliness as factors in the differential provision of neighbourhood care' (paper delivered to Social Administration Association conference, Canterbury, July).

Bulmer, M. (1985a) 'The rejuvenation of community studies: neighbours, networks and policy', *The Sociological Review*, 33(3) (August).

Bulmer, M. (1985b) 'Privacy and confidentiality as obstacles to interweaving formal and informal social care' (London School of Economics and Political Science, mimeo).

Butler, E. W. (1976) *Urban Sociology: a systematic approach* (New York: Harper & Row).

Bytheway, W. R. (1979) *Care in the Street: a study of informal support for frail elderly*

in West Glamorgan (Swansea: University of Swansea Medical Sociology Research Centre, mimeo).
Callow, A. B. Jr. (ed.) (1976) *The City Boss in America* (New York: Oxford University Press).
Caplow, T. and Forman, R. (1950) 'Neighbourhood interaction in a homogeneous community', *American Sociological Review* 15:357–66.
Castells, M. (1977) *The Urban Question* (London: Arnold).
Challis, D. and Davies, B. (1980) 'A new approach to community care of the elderly', *British Journal of Social Work* 10:1–18.
Collins, A. H. and Pancoast, D. L. (1976) *Natural Helping Networks* (Washington D.C.: National Association of Social Workers).
Collison, P. (1963) *The Cutteslowe Walls* (London: Faber & Faber).
Craven, P. and Wellman, B. (1973) 'The network city', *Sociological Inquiry* 43:57–88.
Crossman, R. H. S. (1973) *The Role of the Volunteer in the Modern Social Services* (Sidney Ball Memorial Lecture) (Oxford: Oxford University Press).
Darvill, G. (1983) 'Shuttle diplomacy in the personal social services: interweaving statutory and informal care in a changing Britain', in Pancoast *et al.* (eds) (1983) pp. 239–60.
Dennis, N. (1968) 'The popularity of the neighbourhood community idea', in Pahl (ed.) (1968), pp. 74–92.
Dennis, N., Henriques, F. and Slaughter, C. (1956), *Coal is Our Life* (London: Tavistock).
Dexter, M. and Harbert, W. (1983) *The Home Help Service* (London: Tavistock).
Department of Health and Social Security (DHSS) (1981a) *Care in the Community: a consultative document on moving resources for care in England* (London: DHSS).
Department of Health and Social Security (DHSS) (1981b) *Report of a study on Community Care* (London: DHSS).
Dore, R. P. (1958) *City Life in Japan: a study of a Tokyo ward* (London: Routledge and Kegan Paul).
Dore, R. P. (1983) 'Goodwill and the spirit of market capitalism', *British Journal of Sociology* 34:459–82.
Durant, R. (1939; *Watling: a social survey* (London: P. S. King).
Durkheim, E. (1893, 1933) *The Division of Labour in Society* (New York: Free Press).
Durkheim, E. (1952) *Suicide: a study in sociology* (London: Routledge & Kegan Paul).
Ekeh, P. (1974) *Social Exchange Theory: the two traditions* (London: Heinemann).
Elias, N. and Scotson, J. L. (1965) *The Established and the Outsiders* (London: Frank Cass).
Equal Opportunites Commission (EOC) (1982) *Who Cares for the Carers? Opportunities for those caring for the elderly and handicapped* (Manchester: Equal Opportunities Commission).
Etzioni, A. (1964) *A Comparative Analysis of Complex Organisations* (New York: Free Press).
Fallding, H. (1961) 'The family and the idea of a cardinal role', *Human Relations* 14:329–50.
Festinger, L., Schachter, S. and Back, K. (1950) *Social Pressures in Informal Groups: a study of human factors in housing* (Stanford, Calif.: Stanford University Press).
Field, J. and Hedges, B. (1984) *A National Survey of Volunteering* (London: Social and Community Planning Research).
Finch, J. and Groves, D. (1980) 'Community care and the family: a case for equal opportunities?', *Journal of Social Policy* 9:486–511.
Finch, J. and Groves, D. (eds) (1983) *A Labour of Love: women, work and caring* (London: Routledge and Kegan Paul).

Fischer, C. et al. (1977) *Networks and Places: social relations in the urban setting* (New York: Free Press).
Flew, A. (1980) 'Looking after granny; the reality of community care', *New Society*, 9 October.
Form, W. H. and Nosow, S. (1958) *Community in Disaster* (New York: Harper).
Frankenberg, R. (1957) *Village on the Border* (London: Cohen and West).
Frankenberg, R. (1966) *Communities in Britain* (Harmondsworth: Penguin).
Froland, C. (1980) 'Formal and informal care: discontinuities in a continuum', *Social Service Review* 54(4):572–87.
Froland, C., Pancoast, D. L. et al. (1981) *Helping Networks and Human Services* (London: Sage).
Froland, C., Parker, P. and Bayley, M. (1980) 'Relating formal and informal sources of care: reflections on initiatives in England and America' (Sheffield: University of Sheffield Department of Sociological Studies, mimeo).
Gallie, W. B. (1956) 'Essentially contested concepts', Proceedings of the Aristotelian Society 56 (1955–56): 167–98.
Gans, H. (1961) 'Planning and social life: friendship and neighbour relations in suburban communities', *Journal of the American Institute of Planners* 27:134–40.
Gans, H. (1962) *The Urban Villagers* (New York: Free Press).
Gans, H. (1967) *The Levittowners* (London: Allen Lane).
Gans, H. (1968) 'Urbanism and suburbanism as ways of life', in Pahl (ed.) (1968), pp. 95–118.
Gaylin, W. (ed.) (1978) *Doing Good: the limits of benevolence* (New York: Pantheon).
Gerson, K., Stueve, C. A. and Fischer, C. S. (1977), 'Attachment to place', in Fischer et al. (1977), pp. 139–61.
Gibson, T. (1984) *Counterweight: the neighbourhood option* (London: Town and Country Planning Association).
Ginsberg, J. and Churchman, A. (1983) 'The pattern and meaning of neighbour relations in high-rise housing in Israel', (Tel Aviv: Tel Aviv University Centre for Urban and Regional Studies, Working Paper No. 74), pp. 1–30.
Glass, R. (1948) *The Social Background of a Plan* (London: Routledge and Kegan Paul).
Glasser, I. (1978) 'Prisoners of benevolence', in Gaylin (ed.) (1978).
Gluckman, M. (1963) 'Gossip and scandal', *Current Anthropology* 4:307–16.
Goldberg, E. M. and Connelly, N. (1982) *The Effectiveness of Social Care for the Elderly: an overview of recent and current evaluative research* (London: Heinemann for Policy Studies Institute).
Goldberg, E. M., Mortimer, A. and Williams, B. T. (1970) *Helping the Aged: a field experiment in social work* (London: Allen and Unwin).
Goss, A. (1961) 'Neighbourhood units in British new towns', *Town Planning Review* 32:66–82.
Gottleib, B. H. (ed.) (1981) *Social Networks and Social Support* (London: Sage).
Gottleib, B. H. (1983) *Social Support Strategies: guidelines for mental health practice* (London: Sage).
Gouldner, A. W. (1960) 'The norm of reciprocity: a preliminary statement', *American Sociological Review* 25(2):161–78.
Gouldner, A. W. (1973) 'The importance of something for nothing', in A. Gouldner, *For Sociology* (London: Allen Lane), pp. 260–99.
Grant, G. and Wenger, C. (1983) 'Patterns of partnership: three models of care for the elderly', in Pancoast et al. (1983), pp. 27–51.
Hadley, R., Dale, P. and Sills, P. (1984) *Decentralising Social Services: a model for change* (London: Bedford Square Press).

Hadley, R. and McGrath, M. (1980) *Going Local: Neighbourhood Social Services* (London: National Council for Voluntary Organisations).

Hadley, R. and McGrath, M. (1984) *When Social Services are Local: the Normanton experience* (London: Allen and Unwin).

Hallman, H. W. (1984) *Neighbourhoods: their place in urban life* (Beverly Hills: Sage).

Harbert, W. and Rogers, P. (eds) (1983) *Community-Based Social Care: the Avon experience* (London: Bedford Square Press).

Hareven, T. K. (1982) *Family Time and Industrial Time: the relationship between family and work in a New England industrial community* (Cambridge: Cambridge University Press).

Harris, C. C. (1969) *The Family* (London: Allen and Unwin).

Hatch, S. (ed.) (1983) *Volunteers: patterns, meanings and motives* (London: Policy Studies Institute).

Hawley, A. (ed.) (1968) *Roderick D. McKenzie on Human Ecology* (Chicago: University of Chicago Press).

Heath, A. F. (1976) *Rational Choice and Social Exchange: a critique of exchange theory* (Cambridge: Cambridge University Press).

Hedley, R. (1984) *Neighbourhood Care in Practice* (London: The Neighbourhood Care Action Programme).

Henry, J. (1958) 'The personal community and its invariant properties', *American Anthropologist* 60:827–31.

Hirsch, F. (1977) *Social Limits to Growth* (London: Routledge and Kegan Paul).

Hole, V. (1959) 'Social effects of planned rehousing', *Town Planning Review* 30:166–73.

Holmes, A. and Maizels, J. (1979) *Social Workers and Volunteers* (London: British Association of Social Workers).

Homans, G. C. (1961) *Social Behaviour: its elementary forms* (London: Routledge and Kegan Paul).

Humphrey, R. (1984) *The Excluded and the Involved: a study of voluntary organisations and informal networks* (Goldsmiths College, University of London: Department of Social Science and Administration, mimeo).

Humphrey, R. and Snaith, R. (1982) 'Activate thy neighbour', *Voluntary Action*, Spring 1982, pp. 33–4.

Hunt, A. (1970) *The Home Help Service in England and Wales* (a report by Office of Population Censuses and Surveys, Social Survey Division) (London: HMSO).

Hunter, A. (1974) *Symbolic Communities: the persistence and change of Chicago's local communities* (Chicago: University of Chicago Press).

Hunter, A. and Suttles, G. D. (1972) 'The expanding community of limited liability', in Suttles (1972), pp. 44–81.

Illich, I. et al. (1977) *Disabling Professions* (London: Boyars)

Islington (1977) *The Use of Volunteers in the Social Services Department* (London: London Borough of Islington Social Services Department, Research and Development Section, mimeo).

Jackson, R. M. (1977) 'Social structure and process in friendship choice', in Fischer (ed.) (1977), pp. 59–78.

Janowitz, M. (1970) 'Sociological models and social policy', in *Political Conflict: essays in political sociology* (Chicago: Quadrangle), pp. 243–59.

Janowitz, M. (1977) *Social Control of the Welfare State* (Chicago: University of Chicago Press).

Janowitz, M. and Suttles, G. D. (1978) 'The social ecology of citizenship', in R. C.

Sarri and Y. Hasenfeld (eds) *The Management of Human Services* (New York: Columbia University Press), pp. 80–104.
Johnson, M. and Macdonald, C. (1983) *The Caring Capacity of the Community: the informal network* (Final Report to SSRC) (Newcastle on Tyne: University of Newcastle on Tyne Department of Social Policy).
Johnson, M. L. and Cooper, S. (1984) *Informal Care and the Personal Social Services: an interpretive literature review* (London: Policy Studies Institute, mimeo).
Jones, K., Brown, J. and Bradshaw, J. (1978) *Issues in Social Policy* (London: Routledge and Kegan Paul).
Kapferer, B. (1969) 'Norms and the manipulation of relationships in a work context', in Mitchell (ed.) (1969b), pp. 181–244.
Kapferer, B. (1972) *Strategy and transaction in an African Factory: African workers and Indian management in a Zambian town* (Manchester University Press).
Kardiner, A. and Prebble, E. (1962) *They Studied Man* (London: Secker and Warburg).
Keller, S. (1968) *The Urban Neighbourhood: a sociological perspective* (New York: Random House).
Kingston Polytechnic (1972) *The Buxton Report* (Kingston upon Thames: Kingston Polytechnic Schools of Architecture and Three-Dimensional Design, mimeo).
Knight, B. and Hayes, R. (1981) *Self Help in the Inner City* (London: London Voluntary Service Council).
Krebs, D. L. (1970) 'Altruism: an examination of the concept and a review of the literature', *Psychological Bulletin* 73:258–302.
Kropotkin, P. (1915) *Mutual Aid: a factor of evolution* (London: Heinemann).
Kuper, L. (1953) 'Blueprint for living together', in L. Kuper (ed.), *Living in Towns* (London: Cressett Press), pp. 1–202.
Laumann, E. O. (1973) *Bonds of Pluralism: form and substance of urban social networks* (New York: Wiley).
Leat, D. (1979) *Limited Liability: a report of some Good Neighbour schemes* (Berkhamsted, Herts: The Volunteer Centre).
Leat, D. (1983) *Getting to Know the Neighbours: a pilot study of the elderly and neighbourly helping* (London: Policy Studies Institute Research Paper 83-2).
Lee, T. (1968) 'Urban neighbourhood as a socio-spatial schema', *Human Relations* 21:241–68.
Levin, E., Sinclair, I., and Gorbach, P. (1984) *The Supporters of Confused Elderly Persons at Home* (London: National Institute of Social Work, mimeo).
Levin, E., Sinclair, I. and Gorbach, P. (1986), *Families, Services and Confusion in Old Age* (London: Allen and Unwin).
Litwak, E. and Meyer, H. H. (1966) 'A balance theory of co-ordination between bureaucratic organisation and community primary groups', *Administrative Science Quarterly* 11 (June):31–58.
Litwak, E. and Szelenyi, I. (1969) 'Primary group structures and their functions: kin, neighbours and friends', *American Sociological Review* 34:465–81.
Loudon, J. B. (1961) 'Kinship and crisis in South Wales', *British Journal of Sociology* 12:333–50.
Luhmann, N. (1979) *Trust and Power* (Chichester, Sussex: John Wiley).
McCulloch, A. (1982) 'Philip Abrams – a tribute', *Sociology* 16(1):iii–iv.
McGahan, P. (1972) 'The neighbour role and neighbouring in a highly urban area', *Sociological Quarterly* 13:397–408.
Macmurray, J. (1935) *Freedom in the Modern World* (London: Faber and Faber).
Maguire, L. (1983) *Understanding Social Networks* (London: Sage).

Bibliography

Malinowski, B. (1922) *Argonauts of the Western Pacific* (London: Routledge and Kegan Paul).

Mann, P. H. (1954) 'The concept of neighbourliness', *American Journal of Sociology* 60:163–8.

Marcus, S. (1978) 'Their brother's keepers', in Gaylin (ed.) (1978).

Mauss, M. (1925) 'Essai sur le don: forme et raison de l'échange dans les sociétés archaiques', *Anné Sociologique* n.s. 1:30–186; translated by I. G. Cunnison and M. Mauss, *The Gift* (London: Cohen and West, 1966).

Mead, G. H. (1934) *Mind, Self and Society: from the standpoint of a social behaviourist* (edited with an introduction by Charles W. Morris) (Chicago: University of Chicago Press).

Merton, R. K. (1957) *Social Theory and Social Structure* (New York: Free Press).

Minar, D. W. and Greer, S. (eds) (1969) *The Concept of Community* (Chicago: Aldine).

Mitchell, J. C. (1969a) 'The concept and use of social networks', in Mitchell (1969b), pp. 1–50.

Mitchell, J. C. (ed.) (1969b) *Social Networks in Urban Situations* (Manchester: Manchester University Press).

Mogey, J. M. (1956) *Family and Neighbourhood: two studies in Oxford* (Oxford: Oxford University Press).

Morris, D. and Hess, K. (1975) *Neighbourhood Power: the new localism* (Boston: Beacon Press).

Morris, R. N. (1968) *Urban Sociology* (London: Allen and Unwin).

Mumford, L. (1954) 'The neighbourhood and the neighbourhood unit', *Town Planning Review* 24:256–70.

National Association for the Care and Resettlement of Offenders (NACRO) (1984) *The Safe Neighbourhood Unit: community-based improvement programmes on twelve inner London housing estates* (London: NACRO).

National Commission on Neighbourhoods (1979) *People, Building Neighbourhoods* (Final Report to the President and Congress) (Washington D.C.: U.S. Government Printing Office).

Newby, H. (1979) *England's Green and Pleasant Land* (London: Allen Lane).

Nisbet, R. A. (1969) *The Quest for Community* (New York: Oxford University Press).

Nodding, N. (1984) *Caring: a feminine approach to ethics and moral education* (Berkeley: University of California Press).

Offer, J. (1984) 'Informal welfare, social work and the sociology of welfare', *British Journal of Social Work* 14:545–55.

Pahl, R. E. (1966) 'The rural–urban continuum', *Sociologia Ruralis* 6:299–326 (reprinted in Pahl (ed.) 1968, pp. 263–305).

Pahl, R. E. (ed.) (1968) *Readings in Urban Sociology* (Oxford: Pergamon).

Pahl, R. E. (1970) *Patterns of Urban Life* (London: Longmans).

Paine, R. (1969) 'In search of friendship: an exploratory analysis in "middle class" culture', *Man* 4:505–24.

Pancoast, D. L., Parker, P. and Froland, C. (eds) (1983) *Rediscovering Self-Help: its role in social care* (London: Sage).

Parker, G., Baldwin, S. and Glendinning, C. (1984) *Informal Care and Carers: a research review and recommendations for future research* (York: University of York Social Policy Research Unit Working Paper).

Parker, R. (1981) 'Tending and social policy', in E. M. Goldberg and S. Hatch (eds), *A New Look at the Personal Social Services* (London: Policy Studies Institute Discussion Paper No. 4), pp. 17–34.

Parsons, T. (1951) *The Social System* (London: Routledge & Kegan Paul).
Patterson, S. L. and Twente, E. E. (1971) 'Older natural helpers: their characteristics and pattern of helping', *Public Welfare* 29(4):400–3.
Pember-Reeves, M. S. (1913) *Round About a Pound a Week* (London: Bell).
Personal Social Services Research Unit (PSSRU) (1983) 'Community care', PSSRU Newsletter (Summer): 5–6.
Pfiel, E. (1968) 'The pattern of neighbourhood relations in Dortmund-Nordstadt', in Pahl (ed.) (1968), pp. 135–58.
Pickvance, C. G. (ed.) (1978) *Urban Sociology: critical essays* (London: Tavistock).
Pinker, R. (1979) *The Idea of Welfare* (London: Heinemann).
Pinker, R. (1982) 'An alternative view', in Barclay Report (1982), pp. 236–62.
Pitt-Rivers, J. (1973) 'The kith and the kin', in J. Goody (ed.) *The Character of Kinship* (Cambridge, Cambridge University Press), pp. 89–105.
Poggi, G. (1972) *Images of Society* (Stanford: Stanford University Press).
Power, M. (1980) *The Home Care of the Very Old* (Bristol: University of Bristol Social Care Research Unit, mimeo).
Power, M., Clough, R., Gibson, P. and Kelly, S. (1983) *Helping Lively Minds: volunteer support to residential homes* (Bristol: University of Bristol Social Care Research Unit).
Price, F. V. (1981) 'Only connect? Issues in charting social networks', *Sociological Review* 29:283–312.
Pruger, R. (1973) 'Social policy: unilateral transfer or reciprocal exchange', *Journal of Social Policy* 2:289–302.
Qureshi, H., Challis, D. and Davies, B. (1983) 'Motivations and rewards of helpers in the Kent Community care scheme', in S. Hatch (ed.) (1983), pp. 144–68.
Qureshi, H., Davies, B. and Challis, D. (1979) 'Motivations and rewards of volunteers and informal caregivers', *Journal of Voluntary Action Research* 8(1/2):47–55.
Rees, A. (1950) *Life in the Welsh Countryside* (Cardiff: University of Wales Press).
Reimer, S. (1951) 'Villagers in metropolis', *British Journal of Sociology* 2:31–42.
Reisman, D. A. (1978) *Richard Titmuss: welfare and society* (London: Heinemann).
Report to DHSS (1981) *Patterns of Neighbourhood Care* (end of project report to DHSS by Philip Abrams, Sheila Abrams, Robin Humphrey and Ray Snaith. (London: Office of the Chief Scientist, Department of Health and Social Security.)
Rex, J. and Moore, R. S. (1967) *Race, Community and Conflict: a study of Sparkbrook* (London: Oxford University Press).
Robinson, F. (1977) 'The home help service: an example of organised altruism' (Durham: University of Durham, Rowntree Research Unit, mimeo).
Robinson, F. and Abrams, P. (1977) *What We Know About the Neighbours* (Durham: University of Durham, Rowntree Research Unit, mimeo).
Robinson, F. and Robinson, S. (1982) *Neighbourhood Care: an exploratory bibliography* (Berkhamsted, Herts.: The Volunteer Centre).
Robson, B. T. (1969) *Urban Analysis* (Cambridge: Cambridge University Press).
Ross, E. (1983) 'Survival networks: women's neighbourhood sharing in London before World War 1', *History Workshop Journal* 15 (Spring):4–27.
Sahlins, M. D. (1965) 'On the sociology of primitive exchange', in M. Banton (ed.), *The Relevance of Models for Social Anthropology* (London: Tavistock), pp. 139–236.
Sainsbury, P. and de Alarçon, J. (1974) 'The cost of community care and the burden of the family of treating the mentally ill at home', in D. Lees and S. Shaw (eds), *Impairment, Disability and Handicap* (London: Heinemann), pp. 123–40.
Scarman, Lord (1982) *The Brixton Disorders, 10–12 April 1981* (Harmondsworth: Penguin).

Schwartz, B. (1967) 'The social psychology of the gift', *American Journal of Sociology* 73:1–11.
Seebohm Report (1968) *Report of the Committee on Local Authority and Allied Personal Social Services*, Cmnd 3703 (London: HMSO).
Shulman, N. (1967) 'Mutual aid and neighbouring patterns: the lower town study', *Anthropologica* 9:51–60.
Simmel, G. (1969, first published 1905) 'The Metropolis and Mental Life' in R. Sennett (ed.), *Classic Essays on the Culture of Cities* (New York: Appleton-Century-Crofts), pp. 47–60.
Simpkin, M. (1979) *Trapped Within Welfare: surviving social work* (London: Macmillan).
Sinclair, I., Crosbie, D., O'Connor, P., Stanforth, L. and Vickery, A. (1984) *Networks Project: a study of informal care, services and social work for elderly clients living alone* (London: National Institute of Social Work, mimeo).
Sinclair, I. et al. (forthcoming) *Social Networks and Social Services: a study of informal care, services and social work for elderly people living alone* (London: Allen and Unwin).
Smith, R. A. (1975) 'Measuring neighbourhood cohesion: a review and some suggestions', *Human Ecology* 3(3):143–60.
Snaith, R. (1985) *Mobilising Community Involvement* (Goldsmiths College, University of London, Department of Social Science and Administration, mimeo).
Sorokin, P. A. (1950) *Altruistic love: a study of American Good Neighbours and Christian Saints* (Boston: Beacon Press).
Stacey, M. (1969) 'The myth of community studies', *British Journal of Sociology* 20:134–47.
Suttles, G. D. (1968) *The Social Order of the Slum* (Chicago: University of Chicago Press).
Suttles, G. D. (1970) 'Friendship as a social institution', in G. J. McCall et al., *Social Relationships* (Chicago: Aldine), pp. 95–135.
Suttles, G. D. (1972) *The Social Construction of Communities* (Chicago: University of Chicago Press).
Taub, R. P., Taylor, D. G. and Dunham, J. D. (1984), *Paths of Neighbourhood Change: race and crime in urban America* (Chicago: University of Chicago Press).
Terrill, R. (1974) *R. H. Tawney and His Times: socialism as fellowship* (London: Andre Deutsch).
Thorns, D. C. (1972) *Suburbia* (London: McGibbon & Kee).
Timms, E. (1983) 'On the relevance of informal social networks to social work intervention', *British Journal of Social Work* 13(405–15).
Tinker, A. (1984) *Staying at Home: helping elderly people* (London: HMSO for the Department of the Environment).
Titmuss, R. M. (1968) *Commitment to Welfare* (London: Allen and Unwin).
Titmuss, R. M. (1970) *The Gift Relationship: from human blood to social policy* (London: Allen and Unwin).
Tomeh, A. K. (1964) 'Informal group participation and residential patterns', *American Journal of Sociology* 70:28–35.
Townsend, P. (1963) *The Family Life of Old People* (London: Routledge and Kegan Paul).
Ungerson, C. (1983a) 'Why do women care?', in Finch and Groves (eds) (1983), pp. 31–49.
Ungerson, C. (1983b) 'Women and caring: skills, tasks and taboos', in E. Gamarnikow et al. (eds) (1983), *The Public and the Private* (London: Heinemann), pp. 62–77.

Walker, A. (ed.) (1982) *Community Care* (Oxford: Blackwells and Robertson).
Wallace, C. and Pahl, R. E. (1984) 'Polarisation, unemployment and all forms of work', (University of Kent, Work Behaviour Research Unit, mimeo).
Wallace, W. (1969) *Sociological Theory* (London: Heinemann).
Wallin, P. (1953) 'A Guttman scale for measuring women's neighbourliness', *American Journal of Sociology* 59:243–6.
Warren, D. I. (1981) *Helping Networks: how people cope with problems in the urban community* (Notre Dame, Indiana: University of Notre Dame Press).
Wellman, B. (1979) 'The community question: the intimate networks of East Yorkers', *American Journal of Sociology* 84:1201–31.
Wenger, G. C. (1984) *The Supportive Network: coping with old age* (London: Allen and Unwin).
Whyte, W. H. (1963) *The Organisation Man* (Harmondsworth: Penguin).
Williams, B. (1973) *Morality* (Harmondsworth: Penguin).
Williams, W. M. (1956) *The Sociology of an English Village: Gosforth* (London: Routledge and Kegan Paul).
Willmott, P. (1963) *The Evolution of a Community: a study of Dagenham after forty years* (London: Routledge and Kegan Paul).
Willmott, P. (1984) *Community in Social Policy* (London: Policy Studies Institute).
Willmott, P. and Young, M. (1960) *Family and Class in a London Suburb* (London: Routledge and Kegan Paul).
Wilson, E. (1982) 'Women, the "Community" and the "Family"', in Walker (ed.) (1982), pp. 40–55.
Wirth, L. (1938) 'Urbanism as a way of life', *American Journal of Sociology* 44:3–24.
Wolfenden Report (1978) *The Future of Voluntary Organisations* (London: Croom Helm).
Wrigley, E. A. and Abrams, P. (eds) (1978) *Towns in Societies: essays in economic history and historical sociology* (Cambridge: Cambridge University Press).
Young, M. and Willmott, P. (1972) *Family and Kinship in East London* (Harmondsworth: Penguin) (first published 1957).

Index

Abrams, S., 5, 7, 11, 123, 241, 242
age: of Clients, 165, 166; of Helpers, 160, 161, 162; of neighbours, 68, 69, 84
Allan, G. A., 31, 35, 39–40, 41, 89, 90, 96, 219, 230
altruism, 45, 50, 64–5, 223–4; and reciprocity, 103–17
Anderson, M., 90, 98, 105, 106, 113
Arensberg, C. M., 37
Austen Avenue, 47–52, 83, 86, 246, 247, 252–3

bad neighbouring, 32–3, 74
Bailey, F. G., 31–2, 224
Baldock, P., 46
Banfield, E. C., 32
Barber, B., 116
Barclay Report, 218, 219, 230
Barnes, J. A., 88, 237
Barton, A. H., 9, 29–30
Bates, A., 96
Bayley, M. H., 121, 217, 236
Bayley, M. J., 210, 213, 218
Becker, G. S., 116
Bell, C., 17, 33
beneficence, norm of, 110, 112, 116–17
Berger, B., 38
Berger, P. L., 8
Blau, P., 90, 97, 106, 107, 108
Bloch, M., 8
Boissevain, J., 27, 32, 251
bonding, rules of, 35–6
borrowing and lending, 30, 36, 61, 66–7
Boswell village, 47, 63–71, 83, 86, 87, 230, 246
Bott, E., 88, 89, 96
Bracey, H. E., 28, 30, 31, 32, 36, 41, 42, 96
Bradbury Christian Council Care scheme, 140, 150–2, 181, 182, 255; Clients, 165, 166, 167, 168; Helpers, 162, 164, 165, 179, 191, 192, 193, 198; and neighbourliness, 203; pattern of care, 197, 203; problems, 183, 184, 185, 187–8
Bramson, L., 8
Brandling Good Neighbour scheme, 140, 142–4, 182, 189–90, 255; Clients, 165, 166, 167, 168; Helpers, 162, 164, 165, 179, 191, 192, 193, 198; and neighbourliness, 204; pattern of care, 197, 198–9, 203; problems, 183, 184, 185, 187, 188
Briggs, A., 242
Bulmer, M., 30, 45, 88, 216, 219, 230, 237
Butler, E. W., 37
Bytheway, W. R., 46

Callow, A. B., 93
Caplow, T., 18, 34
care, patterns of, in Neighbourhood Care projects, 194–203
carers, 214–18, 239–42; altruism and reciprocity in, 107, 111, 113, 115, 116–17; central figures, 130, 237; in Good Neighbour schemes, 113–15; see also Helpers
Castells, M., 37, 39
Challis, D., 236, 240
children, 42, 68–9, 75, 81, 84
churches, and neighbourhood care, 114, 138, 142, 143, 150–2, 157
class differences: of Clients, 165, 166; of Helpers, 160–1, 162, 175, 177–80, 194; of neighbours, 39–40, 69, 76; and sources of help, 174; see also middle class; working class
Clients, in Neighbourhood Care schemes, 135, 165–8, 174–5, 190, 191, 254, 256
cohesion of neighbourhoods, 89–90
Collins, A. H., 110–11, 115, 127, 130, 210
Collison, P., 32
colonisation, of Neighbourhood Care schemes, 129–32, 207–8, 232
community care, 3, 6–7, 122, 209; definition, 22–3; see also neighbourhood care
Congreve Hall, 47, 76–82, 83, 85, 86, 87, 246, 247
Craven, P., 88
Crossman, R. H. S., 216

Darvill, G., 216, 218
Dennis, N., 20, 36
density of networks, 88–9, 251
Dexter, M., 235
Dore, R., 36, 43, 116

Index

Dryden Square, 47, 52–7, 83, 86, 246
Durant, R., 41
Durkheim, E., 8, 33, 116, 225, 229

Easethorpe Village Help scheme, 140, 158–9, 182, 204, 255; Clients, 165, 166, 168; Helpers, 158, 159, 162, 164, 179, 191, 192, 193; and neighbourliness, 204; pattern of care, 200–1, 202; problems, 183, 184, 185
East Kinley, *see* Tattworth
Ekeh, P., 106
elderly people, *see* old people
Elias, N., 35
employment patterns, of Helpers, 161, 162, 164, 175
Etherege Terrace, 47, 71–6, 87, 246, 247, 251
Etzioni, A., 95
exchange theory, 105, 106–7
extended families: neighbours as substitute for, 70–1; *see also* kinship ties

Fallding, H., 89
families: and altruism, 115–16; as source of help, 168–9, 172, 173; *see also* extended families; kinship ties
farming community, in Boswell, 64, 68, 70
Festinger, L., 18, 38, 51, 85
Field, J., 235–6
Fielding Close, 47, 57–63, 87, 246, 251
Finch, J., 117
Fischer, C., 27, 90
Flew, A., 214
Form, W. H., 29, 170
formal care, 4; carers, 214–15; and Good Neighbour schemes, 210–11; and informal care, 206–19, 230, 238; and neighbourhood care, 126–33, 136; *see also* social services
Frankenberg, R., 37, 38, 41, 88
friendliness, 28–9, 96
friends, as source of help, 171, 172, 173
friendship, 63, 67, 74, 95–9, 226
Froland, C., 90, 115, 213, 214, 215

Gallie, W. B., 223
Gans, H., 38, 39, 42
Gaylin, W., 224
Gerson, K., 210
Gibson, T., 227
Ginsberg, J., 31
Glass, R., 19–20
Glasser, I., 224
Gluckman, M., 33
Goldberg, E. M., 3, 43, 210, 219, 240
good neighbours, definition of, 49, 53–4, 61, 65–6, 73–4, 79–80; *see also* positive neighbouring
Good Neighbour schemes, 5, 11–13, 44, 74;

and altruism, 111; and carers, 113–15; in Fielding Close, 63; and formal care, 210–11; limitations of, 204–5; methodology of study, 253–4; problems, 185, 190–1; and reciprocity, 107, 112, 113, 115; and Residents, 173–4; and training, 114; *see also* Neighbourhood Care schemes
Goss, A., 20
Gottlieb, B. H., 90
Gouldner, A. W., 108–9, 112, 114
Grant, G., 218
Grantley Neighbourhood project, 140, 146–8, 182, 255; Clients, 165, 166, 167, 168; Helpers, 162, 164, 191, 192, 193; and neighbourliness, 203; problems, 183, 185, 190, 206

Hadley, R., 121, 218, 236
Hallman, H. W., 20, 227
Harbert, W., 218
Hareven, T. K., 105
Harris, C. C., 89
Hatch, S., 117
Hawley, A., 19
Heath, A. F., 106
Hedley, R., 235
help, sources of, 168–75
Helpers, in Neighbourhood Care schemes, 135, 145, 155–6, 157–8, 159, 160–5, 175–81, 191–205
helpfulness, 28, 29, 31
Henry, J., 88
heteromorphic reciprocity, 112; *see also* reciprocity
Hirsch, F., 33, 43, 104–5, 106, 122
Hole, V., 31, 38, 83
Holmes, A., 129
Homans, G. C., 111
Home Help Service, 235
homeomorphic reciprocity, 111–12; *see also* reciprocity
homogeneity, and positive neighbouring, 42
Humphrey, R., 5, 7, 230, 232
Hunt, A., 235
Hunter, A., 8, 20

Illich, I., 224
informal care, 4, 10, 88; carers, 214–15, 217–18, 239–42; colonisation of, 129–32, 207–8; and formal care, 206–19, 230, 238; and kinship ties, 233; and neighbourhood care, 26, 126–33, 136; policies for, 226–42; and reciprocity, 137, 233–4; and religion, 234; *see also* neighbourliness
informal neighbouring, 17–99
intensity of interaction, 34
isolation scores of Clients, 167–8

Index

Jackson, R. M., 97, 98
Janowitz, M., 229
Japan, 36, 116
Jones, K., 232
Johnson, M., 235
Johnson, M. L., 235

Kapferer, B., 34, 89
Kardiner, A., 36
Keller, S., 17, 27, 36, 37, 38, 40, 41, 43, 95, 96, 122
Kingston inquiry, 27, 30
kinship ties, 86, 87–8; in Austen Avenue, 50, 87; in Boswell, 70, 87; in Bradbury, 187–8; of Clients, 166–8; in Dryden Square, 54, 87; in Etherege Terrace, 74–5, 76, 87; in Fielding Close, 62–3, 87; and informal care, 233; and mutual support, 105; in Parsons Green, 154; *see also* extended families
Knight, B., 235
Krebs, D. L., 109–10
Kropotkin, P., 103
Kuper, L., 28, 31, 36, 38, 42, 83, 85, 96

latent neighbouring, 22, 27, 54
Laumann, E. O., 89
Leat, D., 116–17, 214, 235, 240
Lee, T., 20
leisure patterns, 63, 85–6
lending, *see* borrowing and lending
length of residence, *see* residence, length of
Levin, E., 237
Litwak, E., 30, 31, 42, 213, 214
Loudon, J. B., 88
Luhmann, N., 116

McGahan, P., 18, 28, 41
Macmurray, J., 224
Maguire, L., 90
Malinowski, B., 106, 107, 111, 224
manifest neighbouring, 22, 27
Mann, P., 22, 27, 28
Marcus, S., 225
Mauss, M., 106, 109, 224
men as neighbours, 60, 68, 75–6, 84
Merton, R. K., 93
methodology: Good Neighbour schemes, 253–4; Neighbourhood Care schemes, 254–9; Street studies, 245–53
middle class, 85; in Boswell, 69, 70; Helpers, 175, 177–8, 179, 188–9, 198–201; and sociability, 39–40; and social mobility, 70; sources of help for, 174
Minar, D. W., 210
Mitchell, J. C., 88
mobility, 69–70, 77–8, 94, 95
modern neighbouring, 91, 94–5, 176, 177, 226

Mogey, J. M., 22, 28, 36, 45, 83, 96
moral communities, and Good Neighbour schemes, 114
Morris, D., 228
Morris, R. N., 37
mothers: care of elderly, 241–2; with young children, 52–3, 75, 84, 176
Mumford, L., 20

neighbourhood care, 121–219; definition, 22, 23–6; limitations of, 182–205; policies, 226–42
Neighbourhood Care schemes, 4, 5, 12, 14, 95, 122–6, 134–57; Clients, 135, 165–8, 174–5, 190, 191, 254, 256; Helpers, 135, 145, 155–6, 157–8, 159, 160–5, 175–81, 191–205; methodology of study, 254–9; organisational patterns, 136–40, 186–90; patterns of care, 194–203; problems, 183, 184–91, 206; and the social services, 127–33, 143, 145–6, 153–4, 157, 190, 206–7; *see also* Good Neighbour schemes
neighbourhoods, 226; definition, 19–21; physical layout of, 38–9, 76, 77, 84
neighbouring: definition, 21; elements of, 27–33; formal properties of, 33–6; contexts of, 36–43
neighbourliness: definition, 21–2; and Neighbourhood Care schemes, 203–4
neighbours: definition, 17–19, 21; as source of help, 160–71, 172, 173
network analysis, 88–95
Newby, H., 37, 233
newcomers, 83; in Austen Avenue, 48; in Boswell, 66, 67–8, 69, 70, 71; in Etherege Terrace, 75
Nisbet, R. A., 210
Nodding, N., 117, 230
norms, in neighbourhood bonding, 35–6
nursing training, in Good Neighbour schemes, 114

Offer, J., 217
old people, 3, 84, 217–18, 235–6; in Austen Avenue, 51; in Boswell, 64, 65; in Bradbury, 150–1; in Congreve Hall, 80; in Dryden Square, 52, 54, 55–6; in Etherege Terrace, 72, 74–5, 76; in Grantley, 147; neighbourly care for, 116–17; in Skeffington, 144–5; in Stonegate, 122–6

Pahl, R. E., 37, 38, 39
Paine, R., 31, 35
Parker, G., 235
Parker, R., 117, 215, 216, 237
Parsons, T., 126, 214, 215
Parsons Green Neighbourhood Group, 140,

Index

154–6, 181, 182, 207, 239, 255; Clients, 165, 166, 167, 168; Helpers, 155–6, 162, 164, 179, 191, 192, 193; and neighbourliness, 204; pattern of care, 200, 201–2, 203; problems, 183, 184, 185
pattern-variables, in social care, 126, 214
Patterson, S. L., 113
payments: to carers, 240; to Helpers, 138–9, 161, 165, 175, 178, 179, 180, 194, 205, 212
Pember-Reeves, M. S., 92
Pfiel, E., 28, 36, 38
Pickvance, C. G., 37
Pinker, R., 116, 216
Pitt-Rivers, J., 116
place, influence of, 37–9; and layout of neighbourhoods, 38–9, 76, 77, 84
Poggi, G., 116
positive neighbouring, 28–31, 90
Power, M., 210, 235
Price, F. V., 237
privacy, 30, 86
private care, *see* informal care
problem families, 61–2
proximity, 51–2, 83–4
Pruger, R., 116
public care, *see* formal care

Qureshi, H., 117, 236

reciprocity, 10, 226; and altruism, 103–17; in Austen Avenue, 50; and friendship, 97–9; heteromorphic, 112; homeomorphic, 111–12; and informal care, 137, 233–4; and Neighbourhood Care schemes, 135
Rees, A., 37
Reimer, S., 20
relatives, *see* kinship ties
religious beliefs: in Boswell, 69; of carers, 234; of Helpers, 161, 164, 175
residence, length of, 41, 59, 68, 75, 83; *see also* newcomers
Residents: in Good Neighbour schemes, 173–4; in Neighbourhood Care areas, 168–75, 176, 185, 187, 188, 189, 257, 258
Rex, J., 39
Robinson, F., 5, 27, 235
Robson, B. T., 20
Ross, E., 92, 93
rural communities, 37–8, 88; men as neighbours in, 68

Sahlins, M. D., 106
Sainsbury, P., 215
Scarman, Lord, 229
Schwartz, B., 224
Seebohm Reports, 11, 134, 227
Shulman, N., 28, 41, 42

Simmel, G., 38
Simpkin, M., 224
Sinclair, I., 237
Skeffington Visiting Service, 140, 144–6, 182, 225; Clients, 165, 166, 167, 168; Helpers, 145, 162, 164, 165, 179, 191, 192, 193, 195–6; pattern of care, 194; problems, 183, 184, 190
Smith, R. A., 32, 36
Snaith, R., 7, 227, 228
social care, 4, 43, 209; definition, 23; and neighbourhood care, 26, 126–33, 136; philosophy of, 223–6; *see also* formal care; informal care
social class, *see* class differences; middle class; working class
social control, 31–2, 33
social exchanges, 106
social mobility, 70
social networks, 91–5, 250–1
social services: in Boswell, 71; and kinship ties, 88; and Neighbourhood Care schemes, 127–33, 143, 145–6, 153–4, 157, 190, 206–7; Officials, 257–8; role of personnel, 214–15, 216–17; as source of help, 172, 173; *see also* formal care
socialisation, 84–5
sociometric stars, 51, 91, 237
solidarity in neighbouring, 33–6
Sorokin, P. A., 116
Southfield Park Community Link, 140, 156–8, 182, 255; Clients, 165, 166, 167, 168; Helpers, 157–8, 162, 164, 165, 179–80, 188, 192, 193, 198; and neighbourliness, 204; pattern of care, 197, 199–200, 203; problems, 183, 184, 185, 187, 188–9; and the social services, 157, 206
Stacey, M., 45
statutory agencies, *see* social services
Stonegate Home Warden scheme, 122–6, 140–2, 182, 192, 193, 207, 235, 255; Clients, 165, 166, 167, 168, 190; Helpers, 162, 164, 165, 179, 180, 191, 196, 212, 239; and neighbourliness, 203–4, 211; pattern of care, 194, 196, 212; and the social services, 190, 212
Street studies, 44–82; methodology, 245–53
suburbia, 38, 39
Sunniside Good Neighbour scheme, 112, 113, 114, 115, 216
Suttles, G. D., 38, 96, 226

Tattworth Neighbourhood Network scheme, 140, 148–50, 182, 225; Clients, 165, 166, 168; Helpers, 162, 164, 165, 179, 191, 192, 193, 194, 197; and neighbourliness, 204; problems, 183, 184, 190
Taub, R. P., 236

Index

territorial bounding, 238
theories of neighbourliness, 9–10
Thorns, D. C., 28, 38
time, availability of, and Good Neighbour schemes, 114–15
Timms, E., 219
Tinker, A., 240
Titmuss, R. M., 103–4, 223, 224
Tomeh, A. K., 42
Townsend, P., 42, 50, 96
traditional neighbouring, 91–4, 176, 177, 226
training, for neighbourhood care, 114, 239
Trimdon Street Warden scheme, 140, 152–4, 181, 182, 202, 255; Clients, 165, 166, 168; and formal care, 212; Helpers, 162, 164, 179, 192, 193; problems, 183, 184, 185, 186–7
Turkey, reciprocity in, 85

unemployment, 58
Ungerson, C., 117
United States, 93, 115, 227, 228
urbanism, 37–8

voluntary organisations: membership of, 177–9, 180, 188; and neighbourhood care, 149, 150–2, 157, 205, 232–3; as source of help, 173

Walker, A., 22, 235
Wallace, C., 33
Wallace, W., 45
Wallin, P., 18
Warren, D. I., 90
Weber, Max, 214, 225
welfare authorities, *see* social services
Wellman, B., 89, 90
Wenger, G. C., 90, 218, 219, 235, 240, 241
Whyte, W. H., 38, 39
Williams, B., 116
Williams, W. M., 37
Willmott, P., 38, 39, 41, 45, 236
Wilson, E., 117
Wirth, L., 38
Wolfenden Report, 4, 11, 24, 175, 227, 242
women: as carers, 117, 241–2; as Clients, 165, 166; as Helpers, 160, 162, 166, 175; as neighbours, 75–6, 84; *see also* mothers
working class: Helpers, 175, 177, 178, 179, 180, 194–7; and informal care, 88; pattern of care, 194–7, 212; sociability, 39–40; sources of help for, 174

Young, M., 28, 42, 86